Spatial Dimensions of Social Thought

Applications of Cognitive Linguistics
18

Editors
Gitte Kristiansen
Francisco J. Ruiz de Mendoza Ibáñez

Honorary editor
René Dirven

De Gruyter Mouton

Spatial Dimensions of Social Thought

Edited by
Thomas W. Schubert
Anne Maass

De Gruyter Mouton

ISBN 978-3-11-025430-3
e-ISBN 978-3-11-025431-0
ISSN 1861-4078

Library of Congress Cataloging-in-Publication Data

Spatial dimensions of social thought / edited by Thomas W. Schubert, Anne Maass.
  p. cm. − (Applications of cognitive linguistics; 18)
Includes bibliographical references and index.
ISBN 978-3-11-025430-3 (alk. paper)
1. Sociolinguistics   2. Cognitive grammar − Social aspects.
3. Psycholinguistics.   I. Schubert, Thomas W., 1972−   II. Maass, Anne.
P40.S596   2011
304.2'3−dc23
                                                           2011032133

Bibliographic information published by the Deutsche Nationalbibliothek

The Deutsche Nationalbibliothek lists this publication in the Deutsche Nationalbibliografie; detailed bibliographic data are available in the Internet at http://dnb.d-nb.de.

© 2011 Walter de Gruyter GmbH & Co. KG, Berlin/Boston
Typesetting: le-tex publishing services GmbH, Leipzig
Printing: Hubert & Co. GmbH & Co. KG, Göttingen
∞ Printed on acid-free paper
Printed in Germany
www.degruyter.com

Table of contents

Introduction: The interrelation of spatial and social cognition 1
Thomas W. Schubert and Anne Maass

Section A
Spatial dimensions and social thought

Spatial thought, social thought 17
Barbara Tversky

Flexible foundations of abstract thought: A review and a theory 39
Julio Santiago, Antonio Román, and Marc Ouellet

Estimates of spatial distance: A Construal Level Theory perspective .. 109
Nira Liberman and Jens Förster

Embodiment in affective space:
Social influences on spatial perception 129
Simone Schnall

More than a metaphor: How the understanding of power is grounded
in experience 153
Thomas W. Schubert, Sven Waldzus, and Beate Seibt

Section B
Horizontal asymmetries and social thought

Directional asymmetries in cognition: What is left to write about? 189
Anjan Chatterjee

Understanding spatial bias in face perception and memory 211
Nuala Brady

Asymmetries in representational drawing:
Alternatives to a laterality account 231
Jyotsna Vaid

Cultural and biological interaction in visuospatial organization 257
Sylvie Chokron, Seta Kazandjian, and Maria De Agostini

Aesthetic asymmetries, spatial agency, and art history:
A social psychological perspective 277
Caterina Suitner and Chris McManus

Writing direction, agency and gender stereotyping:
An embodied connection 303
Caterina Suitner and Anne Maass

Who is the second (graphed) sex and why? The meaning of order
in graphs of gender differences 325
Peter Hegarty and Anthony F. Lemieux

Index 351

List of Contributors

Anjan Chatterjee. Department of Neurology and the Center of Cognitive Neuroscience, University of Pennsylvania

Sylvie Chokron. CNRS and Unité Fonctionnelle Vision & Cognition, Service de Neurologie, Fondation Ophtalmologique A. de Rothschild, Paris

Nuala Brady. School of Psychology, University College Dublin

Maria De Agostini. U 780 Inserm, Recherche en épidémiologie et biostatistique, Villejuif

Jens Förster. Psychology Department, University of Amsterdam

Peter Hegarty. Department of Psychology, University of Surrey

Seta Kazandjian. Laboratoire de Psychologie & NeuroCognition, CNRS and ERT TREAT Vision, Service de Neurologie, Fondation Ophtalmologique A. de Rothschild, Paris

Anthony F. Lemieux. Purchase College, State University of New York

Nira Liberman. Department of Psychology, Tel Aviv University

Anne Maass. Department of Developmental Psychology and Socialization, School of Psychology, University of Padova

Chris McManus. Research Department of Clinical, Educational and Health Psychology, Division of Psychology and Language Sciences, University College London

Marc Ouellet. Department of Experimental Psychology and Behavioural Physiology, University of Granada

Antonio Román. Department of Experimental Psychology and Behavioural Physiology, University of Granada

Julio Santiago. Department of Experimental Psychology and Behavioural Physiology, University of Granada

Simone Schnall. Department of Social and Developmental Psychology, University of Cambridge.

Thomas W. Schubert. Instituto Universitário de Lisboa (ISCTE-IUL), Centro de Investigação e Intervenção Social, Lisboa, Portugal

Beate Seibt. Instituto Universitário de Lisboa (ISCTE-IUL), Centro de Investigação e Intervenção Social, Lisboa, Portugal

Caterina Suitner. Department of Developmental Psychology and Socialization, School of Psychology, University of Padova

Barbara Tversky. Columbia Teachers College, Stanford University

Jyotsna Vaid. Department of Psychology, Texas A&M University

Sven Waldzus. Instituto Universitário de Lisboa (ISCTE-IUL), Centro de Investigação e Intervenção Social, Lisboa, Portugal

Introduction:
The interrelation of spatial and social cognition

Thomas W. Schubert and Anne Maass

Even though our modern life conditions may sometimes obscure it, it is a simple truth that humans live in real three-dimensional environments in which they move in order to fulfill all their needs. It is not surprising, then, that our nonverbal behavior in this space serves as the medium in which we regulate our social relations. This is the environment for which evolution equipped us, to which all our development is geared. Social relations *take place* in positions and movements, postures and gestures, lines of sight, speed, and other aspects of our movement. Horizontal distance, its change in approach or avoidance, vertical difference and associated looking up or down, being in front vs. being behind while watching or moving, being left or being right – all these topographic aspects can and do mean something in many circumstances. Space is the medium of social interaction – the stage of our social life.

The investigation of the social meaning of space has been in the focus of the social sciences for at least one century. At the dawn of social anthropology, Robert Hertz, a student of Durkheim, published in 1909 an essay on "The preeminence of the right hand" (Hertz, 1909, 1973). It demonstrated the ubiquity of associating *left* and *right* with polarizations of categories essential to social relations. *Good* and *bad*, *moral* and *amoral*, *male* and *female*, *weak* and *strong*, Hertz observed, are associated in many cultures with *right* and *left* in thought, language, and behavior. Hertz already speculated about the origin of these associations, arguing for a complex interaction of biological factors (initial slight physical advantage of the right hand due to brain asymmetry) and cultural processes that are informed by these initial bodily asymmetries, and then interpret and reinforce them. Throughout the twentieth century, eminent scholars, especially cultural anthropologists, have followed up on Hertz' seminal ideas (Evans-Pritchard, 1956; Durkheim, 1912; Needham, 1973; Schwartz, 1981). In modern Western societies, the linguistic association of right and left with good and bad persists, but it has little inferential power (Casasanto, 2009).

In social psychology, lines of inquiry with similarly long traditions on similar topics can be identified. Spatial aspects of social interactions are features of the grand topic of social psychology: how the "imagined, real or implied presence of others" influences thought, feeling and behavior (Allport,

1954). Real presence by definition happens in a spatial context. Imagined presence may often include elaborate spatial images. And even implied presence may have clear spatial aspects. Social psychology has produced a huge body of work investigating such spatial aspects of human interactions, both regarding their production and their impact.

For instance, distance to others has long been recognized as a central feature of social interactions. In 1958, Harlow surprised behaviorists with the finding that infant monkey wanted to be close to a clothed surrogate mother instead of being close to a surrogate that gave milk, but was made from wire. Later, researchers like Hall (1966) and Mehrabian (1972, 1981) developed elaborate analyses of spatial behavior. They, for instance, identified the importance of the personal space around our bodies, roughly the size of our arm reach. Subsequently, social psychologists have used spatial behavior as a proxy for attitudes; for instance, Macrae, Bodenhausen, Milne, and Jetten (1994) assessed seating distance from a chair ostensibly reserved for a skinhead as an index of negative evaluation.

In these cases, the function of spatial distance as a stage for interpersonal interaction is nicely illustrated. However, consider a recent finding from Williams and Bargh (2008). They first asked participants to plot a set of points in a Cartesian coordinate plane. For some participants, the points were far apart, for others, they were close together. Those who had to plot points far apart subsequently judged their emotional attachment to their family as lower! The coordinate plane was neither diagnostic of attachment, nor was it a medium to convey attachment, but still it affected the participants' social thoughts.

Findings like these (and this volume reports many more, see the examples below) raise intriguing new questions: How do spatial aspects affect our social cognitions? How do the meanings associated with spatial dimensions develop? What role do evolution, the makeup of our brain, and language play in this development? What cognitive processes mediate our imbuing of meaning on space? Only in the last few years have researchers started to investigate the role of (often unconscious) processing of spatial information in the social-cognitive domain.

The authors of the present volume all met in 2008 in Venice at an Expert Meeting generously funded by the European Science Foundation and the European Social Cognition Netowork to discuss their different theoretical perspectives, to compare findings from their laboratories and to discuss future developments. The present book reflects the intense and dynamic discussion between researchers who, with diverse methodologies and from diverse theoretical perspectives, approach the same basic question, namely how social and spatial cognition interact and how one supports or constrains the other.

The results converge in the insight that much of social thinking builds upon spatial cognition. This makes social cognition susceptible to influences from spatial cues, and vice versa. A number of such links have been discovered between social and spatial thinking. This book assembles some of the key findings and the theories that generated them. For instance, consider some examples from the chapters of this volume:

> When asked to put stickers representing entities on a paper, most children even at just four years put the stickers on a line, but more abstract concepts were mapped to this line only at a later age: first space, then time, then quantity, then preference. The power of managers is overestimated after thinking about large differences between vertical lines. Words about likely events are understood more quickly when they are written next to arrows pointing at close locations rather than far locations. A backpack will make a hill before you appear steeper – but a sugary drink, and thinking about a close friend will both make it appear less steep.[1]

These findings demonstrate that space plays a role for thinking that goes far beyond it being just a medium for communication. Indeed, it seems that it can become the medium of thinking itself, with spatial and social cognition being closely and intrinsically intertwined. This is the idea behind this book. Although the authors come from a large variety of backgrounds (including art psychology, social and cognitive psychology and cognitive science), they all share the idea that spatial information not only affects what we think, but also the way we think about social reality.

One theoretical approach that is important for a number of chapters in this book is what has been called the embodied cognition approach. By this we do not mean a particular theory or even a particular hypothesis, but the assumption that perceptual and motor systems are not simply input and output modules for a central, "higher level" cognitive modul that does the actual cognition. Instead, the embodied cognition approach assumes that perceptual and motor systems – their general function and their states – shape higher level cognitive functions. In the words of Wilson (2002), it is "the idea that the mind must be understood in the context of its relationship to a physical body that interacts with the world" (p. 625).

A number of different theories are associated with this approach and the label *embodiment* (Wilson, 2002). Volumes that preceded the present one in the Mouton de Gruyter series *Applications of Cognitive Linguistics* and *Cognitive Linguistics Research* have explored this approach (e.g., Hampe

---

[1] These examples were taken from Tverksy, Kugelmaass, and Winter (1991), Giessner and Schubert (2007), Bar-Anan, Liberman, Trope, and Algom (2007), and Schnall, Harber, Stefanucci, and Proffitt (2008).

& Grady, 2005; Sharifian, Dirven, Yu, & Niemeier, 2008; Ziemke, Zlatev, & Frank, 2007). One prominent and early line of argument within the embodiment approach was and continues to be conceptual metaphor theory. It proposed that directly experienced structures are mapped onto concepts that are not directly experienced, and thereby imbue them with meaning and structure (Lakoff & Johnson, 1980, 1999). Many of the above mentioned findings indeed are connected to metaphors that map the relevant conceps in language: Time, quantity, and preference are mapped onto a spatial dimension; power is metaphorically described as up; unrealistic ideas are "far out"; steepness is a metaphor for required effort (see also Landau, Meier, & Keefer, in press).

Yet, this volume also includes a number of findings that show effects of spatial experience on social cognition that are difficult to understand by relying on conceptual metaphor theory alone. Consider these examples:

> It is easier to match the sentence "Peter pushes Paul" to a picture when in this picture Peter is pushing from the left, rather than from the right. Words about the past can be categorized more quickly with the left than the right hand, but the reverse is true for words about the future. In depictions of the Addams family sampled from the Internet, there is an overwhelming tendency to represent the (more agentic) male to the left of the (less agentic) female (82% of all images), whereas this is not the case in depictions of the Simpsons and the Flintstones, where the male is not more agentic than the female. When both scientists and lay persons graph data in diagrams, powerful groups are by far more often graphed on the left, while powerless groups are graphed on the left in only a minority of cases.[2]

What is behind these asymmetries in the horizontal dimension? There are hardly any metaphors about the left and right related to these constructs: While we do map good and bad onto right and left, as described in the introduction, we do not refer to the past as "on the left", and neither to the future as "on the right". Instead, another aspect of language seems to play a major role: The direction in which it is written. Consider three final examples from the present volume:

> When chimeric faces that show different emotional expressions on the left and the right side are interpreted, the left side is typically more relied upon. That left side bias disappears in people who typically read from right to left. Whether you usually read from left to right or from right to left influences where you see the midpoint of a horizontal line, but also where you think is

---

2   These examples were taken fom Chatterjee, Southwood, and Basilico (1999), Torralbo, Santiago, and Lupiáñez (2006), Maass, Suitner, Favaretto, and Cignacchi (2009), and Hegarty, Lemieux, and McQueen (2010).

"straight ahead" when you are blindfolded – tasks that have little to do with reading.[3]

Taken together, these findings suggest that several different mechanisms might be at work in parallel that associate conceptual representations of social and non-social concepts with sensorimotor representations. The chapters in this book demonstrate vividly that in order to understand the impact of space on social cognition, researchers need to combine social cognitive theories and more general theories of cognitive science. This also requires taking findings from cognitive science on non-social topics into consideration. The present volume is an effort to contribute to this endeavor, and to assemble a coherent overview of spatial embodiment effects and theories in the social realm.

Overview of the contributions to this volume

The volume consists of two sections. The chapters in **Section A** bring together findings and theories on the spatial embodiment of concepts and their explanation. These chapters deal with many different spatial aspects and dimensions: grouping, perspective, horizontal and vertical difference, and distance, among others. **Section B** includes chapters that look in more detail at the horizontal dimension: the association of left and right with various processes and concepts, such as horizontal biases in attribution of agency and attention, the influence of brain asymmetries, writing direction, and their outcomes.

The chapters focus on social processes and concepts. However, the chapters invariably go beyond purely social aspects and pay due attention to findings and theory on non-social processes and concepts as well, and with good reason: The embodiment of social concepts, although characterized by some unique features, shares many underlying processes with the embodiment in other areas. As such, we think, it is necessary to integrate spatial aspects of non-social cognition in the study of social cognition. Indeed, the very notion of the influence of spatial cognition in social thought demonstrates the necessity and usefulness of such a broad focus. In both sections, chapters are roughly arranged so that those with a more inclusive focus on general cognitive science precede those with a more specific focus on social concepts and processes.

---

3   Examples are taken from Brady, Campbell, and Flaherty (2005), Vaid and Singh (1989), and Chokron (2003).

Section A starts with a chapter by **Barbara Tversky**. Step by step, she reviews the processes through which we construct a coherent understanding from the raw material of sensation: Objects, categories, orderings, which come together in relations, and on which we look from a specific perspective. She then demonstrates parallel phenomena in the realm of social cognition. The correspondence of spatial and social cognition, she argues, is due the fact that the same perception-action couplings are at work in both areas.

In a comprehensive second chapter, **Julio Santiago, Antonio Román, and Marc Ouellet** take stock of what we know about the embodiment of abstract concepts. They review various versions of conceptual metaphor theory and identify the flexibility of embodiments as a crucial challenge to this family of theories. They review evidence of such flexibility regarding the embodiment of affect, power, magnitude, linear order, and pitch, and conclude that current theories have difficulty explaining, let alone predicting such findings. As a solution, they propose a new theory that emphasizes the role of working memory, and report evidence from tests of this theory.

Nira Liberman and Jens Förster review another general, but very different, theory on the relation between spatial distance and the (more abstract) concepts of social distance, temporal distance, and likelihood. According to Construal Level Theory (Liberman, Trope, & Stephan, 2007), spatial distance is one instance of the more general construct of psychological distance, and it is intrinsically associated with social and temporal distance and likelihood because these are also instances of psychological distance. Liberman and Förster discuss the immense amount of evidence, and, in particular, the perspective of Construal Level Theory on metaphors.

Simone Schnall then reviews a new line of research concerning the influence of social factors on perception of space. Thus, the causal direction between social and spatial cognition is now reversed, with social variables affecting spatial ones rather than vice versa. Feeling alone or socially connected is found to alter basic spatial perceptions, such as estimates of distances and slants. These findings challenge many classic theories, but also some recent theories of embodiment. Not surprisingly, then, the theoretical background used by Schnall is different from that of other chapters, namely Proffitt's view on the economy of action. Besides the breadth and novelty of the reported findings, perhaps the most intriguing aspect of her review is the distinction between judgments in the service of action execution and judgments in the service of action planning – only the latter being influenced by energetic and social factors. Any future comprehensive theory of embodiment has to be able to account for such differences.

The final chapter in Section A by **Thomas Schubert, Sven Waldzus and Beate Seibt** takes a closer look at a specific concept: the embodiment of power. The authors proceed from the assumption that the metaphoric understanding of power as elevation and size in space results from schematization of concrete experiences with larger and powerful others. Based on this assumption, they review evidence from the concrete, nonverbal communication of power to effects of abstracted, schematized, and de-contextualized spatial cues on power judgments. They then review three families of theories that can be drawn upon to explain these findings: Semantic network models, simulation theories, and conceptual metaphor theory. In addition, they discuss the possibility that evolutionarily prepared mechanisms facilitate the learning of essential concepts like power.

The authors of the chapters in **Section B** comprehensively review what is known about horizontal asymmetries in human cognitive processes. **Anjan Chatterjee** provides an overview of his own seminal and recent work on left-right asymmetries in the attribution of agency during our conceptualization of actions and events. From his review of the recent evidence, he concludes that reading and writing habits contribute more to this effect than hemispheric asymmetries. He hypothesizes the existence of a pervasive horizontal schema that, similar to other spatial schemas in the sense of Talmy's (1996), serves to increase efficiency when processing events. He then discusses how such schemas are mentally represented, what their neural underpinnings are, and how they influence the construction of mental models.

Nuala Brady's contribution turns to face perception. She reviews evidence of the curious emphasis on the left half of the face in person perception. In order to understand the causes of this phenomenon, she compares it with horizontal asymmetries in word recognition, and concludes that the two different asymmetries may in fact both be rooted in differential specializations of the brain hemispheres on different scales of spatial details to be considered.

Jyotsna Vaid reviews evidence on horizontal asymmetries in representational drawing, object recognition, and aesthetic preference. She discusses two possible explanations of these differences: differences between the brain's hemispheres, and motor processes due to biomechanical and/or cultural factors. She then reviews to what extent handedness and script direction influence the horizontal asymmetries, and concludes that motor processes may offer the more parsimonious explanation for the available data than brain asymmetries.

Sylvie Chokron, Seta Kazandjian, and Maria De Agostini focus on simple visuospatial tasks such as line bisection, aesthetic preference, and straight-ahead pointing. As the authors of the previous chapters, they point out that horizontal asymmetries – in their case a leftward bias – have generally been attributed to hemispheric differences; however, more recent evidence reported in this chapter shows that reading and writing direction may contribute to these effects, by influencing scanning and salience of stimulus.

Caterina Suitner and **Chris McManus** review a topic that has a long-standing tradition in investigating horizontal biases and their social associations: The use and meaning of left and right spatial positions in paintings. Horizontal biases in different art genres are reported, including portraits, self-portraits, and religious paintings. In their comprehensive chapter, they show that the association of rightward orientation with greater agency probably provides the best explanation for a number of asymmetries identified by art historians and in experimental studies of aesthetic preferences.

In the following chapter, **Caterina Suitner** and **Anne Maass** develop the argument of differential associations of left and right with agency further. In particular, they investigate the cognitive processes underlying this bias and discuss its impact in the area of gender stereotyping. They also relate these findings to the impact of writing direction already discussed in the previous chapters, and conclude that this form of cultural bias may be the major source of the spatial agency bias. They close the chapter with a discussion of the possible causes of the existence of different writing directions, relating them to different types of alphabets which, presumably, put different strains on the two brain hemispheres.

In the final chapter, **Peter Hegarty** and **Anthony Lemieux** apply many of the aforementioned findings to the study of graphs and diagrams. With both archival and experimental data, they show a pervasive and subtle bias to embody the agency of certain (in)groups by placing them on the left side in graphs. This surfaces especially in graphs of gender differences. Their chapter demonstrates the importance of studying spatial embodiments of social concepts not only for an enhanced understanding of social cognition, but also for our understanding of the creation and perpetuation of social inequalities.

Despite the breadth of this volume, important aspects had to remain unexplored. One aspect emphasized in **Section B**, but certainly worthy of further exploration, is the cultural embededdness of spatial groundings of social thought. One such cultural variable is explored in the current volume: the direction of handwriting. Its influence on attention and construction of meaning even in non-linguistic tasks attests to the importance of this notion (see **Tversky**'s and all chapters in **Section B** of this volume). Other culturally meaningful variables such as right vs. left side driving may also be important (Scharine & McBeath, 2002). This underscores that findings from one or a few Western, educated, industrialized, rich, and democratic samples should not be considered representative of the general human population (Henrich, Heine, & Norenzayan, 2010). Cultural influence on metaphors (and their universality) is also touched upon in **Santiago et al.**'s and

Schubert et al.'s chapters. However, the interplay of spatial cognition and metaphors in different cultural environments and languages deserves much more attention. Furthermore, distal causes of such differences need to be addressed. For instance, **Suitner and Maass** (this volume) speculate that characteristics of a language may contribute to whether it is written from left to right or right to left. Similarly, aspects of the physical environment and one's interactions with it will contribute to the development of cultural peculiarities (Uskul, Kitayama, & Nisbett, 2008). In sum, the present volume not only brings together different perspectives on social and spatial bias but it also outlines possible future developments, which, we hope, will stimulate future research endeavors.

A note on theoretical heterogeneity

The extent of the investigated topics and reported evidence already suggests that any one single theoretical perspective would not be able to cover them all. It is worth pointing out that indeed the volume combines many and very different theoretical approaches. We acknowledged earlier that several chapters are influenced by the embodied cognition assumption that lower level perceptual and motor processes shape higher order abstract cognitive processes. Nevertheless, few of the chapters subscribe to one of the more recent embodiment theories in particular. The current volume is more adequately described as a collection of mid-range theories and evidence on the connection of social and spatial thought rather than an attempt to bring forward one particular unified explanation of all of them. In that sense, the evidence in this volume represents a challenge for any theory connecting spatial and social thought, whatever theoretical provinence it comes from. We believe that no current theoretical proposal provides a satisfactory explanation that would cover all parts of the puzzle in this volume.

In this respect, it is particularly relevant that certain assumptions of more specific theories within the embodiment approach have been heavily debated in recent years. This is especially true of the claim that representations in long-term memory are modal, and functionally dependent on the processes that led to their acquisition (i.e., perceptual and motor processes; e.g., Barsalou, 1999, 2008; Glenberg, 1999; Fischer & Zwaan, 2008; Prinz, 2002). Applied to the phenomena discussed in this volume, the question is for instance whether thinking about spatial distance actually and necessarily re-activates mental representations of spatial distance, or just a long-term representation of DISTANT in some arbitrary, non-spatial and quasi-linguistic format, for instance a node labeled DISTANT in a semantic network. This question is especially important when we want to explain the interactions between spatial and social cognition: How does activation of DISTANT lead to construals of events as unlikely, or people as cold (Liberman & Förster, this volume)? Does activation spread in a semantic network, or is a simulation biased?

This question has seen intense debates in recent years. Machery (2007, 2010) argued that current evidence is insufficient to rule out amodal symbols. He notes that direct tests of amodal vs. modal accounts need to be much more complex than what is currently undertaken, and that eventually only falsifications of more specific theories, but not the general claim of amodal or modal symbols may be what can be achieved. Importantly, he also makes the point that most amodal theories actually acknowledge simulation in mental imagery, and thus modal representations in short term memory, to play a functional role. Similarly, Dove (2009) argues against the claim that amodal representations do not exist, and instead for assuming both amodal and modal representations. Interestingly, he emphasizes amodal representations of magnitude, which includes those of distances and sizes, which may become particularly relevant for issues discussed in this volume. Similarly, Mahon and Caramazza (2008) argue for a coexistence of modal and amodal representations in long-term memory. Notably, none of these authors seems to refute the more general embodied cognition claim that sensory-motor processes shape higher order cognition.

What is important for the current volume is to note that the idea underlying it – i.e., the notion that social and spatial cognition are intertwined and influence each other – does not depend on the modal representation hypothesis. Instead, and in line with Machery (2007), this claim could be implemented in a number of both modal and amodal symbol theories. Indeed, the chapters in the current volume remain largely mute concerning this issue. Most authors emphasize like **Schnall** the pragmatic program of the embodied cognition approach, and less the format of representations. **Santiago et al.** in fact propose to focus on working memory and its flexibility and modality, instead of long-term memory. **Liberman and Förster's** concept of psychological distance as a common essence of spatial, social, and temporal distance, and hypotheticality, seems more compatible with an amodal view than a strict modality hypothesis. **Chatterjee** construes a model based on schematized analog representations and their use in mental models, but likewise does not commit to their modal format. **Schubert et al.** compare modal and amodal accounts and acknowledge that the amodal account could in principle account for the reviewed findings. As one anonymous reviewer of this volume put it: "Evidence for spatial influences on social thought (and vice versa) [is] not necessarily evidence for embodiment." Indeed, the field is only now starting to develop stronger tests pitting modal and amodal accounts against each other (Casasanto, 2009).

Having pointed out this issue, we want to shift the focus from a debate perspective back to a discovery perspective (Wegner, 2003): At the current point in the development of this field, contesting the existence of modal representations may distract from the fact that interesting discoveries await those who look for interactions of spatial and social thought. The focus on the computer metaphor and computability of cognition in amodal symbol systems has led to disbelief that the body influences the mind. If we suspend this disbelief, the authors of the current volume argue, and let our imaginations run with the bold idea that social thought is spatial in many respects, we may be rewarded with some interesting insights.

Resumé

This volume developed from a small group meeting in June 2008 in Venice, where all of the first authors of this volume came together and discussed their research thanks to the generous contribution of the European Science Foundation. The meeting surprised its participants constantly with the juxtaposition of two opposing insights: on the one hand the discovery that there are so many spatial effects on social cognition that emerge from such diverse areas of research, many of which entirely unknown to many participants prior to the meeting, and, on the other hand, the surprise that these diverse phenomena all fit together and consistently showed the importance of spatial experience for social thought. Throughout the century, various schools of thoughts in various disciplines, from social anthropology to linguistics to cognitive psychology, have discussed the spatial grounding of social concepts and thought. Brain, society, culture, and language all have been implicated in the underlying processes. With the findings and theorizing in the present volume, we hope to come one step closer to understand how spatial and social thinking determine each other.

Acknowledgements

We are immensely grateful to the European Social Cognition Network (ESCON) and the European Science Foundation (ESF) for providing funding for the Expert Meeting in Venice 2008.

References

Allport, Gordon W. (1954). *The nature of prejudice*. Reading, MA: Addison-Wesley.
Bar-Anan, Yoav, Nira Liberman, Yaacov Trope & Daniel Algom (2007). The automatic processing of psychological distance: Evidence from a Stroop task. *Journal of Experimental Psychology: General, 136,* 610–622.
Barsalou, Lawrence W. (2008). Grounded cognition. *Annual Review of Psychology, 59,* 617–645.
Brady, Nuala, Mark Campbell & Mary Flaherty (2005). Perceptual asymmetries are preserved in memory for highly familiar faces of self and friend. *Brain & Cognition, 58,* 334–342.
Casasanto, Daniel (2009). Embodiment of abstract concepts: *Good and bad in right- and left-handers, 138,* 351–367.
Chatterjee, Anjan, M. Helen Southwood & David Basilico (1999). Verbs, events and spatial representations. *Neuropsychologia, 37,* 395–402.
Chokron, Sylvie (2003). Right parietal lesions, unilateral spatial neglect, and the egocentric frame of reference. *NeuroImage, 20,* S75–S81.
Dove, Guy (2009). Beyond perceptual symbols: a call for representational pluralism. *Cognition, 110,* 412–431.
Durkheim, Emile (1912). Les formes élémentaires de la vie religieuse. Paris: Félix Alcan.
Evans-Pritchard, Edward Evan (1956). *Nuer religion*. Oxford: Clarendon Press.
Fischer, Martin H. & Rolf A. Zwaan (2008). Embodied language – A review of the role of the motor system in language comprehension. *Quarterly Journal of Experimental Psychology, 61,* 860–868.
Giessner, Steffen R. & Thomas W. Schubert (2007). High in the hierarchy: How vertical location and judgments of leaders' power are interrelated. *Organizational Behavior and Human Decision Processes, 104,* 30–44.
Hall, Edward T. (1966). *The hidden dimension*. Garden City, N.Y.: Doubleday.
Hampe, Beate & Joseph E. Grady (Eds., 2005). *From perception to meaning: image schemas in cognitive linguistics*. Berlin, New York: Mouton de Gruyter.
Hegarty, Peter, Anthony Lemieux & Grant McQueen (2010). Graphing the order of the sexes: Constructing, recalling, interpreting, and putting the self in gender difference graphs. *Journal of Personality and Social Psychology, 98,* 375–391.
Henrich, Joseph, Steven J. Heine & Ara Norenzayan (2010). The weirdest people in the world? *Behavioral and Brain Sciences, 33,* 61–135.
Hertz, Robert (1909). La Prééminence de la main droite: étude sur la polarité religieuse. *Revue philosophique, 68,* 553–580.
Hertz, Robert (1973). The preeminence of the right hand. In Rodney Needham (Ed.), *Right and left* (pp. 3–31). Chicago: University of Chicago Pres.
Lakoff, George & Mark Johnson (1980). *Metaphors we live by*. Chicago and London: The University of Chicago Press.
Lakoff, George & Mark Johnson (1999). *Philosophy in the flesh*. New York: Basic Books.

Landau, Mark J., Brian P. Meier & Lucas A. Keefer (in press). A metaphor-enriched social cognition. *Psychological Bulletin*.

Liberman, Nira, Yaacov Trope & Elena Stephan (2007). Psychological distance. In Arie W. Kruglanski & E. Tory Higgins (Eds.), *Social psychology: Handbook of basic principles (2nd ed.)* (pp. 353–381). New York, NY, US: Guilford Press.

Maass, Anne, Caterina Suitner, Xenia Favaretto & Marina Cignacchi (2009). Groups in space: Stereotypes and the spatial agency bias. *Journal of Experimental Social Psychology, 45*, 496–504.

Machery, Edouard (2007). Concept empiricism: a methodological critique. *Cognition, 104*, 19–46.

Machery, Edouard (2010). Précis of Doing without Concepts. *Behavioral and Brain Sciences, 33*, 195–244.

Macrae, C. Neil, Galen V. Bodenhausen, Alan B. Milne & Jolanda Jetten (1994). Out of mind but back in sight. Stereotypes on the rebound. *Journal of Personality and Social Psychology, 67*, 808–817.

Mahon, Bradford Z. & Alfonso Caramazza (2008). A critical look at the embodied cognition hypothesis and a new proposal for grounding conceptual content. *Journal of physiology, Paris, 102*, 59–70.

Mehrabian, Albert (1972). *Nonverbal communication*. Oxford: Aldine-Atherton.

Mehrabian, Albert (1981). *Silent messages*. Belmont, CA: Wadsworth.

Needham, Rodney Ed. (1973). *Right and left: Essays on dual symbolic classification*. Chicago: University of Chicago Press.

Prinz, Jesse J. (2002). *Furnishing the mind. Concepts and their perceptual basis*. Cambridge, MA: MIT Press.

Scharine, Angelique A. & Michael K. McBeath (2002). Right-handers and Americans favor turning to the right. *Human Factors, 44*, 248–256.

Sharifian, Farzad, René Dirven, Ning Yu & Susanne Niemeier (Eds., 2008). Culture, body, and language. Berlin: Mouton de Gruyter.

Schnall, Simone, Kent. D. Harber, Janine Stefanucci & Dennis R. Proffitt (2008). Social support and the perceptionof geographical slant. *Journal of Experimental Social Psychology, 44*, 1246–1255.

Schwartz, Barry (1981). *Vertical classification: A study in structuralism and the sociology of knowledge*. Chicago: University of Chicago Press.

Talmy, Leonard (1996). Fictive motion in language and "caption". In Paul Bloom, Mary A. Peterson, Lynn Nadel & Merrill F. Garrett (Eds.), *Language and space* (pp. 211–276). Cambridge, MA: The MIT Press.

Torralbo, Ana, Julio Santiago & Juan Lupiáñez (2006). Flexible conceptual projection of time onto spatial frames of reference. *Cognitive Science, 30*, 745–757.

Tverksy, Barbara, Sol Kugelmaass & Atalia Winter (1991). Cross-cultural and developmental trends in graphic productions. *Cognitive Psychology, 23*, 515–557.

Uskul, Ayse K., Shinobu Kitayama & Richard E. Nisbett (2008). Ecocultural basis of cognition: Farmers and fishermen are more holistic than herders. *Proceedings of the National Academy of Sciences of the United States of America, 105*, 8552–8556.

Vaid, Jyotsna & Maharaj Singh (1989). Asymmetries in the perception of facial affect: Is there an influence of reading habits? Neuropsychologia, 27, 1277–1287.
Wegner, Daniel M. (2003). Science talk: Discovery and debate. *Dialogue, 18*, 10–11.
Williams, Lawrence E. & John A. Bargh (2008). Keeping one's distance. The influence of spatial distance cues on affect and evaluation. *Psychological Science, 19,* 302–308.
Wilson, Margaret (2002). Six views of embodied cognition. *Psychonomic Bulletin & Review, 9,* 625–636.
Ziemke, Tom, Jordan Zlatev & Roslyn M. Frank (Eds., 2007). *Body, language, and mind. Volume 1, Embodiment.* Berlin, New York: Mouton de Gruyter.

Section A
Spatial dimensions and social thought

Spatial thought, social thought

Barbara Tversky[1]

Abstract

Spatial thought is not an internalized video of experience but rather a construction carved out of experience. Objects, categories, orderings: These constructive processes sharpen, level, add, subtract, simplify, complicate, and distort, not randomly, but in ways that contribute to sense-making. Parallel phenomena appear in social thought. For example, individuals are grouped into categories, and within-category differences are perceived as smaller than between-category differences. Categories are ordered into dimensions that are spatially arrayed from down to up and from left to right in western languages. These correspondences seem to arise from perception-action couplings, and suggest that spatial cognition can serve as a basis for social thought.

1. Basic facts

We can't escape space. Our bodies take up space, perceive in space, and act in space. Our perceptions and our actions are constrained by space, the things in it, the forces acting in it, the changes in it. We begin to act in space and learn about space even before birth. All our senses participate in that learning, contributing to spatial knowledge. Spatial knowledge is supramodal, informed by vision, hearing, touch, kinesthesis, and more. It is essential to survival. If we didn't know how to get food into our mouths and find our way home, survival would be difficult. This does not mean that our spatial knowledge is perfect. On the contrary. Our spatial knowledge is constructed from ele-

---

[1] Gratitude to Thomas Schubert for insightful comments on an earlier version of this paper. Preparation of this chapter and/or some of the research reported were supported by the following grants: NSF BNS 8002012, AFOSR 89-0076, the Edinburgh-Stanford Link through the Center for the Study of Language and Information at Stanford University, Office of Naval Research Grants Number NOOO14-PP-1-O649, N000140110717, and N000140210534, NSF REC-0440103, NSF IIS-0725223, NSF IIS-0905417, NSF IIS-0855995 and the Stanford Regional Visualization and Analysis Center.

ments, reference frames, and perspectives. It must reconcile information from different occasions, elements, reference frames, perspectives, and modalities. Reconciling different sources and different information relies on finding common elements and transforming reference frames and perspectives. The reconciliation is approximate, by no means Euclidean, so that it yields systematic biases and errors (e.g., Tversky, 1981, 2005a, 2005b). Despite the fact that knowledge of space is distorted and biased, it serves us well. This is in part because we often only need approximate information, in part because the different biases are independent and can cancel each other, and in part because spatial knowledge is situated, that is, it is used or invoked in environments that provide constraints and information that can serve as correctives.

Spatial knowledge is so fundamental and useful that it serves as a basis for other knowledge, concrete and abstract (e.g., papers in Gattis, 2001). One reminder of the ubiquity of spatial thinking is the ubiquity of spatial metaphors in language. Just as we can't escape space in perception and action, we can't escape space in communication. Spatial metaphors are evident in the ways we talk (and not just in English). We *grow close* to people or *far apart*; one friend is *at the top* of the class and another *descends* into depression; new research *fields open*, other *areas recede* (e.g., Lakoff & Johnson, 1980). Spatial metaphors are evident in the way we visualize abstract concepts on paper; greater weight, pitch, strength, and rating are graphed higher; connections among concepts in networks are drawn as lines, like paths; cyclical processes are represented as circles, paths that start and end at the same place (e.g., Tversky, 2001; Kessell & Tversky, 2005; Tversky, Kugelmass, & Winter, 1991). Spatial metaphors are evident in gesture, where, as in speech and sketch, things that are good or strong or more numerous are gestured upwards, ideas that are more related are gestured as closer; ideas that are ordered conceptually are ordered in space (e.g., Casasanto, 2009; Goldin-Meadow, 2003; Tversky, Heiser, Lee, & Daniel, 2009). These mappings onto space reveal the nature of thought, concrete and abstract. These mappings, especially to an external space that can be viewed and reviewed, also allow and encourage inference, reasoning, and insight, especially through diagrams and gestures, by applying the impressive, highly-practiced spatial reasoning skills of people to reasoning about abstractions, making the effortful intuitive.

How is spatial knowledge organized? The key is objects and the spatial relations among them. Sounds simple, but determining and characterizing the objects and the spatial relations is subtle, relative, and variable. The clues to how spatial knowledge is organized are as multi-modal as the knowledge itself, from the ways that people act, draw, gesture, and talk. Linguistic analyses have been especially insightful (notably, Clark, 1973;

Lakoff & Johnson, 1980; Miller & Johnson-Laird, 1976; Talmy, 1983, 2000). Language can be counted on to capture the essential objects, features, concepts, actions, states, and the like that are important for human communication. As others have observed, the perceptual processes and representations that serve human action are coopted in the service of conceptual processes and representations (e.g., Clark, 1973; Lakoff & Johnson, 1980; Shepard & Podgorny, 1978). The facts that abstract ideas from a multitude of domains are conveyed by spatial language, that abstract ideas are mapped to the space of the page, that abstract ideas are expressed by spatial gestures imply that it is spatial thinking that is basic, and that abstract thought is built on spatial thought.

Social cognition is no different. Many intriguing phenomena in social cognition have parallels in spatial cognition. What follows is an analysis of some of what is known about human spatial cognition. Paired with that are allusions to analogous effects in social cognition, some demonstrated, some, to this author's limited knowledge, still to be demonstrated. After that are some speculations about how the transfer from spatial to abstract might happen.

As we begin, a few words on some facts of life, as these inexorable facts about humans and the world constrain perception of and action in space, and, therefore, conceptions of space. First *us*. Humans are for the most part upright, with three axes, an elongated asymmetric vertical axis of head and feet and two orthogonal horizontal axes, the asymmetric front-back axis and the nearly symmetric left-right axis. Our perceptual apparatus is oriented forwards, as is our motor apparatus, conferring a strong asymmetry to the body as well as a privileged direction, forwards. We develop and act in a world that has one powerful asymmetric axis, that of gravity. Gravity has profound effects on the way we develop and act as well as on the world we act in (e.g., Clark, 1973; Cooper & Ross, 1975; Franklin & Tversky, 1990). Going against gravity takes time, force, strength, energy, even money. Children get bigger and stronger and more powerful as they mature, and stronger people are on the whole larger, underlying an association of size with power (Schubert, Waldzus, & Giessner, 2009). These correspondences confer a strong asymmetry on the vertical dimension, as well as a privileged direction, upwards. But there is more in the world besides ourselves.

2. Objects: Groups and categories

The world has an overwhelming amount of stuff, and, what's more, that stuff keeps changing, roads, buildings, bridges, trees, fields, mountains, rivers, lakes, people, clouds, seeds, pebbles, grains of sand, How to keep track of all the stuff, how to remember it, how to predict it, how to act toward it, how to make sense of it all require, at a minimum, the same solution: grouping similar things together (e.g., Rosch, 1978). Otherwise there is an unending number of things and no basis for regularities. Even those things mentioned are already grouped and categorized, and named. But how should things be grouped? By similarity, of course, but things are similar and dissimilar in so many different ways. The best categories contain things that not only look alike but also behave alike, or induce similar behaviors from us. Similarity of features helps identification and similarity of behavior helps inference, prediction, and action.

Good categories, then, share many features, and in particular, share the kinds of features that are likely to be important to human life. Knowing that something is a fruit or an animal or mineral allows a range of important inferences about that thing. Common perceptual features, especially shape, which is especially characteristic of objects, allow rapid identification of objects and common functions or behavior allow knowing what the object might do to us or for us (Tversky & Hemenway, 1983, 1984). For these reasons, red things don't make a good category, even if color is salient so that pre-schoolers often prefer to group things by color than by taxonomic category. Little follows from being *red* or *soft* or *elegant*, that is, color does not support many inferences. These "categories" are usually referred to by an adjective added to *thing*. In contrast, good categories, the ones from which many inferences can be made, are typically referred to by nouns. A noun, then, is likely to refer to a category of things that share many features and from which many inferences can consequently be drawn. Using a noun rather than an adjective to describe something indicates that the thing is likely to share many properties with like things. Indeed, nouns induce stronger inferences (a democrat) than adjectives (democratic) in social descriptions (Carnaghi, Maass, Gresta, Bianchi, Cadinu, & Arcuri, 2008).

As noted, good categories of objects share perceptual features that serve human recognition and share behavioral or functional features that serve human action. What about social categories? The important social categories are people, and many categories of people have characteristic perceptual features that are associated with behavior. Age, gender, and the like have salient perceptual features that cue a wide range of behaviors. Dress, too, provides excellent perceptual cues; it is commonly observed that costume and daily attire, not just physicians' white coats or police uniforms, but the even the kinds of t-shirts and shoes and pants worn by people, are a kind of uniform and can be reasonably reliable cues to age, gender, income, profession, politics, and more.

2.1. Bodies

Undoubtedly the most salient and important object in space is the human body, our own and those of others. Bodies and body parts are famously the source of spatial metaphors, social and other: *heads* of committees, someone's *right hand*, the *foot* of a mountain, the *heart* of the matter, the *arms* and *legs* of chairs and institutions. These metaphoric extensions of the names of parts of the body are based as much in function as in appearance.

Grouping into categories, then, has enormous advantages. But there are rarely advantages without disadvantages; category members can vary widely, they are never identical, but categorizing them means treating all instances equally, as if they were the same. This results in overweighting within-category similarity and between-category differences, a process that leads to biases in judgments of distance of things with actual distances in the world. Thus, students in Ann Arbor thought that university buildings were physically closer to each other than they actually were, and physically farther from town buildings than they actually were (Hirtle & Jonides, 1985). Similarly, Israelis estimate the distances between Israeli settlements or between Arab villages to be relatively smaller than the distances between Israeli settlements and Arab villages (Portugali, 1993). Similarly, distances between members within social groups are estimated to be relatively smaller than comparable distances between members of different social groups. Substituting similarity for distance yields parallel distortions in judgments for social categories. That is, members of the same social groups are perceived to be more similar to each other on irrelevant dimensions and more different from members of other social groups (e.g., Quattrone, 1986).

Reducing the vast quantities of information in the world by categorizing is only a first step. A related second step is to recognize similarities and differences in the categories, and thereby to group categories into larger ones as well as subdivide large ones into smaller ones. Categories can be formed at many levels. Hierarchical grouping has similar effects on inferences as grouping. Students in San Diego incorrectly report that San Diego is west of Reno (Stevens & Coupe, 1978). Presumably this is because people cannot remember all the directions among all pairs of cities. Instead they remember the approximate directions among states, and use the larger groups, the states, to infer the directions of the smaller groups, the cities. Since California is for the most part west of Nevada and San Diego is in California and Reno in Nevada, then San Diego must be west of Reno. Wrong. Social inferences are likely to follow the same paths.

3. Perspectives on objects: Zero, one, and more dimensions

Useful categories not only include and exclude, they also contrast with other categories. A basic distinction for mathematics derives from dimensionality, zero, one, two (three, many). For the mind, by contrast, dimensionality depends not on absolute properties of entities but rather on the perspective taken on them (Talmy, 1983). On a map, Paris can be represented as a point, the route from Paris to Nice as a line, and the entire city of Paris can be represented as an area; just as on a map, also in the mind. Paris can also be thought of as a three-dimensional environment in which people live and work, or, adding time, as a four-dimensional space. The perspectives evident in maps and in conceptions are also evident in language, and are evident in abstract thought. The English prepositions *at, on, in* are clues to zero, one, and two-dimensional thinking respectively. For time this gives us: the train arrived promptly *at* 2; he was *on* hold for an hour; she was *in* the meeting until dinner. And now more abstractly: he was *at* rest, *on* drugs, *in* a quandary. What are the more general implications of conceiving of entities, objects, states as dot-like, line-like, or region-like? Does the implied dimensionality in the language that describes these different emotional states indicate or promote different understandings of the emotional states? Persistent states (note the polysemy) metaphorically or literally enclose people, and constrain their perception and action. As has been seen, persistent states nouns induce stronger inferences (a democrat) than attribute-like adjectives (democratic) suggesting that the dimensional perspective may also affect understanding of social situations (Carnaghi et al., 2008).

4. Locating objects

Once objects in space have been identified and conceptualized, they are located. The mind typically locates objects relatively, not absolutely, one object relative to another object or relative to a frame of reference. Both these processes yield systematic distortions (e.g., Tversky, 1981). The reference object or reference frame can distort judgments. For example, distance estimates from ordinary buildings to landmarks are judged smaller than distance estimates from a landmark to an ordinary building, a reliable error that violates any Euclidean model (Sadalla & Staplin, 1980).

There are several explanations for this reliable phenomenon. One is that a landmark comes to represent not only itself, but an entire region, a category if you will. Indeed, the name of the landmark often names the region; in Manhattan, Times Square, in Washington, DC, DuPont Circle. Similarly, when asked where they live, people often give the closest landmark. In more abstract domains, landmark categories are essentially prototypes. Prototypical categories induce a similar bias for perceptual stimuli. For example, people judge that a magenta color patch is closer to a red color patch than vice versa. As for landmarks, prototypes like *red* define a broad category that can include a broad range of instances, in this case, shades of red, like magenta, but not vice versa (Rosch, 1978). The power of prototypes or landmark categories extends further to abstract domains: a son is judged to be more similar to his father than the father to his son, and in the Cold War, North Korea was judged more similar to the People's Republic of China than vice versa (Tversky & Gati, 1978). Prototypical social categories are widespread. There are those represented in languages all over the world: mothers, fathers, leaders, and there are those represented by individuals embodying the defining features. We call others the Einsteins or Stalins of the world, though many prominent social categories enjoy only their Warhol fleeting 15 minutes, the latest rock stars or movie actors. From history to hype, less known scientists, tyrants, rock stars, and movie actors are compared to one or more of the prototypes, a short-hand way to confer the attributes of the prototype to the less known person. Prominent landmarks and prominent people in addition to being unique individuals, become categories whose members are similar in location or in distinguishing characteristics.

4.1. Lines and orders

As we have seen, putting things into groups imposes structure on the world by abstracting and selecting similarities and differences and by reducing the number of different things in the world. A deceptively simple process with far-ranging consequences. Organizing the categories into subcategories, hierarchies of kinds or parts, further simplifies and structures the world. Locating objects with respect to other objects and a frame of reference imposes still more structure. Nevertheless, even more structure is needed. Another seemingly simple way to impose structure on the things in the world is to line them up, much as objects can be naturally lined up on the surface of the world, constructing an ordinal scale. Lining things up imposes an order, putting one thing next to another, raising the issue: how to order, in what direction? Putting things on a line opens the further possibility of putting some pairs of things closer, other pairs of things farther, so that not only the order of objects, but also the distances between them are meaningful, thereby constructing an ordinal scale. Finally, when order and distance are meaningful, this raises the possibility of a natural beginning, a natural zero point, such as the ground, from which height is measured upwards and depth downwards. Zero points may be established ad hoc as well, as when distance to many cities is calculated from a particular one.

Just as humans, even tiny ones, naturally form categories and subcategories, they also naturally form orderings (e.g., Gelman & Gallistel, 1976), and can express those orderings using space. One large project investigated how children and adults group and order related things, concrete and abstract, on the space of a page (Tversky et al., 1991). Children and adults, from preschool to college, from three language cultures, English, Hebrew, and Arabic, were asked to put stickers on paper to indicate spatial, temporal, quantitative, and preference relations. For space, the experimenter placed three small dolls in a row, separated by more than the height of the dolls, and asked the child to put stickers on a page showing the locations of the dolls. The adults put X's. Using the space of the page to show spatial relations was easy for the children. Children at all ages put the stickers in a row, spaced apart. Mapping the more abstract concepts to the page, time, quantity, and preference was more challenging. For time, the experimenter placed a sticker in the middle of the page for lunch, and asked the child to place stickers for breakfast and dinner. For quantity, a handful of candy, a bagful of candy, a shelf full of candy. A few children put the stickers on top of each other, or scattered them all over the page, indicating that they conceived of the entities categorically, for example, all meals or separate meals. They did not represent the underlying temporal dimension that connected the meals or the underlying quantity that connected the amounts. Even so, most children, even at four years, put the stickers on a line, indicating that they conceived of the elements, breakfast, lunch, and dinner or disliked food, OK food, and liked food as lying on a dimension, temporal or preference. Furthermore, the more abstract concepts were mapped to a line at a later age than the more concrete concepts, first space, then time, then quantity, then preference.

4.2. Interval: Mapping distance

Ordering categories on dimensions imposes more structure on the world. However, the human mind also discerns relative distances along dimensions. Paris is closer to Amsterdam than Amsterdam to Stockholm. The height of an ant is closer to that of a spider than the height of a spider to the height of a giraffe. A subsequent study asked children to map interval relations, first spatial relations, and then more abstract relations. Mapping spatial, relations that were interval was easy for children. Even the younger children placed stickers farther apart for dolls placed farther apart. However only older children succeeded in mapping distance for abstract concepts, that is, preserving interval relations, to the space of a page. For time for example, children were asked to place stickers to indicate breakfast, morning snack, and dinner. Mapping relative distance or interval for abstract concepts, time, quantity, and preference, was reliable only for children 11 years or more, and, as for ordinal mapping, in the order of abstractness (Tversky et al., 1991). Thus, even children readily order spatial things and abstract things and can express that ordering using real space. Older children can also express distances between things on abstract dimensions, using real space.

4.3. Perspective: Near to far

For judgments of distance in space, the point of view, the anchor or reference point, biases judgments. In one experiment, students in Ann Arbor were asked to imagine themselves either in San Francisco or in New York City (Holyoak & Mah, 1982). They were then asked to make distance judgments from their viewpoint to a set of cities more or less equidistant along an east-west axis between San Francisco and New York City: Pittsburgh, Indianapolis, Kansas City, Denver, and Salt Lake City. Students exaggerated the distances close to their imagined viewpoint relative to the distances far from their viewpoints. Thus, students imagining themselves in New York judged the distance between New York City and Pittsburgh as greater than students whose imagined viewpoint was San Francisco; conversely, students imagining themselves in San Francisco judged the distance from San Francisco to Salt Lake City as greater than those whose viewpoint was New York City. This error is analogous to a phenomenon in viewing a remote vista: the near distances seem greater than the far ones for several reasons: closer objects occlude farther ones, closer ones subtend larger visual angles, and closer ones are sharper than farther ones. When viewing a landscape, near objects are sharp and clear and distant ones blurry.

Events in time form a landscape, too, that invites perspective, with analogous errors and biases. Events in time bear many analogies to objects or landmarks in space (e.g., Casati & Varzi, 1996; Zacks & Tversky, 2001; Tversky, Zacks, & Hard, 2008). Just as concepts of space are organized around the things in it rather than objective measurable Euclidean coordinates, so concepts of time are organized around the events in it. Just as spatial objects can be viewed as zero, one, two or more dimensions, so temporal events can be viewed as zero, one, two or more dimensions. The temporal landscape gets telescoped from our own perspective; near times are rich and detailed and far times are dim and crowded together (Loftus &

Marberger, 1983; Bradburn, Rips, & Shevell, 1987; Brown, Rips, & Shevell, 1985). The temporal landscape, too, has landmarks, and they draw ordinary events closer to them. Just as landmarks in space draw ordinary buildings to them, temporal landmarks draw events in time towards them. For example, the beginnings and ends of semesters are temporal landmarks. Students judge that the events of a semester happened closer to semester beginnings and ends than they actually did. Ordinary events in time do not have this effect (e.g., Huttenlocher, Hedges, & Prohashka, 1988).

There are parallel effects in social judgments to these effects of spatial perspective. People differentiate those "near" us far more than those "distant" from us, so that the people we know are judged to be highly different from one another whereas those we know less well or not at all are judged more similar to one another (Quattrone, 1986).

4.4. Perspectives: Frames of reference

The mind is remarkably agile, and one of its' tricks is imagining other perspectives, sometimes termed *allocentric* perspectives in contrast to current, *egocentric* perspectives. In fact, people can take a variety of different perspectives on experience, real or imagined (e.g., Levinson, 1996; Tipper & Behrman, 1996; Tversky, 1996).

People imagine unseen perspectives when they provide route directions to others to guide them to a destination. People imagine perspectives that conflict with their own when they tell a person facing them which wine glass is theirs (e.g., Mainwaring, Tversky, Ohgishi, & Schiano, 2003; Schober, 1993). Both these perspectives are embedded in an environment, imagining a point of view within it. Even more remarkably, people can take imaginary perspectives above an environment, an overview or survey perspective, and switch rapidly between overview and embedded perspectives (e.g., Lee & Tversky, 2005; Taylor & Tversky, 1992, 1996). Like a map, an overview perspective captures a large environment and provides the links and spatial relations among its parts, the landmarks within it. It eliminates much detail, notably many features on the terrain. For that reason, a survey perspective is useful for getting an overview of the interrelationships among many different places, landmarks, paths. A survey perspective can also be useful planning, for example, a route that joins two specific places, from here to there. By contrast, an embedded perspective provides detail of the environment within view at a level that allows navigation; as navigation proceeds, the view changes and the perspective is updated. Thus, an embedded perspective is useful for the step-by-step details, the set of procedures for getting from one place to another, after a route has been planned.

A route map or route directions represent both space and time, as it takes time to execute each of the steps. Exact distance and exact time are not typically explicit in route maps or route directions, but good approximations to each can be inferred from experience.

These spatial perspectives, survey and route, have analogues to perspectives on time, to construals of time (e.g., Liberman, Trope, & Stephan, 2007; Trope & Liberman, 2003). A survey or broad overview, a calendar for time like a map for space, provides the interrelations among many different entities, temporal or spatial, events or landmarks. A route provides the step-by-step actions needed to get from one place to another. Since events are rooted in places and actions take time, a route is inherently both spatial and temporal. Route plans don't typically provide exact distances or exact times but good approximations to both can often be inferred (Pazzaglia, Meneghetti, & Tversky, unpublished). Liberman, Trope, and their collaborators have shown broad effects of temporal perspective or as they term it, construals of time, on planning and inference. To transform just one of their many examples to the present analysis, thinking about a meeting (or a paper due) in the far future would be done by a survey perspective, looking at the larger temporal landscape that goes from now until after then. However, when the date approaches (or when we approach the date, depending on the temporal metaphor, moving ego or moving time, adopted), a route perspective would be used to plan the steps taken to arrive at the meeting. In a survey perspective, the each event, like the meeting, would be thought of as a point, along with the other temporal landmarks, whereas in a route perspective, the meeting would be thought of as a duration, one dimension encompassing the day to get there, the days of the meeting, the day to return. Thinking about points in surveys and thinking about regions in routes are quite different; points have far less associated detail.

4.5. Symbolic distance

Putting things into categories allows judgments of belonging or not as well as inferences about properties. Breakfast entails a time of day and a kind of cuisine. Ordering things on a line allows a richer set of judgments and comparisons. The speed of making some judgments and inferences depends on the ordinal distance between entities. For example, when asked which of two animals is more intelligent or more pleasant, people respond faster when the animals are far from each other on the dimension of judgment than when they are close to each other, a phenomenon known as the *symbolic distance effect* (e.g., Moyer & Bayer, 1973; Banks & Flora, 1977; Holyoak & Mah, 1981; Paivio, 1978). The foundations for this effect are again spatial. If things were actually lined up in the world, discerning distance between far objects would be easier than discerning distance between near objects. The effect holds for spatial and abstract comparisons, including, naturally, social comparisons.

4.6. Orientation

Orderings in the mind do not necessarily need an orientation, though they may very well have one. One can know that airplanes are more expensive than cars and cars more expensive than airplanes without orienting that ordering in space. Lines on paper representing orders, however, do need an orientation. Here again spatial cognition provides the foundation for orientation, horizontal and vertical. Aspects of the world and the body favor horizontal and vertical. In the world, the horizon is, of course, horizontal, and gravity forms a vertical dimension that maximally contrasts with the horizontal. As for the body, it is typically upright, that is, vertical (or horizontal, in sleep) and navigates the horizontal world. Moreover, visual acuity is greatest for horizontal and vertical lines. Space, whether on paper or in gesture favors horizontal or vertical orientations for ordering. Written language, accounting, calendars, graphs, and more are typically aligned with horizontal and/or vertical.

4.7. Direction

Orderings need a start point and direction as well as a line. For the vertical axis, there are strong asymmetric embodied and situated forces: the vertical human body, which grows upwards from childhood to adulthood, and gravity, which means that going upwards takes more resources than going downwards. The horizontal axis has no strong asymmetric situated forces. However, there are body and cultural asymmetries that appear to affect horizontal orderings, handedness and reading order.

Previews of associations of the axes and their orderings to meaning appeared in the large international study of mappings by children and adults of spatial, temporal, qualitative, quantitative, and preference relations (Tversky et al., 1991). Time, a relatively neutral concept, was primarily mapped horizontally, and the preferred direction for increases corresponded to writing order, left to right for English and right to left for Arabic. For other dimensions, both vertical and horizontal axes were used. Directionality did not depend on reading order. The only bias was to avoid increases from top to bottom.

4.8. Horizontal biases

Most people in the world are right-handed, a fact that is reflected in language; for example, in English, *sinister* derives from the Latin word for *left* and *dexterity* from the Latin word for *right*. Despite these cultural associations, enduring characteristics of the body affect assignment of meaning to space. Left-handers tend to place the things they like on the left, and right-handers tend to place the things they like on the right (Casasanto, 2009). More surprisingly, temporary characteristics of the body also affect meanings. When sitting on a chair tilting left, people are more likely to endorse left political views (Oppenheimer & Trail, 2010).

Another cultural factor, the order of reading and writing, appears to have even stronger effects on assignment of meaning. Reading order is evident in perception and in action: direction of apparent motion corresponds to reading order (Morikawa & McBeath, 1992) as do directions of perceptual exploration and of drawing (e.g., Chokron & De Agostini, 2002; Nachson, 1985; Vaid, this volume; Vaid, Singh, Sakhuja, & Gupta 2002). It is evident in gesture, notably in relating temporal events (Roman, Casasanto, & Santiago, unpublished). It is also evident in mental representations of number, where, for writers of left-to-right languages, smaller numbers are associated with the left side of space and larger numbers with the right side, called the SNARC effect, for Spatial Numeric Association of Response Code (e.g., Dehaene, 1992). This effect reverses for writers of right to left languages and bias is absent in illiterates (Zebian, 2005). Reading/writing order bias is evident in aesthetic judgments (e.g., Chokron & De Agostini, 2000; Nachson, Argaman, & Luria, 1999) and in emotional judgments (Sakhuja, Gupta, Singh, & Vaid, 1996). For R-L languages, power corresponds to reading order, as evident in a bias to graph data for men prior to, that is, to the right of, data for women (Hegarty, Lemieux, & McQueen, in press).

As readers of this volume know, the reading order bias is evident in diverse and surprising ways for social stimuli. Although surveys of (western) fine art in museums show that faces in portraits typically face left, this effect is stronger for female faces than male (Chatterjee, 2001; McManus & Humphrey, 1973). This has been attributed to a bias, present in readers of languages that proceed from left to right, to put agents of actions on the left and patients of action on the right (Chatterjee, 2001, 2002; Maass & Russo, 2003). This *agency hypothesis* is rooted in syntactic properties of language in that most languages follow subject-verb-object or subject-object-verb. To come full circle, it appears that the favored word order is rooted in action, and in particular, in the temporal order of actions evident in the agent-patient-action order of spontaneous gestural explanations favored across many languages (e.g., Goldin-Meadow, So, Ozyurek, & Mylander, 2008) order. The implication for portraits is that men are more likely to be thought of as agents and women as patients, a trend that seems to be weakening as social norms change (Suitner & Maass, 2007). For readers of left-right languages, left-right motion is perceived as stronger than right-left motion, a trend that reverses for readers of left-right languages (Maass, Pagani, & Berta, 2007). Thus, this seemingly arbitrary, probably accidental, convention of writing from the left or from the right has broad consequences for perception, cognition, emotion, and social expectations.

The right-left (or left-right) axis has a weak asymmetry, consonant with the weak left-right asymmetry of the body and the weaker horizontal asymmetries in the world. The fact that languages are written in both directions is further support for the weakness of the asymmetry. The relative weakness of horizontal asymmetries is also supported by the fact that a cultural artifact, the direction of writing, appears to impose asymmetries of thought. Not so for the vertical, aligned with that powerful asymmetric force, gravity, and in fact, it is probably safe to say that all written languages begin at the top.

4.9. Orientation: Vertical biases

The vertical axis of the world, in stark contrast to the horizontal axis of the world, confers a ubiquitous asymmetry on the world. Living things and many of the artifacts designed for them have a vertical axis of symmetry. It is harder to go up than down, it takes more effort, more strength, more power, more resources. In contrast to time and number, quantity and preference were mapped both horizontally and vertically. In the large study investigating mappings of abstract dimensions to the paper of space, increases in quantity and preference were equally likely to be mapped from left to right and from right to left on the horizontal axis, independent of writing order culture, so the direction of the horizontal did not seem to matter. For the vertical, increases were mapped from down to up, but mapping increases from up to down was avoided, undoubtedly due to the strong correspondences between up and more (Tversky et al., 1991).

The strong vertical bias in spatial mapping is well-known in language and in gesture (e.g. Clark, 1973; Cooper & Ross, 1975; Lakoff & Johnson, 1980; Talmy, 2000). *Up* is associated with good, more, powerful, just about every positive attribute, concrete or abstract, social or not. The origins of the association are again spatial: people grow taller and stronger as they grow older, higher piles of money means more money. Defying gravity takes strength. Happy people stand tall and depressed people slump; correspondingly, people may feel "up" or "down." Good performances are given a thumbs-up. Diagrams follow that bias, those produced by novices and those produced by professionals. For example, almost all the evolutionary charts found in biology textbooks in a large university library put man at the top of the evolutionary tree and the present time at the top of charts of geological eras (Tversky, 2001).

5. Spatial schemas

Spatial thinking is deep and complex. Its structure includes objects, and objects located in space with respect to other objects or reference frames; groups of objects, and groups of groups; orderings of objects or groups, and orderings on orderings; intervals between objects and groups, directions, changes, actions; it includes reference objects, background objects, reference frames, perspectives. This is only the surface, only the beginning, but even that is enough to serve as a foundation for the nuances, richness, and creativity of abstract thought. In addition, we have only considered unsituated, disembodied, cerebral judgments of remembered environments, not judgments in the field that include direct perception of the surrounding environment and direct sensations from the body. Effects of the field have been known for years; for example, when people are asked to adjust the orientation of a stick (rod) to upright in the world, their adjustments are affected by the angle of a frame that encloses the stick (e.g., Witkin, Dyk, Faterson, Goodenough, & Karp, 1962). In the field, for example, people overestimate the slopes of hills, especially when they are carrying heavy backpacks (Proffitt, Stefanucci, Banton, & Epstein, 2003). Nor have we considered the effects of social stimuli and spatial ones, and there are intriguing effects. When people are waiting with friends who will climb with them, they reduce their estimates of the slope of the hill (e.g., Schnall, Harber, Stefanucci, & Proffitt, 2008). Fortunately, this is discussed in this volume (Schnall, this volume).

5.1. Spatial schemas: Abstractions

Direct perception of space does not in itself provide groupings, orderings, dimensions, directions, or distances, nor does it provide the variety of perspectives people are able to take, even perspectives that conflict with the physical point of view of the eyes or the body. Indeed, perspectives other than one's own current physical perspective are often preferred to one's own perspective even when the implicit recipient of the message shares the same perspective (Tversky & Hard, 2009). Spatial reasoning is itself an abstraction from information given in perception. It is the abstractions of space, the cognition of space, not the perception of space that is transferred to abstract concepts. As a start, the objects, foreground and background, relations, frames of reference, perspectives, and more on which reasoning is done are not fixed, but rather selected. Imagine being in a busy city scene. Someone stops you to ask for instructions to a restaurant in view. To give instructions, you select the relevant landmarks from the large array around you; then you select directions, terms of reference, and reference frames, step-by-step (e.g., Levelt, 1989; Taylor & Tversky, 1996). Other judgments, such as counting intersections or restaurants, comparing sizes or distances, estimating time, and more, will lead you to select different information from the scene and organize it in different ways. Many possible objects can be extracted and grouped in many possible ways. Many possible relations can be determined: distance, direction, size, among them. Understanding these relations depends in turn on groupings and orderings, constructs thought imposes on the world.

5.2. Spatial thinking: Perception/action couplings?

Underlying extracting objects, grouping objects, ordering objects comparing objects, groups, orderings and more must be a multitude of processes involving both perception and action. From the classic and profound analyses of Piaget to the most recent treatise on embodied thought comes the insight that both perception and action are involved. Grouping in the mind is undoubtedly connected with grouping in the world, putting similar things together, perhaps into piles, on a surface, and separating different things, an activity that occupies children at play and adults at work. Orderings in the mind are undoubtedly connected with orderings in the world, placing things in order of, say, size or time (e.g., Kirsch, 1995). Taking other perspectives in imagination probably begins with taking other perspectives in the world. Groupings and orderings in the world are easier to make on horizontal surfaces, as they are all around us. Groupings are naturally stretched left-to-right (or vice versa), easier for the hands to arrange and the eyes to see. The same properties of the body and the world make counting easier on horizontal surfaces. What's helpful is to lay things out a single row and to count one by one in a consistent order; the direction of the counting, left to right or right to left, is less consequential. Counting entails two sets of actions, laying out the items, and pointing to each one by one. Both groupings and orderings can additionally capture distance on one or two dimensions, if desired. The perceptual and cognitive processes involved in disembodied spatial thinking, then, are rooted in concrete actions taken in the world, perception-action couplings. Then both the perception and the action, as noted by many thinkers, among them Piaget and Shepard (2001) are internalized and mirrored in thought, underlying the many phenomena reviewed here and in the other papers in this volume. This analysis also points to the close linkage between space and time, as the perception/action couplings take place step by step in time. That space seems to be fundamental (e.g., Boroditsky, 2001) is probably due to the transient nature of time, which does not allow the inspection and reinspection that space allows.

Spatial thinking is inherently complex and abstract. The abstraction and consequent flexibility in spatial thinking allow it to be extended to further abstractions, to concepts and relations that are not inherently spatial, notably social concepts and relations. At its most abstract, thought is fundamentally concrete, if only because concrete thought itself entails abstraction.

References

Banks, William P. & Julianne Flora (1977). Semantic and perceptual processes in symbolic comparisons. *Journal of Experimental Psychology: Human perception and Performance, 3*, 278–290.
Boroditsky, Lera (2001). Metaphoric structuring: understanding time through spatial metaphors. *Cognition, 75*, 1–28.
Bradburn, Norman M., Lance J. Rips & Steve K. Shevell (1987). Answering autobiographical questions: The impact of memory and inference on surveys. *Science, 236*, 158–161.
Brown, Norman R., Lance J. Rips & Steve K. Shevell (1985). The subjective dates of natural events in very-long-term memory. *Cognitive Psychology, 17*, 139–177.
Carnaghi, Andrea, Anne Maass, Sara Gresta, Mauro Bianchi, Mara Cadinu & Luciano Arcuri (2008). Nomina sunt omina: On the inductive potential of nouns and adjectives in person perception. *Journal of Personality and Social Psychology, 94*, 839–859.
Casati, Roberto & Achille C. Varzi (1996). *Events*. Aldershot, England; Brookfield, VT: Dartmouth.
Casasanto, Daniel (2009). Embodiment of abstract concepts: Good and bad in right- and left-handers. *Journal of Experimental Psychology: General, 138*, 351–367.
Chatterjee, Anjan (2001). Language and space: Some interactions. *Trends in Cognitive Science, 5*, 55–61.
Chatterjee, Anjan (2002). Portrait profiles and the notion of agency. *Empirical Studies of the Arts, 20*, 33–41.

Chokron, Sylvie & Marie De Agostini (2000). Reading habits influence aesthetic preference. *Cognitive Brain Research, 10*, 45–49.

Chokron, Sylvie & Marie De Agostini (2002). The influence of handedness on profile and line drawing directionality in children, young, and older normal adults. *Brain, Cognition, and Emotion, 48,* 333–336.

Clark, Herbert H. (1973). Space, time, semantics, and the child. In Timothy E. Moore (Ed.), *Cognitive development and the acquisition of language* (pp. 27–63). New York: Academic Press.

Cooper, William E. & John R. Ross (1975). World Order. In Robin E. Grossman, L. James San, & Timothy J. Vances (Eds.), *Papers from the parasession on functionalism* (pp. 63–111). Chicago: Chicago Linguistic Society.

Dehaene, Stanislaus (1992). Varieties of numerical abilities. *Cognition, 44,* 1–42.

Franklin, Nancy & Barbara Tversky (1990). Searching imagined environments. *Journal of Experimental Psychology: General, 119,* 63–76.

Gattis, Merideth (Ed., 2001). *Spatial schemas and abstract thought.* Cambridge: MIT Press.

Gelman, Rochel & Charles R. Gallistel (1978). *The child's understanding of number.* Cambridge, Mass: Harvard University Press.

Goldin-Meadow, Susan (2003). *Hearing gesture: How our hands help us think.* Cambridge: Belknap Press.

Goldin-Meadow, Susan, Wing-Chee So, Asli Ozyurek & Carolyn Mylander (2008). The natural order of events: How speakers of different languages represent events nonverbally. *Proceedings of the National Academy of Sciences, 105,* 9163–9168.

Hegarty, Peter, Anthony F. Lemieux, & Grant McQueen (in press). Graphing the order of the sexes: Constructing, recalling, interpreting, and putting the self in gender difference graphs. *Journal of Personality and Social Psychology.*

Hirtle, Stephen C. & John Jonides (1985). Evidence of hierarchies in cognitive maps. *Memory and Cognition, 13,* 208–217.

Holyoak, Keith J. & Wesley A. Mah (1981). Semantic congruity in symbolic comparisons: Evidence against an expectancy hypothesis. *Memory & Cognition, 9,* 197–204.

Holyoak, Keith J. & Wesley A. Mah (1982). Cognitive reference points in judgments of symbolic magnitude. *Cognitive Psychology, 14,* 328–352.

Huttenlocher, Janellen, Lawrence V. Hedges & Vincent Prohaska (1988). Hierarchical organization in ordered domains: Estimating the dates of events. *Psychological Review, 95,* 471–484.

Kessell, Angela & Barbara Tversky (2005). Gestures for thinking and explaining. *Proceedings of the Cognitive Science Society Meetings.* Mahwah, NJ: Erlbaum.

Kirsh, David (1995). The intelligent use of space. *Artificial Intelligence, 73,* 31–68.

Lakoff, George & Mark Johnson (1980). *Metaphors we live by.* Chicago: University of Chicago Press.

Lee, Paul U. & Barbara Tversky (2005). Interplay between visual and spatial: The effects of landmark descriptions on comprehension of route/survey descriptions. *Spatial Cognition and Computation, 5*, 163–185.

Levelt, Wilhem J.M. (1989). *Speaking: From intention to articulation.* Cambridge, MA: MIT Press.

Levinson, Stephen (1996). Frames of reference and Molyneux's question: Cross-linguistic evidence. In Paul Bloom, Mary A. Peterson, Lynn Nadel, & Merrill F. Garrett, *Space and Language* (pp. 109–169). Cambridge: MIT Press.

Liberman, Nira, Yaacov Trope & Elena Stephan (2007). Psychological distance. In: E. Tory Higgins & Arie W. Kruglanski (Eds.). *Social psychology: A handbook of basic principles (Vol. 2, pp. 353–383).* New York: Guilford Press.

Loftus, Elizabeth F. & William Marburger (1983). Since the eruption of Mt. St. Helens, has anyone beaten you up? Improving the accuracy of retrospective reports with landmark events. *Memory and Cognition, 11*, 114–120.

Maass, Anne & Aurore Russo (2003). Directional bias in the mental representation of spatial events: Nature or culture? *Psychological Science, 14*, 296–301.

Maass, Anne, Damiano Pagani & Emanuela Berta (2007). How beautiful is the goal and how violent is the fistfight? Spatial bias in the interpretation of human behavior. *Social Cognition, 25*, 833–852.

Mainwaring, Scott D., Barbara Tversky, Motoko Ohgishi & Diane J. Schiano (2003). Descriptions of simple spatial scenes in English and Japanese. *Spatial Cognition and Computation, 3*, 3–42.

McManus, I. Christopher & N. Humphrey (1973). Turning the left cheek. *Nature, 243*, 271–272.

Miller, George A. & Philip N. Johnson-Laird (1976). *Language and Perception.* Cambridge, MA: Harvard University Press.

Morikawa, Kazunori & Michael McBeath (1992). Lateral motion bias associated with reading direction. *Vision Research, 32*, 1137–1141.

Moyer, Robert S. & Richard H. Bayer. Mental comparison and the symbolic distance effect. *Cognitive Psychology, 8*, 228-246.

Nachson, Israel (1985). Directional preferences in perception of visual stimuli. *International Journal of Neuroscience, 25*, 161–174.

Nachson, Israel, E. Argaman & A. Luria (1999). Effects of directional habits and handedness on aesthetic preference for left and right profiles. *Journal of Cross Cultural Psychology, 30*, 106–114.

Oppenheimer, Daniel M. & Thomas E. Trail (2010). Why leaning to the left makes you lean to the left: Effect of spatial orientation on political attitudes. *Social Cognition, 28*, 651–661.

Paivio, Alan (1978). Mental comparisons involving abstract attributes. *Memory and Cognition, 6*, 199–208.

Pazzaglia, Francesca, Chiara Meneghetti & Barbara Tversky (unpublished). *Imagining space and time.*

Portugali, Juval (1993). *Implicate relations: Society and space in the Israeli-Palestinian Conflict.* Dordrecht: Kluwer 1993.

Proffitt, Dennis R., Jeanine Stefanucci, Tom Banton & William Epstein (2003). The role of effort in perceived distance. *Psychological Science, 14*, 106–112.

Quattrone, George A. (1986). On the perception of a group's variability. In Stephen Worchel & William Austin (Eds.), *The psychology of intergroup relations* (pp. 25–48). New York: Nelson-Hall.

Román, Antonio, Daniel Casasanto & Julio Santiago (unpublished). Gesturing the right way about time in two cultures.

Rosch, Eleanor (1978). Principles of categorization. In Eleanor Rosch & Barbara B. Lloyd (Eds), *Cognition and categorization* (pp. 27–48). Hillsdale, NJ.

Sadalla, Edward K. & Lorin J. Staplin (1980). An information storage model for distance cognition. *Environment and Behavior, 12*, 183–193.

Sakhuja, Tripti, Gyan C. Gupta, Maharaj Singh & Jyotsna Vaid (1996). Reading habits affect asymmetries in facial affect judgments: A replication. *Brain and Cognition, 32*, 162–165.

Schnall, Simone, Kent D. Harber, Jeanine K. Stefanaucci, & Dennis R. Proffitt (2008) Social support and the perception of geographical slant. *Journal of Experimental Social Psychology, 44*, 1246–1255.

Schnall, Simone (this volume). Embodiment in affective space: Social influences on spatial perception.

Schober, Michael F. (1993). Spatial perspective-taking in conversation. *Cognition, 47*, 1–24.

Schubert, Thomas W., Sven Waldzus & Steffen R. Giessner (2009). Control over the association of power and size. *Social Cognition, 27*, 1–19.

Shepard, Roger N. (2001). Perceptual-cognitive universals as reflections of the world. *Behavior and Brain Sciences, 24*, 581–601.

Shepard, Roger N. & Peter Podgorny (1978). Cognitive processes that resemble perceptual processes. In William K. Estes (Ed.), *Handbook of learning and cognitive processes* (Vol. 5, pp. 189–237). Hillsdale, N.J.: Erlbaum.

Stevens, Albert, & Patty Coupe (1978). Distortions in judged spatial relations. *Cognitive Psychology, 10*, 422–437.

Suitner, Catherine & Anne Maass (2007). Positioning bias in portraits and self-portraits: Do female artists make different choices? *Empirical studies of the arts, 25*, 71–95.

Talmy, Leonard (1983). How language structures space. In Herbert L. Pick, Jr. & Lynn P. Acredolo (Eds.), *Spatial orientation: Theory, research and application* (pp. 225–282). N.Y.: Plenum.

Talmy, Leonard (2000). *Toward a cognitive semantics (Vols 1 & 2)*. Cambridge, MA: MIT Press.

Taylor, Holly A. & Barbara Tversky (1992). Descriptions and depictions of environments. *Memory and Cognition, 20*, 483–496.

Taylor, Holly A. & Barbara Tversky (1996). Perspective in spatial descriptions. *Journal of Memory and Language, 35*, 371–391.

Tipper, Steven P. & Marlene Behrmann (1996). Object-centered not scene-based visual neglect. *Journal of Experimental Psychology: Human Perception and Performance, 22,* 1261–1278.

Trope, Yaacov & Nira Liberman (2003). Temporal construal. *Psychological Review, 110,* 403–421.

Tversky, Amos & Itamar Gati (1978). Studies of similarity. In Eleanor Rosch & Barbara Lloyd (Eds.), *Cognition and categorization (*pp. 79–98). New York: Wiley.

Tversky, Barbara (1981). Distortions in memory for maps. *Cognitive Psychology, 13,* 407–433.

Tversky, Barbara (1996). Spatial perspective in descriptions. In Paul Bloom, Mary A. Peterson, Lynn Nadel & Merrill Garrett (Eds.), *Language and space* (pp. 463–491). Cambridge: MIT Press.

Tversky, Barbara (2001). Spatial schemas in depictions. In Merideth Gattis (Ed.), *Spatial schemas and abstract thought* (pp. 79–111). Cambridge: MIT Press.

Tversky, Barbara (2003). Navigating by mind and by body. In Christian Freksa, Wilfried Brauer, Christopher Habel & Karl F. Wender (Eds.), *Spatial Cognition III: Routes and Navigation, Human Memory and Learning, Spatial Representation and Spatial Reasoning* (pp. 1–10). Berlin: Springer Verlag.

Tversky, Barbara (2005a). Functional significance of visuospatial representations. In Priti Shah & Akira Miyake (Eds.), *Handbook of higher-level visuospatial thinking.* Cambridge: Cambridge University Press.

Tversky, Barbara (2005b). Visualspatial reasoning. In Keith Holyoak & Robert Morrison (Eds.), *Handbook of Reasoning* (pp. 209–249). Cambridge: Cambridge University Press.

Tversky, Barbara & Bridgette M. Hard (2009). Embodied and disembodied cognition: Spatial perspective taking. *Cognition, 110,* 124–129.

Tversky, Barbara, Julie Heiser, Paul U. Lee & Marie-Paule Daniel (2009). Explanations in gesture, diagram, and word. In Kenny Coventry, John Bateman, & Thora Tenbrink (Eds.), *Spatial language and dialogue* (pp. 119–131). Oxford: Oxford University Press.

Tversky, Barbara & Kathy Hemenway (1983). Categories of scenes. *Cognitive Psychology, 15,* 121–149.

Tversky, Barbara & Kathy Hemenway (1984). Objects, parts, and categories. *Journal of Experimental Psychology: General, 113,* 169–193.

Tversky, Barbara, Solomon Kugelmass & Atalia Winter (1991). Cross-cultural and developmental trends in graphic productions. *Cognitive Psychology, 23,* 515–557.

Tversky, Barbara, Jeffrey M. Zacks, & Bridgette M. Hard (2008). The structure of experience. In Thomas F. Shipley & Jeffrey M. Zacks (Editors), *Understanding events* (pp. 436–464). Oxford: Oxford University Press.

Vaid, Jyotsna (this volume). Asymmetries in representational drawing: Alternatives to a laterality account.

Vaid, Jyotsna & Maharaj Singh (1989). Asymmetries in the perception of facial effects: Is there an influence of reading habits? *Neuropsychologia, 27,* 1277–1286.

Vaid, Jyotsna, Maharaj Singh, Tripti Sakhuja & Gyan C. Gupta (2002). Stroke direction asymmetry in figure drawing: Influence of handedness and reading/writing habits. *Brain and Cognition, 48,* 597–602.

Witkin, Herman A., R.B. Dyk, H.F. Faterson, Donald R. Goodenough & S.A. Karp (1962). *Psychological differentiation.* New York: Wiley.

Zacks, Jeffrey M. & Barbara Tversky (2001). Event structure in perception and conception. *Psychological Bulletin, 127,* 3–21.

Zebian, Samar (2005). Linkages between number concepts, spatial thinking, and directionality of writing: The SNARC effect and the REVERSE SNARC effect in English and Arabic monoliterates, biliterates, and illiterate Arabic speakers. *Journal of Cognition and Culture, 5,* 165–190.

Flexible foundations of abstract thought: A review and a theory

Julio Santiago, Antonio Román, and Marc Ouellet[1]

Abstract

Since the proposal of conceptual metaphors as the representational means for grounding abstract concepts in concrete sensorio-motor experiences, experimental research about this issue is on the rise. The present paper identifies the problem of flexibility as one of the key questions that remains to receive a satisfactory answer, and proposes a psychologically plausible model that offers such an answer. The model is grounded on basic spatial cognition principles, working memory representations and attentional processes. This framework integrates prior results and licenses several new predictions. Direct test of some of these predictions is provided by two recent studies from our lab. Finally, we discuss the implications of this framework for the issues of the manifestation of conceptual metaphors in behaviour, the acquisition of conceptual metaphors, their cross-cultural variation, and the Symbol Grounding Problem.

1. Introduction

When observing a person talking about an abstract idea, say, a psychology professor describing a particular theory, we can often see that her hands depict in the air the concepts she is mentioning as if they were solid, concrete objects (McNeill, 1992). She might, for example, move her hand upwards as if holding a ball-like object. Simultaneous speech make clear that

---

[1] Preparation of this chapter was supported by grant SEJ2006-04732/PSIC, funded by DGI, Ministerio de Educación y Ciencia, Plan Nacional de Investigación Científica, Desarrollo e Innovación Tecnológica (I+D+i), 2006–2009, to Julio Santiago (PI). The authors would like to thank Javier Valenzuela, Daniel Casasanto and Thomas Schubert for their insightful comments on an earlier version of this chapter, to Stephanie Pourcel for her encouragement, to Juan Lupiáñez and Ana Torralbo, and to former and current members of the Psycholinguistics group at the University of Granada who have participated in this enterprise in one form or another.

these solid objects are used to refer to the same concept that is being mentioned. For example, the ball is "presented" to the audience as the speech introduces the name of the theory. Even more interestingly, the solid ball also seems to participate in reasoning involving the concept, as when the theory is compared to a rival theory, held as another ball in the other hand. The professor might then stare to one imaginary ball, then to the other, and compare their weights while she explains why one theory outperforms the other in its fit to available data.

Why are all these concrete concepts called upon when talking about abstract meaning? Are concrete experiences of moving and interacting with the physical world an integral part of abstract meaning? Or are they a more or less optional component that can be called on demand depending on the requirements of the situation (say, for improving understanding in the addressee or performing certain reasoning tasks)?

This question is the Symbol Grounding Problem (Harnad, 1990), and it constitutes a central topic in cognitive science (Barsalou, 1999; Glenberg, 1997; Harnad, 1990; Johnson-Laird, 1983; Lakoff & Johnson, 1999; Evans, Bergen & Zinken, 2008): how are concepts grounded in the external world? How is the internal representational machinery of the mind brought to bear on the objects and events that surround the individual? Within this general frame, many authors agree that the grounding of abstract concepts constitutes the hardest part. How can we think about things we have never experienced? How can the concepts of DEMOCRACY, FUTURE, or CONCEPT be entertained, let alone their references resolved?

The notion of embodiment has been offered as a possible solution to this problem. In what follows we first outline the version of embodiment that will be scrutinized in this paper, based on the idea of conceptual metaphors, what we will call the Solid Foundations View. We then identify the problem of cognitive flexibility as one of the most challenging questions for the Solid Foundations View, and undertake a literature review of research from several different traditions which can be related mostly to primary conceptual metaphors. We will keep the review focused on tasks involving literal or highly conventional language, including numbers, or without a linguistic component. Related research on figurative language processing will be mentioned only in passing.

Contrary to expectations from this view, available evidence shows a surprising degree of flexibility in conceptual metaphoric mappings, and points to a number of mediating factors. Cognitive flexibility opens questions regarding how specific mappings are selected and used in particular occasions. The main goal of the present paper is to offer an answer to these questions that grants cognitive flexibility a central theoretical role, instead of treating it as a nuisance. A main consequence of this approach will be to bring working memory to the explanatory forefront, leaving semantic long term memory in the background, just the opposite situation to what is currently the norm in the embodiment literature.

We show how the theory can integrate prior results, points to several factors that mediate the flexibility in the manifestation of conceptual projections, and generates several new predictions. We then draw on our own research to provide support for the theory. Finally, we end with a discussion of the implications of the theory for the issues of the acquisition of conceptual metaphors, their cross-linguistic and cross-cultural variations, and the Symbol Grounding Problem.

2. The Solid Foundations View of abstract concepts

The Solid Foundations View of abstract concepts has its origins in Conceptual Metaphor theory, which emerged within cognitive linguistics with a stronger focus on representation than on processing (Lakoff & Johnson, 1980, 1999; Gibbs & O'Brien, 1990; Johnson, 1987). In this view, concrete conceptual domains, which arise by direct experience in interaction with the world, are characterized by their image schematic structure (see also Mandler, 1992). Image schemas are perceptuo-motor gestalts such as SOURCE-PATH-GOAL, which arise from repeated situations in which movement from a source point to an end point is observed, experienced or imposed onto something. Other proposed image schemas include CENTER-SURROUND, CONTAINMENT, or BALANCE (Johnson, 1987). Image schemas provide relational structure to concrete conceptual domains. All other concepts are hypothesized to be structured through metaphoric mappings from these concrete domains. Such mappings arise also because of experienced correlations between the processing of the concrete and the abstract domains.

As an example, the domain of time (at least in one of the meanings of the polysemous term "time", see Evans, 2004) is proposed to borrow extensively from the domain of space, such that time is understood as the PATH along which the observer moves from one SOURCE location in the back (the past) towards another GOAL location in front (the future). This primary metaphor has been termed TIME IS MOTION, and arises from repeated correlations between the experience of motion and the passing of time. Some other proposed primary metaphors are MORE IS UP, HAPPY IS UP, or KNOWING IS SEEING (Lakoff & Johnson, 1980, 1999), which are embodied in experienced correlations between height and amount of substance, between body posture and emotion (positive or negative), and between the act of seeing and the experience of knowing. More complex concepts are in turn built up metaphorically through combinations of metaphors, such as, e.g., LOVE IS A JOURNEY or THEORIES ARE BUILDINGS.

Embodiment is thus something akin to the foundations of a building. Under this view, the human conceptual apparatus may look like the Empire State Building (Figure 1), a rock-solid structure where upper (more abstract) floors are supported by lower (more concrete) floors, which ground the whole structure firmly on the experiential terrain. The progressive bottom-up support is both intended as a metaphor for the adult conceptual system and for its ontogenetic development (Lakoff & Johnson, 1980, 1999; Mandler, 1992). This is the central tenet of the theoretical family that we refer to as the Solid Foundations View. Conceptual Metaphor Theory constitutes its strongest formulation.

In this view, all meaning is embodied in the sense that it all refers more or less directly to basic image schemas, which are abstracted in turn from perceptuo-motor experiences. There is a strict directionality implied here:

Figure 1. The Solid Foundations View of abstract concepts (photograph by wallyq, some rights reserved).

more abstract domains borrow structure from more concrete domains, but concrete domains do not borrow from abstract domains. We will refer to this assumption as the Strict Directionality Hypothesis heretofore. It should be noted that, under this formulation of the hypothesis, it implies both an ontogenetic asymmetry (more abstract concepts develop from more concrete concepts) and a representational asymmetry (more abstract concepts are represented in terms of more concrete concepts).

The power of metaphoric mappings for substantiating abstract thought lies in their ability to guide inferences and construct new meaning. To stay with the example of time, our bodily experience of passing time affords very few inferences by itself. Once time is mapped onto spatial motion, the imported structure allows a much richer set of inferences, i.e., one can ask what event is farther away in the future or in the past, whether it is possible for events to travel in circles and occur again in cyclic fashion, and so on. Hence, metaphoric structure helps reasoning and problem solving. Finally, conceptual metaphors allow extending meaning along novel lines which are consistent with the established mapping, as when we wonder whether we will be marching, stumbling or sliding into the future.

The original linguistic evidence stemmed from the analysis of patterns of idiomatic use in language. Lakoff and Johnson (1980) observed that conventional expressions can be grouped together in families which suggests a common underlying metaphoric structure. For example, sentences like "we are years ahead of them", "that was a long time back", or "he is advancing quickly towards a great future", all share the underlying TIME IS MOTION metaphor. This systematicity was unexpected from the standard semantic analysis of idioms, which sees them as frozen complex lexical items whose meaning must be listed as a whole in the mental lexicon (Cruse, 1986). Even more convincing was the fact that these hypothetical conceptual metaphors would allow idiomatic meanings to be extended in novel ways (as in the phrase "a remnant from a misty past") without compromising their comprehensibility. They also noted that it is very often the case that people speak about an abstract concept in terms of a more concrete one, but rarely they do it in the opposite way.

The analysis of polysemy provided another important source of support for these original insights. In the standard analysis, polysemy is captured by listing different senses of a word, as if they were just homonyms (e.g., Katz & Fodor, 1963; Cruse, 1986). However, meaning extensions of polisemous words often follow the lines established by conceptual metaphors (see, e.g., Tyler & Evans, 2001). These lines seem to be also important organizing principles for semantic change over time (Sweetser, 1990).

Gesture also provides many examples of abstract concepts being instantiated as concrete examples of image schemas, both in spontaneous gestures made along spoken language (McNeill, 1992; McNeill & Duncan, 2000; Núñez & Sweetser, 2006) and as stored lexical items in signed languages (Taub, 2000, 2001).

However, given its observational nature, these kinds of evidence, although intuitively compelling, cannot be taken as definitive evidence for the psychological reality of conceptual metaphors (Murphy, 1996, 1997). So far, the argument for the proposed causes of linguistic patterning (regularities of thought) relied only on theoretical parsimony. Parsimony, though, is only a heuristic strategy in science. In order to establish a causal relation between thought and language, it is necessary to use experimental methods. However, the Conceptual Metaphor View is not stated as a processing model, and as such, it cannot make predictions on performance in behavioural tasks of the kind used in psychological experiments. Therefore, a psychological version of it was devised by Boroditsky (2000), the Metaphoric Structuring View.

The Metaphoric Structuring View adopts the central idea of the progressive building of more abstract (less clearly delineated) conceptual domains on the foundations of more concrete (clearly delineated) domains. From there, interactions between the online processing of concrete and abstract concepts are predicted. Boroditsky (2000) also accepts the Hypothesis of Strict Directionality from concrete to abstract domains, and uses it to predict the shape of that interaction. She distinguishes two versions of Metaphoric Structuring. The Strong Version assumes that the source concrete domain is automatically activated by aspects of the situation, and it is then used to structure the abstract domain, so framing its understanding and reasoning about. The Weak Version maintains that, after repeated use, the relational structure of the source domain may be stored at the abstract domain, allowing the processing of the latter without having to activate the former. Under the Weak Version, once a conceptual metaphor is well established, no further influences of the processing of the abstract domain are expected on the processing of the concrete domain. Processing the concrete domain should influence concurrent performance based on the abstract domain, but the opposite should not hold. Boroditsky (2000) observed asymmetrical priming effects, which have since been replicated in several studies (e.g., Casasanto & Boroditsky, 2008; see discussion below), and thus rejected the Strong Version.

Although agreeing on the basic structuring of the conceptual system, it is important to note that Boroditsky (2000, and in later writings) does not sustain the ontogenetic view posed by Lakoff and Johnson (1980, 1999). Under her view, the determinant factor for the development of metaphoric mappings is language, and not experiencial correlations between the processing of the concrete and abstract domains. The metaphorical expressions present in language motivate the generation of analogies and guide the mapping of structure across concrete and abstract domains. Therefore, although the Weak Metaphoric Structuring Version is mainly related to the online processing of abstract concepts, it comes associated to an ontogenetic view of its own that places language at the origin of conceptual metaphors.

A final, intermediate version has been recently put forward by Casasanto (2008; Casasanto & Boroditsky, 2008; Casasanto, 2009), which we will call the Integrated Metaphoric Structuring View. It accepts the tenets of the Weak Metaphoric Structuring View, but suggests that both experiential correlations and linguistic metaphors play a role in the development of conceptual mappings. Perceptuo-motor experiences provide the ground for universal conceptual metaphors and language enters the picture later to strengthen some mappings and weaken others. So far, only one clear dissociation between these two sources of conceptual mappings has been reported (Casasanto, 2009): whereas right-handers associate positive emotional valence with right space and negative valence with left space, in agreement with both linguistic-cultural conventions and bodily experiences, left-handers show the opposite association. The mapping in left-handers must arise, therefore, only from perceptuo-motor experience, against the tide of language and culture. Figure 2 shows the family tree of the Solid Foundations View.

Summing up, the Solid Foundations View seems to provide a neat description of how abstract concepts are grounded, by resorting to mappings from more concrete concepts, and suggests two possible mechanisms for their acquisition: experiential correlations and linguistic influence. But before we turn to its problems, a quick note is in order about its relation to the other main tradition in the study of the embodiment of abstract concepts, the Simulation View. This approach posits that all concepts are represented by means of the enactment of detailed mental simulations, with

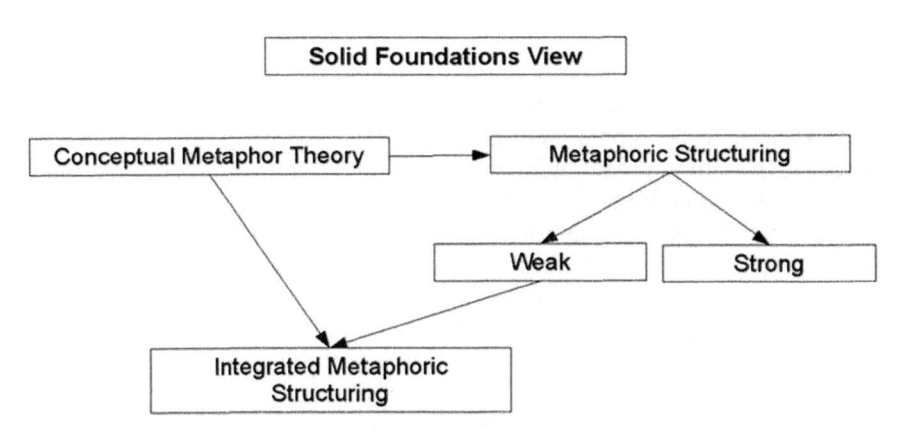

Figure 2. Family tree of the Solid Foundations View

extensive involvement of perceptuo-motor representations (Barsalou, 1999, 2003; Barsalou, Simmons, Barbey & Wilson, 2003; Glenberg, 1997; Gibbs, 2003). Most of the research within this tradition has been concerned with the processing of words and sentences with concrete meanings (see Zwaan, 2004, for a review). Regarding abstract concepts, Barsalou (1999; Niedenthal, Barsalou, Winkielman, Krauth-Gruber & Ric, 2005) has argued that their processing can be accounted for with very little resort to metaphor. Instead, the content of an abstract concept is constituted by concrete concepts and basic image schemas which are part of the perceptual, motor and introspective activations that form its experiencial basis. That is, abstract concepts are directly represented in terms of complex combinations of concrete concepts (with the important addition of introspective events within this category). This is an even stronger position than the Strong Metaphorical Structuring View, one that fails to see a representational difference between concrete and abstract levels. Strict directionality effects argue, therefore, against this position. However, Barsalou (1999) was careful not to deny the possibility of metaphoric structuring for some abstract concepts, and a more prominent role has been acknowledged by other proponents of the Simulations View (e.g., Zwaan, 2004).

3. The problem of cognitive flexibility

The picture laid by the Solid Foundations View is complicated by the fact that many primary conceptual metaphors can be used to structure a given abstract concept in different occasions, both by a single individual and across languages and cultures. Conceptual Metaphor Theory suggests that abstract concepts are grounded through experiential correlations in primary metaphors, which in turn are grounded in perceptuo-motor correlations, such as watching an object to move from one location to another. Such experiences are supposed to be determined by the characteristics of human bodies and their perceptual and motor systems, as well as by the characteristics of the environment with which humans interact. Therefore, image schemas should be basically universal. From there, it arises the expectation of universal primary metaphors (see Rakova, 2002, and Koveczes, 2005, for discussions). By including the possibility of language influences on conceptual mappings, the two current versions of Metaphoric Structuring (Weak and Integrated) are, in principle, better equipped to deal with crosslinguistic variability, but not with within-subject moment-to-moment variability. Another expectation that follows from the Solid Foundations View is that the influence between the processing of concrete and abstract domains should be asymmetrical, with a stronger influence from concrete to abstract and small or null influence from abstract to concrete. Available data also cast doubt on this prediction. Finally, the fact that all of them assume associative learning mechanisms also leads them to expect gradual acquisition of abstract concepts through repeated practice. This contrasts with the surprisingly fast learning rate that sometimes is attested.

As the upcoming review will reveal, there is an impressive degree of flexibility in conceptual mappings, both within and across languages and cultures. Alternative conceptual metaphors can be selected with high ease and speed, as well as old mappings replaced by new ones. The directionality of the cross-domain effect can also be altered. The present review will also point out several factors which seem to mediate the manifestation of that cognitive flexibility in behaviour. Because of its extensive study, we will start this review focusing on the conceptual domain of time, and then expand the conclusions by looking at other conceptual domains.

3.1. Cognitive flexibility in the domain of time

Within-subject flexibility

The conceptual metaphor of time which has so far received most attention in the literature maps past to locations in the back of the observer, future to locations in her front, and time to forward motion from past to future. This mapping has been termed the "ego-moving" metaphor (Clark, 1973). However, conventional language often shows the use of a different time metaphor, the "time-moving" metaphor, as in the sentence "Christmas is quickly approaching". In this mapping, time is also motion along a front-back PATH, but it is time units what move. The observer stands still as future time units approach her, pass her by and proceed into the past. Of central importance, only one mapping seems to be used to structure time in each given occasion, a choice which can have non-trivial consequences for thought. For example, the sentence "Next Wednesday's meeting has been moved forward two days" is ambiguous (McGlone & Harding, 1998; Boroditsky, 2000). If the listener uses the ego-moving metaphor, the meeting will be held next Friday. If the time-moving metaphor is used, the meeting is scheduled for next Monday. The chosen mapping helps framing the problem, and therefore affects its solution.

There is also supporting experimental evidence. McGlone and Harding (1998) presented a context of sentences referring to the time of events from either the ego-moving or the time-moving perspective. Participants judged whether each sentence was true or false with respect to a given temporal reference. When the last sentence changed perspective, decision times increased. In a second experiment, prior context affected how the ambiguous sentence "The meeting has been moved forward two days" was interpreted. Boroditsky (2000) obtained similar results using spatial primes in which a person moves toward an object (ego-moving) or an object moves toward a person (time-moving). Gentner, Imai and Boroditsky (2002) observed a congruency effect in reaction times in a task in which participants read a context written from one or the other perspective, and judge whether the mentioned event is past or future with respect to a reference event. Boroditsky and Ramscar (2002) extended the primes to actual experiences of motion by asking the "meeting" question to people at different points of a trip by flight, train or along a lunch line, and showed that the spatial experience of motion is able to prime the choice of an ego-moving perspective as long as people are actively paying attention to those spatial experiences.

Recently, a third type of spatial mapping has been emphasized by Núñez and Sweetser (2006), Núñez, Motz and Teuscher (2006) and Moore (2006). Núñez et al. named it the "time reference point" (time-RP) metaphor. When it is used, the sequence of events does not refer to any observer co-located with the present, but only to the order of events in itself (as in expressions like "Monday precedes Tuesday"). Núñez et al. (2006) were able to prime the use of a Time-RP perspective by means of displays of sequences of cubes moving horizontally, without including any ego that could be used as reference point. This mapping can be applied, in principle, to any spatial axis (front-back, left-right or up-down), as long as anteriority is mapped to the beginning of the sequence of events and posteriority to subsequent positions. However, gestural evidence obtained by Núñez and Sweetser (2006) suggests that the left-right spatial axis is often used to ground the Time-RP metaphor, which takes us to as yet another variant of the question of flexibility.

An interesting consequence of the experimental research on conceptual metaphors has been the discovery of mappings that are not attested in linguistic expressions, and therefore, have escaped the attention of linguists. A chief example is the TIME IS MOTION metaphor that maps time onto the left-right spatial axis, instead of the more investigated front-back axis. In his review of cross-linguistic metaphors for time, Radden (2004) concluded that there seems to be a total lack of linguistic conventions that refer to the left-right dimension in speech about time in any language. Signed languages seem to be the only exception to this rule (Emmorey, 2001). In contrast, we are all used to the conventional association of time to the horizontal axis in graphs, increasing from left to right. Comic strips and written language also flow from left to right in English, Spanish, and many other languages.

Tversky, Kugelmass and Winter (1991) asked English, Hebrew and Arab children to place three stickers on a paper to represent triads of concepts.

Some of these concepts were events organized along time, such as breakfast-lunch-dinner. English children were extremely consistent in placing the three stickers along a horizontal line with a left-to-right progression of events (see also Koerber & Sodian, 2008, for analogous results with German children). What could be the experiental basis of such a left-right temporal mapping? In the Tversky et al. (1991) study, Arab children were as consistent in mapping events to space in a right-to-left manner, which points to exposure to reading-writing direction and other graphical conventions as a chief candidate. (Hebrew children performed somewhere in between, what the authors adscribed to their greater exposition to English and other left-to-right orthographies.)

Recent studies have replicated the left-right effect with less explicit tasks. Núñez and Sweetser (2006) observed that gestures for ordered sequences of events were always from left-to-right in speakers of Aymara and Spanish. Santiago, Lupiáñez, Pérez and Funes (2007) presented Spanish adverbs and tensed verbs referring to past or future at left or right positions of a computer screen. Participants judged whether the words referred to past or future by pressing a left or a right key. Latencies were faster when past words were presented on the left or responded to with the left key, whereas the reverse was true for future words. Recent work using analogous procedures suggests that visual narratives such as movie clips (Santiago, Román, Ouellet, Rodríguez & Pérez-Azor, 2008) and short temporal intervals (Vallesi, Binns & Shallice, 2008) are also represented as running from left to right in the mind. Ouellet, Santiago, Israeli and Gabay (2010) have also shown that Hebrew speakers show a reversed right-to-left mapping. Furthermore, Weger and Pratt (2008) and Ouellet, Santiago, Funes and Lupiáñez (2010) have been able to show that the mere activation of the concepts of past and future by means of centrally presented words facilitates the processing of subsequent stimuli presented at left and right locations, respectively.

So far, no studies have addressed whether the ego-moving or time-moving perspectives are equally applicable to the left-right movement of time, but nothing seems to prevent it. Thus, the reviewed evidence suggests that, when time is conceptualized as motion in space, it may move along the front-back and left-right axes, and taking three different perspectives: ego-moving, time-moving and time-RP.

Are these really different conceptual mappings? As Lakoff and Johnson (1980, 1999) pointed out, the ego-moving and time-moving metaphors are just a figure-ground reversal of each other, a frequent phenomenon attested in many other metaphor pairs as well as in literal motion. This argument can be extended to the time-RP metaphor, which would result from taking the perspective of an observer located outside the sequence of events. Even the left-right TIME IS MOTION metaphor could be seen as a minor derivation of the same underlying schema and, perhaps, be explained by an integrated Conceptual Metaphor account. Nevertheless, it is easy to find in language other common metaphors for time which are radically inconsistent with the TIME IS MOTION metaphor, such as TIME IS MONEY. This latter metaphor forms itself a complex with other consistent metaphors, such as TIME IS A SUBSTANCE (as when asking "how much time do you have?", Lakoff & Johnson, 1980). Temporal metaphors, therefore, show an impressive degree of flexibility within a single individual, language and culture.

Cross-linguistic and cross-cultural flexibility

Within-subject flexibility is coupled with wide cross-linguistic and cross-cultural variation. Continuing with the TIME IS MOTION metaphor, languages and cultures differ in their preference for the use of some spatial axis over others. Moreover, sometimes these preferences are variations of the TIME IS MOTION metaphor, whereas some other times they are mediated by inconsistent metaphors.

Linguistic and anthropological evidence regarding the horizontal front-back axis suggests that speakers of English, Spanish and many other languages (see Malotky, 1983, for Hopi; Alverson, 1994, for Mandarin, Hindi and Sesotho; Ozçaliskan, 2003, for Turkish; see Radden, 2004, for a review) find intuitively compelling that future should be located in front of us and past behind, because we move in space towards locations that will be reached in the future and leave behind the places visited in the past. In contrast, many languages place the future behind and look ahead to the past. This mapping is common in some South American languages, and it seems to be mediated by a non-spatial metaphor, SEEING IS KNOWING: the past is something already known, and it can therefore be "seen" clearly, whereas the future is always a possibility state which cannot be "seen" definitely (see Núñez & Sweetser, 2006, for Aymara; and Klein, 1987, for Toba; there is also some evidence that Hawaiian is also within this language type: Karme'eleihiwa, 1992, cited in Clifford, 2004).

The vertical spatial axis is also used by some languages to express time, at least as an option. English resorts to this axis in expressions like "Christmas is coming up" (Lakoff & Johnson, 1980). There is a time metaphor in Zapotec in which the days and months increase upwards in the vertical dimension, so it is common to refer to the prior month as the down month and to the next month as the up month (MacLaury, 1989). This past-down future-up mapping is probably mediated by the conceptual metaphor MORE IS UP and its experiential basis in image schemas of growing pile size as matter accumulates (Lakoff & Johnson, 1980). Boroditsky (2001, citing Scott,

1989) asserts that Chinese also has a vertical time metaphor, but in the opposite direction, past being up and future down. No image schematic basis for such a mapping is offered, although it might be based on writing direction.

Finally, as mentioned above, the left-to-right mapping of time is attested in conventional linguistic usage only in signed languages (Emmorey, 2001). That this mapping is based on reading habits and graphic conventions is supported by the fact that Jordanian Sign Language conventionally uses a right-to-left temporal mapping instead (Emmorey, 2002). Experimental evidence in the same direction is provided by Tversky et al. (1991, see above).

A sizeable literature now supports that reading direction and graphical conventions constitute an important source of perceptuo-motor experiences which may be used to ground conceptual domains. They exert subtle influences on perception (Dreman, 1977), attention (Spalek & Hammad, 2005), motor control and memory (Nachson, 1981), and preferences for physical stimuli (McManus & Humphrey, 1973). Such an effect seems to extend into the conceptual realm: English speakers have a left-to-right bias when thinking of the agent and patient roles of a sentence: the agent tends to be imagined to the left of the patient. Moreover, actions like "push" or "pull" tend to be imagined flowing from left to right (Maher, Chatterjee, Gonzalez-Rothi & Heilman, 1995; Chatterjee, Maher, Gonzalez-Rothi & Heilman, 1995; Chatterjee, Southwood & Basilico, 1999; see also Rinaldi & Pizzamiglio, 2006, for related evidence). The association of this bias to reading direction has been shown by Maas and Russo (2003), comparing adult native speakers of Arabic and Italian, and Dobel, Diesendruck and Bölte (2007), comparing adult and preschool speakers of German and Hebrew. However, there are also two published studies which fail to replicate this result: Barrett, Kim, Crucian and Heilman (2002) with right-to-left vertical Korean readers, and Altmann, Saleem, Kendall, Heilman and Rothi (2006) with Arab readers.

Finally, there is also some evidence suggesting cross-linguistic variation in perspective use: Dahl (1995) argues that Malagasy does not use the ego-moving perspective at all.

Sometimes, cross-linguistic differences are a matter of degree. For example, Levine (1997) describes wide, but gradual, variations in the use of the TIME IS MONEY metaphor across the world's cultures. Another example is provided by English and Greek, both of which show the use of the TIME IS MOTION and TIME IS A SUBSTANCE metaphors in conventional language, but the former predominates in English and the latter in Greek (Casasanto, 2008).

Because of its reliance on universal perceptuo-motor experiences as the most basic grounding of abstract concepts, cross-linguistic and cross-cultural flexibility is unexpected from Conceptual Metaphor Theory. However, as mentioned above, the two Metaphoric Structuring Views (Weak and Integrated) can account for linguistic relativity effects. Boroditsky (2001) proposed that language may influence the selection of image schemas from the concrete domain that are used to structure the abstract domain in a given occasion. As repeated use produces those schemas to be independently stored within the abstract domain, language habits may affect which schemas are finally selected to structure the target domain. In sum, how people talk may affect how people think. Consistently with this assertion, Boroditsky (2001) showed that vertical spatial primes were more effective than horizontal primes to affect a temporal judgment task in Chinese than in English speakers (but see Chen, 2007, January & Kako, 2007, and Tsé & Altarriba, 2008, for three failures at replicating this result). Casasanto (2008) describes a study which compared English and Greek speakers in the ability of the length of a growing line or the amount of water in a filling container to bias estimations of the duration of the event. Coherent with the predominant linguistic patterns of their languages, English speakers' time estimation was affected by length and unaffected by quantity, whereas the opposite pattern was observed for Greek speakers.

Although this is suggestive evidence for an effect of language on conceptual organization, these data pose a logical problem for both Metaphoric Structuring Views, as they are now faced with explaining how those conceptual mappings get initially into language. One possibility comes from the "career of metaphor" hypothesis proposed by Bowdle and Gentner (2005) in the context of metaphor comprehension. They proposed that novel linguistic metaphors (e.g., "a ballerina is a butterfly") are initially processed as literal comparisons ("ballerinas are like butterflies"), which implies the simultaneous activation of source (butterfly) and target (ballerina) concepts and the alignment of their relational structures and content. With repeated use and conventionalization, an abstract category is created that refers directly to the metaphorical meaning of the target concept (something that moves delicately tracing beautiful figures). Thereafter, metaphoric statements are understood as categorizations (ballerinas are something that moves delicately tracing beautiful figures), often making little contact with the source concept from which the new category was abstracted (butterflies). In this argument, ballerina and butterfly can be readily substituted by time and space. Metaphoric mappings that occur frequently in language can lead to novel conceptual metaphors. Once conventionalized, they can be processed on their own terms, without activating the source domain (see consistent evidence by Gentner & Boronat, 1991, cited in Gentner et al., 2002, and Keysar, Shen, Glucksberg & Horton, 2000). Though attractive, this hypothesis is in need of closer scrutiny. How conceptual mappings get initially into language remains so far an open question for these views.

Flexibility in the directionality of the cross-domain mapping

Prior sections show that wide cognitive flexibility is attested in temporal conceptual metaphors, both within the individual and across languages and cultures. Moreover, it is also possible to make a case for flexibility in the directionality of the cross-domain influence of space and time. Studies of the TIME IS MOTION metaphor have provided what seems strong support for Strict Directionality. Boroditsky (2000) used drawings and sentences depicting either the ego-moving or the object-moving perspective for both spatial motion and temporal "motion". After seeing one of the primes, participants responded to a spatial or temporal version of the ambiguous "meeting" question. She found that spatial primes were effective in biasing both spatial and temporal reasoning, whereas temporal primes were only effective for temporal targets (see also Kemmerer, 2005, for related neuropsychological evidence).

Casasanto and Boroditsky (2008) provided even more convincing evidence using tasks with no linguistic component. Building upon prior developmental observations by Piaget (1927/1969), they presented growing lines of varying lengths and durations, and asked their participants to estimate either spatial extent or duration. Consistent with the Hypothesis of Strict Directionality, the length of a growing line affected its perceived duration, but there was no influence whatsoever of growing time on perceived line length. In search of an influence of time on space, these authors also used moving dots and stationary lines of varying lengths, but the pattern of results remained constant.

However, Teuscher, McQuire, Collins and Coulson (2008) observed priming effects from both spatial and temporal sentences on ERPs time-locked to a subsequent spatial display showing movement of an object towards a schematic person or viceversa. Space-space priming produced an early ERP component, and more importantly, time-space priming generated a later semantic component. Moreover, the studies by Weger and Pratt (2008) and Ouellet, Santiago, Funes and Lupiáñez (2010) found effects of centrally presented past and future words on the subsequent spatial discrimination of stimuli presented at left or right locations. These studies showcase effects of the processing of the abstract conceptual domain on the concrete domain and, therefore, stand against the Strict Directionality Hypothesis.

Finally, two old phenomena from the field of psychophysics, with the rather uninformative names of Tau and Kappa effects (see Jones & Huang, 1982, for a review), suggest that it may be possible to find effects of time on space in tasks which are very similar to those used by Casasanto and Boroditsky (2008). Tau and Kappa effects have been most often tested in conditions in which three succesive discrete stimuli are presented at different points along an imaginary line, defining two spatial and two temporal intervals. The most common task is to adjust either the location or the time of the central stimulus until spatial and temporal intervals appear equal to the observer. The Kappa effect (Cohen, Hansel & Sylvester, 1953) consists in the influence of the spatial intervals on the perceived temporal intervals, and is therefore consistent with the Strict Directionality Hypothesis. When the first spatial interval is longer than the second, participants lengthen the timing of the central stimulus, and the result is an overestimated first temporal interval with respect to the second interval even though their goal is to make them equal. The Tau effect (Helson & King, 1931) is the mirror image of the Kappa effect: when asked to make both spatial intervals equal, their durations produce corresponding shifts in the spatial estimations. The Tau effect would thus seem to contradict the null time-to-space influence observed by Casasanto and Boroditsky (2008). As Casasanto and Borodistky (2008) argue, it is still unclear whether this contradiction is real or just an artifact from small differences in the methods used. As with so many other questions left open by this review, more research is needed.

It is important to note that, by letting language to take a guiding role in the selection of conceptual mappings, the two Metaphoric Structuring Views also open a possibility for the structure of the abstract domain to affect processing about the concrete domain. If the abstract domain is talked about in terms of the concrete domain, then its structure may be used to organize thinking about the concrete domain. It is possible to talk about space *qua* time, as in "The station is only five minutes away", although the reversed mapping is way more frequent (Boroditsky, 2001; Casasanto & Boroditsky, 2008). This view, therefore, also promotes a weaker version of cross-domain influences, one which we will call the Lenient Directionality Hypothesis. Under this view, asymmetric influences across domains are expected not because of the progressive building of abstract domains from more concrete domains. Instead, they may result simply because it is more common to talk about the abstract domain in terms of the concrete one than the opposite. Of course, this frequency difference may well have deep roots in the conceptual building of the domain of time from the domain of space ... or not. Anyhow, the Lenient Directionality Hypothesis opens the possibility of finding effects of time on space under some circumstances: when people talk more often about the concrete domain in terms of the abstract domain than the opposite. Under the typical situation in which the concrete domain predominates over the abstract in linguistic patterns, asymmetrical but not necessarily strictly directional influences are expected (Casasanto & Boroditsky, 2008). The problem is to submit this hypothesis to a fair test, as it is necessary to show that the processing of both domains

Quick learning of new mappings

A final kind of flexibility in conceptual metaphors has to do with the speed at which new mappings can be acquired. Current Metaphoric Structuring Views suggest that an associative mechanism working through repeated uses of the same mapping increases the probability of activating it again the next time the conceptual domain is processed, leading to the establishment of habits of thought. The more practised a mapping is, the stronger the habit. As a corollary of this position, stronger habits should show an important resistance to change, and only extended practice with new mappings may be able to overcome them. However, this is far from being the case.

Both Boroditsky (2001) and Casasanto (2008) describe experimental studies in which they trained English participants to think about time using a new conceptual mapping. Although both report comparable results, the former study provides a clearer case, as English speakers were trained to use a past-up future-down mapping which is never attested in the English language. The results showed that only 90 training trials (one sentence per trial) were enough to remove the horizontal priming effect characteristic of untrained English participants and to make them indistinguishable from native Chinese speakers in the spatial priming task. Such results are in starkling contrast with Boroditsky's (2001) own data (Experiments 1 and 2), which were obtained from Mandarin-English bilinguals attending college in the US, that is, after many years of inmersion into English. Actually, the main predictor of the typically Chinese vertical bias was the age of English acquisition, and not the length of English exposure. If about 10 years of intensive experience with English metaphors are not able to turn Mandarin speakers into English speakers, how is it possible that 90 trials suffice to turn English speakers into Mandarin speakers?

We contend that these results are unexpected from the workings of an associative mechanism. In the sections below, we will see more examples of quick learning of new mappings in conceptual domains other than time. The learning mechanism must be of a kind that allows much faster learning than usual associative mechanisms do. A category induction mechanism of the kind proposed by Bowdle and Gentner (2005) may make a better job, as it is known that new categories can be formed on-the-fly with extreme flexibility and little effort (e.g., Barsalou, 1983). Indeed, Bowdle and Gentner (2005) were able to find traces of such a category learning process after only three training trials with a novel metaphor.

Fast and flexible learning also integrates more smoothly with the fact that switching between alternative mappings for a given conceptual domain is, at least sometimes, also fast and easy (e.g., McGlone & Harding, 1998; Gentner et al., 2002). The resulting picture of how the mind recruits and uses conceptual metaphors starts to look way more flexible than expected, even under the Metaphoric Structuring Views.

To summarize, the present review of research on conceptual metaphors of time has revealed a massive degree of cognitive flexibility. First, several alternative mappings are available to each individual within a single language and culture, as well as across different languages and cultures. The alternatives can vary in about every possible parameter: they can resort to different source domains to generate wholy inconsistent mappings; when they rely on the domain of space, they can map to all three spatial axes, to both poles within each axis, and taking each possible perspective. Second, there are clear effects of space on time, as well as effects of time on space, although the studies which have assessed both directionalities only report the former. Third, new conceptual metaphors can be acquired at an impressive speed, even in the face of highly practiced, life-long conceptual mappings for the same abstract domain.

Regarding the factors that mediate the manifestation of one or another conceptual mapping, reviewed studies point out the relevance of an attended supporting context (priming), of habitual exposure, use of linguistic expressions, and graphic cultural conventions.

This degree of flexibility poses a central problem to Conceptual Metaphor theory. Its psychological siblings, the Weak and Integrated Metaphoric Structuring Views, fare better in the face of the evidence by letting language play a shaping role in the establishment of conceptual mappings and their directionality. Frequent language patterns lead to specific conceptual mapping habits, which may lead to the presence of alternative conceptual mappings both within a language and across languages. In the standard case in which the abstract domain is talked about in terms of the concrete domain more often than the converse, this view predicts asymmetric, stronger influences of the concrete domain on the abstract domain, which so far seems consistent with the evidence. However, under the assumed associative mechanism, the Metaphoric Structuring Views do not seem to be able to account for the easiness with which people are able to switch between alternative, simultaneously available mappings, nor for the speed at which old and highly practiced mappings can be replaced by new ones. Proposals by Bowdle and Gentner (2005) on a "career of metaphor" could be fruitfully incorporated. Many questions remain to receive a definite answer, and among them, how is a metaphor selected out of the available alternatives in a given occasion figures prominently.

We now turn to evaluate whether available research on other abstract domains leads to consistent conclusions.

3.2. Cognitive flexibility in the domain of affective evaluation

The conceptual domain of emotional evaluation (positive-negative valence) also shows important within-individual flexibility, participating in several conceptual metaphors. A first one relates emotional evaluation to vertical space: positive evaluations are up and negative ones are down (which Lakoff & Johnson, 1980, called HAPPY IS UP, based on sentences like "I'm feeling down today". We will name it POSITIVE IS UP because the metaphor applies not only to emotions, but to all positively evaluated concepts). The psychological reality of this vertical conceptual mapping is supported by several studies. Förster and Stepper (2000, exp. 1) reported that the learning of positive words was facilitated by adopting an upright posture, whereas negative words were facilitated by a back-rounded posture. This study suggests a possible body-based image schema motivating the mapping, which agrees with proposals by Lakoff and Johnson (1980). Consistently, Meier and Robinson (2004) observed that positive and negative words were evaluated faster when presented in the upper and lower parts of the screen, respectively, and Crawford, Margolies, Drake and Murphy (2006) showed that memory for location of positively valenced pictures is biased upwards relative to negative pictures (see also Weger, Meier, Robinson & Inhoff, 2007). Finally, Meier and Robinson (2006) reported that neurotic and depressive feelings were associated with faster detection of targets in lower spatial positions.

Evaluation also participates in two more space-conceptual mappings along the horizontal plane. The first one locates positive concepts close to self and negative concepts in far space. Lakoff and Johnson (1999) talked of a highly related metaphor: INTIMACY IS CLOSENESS (found in linguistic expressions such as "they are close friends" or "they feel far apart from each other"). Its image schematic foundation can probably be found in the approach-avoidance tendencies generated by positive and negative stimuli. Cacciopo, Priester and Berntson (1993) found that ideographs are evaluated more positively if the participant is simultaneously performing an arm flexion (approach) rather than an arm extension (avoidance). It is also faster to respond to positive words by pulling a lever and to negative stimuli by pushing it (Chen & Bargh, 1999; see also Tops & de Jong, 2006). Evaluations activate approach-avoidance reactions to such a high degree that congruency effects have been observed using a lexical decision task (Wentura, Rothermund & Bak, 2000) and even when the task is just to detect the presence of a word on the screen (without any need to read it; Chen & Bargh, 1999).

It has also been shown that approach-avoidance reactions are able to exacerbate preexisting valence differences (Centerbar & Clore, 2006).

The second mapping locates positive in right space and negative in left space (McManus, 2002). It is widely manifested in language (e.g., "sinister" comes from the latin word for "left") and its experiential basis is related to the greater fluency and easiness with which right-handed people interact with right space. Strong support for this assertion comes from Casasanto (2009), who found that lefties show the opposite association. It is also incorporated in a great many cultural conventions (e.g., burial patterns, arrangement of houses and churches, see McManus, 2002, for a review).

The evaluative positive-negative dimension therefore participates in three different space-conceptual mappings: POSITIVE IS UP, POSITIVE IS CLOSE and POSITIVE IS RIGHT, but little is known of the factors that guide the choice of one or another mapping in a particular situation. A study by Markman and Brendl (2005; see also van Dantzig, Zeelenberg & Pecher, 2009) adds to this flexibility by showing that the reference point (or deictic origin) on which the close-far horizontal space is centered can be freely moved onto an object different from self. Valenced words were evaluated by means of a pull-push joystick movement. The words were presented on the screen within a visual context which gave the impression of depth (a visual corridor). The participant's name was presented at an intermediate distance in the corridor, and words could appear either below the name ("closer" to the participant) or above ("farther" than the name). The response requirement was always anchored on the name of the participant: to move the joystick towards or away from the name depending on word valence. In this situation, the well-known approach-avoidance congruity effect was replicated with respect to the position of the participant's name on screen, and not with respect to the physical position of the participant. In a very clean manipulation, Seibt, Neumann, Nusinson and Strack (2008, Exp. 3) instructed their participants to either move their hand toward the word on the screen (approach) or away from it (avoidance), or to move the hand towards self (approach) or away from it (avoidance). The former instructions centered the deictic origin on the word, whereas the latter centered it on the participant. Word valence again interacted with approach-avoidance reactions as defined with respect to the current deictic origin.

Emotional evaluation has also been shown to participate in one additional conceptual metaphor based on a non-spatial domain: brightness, which maps positive with bright and negative with dark. As for the POSITIVE IS RIGHT mapping, the POSITIVE IS BRIGHT metaphor is not discussed by Lakoff and Johnson (1980, 1999), although it is easy to find linguistic traces of it (e.g., "dark ages", "Darth Vader was attracted by the dark side of the Force"). Meier, Robinson and Clore (2004) showed that evaluative judgments to positive words are facilitated when presented in a bright versus dark font, and the converse occurs for negative words. In contrast to the highly automatic, nearly mandatory effects of evaluative meaning on approach-avoidance reactions discussed above, when the task was to judge the brightness of the font or to perform a lexical decision on the word, the effect disappeared. However, soon thereafter Meier, Robinson, Crawford and Alhvers (2007), using more ambiguous brightness stimuli, observed effects of a prior evaluation judgment on its perceived brightness.

Actually, coming back to the POSITIVE IS UP metaphor, the domain of emotional evaluation provides the clearest available case against both the Strict and the Lenient Directionality Hypothesis. The experiments 2 and 3 in Meier and Robinson (2004) study are very close to provide a fair comparison between effect sizes in the two directions of a cross-domain interaction: the effect of vertical space on affective evaluation and its converse. This contrast is made even more interesting by the fact that the domains of emotional evaluation and space show a sharp difference in the frequency of linguistic expressions talking about each one in terms of the other (i.e., positive-negative emotions are often talked about using spatial terms like "up" or "down", whereas it is hardly possible to talk about space in terms of emotions, e.g., "it was a very sad cave" meaning a deep cave). Therefore, both versions of the Directionality Hypothesis make the same prediction: space should influence evaluation whereas evaluation should not affect space. In contrast, Meier and Robinson's (2004) second experiment presented positive and negative words centrally to be affectively judged, followed by the presentation of a stimulus ("p" or "q") at either upper or lower locations to be recognized. Their third experiment presented a stimulus ("++++") at either upper or lower positions to be located (participants responded vocally), followed by the central presentation of the same words to be evaluated. The former experiment found a clear priming effect of evaluation on space, whereas the latter found nothing.[2] We take these results to be clear evidence of the possibility of finding bidirectional cross-domain effects in spite of asymmetrical linguistic habits, although it could still be argued that the procedures were not exact reversals of each other

---

2 It is surprising that the authors actually defended the opposite interpretation of their results, supporting the Strict Directionality Hypothesis. They state: "... one can make spatial discriminations without activating affective metaphors" (p. 244). However, their procedures are analogous to priming studies such as Boroditsky (2000) and others reviewed above, where processing spatial primes did affect subsequent processing of the temporal domain, and temporal primes did not affect the processing of spatial targets.

and that the relative cleanliness of within-dimension processing was not explicitly assessed.

To summarize, reseach on the conceptual domain of affective evaluation provides clear examples of flexibility at the individual level, having been related to at least four alternative mappings: to upper and lower space in the vertical axis, to close and far regions from deictic origin, to left and right space in the horizontal axis, and to bright and dark visual stimuli. Moreover, by resorting to a different source domain, the fourth mapping is wholly inconsistent with the prior three. Reviewed evidence also suggests that the location of the deictic origin where the spatial axes are centered can be freely moved to other locations distinct from ego. Finally, it is possible to observe influences of the abstract domain on the concrete domain, which are stronger than in the opposite direction, supporting flexibility also in the directionality of the cross-domain mapping.

Regarding the mediating factors that affect flexible use of conceptual mappings, the relative automaticity of the mapping is important: positive and negative stimuli generate automatic approach-avoidance reactions, whereas their mapping to vertical space or brightness is less automatic.

3.3. Cognitive flexibility in the domain of social power

A conceptual metaphor which has received much attention by social psychologists maps power and status to the vertical dimension (Lakoff & Johnson, 1980, called it CONTROL IS UP; see Fiske, 1992, for a wider conceptual framework of social relations). In this mapping, powerful entities are located in upper space, powerless entities in lower space, as attested in many conventional linguistic expressions (i.e., "the decision came from above"). As for time, the mapping of control is continuous (Chiao, Bordeaux & Ambady, 2004), leading to a power gradient and rich inferential possibilities.

Schubert (2005) presented group labels such as "professor" and "student" to be judged as powerful or powerless. Words appeared either above or below the center of a computer screen, and responses were given by means of the up and down arrow keys. Both dimensions produced a congruency effect. Giessner and Schubert (2007) found consistent results manipulating the vertical extent of organization charts on judgments of the leaders' power. Schubert (2005) suggests that the image schematic basis of this mapping have to do both with bodily experiences (powerful people are bigger and taller, and feeling threatened or protected by a bigger person is probably a universal experience) and a complex of cultural conventions, from the arrangement of athletes on the podium to the location of bosses' offices in the upper floors of buildings. Schubert, Waldzus and Giessner (2009) reported data supporting that this metaphor should be actually understood as POWER IS BIG: in a power judgment task, they found congruency effects for words referring to powerful and powerless groups presented in big and small font sizes.

Schubert (2005) was very careful in dissociating these effects from those of the POSITIVE IS UP metaphor. Although the dimensions of power and evaluation are often positively correlated, he was able to find a set of powerful but negative words (e.g., "dictator"). Judgments of power on this set of words were facilitated when presented in the upper position of the screen. In contrast, when the judgment was about evaluation, performance was better when presented in the lower position. This is a clear example of cognitive flexibility in the selection of space-conceptual mappings depending on task requirements.

The study by Schubert et al. (2009) also provides an example of quick learning of new conceptual mappings which are inconsistent with previously active and highly practiced mappings. As mentioned above, power judgments of words were automatically affected by font size. However, when the proportion of incongruent trials (powerful labels presented in small font, powerless labels in big font) was increased to two thirds and participants were informed about it, only 48 trials (38 incongruent) were enough to reverse the congruency effect in a subsequent test. Aspects of the results indicated that there had been a real learning process underlying the change and not just a strategic change. Furthermore, the outcome of this process was not only the elimination of a prior bias, but the creation of a new bias in the opposite direction. Only participants who were informed about the high proportion of incongruent trials showed the fast remapping, suggesting that voluntary attention to the relevant dimensions and mappings is an important factor involved.

Finally, there are also some hints of bidirectional influences between vertical space and/or physical size and social power, as several studies have shown that estimates of how tall a person is are biased by that person's power (Dannemaier & Thumin, 1964; Higham & Carment, 1992; Wilson, 1968).

To sum up, research on the conceptual metaphor of power has supported its mapping to vertical space and/or physical size; the possibility of reverting, in just a few training trials, prior life-long associations grounded in very basic bodily experiences as well as on a complex of cultural conventions; and the existence of bidirectional cross-domain influences. It has also revealed two important factors mediating the flexible deployment and learning of conceptual mappings: task requirements (such as being asked to judge affective evaluation vs. power) and voluntary attention to the relevant domains and mappings.

3.4. Cognitive flexibility in the domain of magnitude

Another vertical metaphor with some experimental support is MORE IS UP, which Lakoff and Johnson (1980) suggested from examples like "My income rose last year" and "If you are too hot, turn the heat down". They also suggested that its image schematic basis came from experiences of piling up objects and observing the level to go up. In agreement with this suggestion, Josephs, Giesler and Silvera (1994) showed that pile size biased judgments of proofreading performance. Gattis and Holyoak (1996) found that graphs are easier to understand and reason about when the increase in quantity of a variable is mapped to an increase in slope.

Some studies in the domain of numerical cognition can also be interpreted as consistent with this metaphor. Numbers convey both magnitude information (4 is greater than 3) and ordinal information (4 comes after 3). It is common in many languages to refer to numbers using a vertical metaphor ("a high number", "a low number"). Ito and Hatta (2004) used a parity judgment task (discriminate whether a number is odd or even), and showed that it is faster to press an upper key in a desktop keyboard to respond to relatively larger numbers, and to press a lower key to respond to smaller numbers. Schwarz and Keus (2004) found a similar result using saccadic eye movements instead of manual keypresses, thereby confirming the existence of a vertical analogue of the Space-Number Association of Response Codes (SNARC) effect first reported by Dehaene, Bossini and Giraux (1993; to be discussed below in detail).

The vertical SNARC studies cannot differentiate whether it is ordinal sequence or magnitude what is associated with the vertical spatial dimension. Neither they can tell us whether the relevant spatial dimension is the vertical axis or physical size (in which case the metaphor should be rephrased as MORE IS BIG). Another discovery in the domain of numerical cognition is more diagnostic: the effects of numerical magnitude on planning the size of a manual response. Lindemann, Abolafia, Girardi and Bekkering (2007) presented small (1, 2) and large numbers (8, 9) in a parity judgment task. Participants were asked to give their responses either by grasping a small rod with a precision grip with the index and middle fingers or by grasping a big rod using a power grip with the whole hand. Precision grips were initiated faster in response to small numbers and power grips to large numbers, even though magnitude was completely irrelevant to the task. Badets, Andres, Di Luca and Pesenti (2007) visually presented a vertical rod on a screen and asked their participants to estimate whether they could grasp it lengthways between their index and middle fingers. Each trial was preceded by a small (2) or large (8) number, or a neutral symbol ($) to be named aloud. The small number shifted the estimation distribution down, and the large number shifted it up, with the neutral symbol in between. These two studies provide another clear example of directional influences from the abstract to the concrete dimension of a conceptual metaphor, against the Strict Directionality Hypothesis, although they do not compare the relative sizes of both directions of the cross-domain effect.

A fair comparison of the sizes of the cross-dimensional effect in both directions has been provided in the context of a third research line in numerical cognition: the size congruity effect. In a typical experiment, the participant is asked to compare two numbers which differ in magnitude and physical size. The relation between the two dimensions defines a congruent condition (e.g., 2-8), an incongruent condition (2-8) and a neutral condition (2-8). The original report by Besner and Colheart (1979) instructed participants to decide which of the two numbers was of greater magnitude while ignoring their physical sizes. In accord with expectations from a MORE IS BIG metaphor, physical size interfered with magnitude judgments.

Furthermore, several studies have shown the converse influence of number magnitude on judgments of physical size (Henik & Tzelgov, 1982; see Pansky & Algom, 1999, for detailed references). Recent work has shown that the relative discriminability and salience of physical size and numerical magnitude determines which one will affect the processing of the other. Discriminability has to do with the "resolution" at which a conceptual dimension is sampled to select values for use in an experiment. Pansky and Algom (1999, see also Pansky & Algom, 2002; and Schwarz & Ischebeck, 2003) noted that prior research always used between seven and nine different numbers, whereas size was often manipulated in only two or three levels. The range and dispersion of values was thus greater for number than size, making number more discriminable. In several experiments, they manipulated systematically the relative discriminability of both dimensions, by equalling the number of levels while varying dispersion of values. Overall, the most discriminable dimension interfered with the processing of the less discriminable dimension. When both dimensions were equally discriminable, cross-dimensional interference was always symmetrical and its size was very small or null.

Regarding stimulus salience, Fitousi and Algom (2006) presented number and size information at different spatial locations, by using a fixed font for numerals and a varying length line appearing below the numeral. Stimulus salience was manipulated varying the size of the numeral and the line (i.e., to make the number dimension more salient, all numbers appeared in a greater font, and the lines varied around a smaller mean length). The more salient dimension always interfered with the less salient dimension.

The previous studies (Pansky & Algom, 1999; Fitousi & Algom, 2006) provide assessments of the relative size of both directions of the cross-domain effect between physical size and numerical magnitude under perfectly comparable conditions. Indeed, they only differ in the assignment of conceptual dimensions to being relevant (used to guide responding) or irrelevant. In these conditions, discriminability and salience switch the directionality of the cross-domain effect. These studies provide convincing evidence against the Strict Directionality Hypothesis. However, as it is (roughly) as common to talk about numbers in terms of size (e.g., "a small number") as to talk about size in terms of numbers (e.g., "that was a 500 squared meters house"), the Lenient Directionality Hypothesis predicts symmetrical cross-domain effects.

To wrap up, research on the domain of magnitude has shown a conceptual mapping between magnitude and vertical space or physical size. Studies on numerical magnitude have also shown parallel bidirectional cross-domain effects that stand against the Strict Directionality Hypothesis but can be accounted for by its Lenient version. Moreover, they have isolated several important factors that mediate the observed directionality: relative discriminability and stimulus salience.

3.5. Cognitive flexibility in the domain of linear order

Linear order or sequence order is a conceptual domain that has strong links with the domain of time. Actually, it can be said that most studies discussed in the section on time could also be included in this one. Our treatment of time focused on its two main correlates, event order and duration, often conflating them. We didn't try to make a systematic distinction between them because it is possible to argue that both can be reduced to a common kind of representation which segments the continuous flow of time in a sequence of discrete time units, therefore an ordered sequence of events (this assumption underlies most current models, both for extended sequences, e.g., Boroditsky, 2000, and short intervals, e.g., Ivry & Richardson, 2002).

However, there are other kinds of ordered sequences which have nothing to do with time, at least in principle. They are constituted by arbitrary sequences of elements, which may refer to an intrinsically ordered conceptual domain or not. For example, the letters of the alphabet are ordered only by convention. In contrast, numbers, days of the week and months of the year refer to an intrinsically ordered domain (magnitude or time). At one level, all of these sequence types require the representation of an arbitrary series of concepts defined by their position in the sequence and their order relations with the other elements of the sequence (e.g., Tuesday derives its meaning from its position within the sequence of weekdays). Some sequences, like the alphabet, weekdays or months, are short and overlearned. For other sequences, like the numbers, there are combinatorial mechanisms that, from a small ordered set, are able to generate an infinite extension of the sequence.

Given the similarities between time and these other ordered sequences, it comes as no surprise that they all display similar conceptual mappings onto space. We will review first literature about the mental representation of number sequences, and then proceed to the other types of ordered sequences (months, weekdays, alphabet letters ...).

Numerical sequences

Two effects support that numbers are represented in some kind of analogical format (Dehaene, Dehaene-Lambertz & Cohen, 1998): the semantic distance effect (more difficult discrimination of numbers which are closer together than of numbers farther apart), and the number size effect (worse discrimination of numbers as their numerical size increases, a numerical counterpart of Weber's law). Interestingly, this analogical number line extends in mental space from left to right, as it was the case for the mental time line. Dehaene et al. (1993) found that people are faster to respond to small numbers with the left than the right hand, and to larger numbers with the right than the left hand, which they called the Space-Number Association of Response Codes (SNARC) effect. The name presupposes that the effect is an association between numbers and response codes, but studies using lateralized presentation of numbers (Keus & Schwarz, 2005; Zebian, 2005) and the priming studies discussed below support that it indexes a central analogical representation instead. In the years so far, a considerable literature on the SNARC effect has amassed (see Fias & Fischer, 2005, for a review), with several results which are directly relevant to the question of cognitive flexibility in conceptual metaphors.

Numerical order shows cross-cultural and cross-linguistic flexibility in its conceptual mappings. In direct correspondence with findings in the domain of time, the directionality of the number line seems to be affected by reading and writing direction, as the effect fades and even reverses in users of languages with right-to-left writing (Dehaene et al., 1993; Gevers & Lammertin, 2005; Shaky & Fischer, 2008; Shaki, Fischer & Petrusic, 2009; Zebian, 2005).

Wide flexibility within the individual is also attested. In a questionnaire study by Seron, Pesenti and Nöel (1992), 27 out of 194 people reported to have systematic images for numbers, which were aroused by merely seeing a number, and to use them when performing calculations. A variety of configurations were reported, including a majority of lines that could be vertical, horizontal, or having turns at key points (e.g., decades). Currently, there is experimental support in the general population for both horizontal (Dehaene et al., 1993) and vertical number lines (Ito & Hatta, 2004; Schwarz & Keus, 2004). As discussed in the prior section, though, the vertical mapping in these studies might be mediated by the association of number stimuli with another conceptual dimension, magnitude, and not with linear order. The study by Hung, Hung, Tzeng and Wu (2008) does not suffer from this potential confound. Using Chinese readers, they showed that the type of numerical notation (either Indo-Arabic or Chinese number characters) in which numbers were presented was able to induce a different spatial mapping: Indo-Arabic numbers generated a standard SNARC effect, indicating left-to-right mapping, whereas Chinese numbers generated a vertical SNARC suggesting a top-to-bottom directionality (larger numbers located in lower space). These results also strengthen the case for the direction of ortography and graphic conventions as causes of this spatial conceptual metaphor. Some studies have also supported a circular clock-face representation for numbers up to 10–12 (Bächtold, Baumüller & Bruger, 1998; Ristic, Wright & Kingstone, 2006; see discussion below). In some individuals numerical images are so automatic and systematic that they are categorized as a type of synaesthesia. Sagiv, Simner, Collins, Butterworth and Ward (2006) observed wide variation in preferred patterns, and were able to show SNARC effects tailored to the preferred pattern in each of five synaesthetes. Finally, a mapping of small numbers to close and large numbers to far peripersonal space have also been reported (Santens & Gevers, 2008).

Indo-Arabic numerals have also been able to facilitate subsequent spatial processing, showing a directional effect from the abstract to the concrete domain. Just looking to a centrally presented digit was enough to speed up processing of the corresponding spatial location (small numbers facilitated left space, large numbers facilitated right space) both in a detection task (Fischer, Castel, Dodd & Pratt, 2003), and an order decision task (say which of two lateralized stimuli has been presented first; Casarotti, Michielin, Zorzi and Umiltá, 2007). Other studies have shown the corresponding influence of a spatial prime on a numeric task (Keus & Schwarz, 2005; Stoianov, Kramer, Umiltá & Zorzi, 2008). Once again, no direct comparison of the sizes of both directions of the cross-domain effect is available.

It is interesting to note that, if only linguistic habits are taken in consideration, the Lenient Directionality Hypothesis would predict an asymmetrical influence between space and number, with number having stronger effects on space than the opposite. In another interesting parallel with left-right metaphors of time, it is common to say things like "the town was 20 Km away", but linguistic expressions like "2 is to the left of 6" or "when a right number is substracted from a left number" (meaning substracting a larger from a smaller number) are hardly ever attested. However, left-right space is conventionaly used to represent numerical order in charts and written language. If cultural conventions are included together with linguistic habits as a source of guidance for conceptual mappings, the Lenient Directionality Hypothesis probably predicts symmetrical effects between space and number.

Research on the SNARC effect has pointed out several mediating factors in the manifestation of space-number influences. Firstly, different number codes activate the mental number line to different extents. The association of numbers with space is strongest for Indo-Arabic numerals, even in implicit tasks such as parity judgment. Verbal numerals and other number codes produce smaller or non-significant effects instead (Dehaene et al., 1993; see also Razpurker-Apfeld & Koriat, 2006, for related evidence). This could be the result of practice, as when numbers are presented as an ordered sequence (e.g., on rulers, charts, and so on) they are most often written in Indo-Arabic format. A second one concerns the simultaneity of spatial and numerical processing. Stoianov et al. (2008) reasoned that a spatial stimulus may be processed faster than a numerical stimulus. Correspondingly, they showed that a visual stimulus located at the left or right of fixation presented before a central number (e.g., "2") does not speed up a compatible response to the number (a left hand keypress). In contrast, if the spatial prime is presented a short time (59 ms) after the number, facilitation is observed. A third factor is voluntary choice of the spatial image for numbers. Bächtold et al. (1998) reported that it is possible to change the association of number to space just by instructing participants. When they asked their participants to conceive of numbers "as on a ruler", a normal left-right SNARC effect was found. However, when the instruction was to conceive of numbers "as on a clockface", a reversed SNARC appeared, with faster left reactions to larger numbers and right reactions to smaller numbers (see Galfano, Rusconi & Umiltá, 2006; and Ristic et al., 2006, for analogous results).

SNARC studies have also provided evidence on a phenomenon that we will call *coherence interactions*, anticipating the interpretation that the theory to be presented in this paper will give to this family of effects. When people have to carry out two tasks simultaneously, both of which resource to an underlying spatial mental representation, people tend to align those representations to make them cohere, or to use a single common spatial representation. Notebaert, Gevers, Verguts and Fias (2006) presented digits centrally in either black or red font, randomly mixed. If the digit was black, participants performed a so-called inducer task: number comparison. One group was instructed to respond to digits smaller than five with the left hand and to larger digits with the right hand. A second group used the reversed mapping. The effect of the inducer task was assessed on a concurrent, diagnostic task: font judgment. If the digit was red, participants judged whether the digit was in normal font or in italics.

The first group (small numbers assigned to the left hand, large numbers to the right hand) showed a standard SNARC effect in the font judgment task. The second group (small numbers assigned to the right hand, large numbers to the left) showed a reversed effect in the diagnostic task. In other experiments, these authors found that the metaphorically incongruent number comparison task can induce reversals in purely spatial tasks (i.e., discriminating the color of a lateralized circle), and that incongruent spatial tasks can also induce reversals in number tasks. The important factor seems to be the overall coherence of the mappings simultaneously active during the experiment.

Are coherence interactions the automatic result of simultaneous activation of two different spatial mappings, or do they need some time to develop, and perhaps some practice? Another study supports the latter possibility. Lindemann, Abolafia, Pratt and Bekkering (2008) used a parity task with centrally presented digits. Each trial started with the presentation of a sequence of three numbers to be memorized, which could be in ascending (3-4-5), descending (5-4-3) or no order (5-3-4). At the end of each trial, memory of digit location within this sequence was tested. When each type of trial was presented in a separate block, a standard SNARC effect was found for ascending and disordered sequences, but it was eliminated in the descending condition. This change was observed in blocks of only 72 trials. When the three types of trials were randomly mixed, comparable SNARC effects obtained in all conditions. This study suggests that a coherent spatial representation between all concurrently active spatial mappings is not an automatic result. Instead, it looks like an strategic effect which needs some time and practice to develop, though not much. A bit longer practice would probably lead to a complete reversal of the SNARC effect, like in the Notebaert et al. (2006) study using 384 trials-long blocks.

Other sequence types

Although numbers and other kinds of arbitrary sequences such as weekdays or months show important conceptual commonalities, the experimental evidence regarding the latter is not so clear-cut. Gevers, Reynvoet and Fias (2003) found SNARC-like effects for letters of the alphabet and months, Gevers, Reynvoet and Fias (2004) found them for weekdays, and Dodd, Van der Stigchel, Leghari, Fung and Kingstone (2008) found them for all three kinds of ordinal sequences. However, Dehaene et al. (1993) failed to find a SNARC effect based on the alphabet, and Price and Mentzoni (2008) were unable to find it for representations of months.

Probably, the inconsistent results are related to the wide flexibility attested in these mappings within and across individuals, which is particularly strong for months sequences. Seymour (1980) report questionnaire and experimental evidence suggesting that months can be represented along horizontal and vertical lines as well as circularly. Some of his participants showed preferences for one particular spatial mapping, with all mappings being preferred by more or less equal numbers of people. In contrast, linear horizontal mappings were most frequently preferred for weekdays and the alphabet, and circular arrays were preferred for seasons of the year (see also Seron et al., 1992, for analogous results). As with numbers, there are also month-space-synaesthetes (Price & Mentzoni, 2008; Smilek, Callejas, Dixon & Merikle, 2007), a condition which often associates with number-space and colour synaesthesia (Sagiv et al., 2006). Month-space synaesthetes prefer circular patterns, but the specific location of months within them varies widely. In full agreement with data from number-space-synaesthesia, idiosyncratic spatial patterns produce corresponding congruency effects (Price & Mentzoni, 2008) and attentional biases (Smilek et al., 2007).

Sequences of different types also seem to differ in automaticity of access. Gevers et al. (2003) reported that months interact with space even when month order is not task relevant (judging whether the month ended with 'R'). In contrast, letters show a markedly reduced effect when participants make order irrelevant judgments (consonant-vowel classification). Dodd et al. (2008) found that letters, months and weekdays induced spatial shifts of attention only when the processing of ordinal information was task relevant.

Overall, studies on linearly ordered sequences support the following conclusions. There are cross-linguistic and cross-cultural variations, coupled with wide within-individual variation. Clear bidirectional effects between the concrete and abstract domains are observed, against the Strict Directionality Hypothesis. Several factors mediating the manifestation of cross-domain influences have been isolated, namely, associative strength from number format, temporal overlap between the processing of both domains, voluntary choice of spatial shape and number-to-shape mapping, coherence interactions with other spatial mappings concurrently in use in the task at hand, and intrinsic differences in the automaticity of a given conceptual mapping.

3.6. Conceptual flexibility in the domain of pitch

Musical pitch is another dimension that is often talked about in spatial terms (a tone can be "high" or "low"), and this mapping affords the inferential possibilities characteristic of other continuous conceptual mappings. Other cultural conventions, like standard musical notation, also support this mapping in musically literate minds. There are also cultural conventions which support a left-to-right mapping of pitch onto space. For example, Lidji, Kolinsky, Lochy and Morais (2007) suggest that the piano keyboard acts as a cultural artifact for representing tone, having a wide influence in the minds of both musicians and non-musicians.

There is experimental evidence suggesting a spatial mental representation of pitch. Cohen, Hansel and Sylvester (1954), in a study on the Tau effect, found an effect of temporal intervals on pitch judgment. They presented three tones and asked participants to adjust the frequency of the middle tone such that it would be intermediate between the initial and final tones. The pitch distance between tones presented within a shorter time interval was perceived to be smaller, and therefore, the pitch of the intermediate tone was adjusted to be closer to the pitch of the tone presented after the larger interval. Cohen et al. (1954) contended that these results show that Tau effects have nothing to do with space, being instead a general characteristic of all linearly ordered mental events. Jones and Huang (1982) counterargued that it is more correct to assume that pitch is underlyingly spatialized, and the auditory Tau effect is just a variant of the purely spatial Tau effect.

Pitch can map onto both vertical and horizontal spatial axes, indicating important within and between participants flexibility. Relevant studies also point out several mediating factors which agree with evidence from other conceptual metaphors discussed so far. Rusconi, Kwan, Giordano, Umiltá and Butterworth (2006) and Lidji et al. (2007) found spatial compatibility effects for both axes in an explicit pitch judgment task (discrimination of high versus low tones by pressing up-down or left-right keys) in musically untrained participants. When an implicit task was used (discrimination of the instrument playing the tone), only trained musicians showed space-pitch compatibility effects in both axes, whereas untrained participants showed the effect only in the vertical axis, indicating that the vertical mapping is more intuitive and automatic than the horizontal (see also Repp & Knoblich, 2007). The whole pattern of results was clearer in Lidji et al. (2007) than in Rusconi et al. (2006), probably because the former used tones encompassing a wider range, thereby increasing the discriminability of the dimension of pitch.

The pattern of results suggests that pitch can be mapped quite automatically onto the vertical dimension. It can also be mapped onto the horizontal dimension if potentiated by practice or by task requirements (making pitch an explicit part of the task). Pitch discriminability also seems to mediate the manifestation of cross-domain effects, specially when the task does not require explicit processing of pitch.

3.7. Conclusions about cognitive flexibility in conceptual metaphors

In the first half of the paper we have undertaken a review of a wide landscape of research often coming from disparate traditions, and comprising a variety of (mainly primary) conceptual metaphors. It is surprising, therefore, how consistent the resulting picture is. Overall, conceptual metaphors are characterized by the existence of alternative mappings for the same abstract dimension which are available to the same individual or to individuals with different training histories, speaking different languages and/or being exposed to different cultural conventions. Moreover, cross-domain interactions do not always run exclusively in the direction from the concrete to the abstract domain, but very clear reversed influences are often found. There are even some hints (limited so far to the domain of affective evaluation) that it is possible to find cases of stronger influences from abstract to concrete despite more frequent linguistic patterns phrased the opposite way (using concrete terms to talk about abstract terms). Finally, this picture of wide, but lawful, flexibility is complemented by evidence showing a very fast and easy learning of new mappings in the place of life-long, highly practiced mappings.

Several questions naturally follow: how are image schemas or simpler metaphors originally selected to structure new conceptual domains, out of the many potential candidates? How can new image schemas or metaphors be selected for application to a given conceptual domain which already has metaphoric conceptualisations in place? How do people choose which metaphor to activate in a given context? How do language and culture affect which metaphoric mappings are used?

A first step toward answering these questions requires the isolation of factors mediating the manifestation of a given mapping and the directionality of the cross-domain influence. The reviewed studies have exposed a complex set of them. Many of their effects seem to have an important degree of generality across different conceptual mappings. These factors include: 1) the intrinsic "strength" or automaticity of a given mapping and/or its practice level (it is unclear whether these two factors are separable); 2) the discriminability and salience of the stimuli used in the tasks; 3) the "strength" or automaticity with which the code conveying the concepts activate the conceptual dimension; 4) the presence of a priming context; 5) the degree of simultaneity in the processing of both dimensions; 6) the degree to which attention is either voluntarily or automatically drawn to the mapping or to either dimension; 7) the requirements on conceptualization imposed by the task; 8) the voluntary choice of imagistic conceptualization (which may recur to images more complex than linear or circular forms); 9) the coherence interactions in which the activated dimensions may enter; 10) the degree of conventionality of linguistic patterns used to talk about them; 11) their frequency; and 12) the existence of related cultural conventions.

The global picture is marked by cognitive flexibility to a much greater extent than it could be expected from Conceptual Metaphor Theory (Lakoff & Johnson, 1980, 1999). The degree of flexibility, especially when it comes to the directionality of the cross-domain effect, is such that we contend it cannot be accounted for by the two Metaphoric Structuring Views (Weak and Integrated) either (Boroditsky, 2000; Boroditsky & Casasanto, 2008; Casasanto, 2008), although a definitive test is still to come.

In order to see the deeper implications of the global picture, it is worthwhile to go back to the original motivation of the whole Solid Foundations View: the grounding of abstract concepts on the solid foundations provided by concrete concepts, in a recursive mapping leading down to the most basic universal image schemas and perceptuo-motor experiences. Conceptual Metaphor Theory, as formulated by Lakoff and Johnson (1980, 1999), constitutes the strongest version of such an enterprise. It does a good job at accounting for many linguistic patterns, but when its empirical base is widened to include behavioural experiments, it is faced with a problem for which it is not well equipped: how are several alternative mappings for a single domain learned, and how is one of them selected in a given occasion. Its psychological version, the Weak Metaphoric Structuring View (Boroditsky, 2000), held a better potential for providing such an account, as typically psychological factors such as priming and attention were allowed to enter the scene, though still the theory was far from providing a processing model. It also changed the ontogenetic theory, postulating a causal role for language experience at the expense of image schemas and perceptuo-motor experiences. The Integrated Metaphoric Structuring View (Casasanto & Boroditsky, 2008; Casasanto, 2008) came to acknowledge both sources of developmental influences on conceptual metaphors. Strict or Lenient Directionality remained as an essential part of the theory, and asymmetric cross-domain effects came in handy to serve as an empirical index for the progressive building of abstract over concrete domains. The Metaphoric Structuring Views could also be supplemented with a category formation mechanism (Bowdle & Gentner, 2005) instead of an associative learning mechanism to be able to account for quick learning of new mappings and their conventionalization into language.

Two points should be emphasized here. Firstly, linguistic experience (the frequency with which a conceptual domain is talked about in terms of another) and whatever learning mechanism is chosen do not by themselves assure that abstract domains will be structured by reference to more concrete domains. They can just as well serve to make analogies across two equally concrete or abstract concepts, or even support the "grounding" of concrete concepts onto abstract ones. Therefore, they fail in their goal of securing a solid foundation for abstract concepts onto experiential ground. Secondly, the inclusion by the Integrated Metaphoric Structuring View of experiential correlations as a main source of conceptual mappings which later come to be modified by the modulatory influence of language falls short of its explanatory goal of accounting for both universal and relativistic patterns. As long as language is granted the ability to choose from several available experiential grounds, making some of them salient and hiding others as if not experienced at all (or even establishing completely new, creative mappings), the role of language comes to be as causal as it is assumed by the Weak Metaphoric Structuring View (see also Rakova, 2002, for related arguments about the difficulty of reconciling universalism and relativism under a Solid Foundation View of concepts).

As a consequence, current Metaphoric Structuring Views need the asistance of another factor to make sure that these mechanisms work to place abstract concepts on solid concrete ground. This factor may be the fact that concrete concepts are more clearly delineated and structured than abstract concepts, and therefore there is an important tendency to use the former to help our thinking about the latter instead of the other way around. This difference predicts asymmetric cross-dimensional effects, which thus remain as a key index of the progressive building of abstract thought on concrete, solid foundations. The present review suggests that this prediction may not be held by the data, although the definitive test is still to be carried out.

Let us for a moment grant that available evidence supports unambiguously that bidirectionality in cross-domain interactions is the rule instead of the exception. What could now serve as the empirical index of how concrete or basic a conceptual dimension is? Put in other words, what empirical evidence could show that space, for example, is more concrete than time? Or, to give a more compelling example, that space is more concrete than pitch? Lacking an accepted criterium, we are left with a very different picture of how human conceptualization may work: one that would plainly accept that concepts at the first floor could be grounded by concepts at the roof (Figure 3).

The remaining part of this chapter constitutes an effort to provide a theory that takes cognitive flexibility seriously, bringing the processing dynamics that occur in the mental workplace to the forefront. Abstract thinking is to be severed from abstract long-term representations, and studied in its own terms. The central concern of the theory is to give an account of how conceptual domains are represented and processed in working memory in order to carry out successfully the kind of tasks reviewed above. Such an account is based on well-established psychological principles regarding spatial attention, spatial language, and working memory. With the help of some reasonable assumptions about long-term learning, the theory suggests a way in

Figure 3. A Flexible Foundations View of abstract concepts (photograph by Kevin Pammet, all rights reserved, reproduced with permission).

which working memory and long-term memory are connected, thereby also providing some hints about the long-term representation of conceptual metaphors. In what follows, we first describe the theory and some efforts explicitly aimed at testing it. In the final sections, we will explore the implications of the model for the manifestation of conceptual metaphors and the directionality of the cross-domain effect, the long-term learning of new conceptual mappings, and cross-linguistic and cross-cultural relativity issues. We will end by stepping back again and considering what expectations can be held from this view to solve the Symbol Grouding Problem.

4. A Flexible Foundations theory of metaphoric reasoning

A central aim of this second half of the paper is to present a psychological model of abstract reasoning using metaphoric projections. Many conceptual metaphors use space as a source domain to help us think about more abstract domains. Although the model can be generalized to a variety of source domains, it focuses on spatial conceptual metaphors in its current formulation. We first go through a short discussion of relevant principles in spatial cognition and attention. Then we introduce the main representational and processing assumptions about working memory. Next, we draw predictions and describe some empirical studies explicitly aimed at testing them.

4.1. Basic principles of spatial language and spatial attention

Spatial deixis, or pointing with words, requires selecting an object to work as an anchor or relatum (Levelt, 1989). In a simple type of deixis, no more than a relatum is needed (e.g., "bring that ball here" in which "here" refers to the proximity of the speaker). The relatum may be the speaker or it might be another object including the addressee ("put that ball close to you"). Garnham (1989) called this a *basic* relation. In more complicated forms of deixis, a coordinate system or reference frame is imposed on the relatum (see Levelt, 1989; Landau & Jackendoff, 1993; Levinson, 1996). When the relatum is the speaker (as in "put the ball to my left"), the reference frame is called a *deictic frame*. When the relatum is another object as in ("put the ball to the left of the chair"), the reference frame is called *intrinsic*. Levinson (1996) distinguishes a third type of reference frame: an *absolute* frame, which can be exemplified by the terms north, south, east, west. Finally, after setting a reference frame, spatial linguistic terms define a region of acceptability or spatial template (Landau & Jackendoff, 1993; Carlson-Radvansky & Logan, 1997) which is applied onto the frame (e.g., the English preposition "above" defines a region above but not in touch with an object, while "on" defines a region which is above and in touch with the object).

Logan (1995; Logan & Sadler, 1996) distinguished several processing operations which must be carried out when locating an object by means of a relatum and a reference frame. The reference frame must be created with the relatum at its origin, its axes must be aligned with intrinsic characteristics of the relatum, so that the up-down left-right and front-back dimensions are properly oriented, and its scale set. Spatial frames can also be moved and rotated in such a flexible way that Logan (1995) contended that they are part of the machinery of attention.

Much research suggests that in each moment there are several active spatial frames in competition (Carlson-Radvansky & Irwin, 1993, 1994; Carlson-Radvansky & Logan, 1997). Carlson-Radvansky and Irwin (1994) presented sentences using the term "above" and a picture of a relatum with an intrinsic vertical axis (e.g., a tree) and a located object (e.g., a ball). Sometimes the relatum was upright, such that viewer-centered, environment-centered and object-centered frames were aligned. In other occasions the relatum was rotated, such that the object-centered frame was misaligned with the other two. In a final experiment, some groups carried out the task with the heads tilted, thus dissociating the viewer-centered frame from the environment-centered frame. In all cases, sentence to picture matching times gave signs of being affected simultaneously by competition between multiple reference frames, and not only by the one guiding the yes/no response.

Carlson-Radvansky and Irwin (1994) also found that co-activated frames vary in their salience: the environment-centered frame exerted a stronger influence than the object-centered frame, whereas the viewer-centered frame did not have a significant effect. Frame salience and competition were affected by instructions to a certain extent, but it was not possible to override them completely. The salience of spatial reference frames can also be affected by factors such as the presence of salient cues (Li & Gleitman, 2002; Levinson, Kita, Haun & Rasch, 2002) or patterns of alignment and mis-alignment between frames (e.g., Shelton & McNamara, 2001). The dimensions within a reference frame also vary in salience: the vertical dimension is more salient than front-back and left-right (Rock, 1973). Some theorists suggest that this is because verticality is determined by gravity, upright posture, body symmetry and other very salient and consistent signals (Levelt, 1989). This is not the case with the horizontal left-right and front-back axes. Correspondingly, Franklin and Tversky (1990; see also Logan, 1995) found that it was faster to find objects along the vertical dimension than along the two horizontal dimensions. Finally, Carlson and Van Deman (2008) showed that it is possible to prime separate frame components, suggesting that it is possible to access selectively a single axis, with or without specification of its poles, or a whole frame. More salient frames tend to be activated as a whole, whereas less salient frames can be partially activated.

Because of this flexibility, spatial representations and mechanisms seem very well endowed to explain many of the types of interactions and some of the intervening factors that were described in our prior review of cross-domain conceptual mappings. The mental workspace may contain many simultaneous spatial frames of reference which can be set up and moved with an impressive degree of flexibility, which affect spatial processing depending on perspective or deictic origin, and with intrinsic variations in automaticity or "strength". The following section builds on these conclusions to present a view of working memory which can provide a coherent account of prior evidence regarding conceptual metaphor processing, as well as make several new predictions.

4.2. Mental working spaces, activation, and coherence mechanisms

In this section, we sketch a theoretical framework which makes use of attentional and linguistic mechanisms working on embodied representations of abstract meaning in a mental workplace. Most of its postulates are not new. To the contrary, there is wide agreement on many of them. The framework is thus offered as an integration of theoretical ideas that so far have not been put together in a coherent way, and as a heuristic tool to guide future research and theorizing about conceptual metaphors.

It should be emphasized at the outset that the view of working memory to be described here has very little in common with the view advocated by Alan Baddeley and coworkers (see Baddeley, 2007, for a recent review). Baddeley's Working Memory is a system composed of unimodal, separate and distinct subsystems. In our view, working memory is instead a multimodal, highly integrated system which combines the outputs of perception, language and memory into a complex representation which is able to guide situated action.

A first postulate of the model is a mental workspace endowed with both structure and content. Structure is provided by both structural dimensions and image schemas, constituting the scaffolding on which concrete contents are placed (Johnson-Laird, 1983; Fauconnier, 1985; Jackendoff, 2002; Talmy, 2000). All kinds of elements have activation levels which determine their inclusion in the mental space or model and their ability to interact with other elements (we use the terms "mental space" and "mental model" as synonyms).

Following Johnson-Laird (1983), we assume that there is a basic mental space which is directly linked to our perceptual experiences. Its reference frames are constructed with the three perpendicular dimensions of physical space. It also contains representations of objects located in space and the observer's viewpoint or deictic origin. Spatial location is coded by means of reference frames, which define positions with respect to reference points. Image schemas such as CONTAINMENT or SUPPORT can also be added, if activated, to provide further structure. Individual contents (physical objects) are located within the structure, therefore holding varying types of relations between them.

The perceptual space holds a representation which is analogous to the outer reality. Representations of objects and reference frames in this space can be located, moved, rotated and contemplated from another viewpoint at will, thereby allowing many visuospatial inferences. The perceptual space is probably constructed in very similar ways by many animal species, and its basic design characteristics are in all likelihood universal in humans.

In line with other theorists, we assume that the mind creates and uses a variety of mental spaces for different purposes, including navigating, reasoning, and using language (Johnson-Laird, 1983; Fauconnier, 1985; Fauconnier & Turner, 2002; Jackendoff, 2002). Following Johnson-Laird's analysis (1983), the evolution of language in humans brought up the possibility of labelling the contents within the mental space. The linguistic labels then became the key factor for determining element identity, overriding physical similarity and other perceptually based cues. In the mental space, a black dot on a white field may be a person, a fly, a planet or whatever it is labelled to be. We suggest that the capacity of holding and manipulating abstract thoughts through spatial conceptual metaphors depends crucially on labelling representations of physical objects with abstract labels and locating those "abstract" objects on the physical dimensions of space, which in turn can also hold abstract labels such as time or emotional evaluation.

Linguistic labelling is able to support the distinction between types and tokens, i.e., some object in the model may be labelled either as representing the category CAR or just a specific car (see Jackendoff, 1983, 2002, for discussion of the distinction between types and tokens and the intricacies of their representation in short and long term memory). However, because the mental workplace still retains the design of the perceptual model, the labelled object in the mental space must be a concrete object taking a concrete shape and located in a particular point of the structural scaffolding. It holds concrete relations with other objects, even if those relations are within dimensions with abstract labels. When we think of "cars" in general, we still represent them by means of particular instances in the mental space. This is in agreement with the wide literature on language comprehension and embodiment within the Simulation tradition (e.g., Stanfield & Zwaan, 2001; Zwaan, Stanfield & Yaxley, 2002). It also accounts for the abundance of metaphoric gesture accompanying speech, as in the psychology professor example that opened this chapter (McNeill, 1992). Our contention is that the grounding of meaning arises necessarily from the fact that the design characteristics of the mental workplace are the same that developed to represent the perceptual world. In other words, the mental space used for abstract thought is essentially the same as the one that is used for perceiving and acting on the environment.

We suggest that the acquisition of language did not lead to any substantial change in the way mental spaces are built: the reference frames hold a maximum of three perpendicular structural axes, they contain representations of concrete objects and they are structured by the same kind of image schemas. The objects, dimensions and schemas labelled as abstract concepts gain new characteristics from their abstract meaning, keeping at the same time many of their perceptually based properties. As a result, they can be used to support abstract reasoning. For example, after a vertical axis is labelled as the social dimension of power, objects representing people can be located at different heights of this dimension. Apart from allowing perceptual judgments of "social distance", it also supports judgments of, say, who should show respect to whom with only a glimpse at the mental space.

The social power example shows a counter-intuitive property of mental spaces. Even though the reference frames are constrained to have a maximum of three perpendicular axes because of their basic perceptual nature, there may be more than one active frame with different labels. Imagine a scene in which a soldier talks to his captain. While both persons are located (more or less) at the same height in the physical vertical dimension, they are located at different heights of the social power vertical dimension. Contents may be located simultaneously at different points of the "primary" physical vertical dimension and the "secondary" social hierarchy vertical dimension. When in a model there are both primary and secondary dimensions, primary dimensions have priority over secondary in determining how the model is seen from the perspective of the observer (although secondary dimensions may induce subtle biases). When the model only requires the inclusion of secondary dimensions, they may determine how it physically looks like. If asked to think of ranks in the army, participants probably set up a mental model with rank-labelled objects (e.g., LIEUTENANT, CAPTAIN, COLONEL, GENERAL) arranged along a vertical axis labelled rank.

A central property of the contents of the mental working space at any given time is their degree of activation. When a mental representation gathers enough activation, it is on the focus of attention. This notion of focus is wider than that used in space-based theories of visual attention (e.g., Posner, 1980), being closer to the notion of discourse focus (Levelt, 1989). Representations which are above a certain threshold, and therefore in focus, are processed in a more efficient way. They are also able to exert effects which are forbidden to out-of-focus (or below-threshold) representations, such as guiding further processing, directing attentional mechanisms, or interacting with other relevant representations for establishing global coherence (to be discussed below). They can also be subjected to voluntarily controlled goal-directed manipulation. Variations in activation affect the degree to which in-focus representations participate in these kinds of above-threshold interactions. Representations activated below threshold can be said not to be part of the mental space, although they can participate in a variety of below-threshold interactions (MacKay, 1987).

Many different factors can affect the degree of activation of a representation. Some are exogenous factors, such as the greater salience of the vertical dimension of space (Rock, 1973; Franklin & Tversky, 1990). Another example is the intrinsic ability of symbolic signals such as linguistic spatial terms ("above", "below", "left", "right"), arrows (Hommel, Pratt, Colzato & Godijn, 2001; Mayer & Kosson, 2004), eye gaze and body parts (Ansorge, 2003; Friesen & Kingston, 1998, 2003) to capture and direct attention to particular spatial locations even without predictive power. Concepts can be called up by stimuli in different formats, which may have different intrinsic capacity to activate their representations (e.g., Arabic numerals versus number words, Dehaene et al., 1993). This intrinsic capacity is strongly linked to extended practice and automaticity of processing (for modern views on automaticity, see Anderson, 1982; Logan, 1988). When the input is linguistic, the devices by which language controls attention deployment to certain representations over others become crucial (Talmy, 2000, 2003; Taube-Schiff & Segalowitz, 2005). Stimulus characteristics such as abrupt onset, parafoveal location, unpredictable movement and so on, which are able to automatically capture attention toward a stimulus (Ruz & Lupiáñez, 2002), and explicit task requirements also increase the activation of its associated representation. Finally, endogenously controlled factors and voluntary will (Posner, 1980; Jonides, 1981; Jonides & Yantis, 1988) may also boost the level of activation of particular representations. These different sources of activation enter into a weighted sum which renders the total activation of a given element in the mental working space. All these attentional factors can also affect the choice of deictic origin, i.e., the point from which the subject views the mental model.

A final component of the theory is a mechanism aimed at reducing the total number of degrees of freedom present in the mental space. Somehow, this coherence mechanism tries to satisfy simultaneously the many constraints that the contents of the mental space pose to each other, making the global representation stable and coherent (see Thagard, 2000, for a general treatment of coherence). Many inferences are automatically drawn as part of the workings of this mechanism: the representations may be changed, new contents brought up and others deleted, and structural dimensions may be conflated. The resulting representation is maximally informative and useful for the task at hand with the minimum storage cost and processing load. This mechanism is similar in spirit to the rules of good shape proposed by Gestalt theorists (Kohler, 1929), to the idea of equilibrium in integration networks of mental spaces (Fauconnier & Turner, 2002), and to the constraints of Optimality Theory (see Archangeli & Lagendoen, 1997, for a review). It is also consistent with the rules that guide the mesh of affordances in Glenberg's theory (Glenberg, 1997; Glenberg & Robertson, 2000) or the creation of simulations in Barsalou (1999, 2003; Barsalou et al., 2003), as well as with the relevance-creating mechanisms of Relevance Theory (Sperber & Wilson, 1986). It may be argued that all the studies which find congruency effects between task dimensions provide supporting evidence for a coherence mechanism of some kind.

An important point to note is that setting up and maintaining a mental model is something that takes effort. The amount of effort is determined by the complexity of the model in ways that relate to the number of elements which are not consistent with other elements in the model (Johnson-Laird, 1983). This supports the expectation that people will always try to set up only the minimally complex mental model which allows dealing satisfactorily with the situation at hand. Such principle of rationality pervades both strategic planning of one's behaviour and interpretation of the behaviour of others (Grice, 1975; Shank & Abelson, 1977). In the current context, it is a necessary ingredient to be able to extract predictions from the theory. We postulate that searching for coherence in the model is effortful too, so whether it is worthwhile to pursue a coherent model will be strategically chosen depending on the situation. Nevertheless, coherence reduces global complexity and mental effort, which makes it a useful strategy in many situations. People will always try to arrive at a model that maximizes simplicity and coherence and minimizes effort, in the context of current goals and circumstances.

A final central assumption of the present theory is that the coherence mechanism exists only in working memory. It works against having inconsistent mappings simultaneously active within a mental model. However, mental models using inconsistent mappings can be built on different occasions. If each successful use of a model is committed to long term memory, and its internal mappings are strengthened through repeated use, a variety of inconsistent mappings for the same conceptual dimension will reside in long term memory side by side, without conflict. They are only pressed to be consistent when simultaneously activated and entered into a single mental model in working memory.

To summarize, working memory is a multimodal, integrated, optimally coherent and detailed mental space, populated by labelled elements (objects, structural dimensions and image schemas), which is aimed at maximazing goal attainment with a minimum mental effort. The ontology of the mental workspace, the selected structural and content units, their labelling and concrete shapes, their positioning into the structure, their relative degree of activation, and finally, the kind of coherence interactions established among all of these elements, are the chief factors which determine which behaviour will be observed in a given experimental task.

4.3. Testing the theory

A central prediction of the present framework is that the key aspect that governs the manifestation of conceptual metaphors in behaviour relates to the simultaneous inclusion of both the abstract and concrete dimensions within the current working mental model, such that both sets of dimensions are able to constraint each other. The theory predicts that the more salient dimension will be able to interfere to a greater extent with the less salient dimension, and therefore they will interact when the coherence mechanism is applied to the model. This mechanism reorganizes the contents of the model to produce a maximally coherent overall description of the situation, which in turn provides guidance for coping with that situation with a minimal mental effort. If the response is based on the less salient dimension, (in)congruency effects are expected. More succinctly, manipulating the degree of activation of both the concrete and abstract dimensions will affect their ability to interact, and therefore the finding of conceptual metaphoric effects on behaviour. We now turn to research aimed explicitly at testing this suggestion. We will describe two so far unpublished experiments, and discuss in detail other relevant work from our lab (Torralbo, Santiago & Lupiáñez, 2006).

Other important predictions follow from the distinction between working memory and long term memory, the long term storage of working memory models with practice and repetition, and the postulate that only working memory struggles to be internally coherent, whereas long term memory can be populated with contradictory representations without conflict. The implications of these assumptions will be followed up in the final sections of this chapter.

Experiments on the vertical axis and voluntary attention. Santiago, Ouellet, Román and Valenzuela (2011) focused on affective evaluation using words relevant to the HAPPY IS UP conceptual metaphor. Participants read Spanish emotion words, such as "feliz" (happy) and "triste" (sad), and were asked to judge whether the word referred to a positive or negative emotion. A silhouette of a human face looking rightwards was presented centered on the screen, and words were presented either above or below the face (see Figure 4).

The procedure is analogous to that used by Meier and Robinson (2004, exp. 1), with a single difference: word location was not cued just before word presentation. Therefore, it is possible that our experiment does not activate the vertical spatial dimension to the same extent. Consistent with this suggestion, both space and affective evaluation affected response latency (with faster responding to upper than lower words, and to positive than negative words), but there were no traces of an interaction between them. In other words, the congruency effects observed by Meier and Robinson (2004) between the up-down and the positive-negative dimensions was not replicated.

Figure 4. Stimuli used in Santiago et al. (2011).

Experiment 2 tried to increase the amount of attention voluntarily paid to the spatial dimension by changing the instructions given to participants. A paragraph was added to the instructions explaining that there would be a secondary task to be carried out simultaneously: a greater number of words would be presented at one of the two screen positions; at the end of the session, they should report at which position there were more words. The task was presented as a difficult task because the number of words at each position would be only slightly different. Actually, as in Experiment 1, there were exactly 50% words at each site. If the reason why no spatial-conceptual interactions were found in the first experiment has to do with the processing of the literal spatial up-down dimension, this manipulation should make participants to pay attention to the position where words are presented, thereby increasing the activation of this dimension. The dimension of space should then be included in the model, entering into coherence interactions with the other active conceptual dimension of affective evaluation. Note that the conceptual processing side of the task (judging emotional valence) remains untouched by this manipulation.

During debriefing, many participants in Experiment 2 reported that they started the session trying to keep a count of words at one of the two positions, but many of them acknowledged that after a while they felt that the difference was too small and gave up the secondary task during the experiment. It is therefore possible that participants followed the instructions at the beginning of the experiment, but then changed to perform in a fashion which would be analogous to Experiment 1. As the experiment consisted of two identical blocks of trials, we looked at them independently.

As suspected, position and meaning interacted only in the first block of the experiment, whereas the second block showed no traces of such interaction. The size of the spatial-conceptual congruency effect (obtained by substracting the congruent conditions positive-up and negative-down from the incongruent conditions positive-down negative-up) amounted to 27 ms in the first block and shrinked to -7 ms in the second block (see Figure 5).

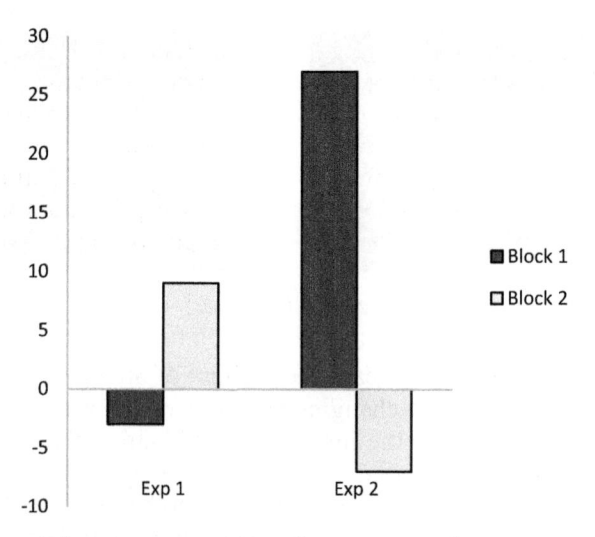

Figure 5. Size of the congruency effect (incongruent minus congruent conditions) in each half of Experiments 1 and 2 of Santiago et al. (2011).

Therefore, the voluntary allocation of attention to the vertical axis produced detectable effects of the spatial conceptual metaphor underlying the processing of emotional meanings. This study provides evidence for the hypothesis that concrete dimensions need to be salient enough to be able to interact with concurrently processed abstract dimensions. An interesting point to note is that this study differs from others which also show effects of voluntary strategies (e.g., Bachtöld et al., 1998; Galfano, Rusconi & Umiltá, 2006; see review above) in that we did not instruct our participants where to locate the positive and negative poles of the evaluative dimension, but just to attend to the whole dimension. This suggests that attention is only a mediating factor, and not the only cause of the observed pattern.

Experiments on the horizontal axes and automatic attention. Another series of experiments from our lab (Torralbo, Santiago & Lupiáñez, 2006) used a similar logic but manipulated attention through automatic means. This study focused on the temporal metaphor TIME IS MOTION. As reviewed above, there is experimental evidence supporting two variations of this metaphor in Western left-to-right writing cultures: one that maps future onto front space and past onto back space (e.g., Boroditsky, 2000) and another that maps past onto left space and future onto right space (Santiago et al., 2007, among others, see above). Spanish words (tensed verbs and temporal adverbs) were presented on a screen and participants gave a speeded judgment of whether the word referred to the past or to the future. The crucial aspect of the procedure was that the spatial arrangement of objects on the screen allowed the simultaneous application of both the back-front and left-right time metaphors. A silhouette of a human profile was presented centered on the screen, facing either rightwards or leftwards. Words were presented within a balloon either to the right or to the left of the silhouette (see Figure 6). Participants were instructed to judge whether the "person" was thinking of her past or her future. In this situation, if the deictic origin is placed on the silhouette, past and future words are presented in its back and front space. If the deictic origin is placed on the participant, past and future words are presented in left and right space. Because the silhouette changes its direction of sight randomly from trial to trial, and because all words are presented at both the left and right locations, both frames (the back-front and left-right axes) are orthogonal. Note that both axes are also equally irrelevant to the conceptual task (judging the words' temporal reference).

The first experiment used a vocal response: people pronounced "pasado" (past) or "futuro" (future). In this situation, we predicted that the left-right spatial dimension would not be included in the model, because it has a low intrinsic salience (Franklin & Tversky, 1990), it is not being voluntari-

Figure 6. Sample of stimuli from Torralbo et al. (2006). All eight combinations of left-right word presentation and left-right face direction were used.

ly focused, and nothing in the task requires it. In contrast, the back-front dimension would enjoy a high level of activation, because both faces and random changes automatically attract attention (Friesen & Kingstone, 2003). Out of the two spatial conceptual mappings available for time in long term memory, the search for a maximally consistent mental model would most likely select the back-past front-future metaphor in this situation. Therefore, the temporal meaning of words should interact with the position occupied by the word in the back-front axis of the silhouette: future words should be responded to faster when presented in front of the face and past words when presented behind the face, independently of whether these positions were to the left or to the right of the screen.

The results supported this prediction: words presented at metaphorically congruent positions in the front-back spatial frame were 15 ms faster than words presented in incongruent positions, a statistically significant result. In contrast, words presented at congruent positions in the participant-centered left-right spatial frame were a non-significant 2 ms slower than words at incongruent positions.

In a second experiment, the salience of the left-right frame was increased through exogenous-automatic means by changing to manual responding using left and right keys. This task requirement should force the inclusion of the left-right spatial dimension into the mental model of the task. We expected that the high activation of this spatial frame would bias the results of the coherence mechanism in two ways: first, the conceptual mapping of time onto the left-right dimension would be selected; and second, the deictic origin would be moved from the face in the screen onto the participant. In this situation, it was predicted that the processing of word meanings would be speeded up only in positions congruent with the left-right conceptual metaphor, and not with the back-front mapping.

The results again supported the expectations: past words presented on the left and future words presented on the right were now 14 ms faster than the same words presented in the opposite positions. Moreover, the back-front axis lost all trace of its former effect, which came down to a non-significant -5 ms (see Figure 7).

Torralbo et al. (2006) results provide strong support for several claims of the present theoretical framework. First of all, they show that several inconsistent conceptual metaphors can coexist in long term memory and be selected and used in different occasions. Note that we did not instruct participants about where to locate the poles of the time dimension, which again supports that the choice is based on stored mappings. Second, only one of those inconsistent mappings can be used on a given occasion (unless they are somehow blended, Fauconnier & Turner, 2002). Third, there is a great deal of cognitive flexibility in the selection of conceptual metaphors, as much as it is

Flexible foundations of abstract thought 87

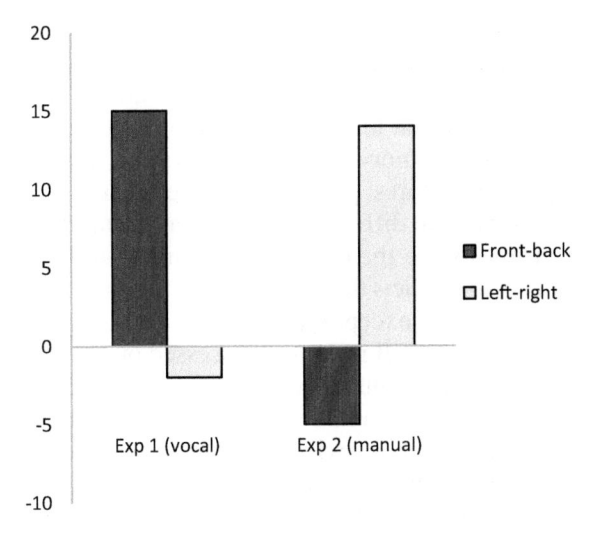

Figure 7. Size of the congruity effect (incongruent minus congruent conditions) for each reference frame (face intrinsic front-back or observer-relative left-right) in Experiments 1 (vocal response) and 2 (manual response) of Torralbo et al. (2006).

attested in non-metaphorical spatial cognition. This points to the intervention of basic attentional mechanisms which treat metaphorical dimensions in a similar way to how they treat concrete, perceptually-based dimensions. Fourth, the search for a globally coherent mental model is an important force molding the final shape of the mental model. Finally, these results, taken together with the experiments by Santiago et al. (in preparation) support the idea that both endogenous-controlled and exogenous-automatic attentional factors affect the degree of activation of the elements of the mental model and the choice of deictic perspective, thereby modulating its interactions.

5. Implications and extensions

5.1. The manifestation of conceptual metaphors in behaviour

A central prediction of the present theory is that the manifestation of spatial conceptual metaphors depends on the simultaneous presence in working memory of both spatial and abstract concepts, their relative activation and their coherence interactions. This kind of interactions explain why it is possible to observe the manifestation of a spatial-conceptual mapping when the degree of activation of the associated (irrelevant) spatial dimension is increased in the experiments just described. The theory also allows a unified explanation of the studies reviewed in the first part of this paper.

The present theoretical framework readily accounts for the availability of several alternative, and often inconsistent, mappings for a given conceptual domain in the long term memory of a single individual, as well as across individuals, languages and cultures: people can conceptualize an abstract domain in wholly different ways in different occasions and learn them all. They are only constrained not to use them at the same time within a single mental model. The theory also predicts that bidirectional interactions across domains will be the rule and not the exception, and poses clear conditions: whenever the effect of the more active dimension is assessed on the less active dimension while both of them are simultaneously active in a mental model. Finally, the theory supports a very fast use of new mappings in the face of life-long habits: although practiced habits will tend to be used all other factors being equal, people have an enormous control on their conceptualizations of situations in working memory. For example, insight problem solving is based on the sudden set up of a new, and successful, mental model for a problem, often after giving signs of trying many alternative configurations. As soon as a new way of conceiving a problem proves useful, it tends to be learned immediately and used in subsequent occasions (see, e.g., Dunbar, 1998).

The theory is also able to account for the influence of all mediating factors isolated along our review of relevant literature, and suggests that they can be grouped into three main categories:

a) Factors affecting the strength with which activating a given abstract concept primes a particular metaphoric mapping (i.e., the strength of the habit of thinking about an abstract domain in terms of another in a particular configuration): practice of the mapping, degree of conventionality and frequency of consistent linguistic patterns and cultural conventions fall here. The three factors can be actually subsumed under the first, as habitual language is just a source of pressure to practice a mapping. Other sources are possible. For example, mapping affective valence to the close-far dimension has a higher degree of automaticity than alternative mappings probably because it supports approach-avoidance reactions, which are relevant and useful in a greater proportion of valenced situations.

b) Factors affecting the strength with which aspects of the task activate an underlying conceptual dimension: this includes variations in the efficacy of different codes (e.g., number concepts being activated more strongly from Indo-Arabic numerals than from number words), perceptual salience, perceptual discriminability, priming context, task requirements, and degree of attention voluntarily paid to or automatically attracted by the stimulus. Voluntary attention is in turn mediated by factors like instructions, goals, motivation, etc., and exogenous attention is affected by factors like abrupt onset, parafoveal location, predictability and so on.

c) Factors affecting coherence interactions between dimensions within a mental model: relative activation (related to a and b), simultaneity of processing, availability of enough time and motivation to adopt stricter coherence strategies.

d) Factors affecting the choice of perspective or deictic origin from which the mental model is considered: this set includes many of the factors mentioned in a–c, being specially relevant both exogenous and voluntary attentional factors.

5.2. The acquisition of conceptual metaphors

The present theory suggests that the most important factor for the establishment of new conceptual metaphoric associations between two semantic dimensions is their being simultaneously included in an active mental model (similar claims have been proposed from research on implicit learning and automaticity: Jiang & Chun, 2001; Jiménez & Méndez, 1999). By coexisting in working memory, a spatial and a conceptual representation become associated. Once this space-conceptual association is stored, there will be a tendency towards using it again in the future. The more frequent the association, the greater this trend.

Nothing precludes storing of conflicting space-conceptual mappings in semantic memory, as the result of different learning experiences. Only individual mental spaces are constrained to be globally coherent. Once a particular mapping is stored, it may be activated and it can then place constraints on the final shape of mental models in which that concept intervenes. When there are conflicting mappings for a given concept, the use of one or the other in the model is affected by the factors influencing degree of activation, and by coherence interactions with other elements in the model.

Let's follow in detail the acquisition process of a conceptual metaphor using the source domain of space. People often use spatial strategies to solve problems. For example, if participants are asked to press a left button when a red square is presented and a right button when the square is green, probably many of them will generate a mental model in which the label RED is assigned to a concrete object located to the left and the label GREEN to an object on the right in the left-right spatial dimension. The mentally represented object might be a written word, a coloured patch or anything that the person finds useful. The important point is that, being labelled as RED, it will be used to stand for the concept of "redness". The repeated use of this spatial-conceptual mapping would lead to the storage of a permanent association between RED and left space and GREEN and right space in long term semantic memory. Further practice will strengthen the association and make its use more likely in new situations.

De Hower (2004) actually carried out a very similar manipulation. He trained participants to say "cale" to a leftward arrow or the word "left" and to say "cole" to a rightward arrow or the word "right". In a subsequent block, participants were to say "cale" to a blue square and "cole" to a green square. A clear Simon effect emerged: blue squares were responded to faster when presented on the left side, and green squares were faster on the right side. The effect was thus mediated by the prior association of "cale" to left space and "cole" to right space (see also Pellicano, Vu, Proctor, Nicoletti & Umiltà, 2008).

The general claim is that whatever dimensions, schemas and contents are simultaneously active in working memory, they will enter into coherence interactions and become an optimally coherent mental model. The model will be later committed to long term memory. This mechanism provides a way for acquiring initial content for an abstract continuous dimension, such as TIME and EVALUATION, through the kind of experiential correlations that are assumed to underly many conceptual metaphors. If attention is simultaneously paid to forward movement of the person in the front-back dimension and to the impression of duration, both dimensions may be included into a coherent model, which will export a lot of spatial structure to the domain of time. Storing many similar models will entrench this spatio-temporal conceptual mapping in semantic memory.

The concrete domain may be included in the model based on actual perceptuomotor input, as in the example above, or by linguistic input, both through its literal content, through presuppositions, or through derived pragmatic inferences. Language may also influence mental model construction by inducing a particular perspective, directing attention and increasing the level of activation of some contents over others (see discussion below). In the same vein, a metaphoric mapping can be acquired through exposition to cultural "reifications" of the metaphor, as those placing powerful people like professors, executives, kings or winners in higher positions on daises, buildings, thrones or podiums (Schubert, 2005).

For similar reasons, cultural practices such as orthographic direction and graphic conventions can induce horizontal conceptual mappings of linear order and time (e.g., Tversky et al., 1991), numerical sequences (Dehaene et al., 1993) and agent-patient relations and action directionality (e.g., Chatterjee et al., 1995; see the review section), even though they are just arbitrary cultural choices. Mental models of events are constructed from text, comic strips, charts and so on. These models use a left-to-right strategy as a consequence of the search for a maximally coherent model of the entire situation, including both the spatial linearisation of the input and the meaning of its parts. Reading habits also produce attentional and scanning biases which can operate on inner space when mental models are created for other reasons. As a result, the spatialization of meaning falls into place just because of pure co-occurrence coupled with the strong human tendency to build coherent mental models.

Support for this suggestion is provided by Jahn, Knauff and Johnson-Laird (2007), who showed that when participants receive a description like "a table is between the TV and a chair", they tend to form a model which locates the TV on the left, then the table in the center, and the chair on the right, although this arrangement does not necessarily follow from the premises. A current study in our lab is testing whether Arabic readers show the opposite bias in mental model construction, which would support its more than likely relation with reading habits. If so, the model construction bias will support our contention that a conceptual metaphor can be learned just by repeated experiences with fully arbitrary mappings.

Finally, it is also possible to learn radically new ways of understanding a concept for which there is already knowledge in place. Learning proceeds just as when there is no prior knowledge: a creative mental model is set up from scratch. If it succeeds, the same strategy will probably be used in similar tasks in the future, producing similar memory traces. These will create a new cluster and contribute to the development of a new conceptual schema in semantic memory. How much and how easily it will be activated in the future will depend on its effectiveness, as well as on the mediating factors listed above.

Summing up, in our view the repeated construction of coherent mental models in working memory underlies the internal organisation of concepts in semantic memory. Whatever representations are simultaneously entered into a mental model are subjected to coherence interactions that may involve cross-domain projections. Mental models leave memory traces and similar traces cluster together to form new conceptual metaphoric projections in long term semantic memory.

5.3. Metaphoric structuring and linguistic relativity

As the present chapter has emphasized, there are many ways to construe internally coherent conceptual structures using the reservoire of universal image schemas. Why some languages and cultures choose a particular configuration while others choose a different one? The present theory points to three sets of causes.

Firstly, mental models are built as a tool for dealing with situations and solving problems. Only the metaphoric construals which offer useful solutions to everyday problems have the potential to be repeatedly used. Levine (1997), in his thorough description of cross-cultural variations of the non-spatial TIME IS MONEY metaphor, makes a compelling case for the social and economic usefulness of this metaphor (see also Alverson, 1996).

Secondly, the factors governing the inclusion of structural and content elements in mental models influence which subset of all potentially useful construals of abstract meanings is instantiated in a culture. Some elements have intrinsically greater salience (or activation levels) as, e.g., the vertical dimension, and these are expected to be universally more influential and less variable in the construction of abstract meanings. Other factors are expected to vary widely across languages and cultures, because of variations in the many endogenous and exogenous means by which attention is deployed to certain elements over others.

Language is a chief tool for the control of attention. Talmy (2003) mentions over 50 different linguistic mechanisms that increase or decrease attention to a certain type of linguistic entity. For example, speakers of Turkish must pay attention to whether an event has been witnessed or non-witnessed, as this distinction is obligatorily encoded in the verb flexion. Speakers of many other languages have optional ways to express this distinction, but they are not forced to do it every single time a verb is produced (Slobin, 1996). This is a linguistic attentional factor which forces an element to be included in the mental model of the situation. Other factors may exert only gradual influences (Talmy, 2003). Powerful cognitive habits may be developed because of bidirectional influences between language and attention. For example, the availability of linguistic labels directs attention to certain features of the outer world (e.g., object shape), tuning the attentional mechanism to those features and so boosting the learning of new labels based on the same features (Landau, Smith & Jones, 1998; Smith, Jones, Landau, Gershkoff-Stowe & Samuelson, 2002). A similar mechanism may explain the exclusive use of absolute frames of reference in languages lacking deictic and intrinsic spatial terms (see Majid, Bowerman, Kita, Haun & Levinson, 2004, for a review). The currently booming research on linguistic relativity takes as one of its foundations the idea that by means of mechanisms of this kind, languages may instill cognitive habits, therefore leading to systematic differences in the way reality is conceptualized (Hunt & Agnoli, 1991; Slobin, 1996; Gentner & Goldin-Meadow, 2003; Casasanto, 2008).

In the terms of the present theory, these cognitive habits lead to the routinary inclusion or rejection of certain elements (both structural and content) in mental models. Moreover, the theory leads to a more general prediction:

cross-cultural variations in factors affecting mental model construction may lead to relativity effects even if such variations are not manifested in language. The differences in conceptual left-right biases observed across cultures using a left-to-right versus a right-to-left writing system are a relevant example.

A third factor which the present theory points at is coherence. Although in the theory there is no such a thing as a coherence mechanism to be applied to the contents of long-term memory, the fact that several abstract concepts are often simultaneously part of a given mental model will expose them to the short-term coherence mechanism. This will foster the development of clusters of conceptual metaphors which are internally consistent, even though they may be radically inconsistent with the members of another cluster. As an example, Klein's (1987) analysis of time in Toba suggests that this language distinguishes a near future, approaching the speaker from behind; a near past, going away in front of her; and a remote past and future, which are linguistically indistinguishable. In Toba, the remote past is of the same nature as the remote future, supporting a cyclical understanding of time over long periods. Klein (1987) argues that similar patterns of linguistic uses can be found in Toba's understanding of death as leading to a return to life, and in their kinship terms, which group together in a single category future relatives with those who are no longer relatives (because of divorce or death).

To sum up, the present theory suggests that the factors underlying cross-linguistic and cross-cultural differences in metaphoric structuring can be grouped into three main categories: 1) social and economic usefulness of a given mapping; 2) attentional foregrounding of their components, both structure and content, by endogenous and exogenous means, with language playing an important but not exclusive role; and 3) patterns of coalescence with other metaphoric mappings already in use in the culture. These are the same organising principles for metaphoric structuring of concepts within a single culture and language, although less variation is expected because many of these factors are kept constant in this context.

5.4. Symbol grounding through conceptual metaphors

As a closing note of a general character, it should be emphasized that the present theory represents a move from the focus on long term memory structures that characterizes most current approaches to conceptual metaphor, to a focus on working memory representations and processes.

Stability is the hallmark of the contents of long term semantic memory. Thinking of conceptual metaphors as long term memory structures leads to a view of abstract concepts as embodied through pre-wired, solid, stable connections to more basic perceptuomotor schemas. The human conceptual system would thus be analogous to a building (Figure 1), where relations of support underlie the progressive abstractness of concepts, a proposal we termed the Solid Foundations View.

However, our review of the literature suggests that available evidence supports a more flexible view. Flexibility is the hallmark of working memory and attentional processes. In our view, centered on conceptual processing taking place in working memory, content representing abstract concepts sometimes participates in projections from and to content representing more concrete domains. They are flexible projections, chosen out of the available possibilities (or even created anew) to best fit into the overall current mental model and generate the best adaptation to the situation and task at hand. In other occasions, concepts are understood in terms of other concepts which are at the same level of abstractness, or even in terms of more abstract concepts.

The important point is that all of them are mentally represented by means of concrete contents, as the mental workspace is bound to be populated only by concrete representations, however labeled. The mental space is basically a perceptual space, and its contents can be built from both the senses and long term memory, providing a grounding for the concepts residing in memory. It is also a flexible grounding: concepts are embodied at the moment of thinking about them.

The central postulates of the present theory do not say much about conceptual representation in semantic long-term memory. A possible solution to the basic categorization problem (how to decide whether a mental model entity is to be properly labelled as an instance of a given concept), when the entity has been introduced in the model as a result of activating a concept in long term memory, consists in tracing the source concept, which will provide perfect labelling (Barsalou, 1999). However, when the entity is introduced from perceptual data, the theory says nothing about how memory search and concept activation is carried out. To reiterate, the present theory is not about semantic memory but working memory. If concepts were represented in semantic memory as disembodied feature lists or propositions, it would probably make no strong difference to the central tenets of the current theory.

With the additional assumption that working memory is the entry gate to long term memory, and that mental models are saved to memory after each successful use, then the theory predicts that semantic memory representations would also be based on perceptual-motor representations to a significant extent, as proposed by Barsalou (1999). This assumption also suggests that conceptual mappings are an essential part of long-term memory. The

Flexible foundations of abstract thought 95

Figure 8. Semantic memory from the Flexible Foundations View (photograph by CATIC-TEDer, some rights reserved).

fact that, given the activation of a conceptualization (e.g., about time passing), a particular mapping of it is observed (e.g., past-left and future-right, but not the other way around), suggests that the form of the mapping was stored in long-term memory. However, nothing suggests that conceptual mappings will necessarily proceed in the direction of concrete to abstract domains. The resulting picture of the human semantic memory system looks more like the Nest than like the Empire State (Figure 8).

Reasonable as it is, the posited connection between working and long term memory is still in need of independent evidence to substantiate it. The present theory suggests that showing that detailed mental simulations (models) are generated in language and reasoning tasks (as it has been repeatedly shown by defendants of the Simulation View, see, e.g., Glenberg & Kaschak, 2002; Richardson, Spivey, Barsalou & McRae, 2003; Stanfield & Zwaan, 2001; Zwaan et al., 2002) does not entail that their semantic memory representations take the form of perceptual symbols. Theorizing in this field is in need of developing more direct indexes of semantic representation in long-term memory. Bringing cognitive flexibility to the forefront leads to giving working memory the credit it deserves in the explanation of behavioural facts. After doing so, researchers will need to exert special care when trying to draw inferences about semantic memory from those facts.

6. Conclusions

In the present chapter, we have reviewed the available evidence for the Solid Foundations View of abstract concepts, with a special focus on spatial conceptual metaphors and literal-conventional-numerical language, and presented a theoretical framework which is consistent with proposals in wide areas of psychology and linguistics. This model embraces what we call a Flexible Foundations View instead. It has at its center 1) the distinction between long-term memory and a mental workspace endowed with both structure and content; 2) the notion of degree of activation as the main factor guiding inclusion in the model and interactions with other elements; and 3) a mechanism which struggles to turn the final mental model into a maximally coherent representation. The presumed design characteristics of the human mental workspace are grounded in a plausible, if simplified, account of how the universal perceptual mental space of apes may have been expanded by the acquisition of language. Finally, it includes also some simple but sensible assumptions about how learning develops from concrete episodes.

We have shown how this model is able to account for the reviewed data from several different research lines, and to provide a principled answer to some theoretically conflicting issues within the Solid Foundations tradition, chiefly the questions of 1) how an abstract concept may be simultaneously structured by means of contradictory metaphoric mappings both within a single individual and across cultures and languages; 2) how a given conceptual mapping is selected for use in the face of alternatives. The theory also provides a unified framework to think about the learning of new conceptual mappings and about the generation of cross-linguistic differences.

We have also illustrated at several points that the theory may generate non-trivial predictions. We have also provided experimental data that test one of the main assertions of the model: that both endogenous and exogenous attentional factors mediate the interaction between irrelevant spatial dimensions and relevant abstract dimensions of the processing task.

Finally, we have shown how a different view of the question of symbol grounding and embodiment arises from the present postulates, a view that emphasizes how concepts are embodied at the moment of thinking about them, of using them to solve specific problems, over the focus on long-term memory representations that characterizes most current views about this topic.

Although much work remains to be done before a fully specified computational model can be developed, we hope that this paper provides some useful ideas to foster further theoretical and empirical developments on the topics of conceptual metaphor and symbol grounding.

References

Altmann, Lori J.P., Ahmad Saleem, Diane Kendall, Kenneth M. Heilman & Leslie J.G. Rothi (2006). Orthographic directionality and thematic role illustration in English and Arabic. *Brain and Language, 97*, 306–316.

Alverson, Hoyt (1994). *Semantics and experience: Universal metaphors of time in English, Mandarin, Hindi, and Sesotho.* Baltimore, MD: The Johns Hopkins University Press.

Alverson, Hoyt (1996). From "storied time" to "clock time" in economic globalization at the new millenium. In: Julius T. Fraser & Marlene P. Soulsby (Eds.), *Dimensions of time and life: Selected papers from the 8th Conference of the International Society for the Study of Time.* Guilford, CT: International Universities Press.

Anderson, John R. (1982). Acquisition of cognitive skill. *Psychological Review, 89*, 369–406.

Ansorge, Ulrich (2003). Spatial Simon effects and compatibility effects induced by observed gaze direction. *Visual Cognition, 10*, 363–383.

Archangeli, Diana & D. Terence Langendoen (1997). *Optimality Theory. An Overview.* Oxford: Blackwell.

Bächtold, Daniel, Martin Baumüller & Peter Brugger (1998). Stimulus-response compatibility in representational space. *Neuropsychologia, 36*, 731–735.

Badets, Arnaud, Michael Andres, Samuel Di Luca & Mauro Pesenti (2007). Number magnitude potentiates action judgements. *Experimental Brain Research, 180*, 525–534.

Barrett, Anna M., Kim, Manho, Crucian, Gregory P., Heilman, Kenneth M. (2002). Spatial bias: Effects of early reading direction on Korean subjects. *Neuropsychologia, 40*, 1003–1012.

Barsalou, Lawrence W. (1983). Ad hoc categories. *Memory & Cognition, 11*, 211–227.

Barsalou, Lawrence W. (1999). Perceptual symbol systems. *Behavioral and Brain Sciences, 22*, 577–660.

Barsalou, Lawrence W. (2003). Situated simulation in the human conceptual system. *Language and Cognitive Processes, 18*, 513–562.

Barsalou, Lawrence W., W. Kyle Simmons, Aron K. Barbey & Christine D. Wilson (2003). Grounding conceptual knowledge in modality-specific systems. *Trends in Cognitive Science, 7*, 84–91.

Besner, Derek & Max Coltheart (1979). Ideographic and alphabetic processing in skilled reading of English. *Neuropsychologia, 17*, 467–472.

Boroditsky, Lera (2000). Metaphoric structuring: Understanding time through spatial metaphors. *Cognition, 75*, 1–28.

Boroditsky, Lera (2001). Does language shape thought?: Mandarin and English speakers' conceptions of time. *Cognitive Psychology, 43*, 1–22.

Boroditsky, Lera & Michael Ramscar (2002). The roles of body and mind in abstract thought. *Psychological Science, 13*, 185–189.

Bowdle, Brian F. & Dedre Gentner (2005). The career of metaphor. *Psychological Review, 112*, 193–216.

Cacciopo, John T., Joseph R. Priester & Gary G. Berntson (1993). Rudimentary determinants of attitudes II. Arm flexion and extension have differential effects on attitudes. *Journal of Personality and Social Psychology, 65*, 5–17

Carlson, Laura A. & Shannon R. Van Deman (2008). Inhibition within a reference frame during the interpretation of spatial language. *Cognition, 106*, 384–407.

Carlson-Radvansky, Laura A. & David E. Irwin (1993). Frames of reference in vision and language: Where is above? *Cognition, 46*, 223–244.

Carlson-Radvansky, Laura A. & David E. Irwin (1994). Reference frame activation during spatial term assignment. *Journal of Memory and Language, 33*, 646–671.

Carlson-Radvansky, Laura A. & Gordon Logan (1997). The influence of reference frame selection on spatial template construction. *Journal of Memory and Language, 37*, 411–437.

Casarotti, Marco, Marika Michielin, Marco Zorzi & Carlo Umiltá (2007). Temporal order judgment reveals how number magnitude affects visuospatial attention. *Cognition, 102*, 101–117.

Casasanto, Daniel (2008). Who's Afraid of the Big Bad Whorf? Crosslinguistic Differences in Temporal Language and Thought. *Language Learning, 58*, 63–79.

Casasanto, Daniel (2009). Embodiment of Abstract Concepts: Good and bad in right- and left-handers. *Journal of Experimental Psychology: General, 138*, 351–367.

Casasanto, Daniel & Lera Boroditsky (2008). Time in the mind: Using space to think about time. *Cognition, 106*, 579–593.

Centerbar, David B. & Gerald L. Clore (2006). Do approach-avoidance actions create attitudes? *Psychological Science, 17*, 22–29.

Chatterjee, Anjan, Lynn M. Maher, Leslie Gonzalez-Rothi & Kenneth M. Heilman (1995). Asyntactic thematic role assignment: The use of a temporal-spatial strategy. *Brain and Language, 49*, 125–139.

Chatterjee, Anjan, M. Helen Southwood & David Basilico (1999). Verbs, events and spatial representations. *Neuropsychologia, 37*, 395–402.

Chen, Jenn-Yeu (2007). Do Chinese and English speakers think about time differently? Failure of replicating Boroditsky. *Cognition, 104*, 427–436.

Chen, Mark & John A. Bargh (1999). Consequences of automatic evaluation: Immediate behavior predispositions to approach or avoid the stimulus. *Personality and Social Psychology Bulletin, 25*, 215–224.

Chiao, Joan Y., Andrew R. Bordeaux & Nalini Ambady (2004). Mental representations of social status. *Cognition, 93*, B49–B57.

Clark, Herbert H. (1973). Space, time, semantics, and the child. In: Moore, T.E. (ed). *Cognitive development and the acquisition of language*. New York, NY: Academic Press.

Clifford, James (2004). Traditional futures. In: Mark S. Phillips & Gordon Schochet (Eds.), *Questions of Tradition* (pp. 152–168). Toronto: University of Toronto Press.

Cohen, John, C.E.M. Hansel & J.D. Sylvester (1953). A new phenomenon in time judgment. *Nature, 172*, 901.

Cohen, J., C.E.M. Hansel & J.D. Sylvester (1954). Interdependence of temporal and auditory judgments. *Nature, 174*, 642.

Crawford, L. Elizabeth, Skye M. Margolies, John T. Drake & Meghan E. Murphy (2006). Affect biases memory of location: Evidence for the spatial representation of affect. *Cognition and emotion, 20,* 1153–1169.
Cruse, D. Alan (1986). *Lexical semantics.* Cambridge: Cambridge University Press.
Dähl, Oyvind (1995). When the future comes from behind: Malagasy and other time concepts and some consequences for communication. *International Journal of Intercultural Relations, 19,* 197–209.
Danenmaier, W.D. & F.J. Thumin (1964). Authority status as a factor in perceptual distortion of size. *Journal of Social Psychology, 63,* 361–365.
De Hower, Jan (2004). Spatial Simon effects with nonspatial responses. *Psychonomic Bulletin & Review, 11,* 49–53.
Dehaene, Stanislas, Serge Bossini & Pascal Giraux (1993). The mental representation of parity and number magnitude. *Journal of Experimental Psychology: General, 122,* 371–396.
Dehaene, Stanislas, Ghislaine Dehaene-Lambertz & Laurent Cohen (1998). Abstract representations of numbers in the animal and human brain. *Trends in Neurosciences, 21,* 355–361.
Dobel, Christian, Gil Diesendruck & Jens Bölte (2007). How writing system and age influence spatial representations of actions. *Psychological Science, 18,* 487–491.
Dodd, Michael D., Stefan Van der Stigchel, M. Adil Leghari, Gery Fung & Alan Kingstone (2008). Attentional SNARC: There's something special about numbers (let us count the ways). *Cognition, 108,* 810–818.
Dreman, S.B. (1977). A review of directionality trends in the horizontal dimension as a function of innate and environmental factors. *Journal of General Psychology, 96,* 125–134.
Dunbar, Kevin (1998). Problem solving. In William Bechtel & George Graham (Eds.), *A companion to Cognitive Science (pp. 289–298).* London, England: Blackwell.
Emmorey, Karen (2001). Space on hand: The exploitation of signing space to illustrate abstract thought. In: Merideth Gattis (Ed.), *Spatial Schemas and Abstract Thought.* Cambridge, MA: MIT Press.
Emmorey, Karen (2002). *Language, Cognition, and the Brain: Insights from Sign Language Research.* Mawah, NJ: Lawrence Erlbaum Associates.
Evans, Vyvian (2004). How we conceptualise time: Language, meaning and temporal cognition. *Essays in Arts and Sciences, 33,* 13–44 (to be reprinted in *The Cognitive Linguistic Reader.* Equinox).
Evans, Vyvian, Benjamin Bergen & Jörg Zinken (2008). The cognitive linguistics enterprise: An overview. In: Vyvian Evans, Benjamin Bergen & Jörg Zinken (Eds.), *The Cognitive Linguistics Reader (pp. 2–36).* Equinox Publishing Company.
Fauconnier, Gills (1985). *Mental spaces.* Cambridge, MA: MIT Press.
Fauconnier, Gills & Mark Turner (2002). *Conceptual blending and the mind's hidden complexities.* New York, NY: Basic Books.

Fias, Wim & Martin H. Fischer (2005). Spatial representation of numbers. In: Jamie I.D., Campbell (Ed.) *Handbook of Mathematical Cognition.* New York, NY: Psychology Press.
Fischer, Martin H., Alan D. Castel, Michael D. Dodd & Jay Pratt (2003). Perceiving numbers causes spatial shifts of attention. *Nature Neuroscience, 6,* 555–556.
Fiske, Alan P. (1992). The four elementary forms of sociality: Framework for a unified theory of social relations. *Psychological Review, 99,* 689–723.
Fitousi, Daniel & Daniel Algom (2006). Size congruity effects with two-digit numbers: Expanding the number line? *Memory & Cognition, 34,* 445–457.
Förster, Jens & Sabine Stepper (2000). Compatibility between approach/avoidance stimulation and valenced information determines residual attention during the process of encoding. *European Journal of Social Psychology, 30,* 853–871.
Franklin, Nancy & Barbara Tversky (1990). Searching imagined environments. *Journal of Experimental Psychology: General, 119,* 63–76.
Friesen, C.K. & A. Kingstone (1998). The eyes have it!: Reflexive orienting is triggered by nonpredictive gaze. *Psychonomic Bulletin & Review, 5,* 490–495.
Friesen, Chris K. & Alan Kingstone (2003). Abrupt onsets and gaze direction cues trigger independent reflexive attentional effects. *Cognition, 87,* B1–B10.
Galfano, Giovanni, Elena Rusconi & Carlo Umiltá (2006). Number magnitude orients attention, but not against one's will. *Psychonomic Bulletin and Review, 13,* 869–874.
Garnham, Alan (1989). A unified theory of the meaning of some spatial relational terms. *Cognition, 31,* 45–60.
Gattis, Merideth & Keith J. Holyoak (1996). Mapping conceptual to spatial relations in visual reasoning. *Journal of Experimental Psychology: Learning, Memory, and Cognition, 22,* 231–239.
Gentner, Dedre & Susan Goldin-Meadow (2003). Wither Whorf. In: Dedre Gentner & Susan Goldin-Meadow (Eds.), *Language in mind: Advances in the study of language and thought.* Cambridge, MA: MIT Press.
Gentner, Dedre, Mutsumi Imai & Lera Boroditsky (2002). As time goes by: Evidence for two systems in processing space-time metaphors. *Language and Cognitive Processes, 17,* 537–565.
Gevers, Wim & Jan Lammertin (2005). The hunt for SNARC. *Psychology Science, 47,* 10–21.
Gevers, Wim, Bert Reynvoet & Wim Fias (2003). The mental representation of ordinal sequences is spatially organized. *Cognition, 87,* B87–B95.
Gevers, Wim, Bert Reynvoet & Wim Fias (2004). The mental representation of ordinal sequences is spatially organised: Evidence from days of the week. *Cortex, 40,* 171–172.
Gibbs, Raymond W. (2003). Embodied experience and linguistic meaning. *Brain and Language, 84,* 1–15.
Gibbs, Raymond & Jennifer O'Brien (1990). Idioms and mental imagery: The metaphorical motivation of idiomatic meaning. *Cognition, 36,* 35–68.
Giessner, Steffen R. & Thomas W. Schubert (2007). High in the hierarchy: How vertical location and jugments of leaders' power are interrelated. *Organizational Behavior and Human Decision Processes, 104,* 30–44.

Glenberg, Arthur M. (1997). What memory is for. *Behavioral and Brain Sciences, 20*, 1–55.
Glenberg, Arthur M. & Michael P. Kaschak (2002). Grounding language in action. *Psychonomic Bulletin & Review, 9*, 558–565.
Glenberg, Arthur M. & David A. Robertson (2000). Symbol grounding and meaning: A comparison of high-Dimensional and embodied theories of meaning. *Journal of Memory and Language, 43*, 379–401.
Grice, Paul (1975). Logic and conversation. In Peter Cole & Jerry L. Morgan (Eds.), *Syntax and Semantics 3: Speech Acts* (pp. 41–58). New York: Seminar Press.
Harnad, Stephen (1990). The symbol grounding problem. *Physica D, 42*, 335–346.
Helson, Harry & Samuel M. King (1931). The *tau* effect: An example of psychological relativity. *Journal of Experimental Psychology, 14*, 202–217.
Henik, Avishai & Joseph Tzelgov (1982). Is three greater than five: The relation betwen physical and semantic size in comparison tasks. *Memory & Cognition, 10*, 389–395.
Higham, Philip A. & D. William Carment (1992). The rise and fall of politicians: The judged heights of Broadbent, Mulroney and Turner before and after the 1988 Canadian federal election. *Canadian Journal of Behavioral Science, 24*, 404–409.
Hommel, Bernhard, Jay Pratt, Lorenza Colzato & Richard Godijn (2001). Symbolic control of visual attention. *Psychological Science, 12*, 360–365.
Hung, Yi-Hui, Daisy L. Hung, Ovid J.-L. Tzeng & Denise H. Wu (2008). Flexible spatial mapping of different notations of numbers in Chinese readers. *Cognition, 106*, 1441–1450.
Hunt, Earl & Franca Agnoli (1991). The Whorfian hypothesis: A cognitive psychology perspective. *Psychological Review, 98*, 377–389.
Ito, Yasuhiro & Takeshi Hatta (2004). Spatial structure of quantitative representation of numbers: Evidence from the SNARC effect. *Memory & Cognition, 32*, 662–673.
Ivry, Richard & Thomas C. Richardson (2002). Temporal control and coordination: The multiple timer model. *Brain and Cognition, 48*, 117–132.
Jackendoff, Ray (1983). *Semantics and cognition*. Cambridge, MA: MIT Press.
Jackendoff, Ray (2002). *Foundations of language: Brain, meaning, grammar, evolution*. Oxford, UK: Oxford University Press.
Jahn, Georg, Markus Knauff & Philip N. Johnson-Laird (2007). Preferred mental models in reasoning about spatial relations. *Memory & Cognition, 35*, 2075–2087.
January, David & Edward Kako (2007). Re-evaluating evidence for linguistic relativity: Reply to Boroditsky (2001). *Cognition, 104*, 417–426.
Jiang, Yuhong & Marvin M. Chung (2001). Selective attention modulates implicit learning. *Quarterly Journal of Experimental Psychology, 54A*, 1105–1124.
Jiménez, Luis & Cástor Méndez (1999). Which attention is needed for implicit sequence learning? *Journal of Experimental Psychology: Learning, Memory and Cognition, 25*, 236–259.

Johnson, Mark (1987). *The body in the mind.* Chicago, IL: The University of Chicago Press.

Johnson-Laird, Philip (1983). *Mental Models.* Cambridge, MA: Cambridge University Press.

Jones, Bill & Yih Lehr Huang (1982). Space-time dependences in psychophysical judgement of extent and duration: Algebraic models of the tau and kappa effects. *Psychological Bulletin, 91,* 128–142.

Jonides, John (1981). Voluntary vs. automatic control over the mind's eye movement. In: J. Long & A. D. Baddeley (Eds.), *Attention and Performance IX.* Hillsdale, NJ: Erlbaum.

Jonides, John & Steven Yantis (1988). Uniqueness of abrupt visual onset in capturing attention. *Perception and Psychophysics, 43,* 346–354.

Josephs, Robert A., R. Brian Giesler & David H. Silvera (1994). Judgment by quantity. *Journal of Experimental Psychology: General, 123,* 21–32.

Katz, Jerrold J. & Jerry A. Fodor (1963). The structure of a semantic theory. *Language, 39,* 170–210.

Kemmerer, David (2005). The spatial and temporal meanings of English prepositions can be independently impaired. *Neuropsychologia, 43,* 797–806.

Keus, Inge M. & Wolf Schwartz (2005). Searching for the functional locus of the SNARC effect: Evidence for a response-related origin. *Memory & Cognition, 33,* 681–695.

Keysar, Boaz, Yeshayahu Shen, Sam Glucksberg & William S. Horton (2000). Conventional language: How metaphorical is it? *Journal of Memory and Language, 43,* 576–593.

Klein, Harriet (1987). Time in Toba. *Word, 38,* 173–185.

Koerber, Susanne & Beate Sodian (2008). Preschool children's ability to visually represent relations. *Developmental Science, 11,* 390–395.

Kohler, Wolfgang (1929). *Gestalt psychology.* New York, NY: Liveright. (Spanish translation: 1972. Madrid: Biblioteca Nueva).

Kövecses, Zoltan (2005). *Metaphor in culture.* Cambridge: Cambridge University Press.

Lakoff, George & Mark Johnson (1980). *Metaphors we live by.* Chicago, IL: The University of Chicago Press.

Lakoff, George & Mark Johnson (1999). *Philosophy in the flesh: The embodied mind and its challenge to Western thought.* New York, NY: Basic Books.

Landau, Barbara & Ray Jackendoff (1993). "What" and "where" in spatial language and cognition. *Behavioral and Brain Sciences, 16,* 217–265.

Landau, Barbara, Linda B. Smith & Susan Jones (1998). The importance of shape in early lexical learning. *Cognitive Development, 3,* 299–321.

Levelt, Wilhem J.M. (1989). *Speaking: From intention to articulation.* Cambridge, MA: MIT Press.

Levine, Robert (1997). *A geography of time.* New York, NY: Basic Books.

Levinson, Stephen (1996). Frames of reference and Molineaux's question: Cross-linguistic evidence. In: Paul Bloom, Mary A. Peterson, Lynn Nadel & Merrill F. Garrett (Eds.), *Language and space.* Cambridge, MA: MIT Press.

Levinson, Stephen, Sotaro Kita, Daniel B.M. Haun & Björn H. Rasch (2002). Returning the tables: Language affects spatial reasoning. *Cognition, 84,* 155–188.
Li, Peggy & Lila Gleitman (2002). Turning the tables: Language and spatial reasoning. *Cognition, 83,* 265–294.
Lidji, Pascale, Régine Kolinsky, Aliette Lochy & José Morais (2007). *Journal of Experimental Psychology: Human Perception and Performance, 33,* 1189–1207.
Lindemann, Oliver, Juan M. Abolafia, Giovanna Girardi & Harold Bekkering (2007). Getting a grip on numbers: Numerical magnitude priming in object grasping. *Journal of Experimental Psychology: Human Perception and Performance, 33,* 1400–1409.
Lindemann, Oliver, Juan M. Abolafia, Jay Pratt & Harold Bekkering (2008). Coding strategies in number-space: Memory requirements influence spatial-numerical associations. *Quarterly Journal of Experimental Psychology, 61,* 515–524.
Logan, Gordon D. (1988). Toward an instance theory of automatization. *Psychological Review, 95,* 583–598.
Logan, Gordon (1995). Linguistic and conceptual control of visual spatial attention. *Cognitive Psychology, 28,* 103–174.
Logan, Gordon & Daniel D. Sadler (1996). A computational analysis of the apprehension of spatial relations. In: Paul Bloom, Mary A. Peterson, Lynn Nadel & Merrill F. Garrett (Eds.), *Language and space.* Cambridge, MA: MIT Press.
Maas, Anne & Aurore Russo (2003). Directional bias in the mental representation of spatial events: Nature or culture? *Psychological Science, 14,* 296–301.
MacKay, Donald G. (1987). *The organization of perception and action.* New York, NY: Springer-Verlag.
MacLaury, Robert E. (1989). Zapotec body-part locatives: Prototypes and metaphoric extensions. *International Journal of American Linguistics, 55,* 119–154.
Maher, Lynn M., Anjan Chatterjee, Leslie Gonzalez-Rothi & Kenneth M. Heilman (1995). Agrammatic sentence production: The use of a temporal-spatial strategy. *Brain and Language, 49,* 105–124.
Majid, Asifa, Melissa Bowerman, Sotaro Kita, Daniel B.M. Haun & Stephen Levinson (2004). Can language restructure cognition? The case for space. *Trends in Cognitive Science, 8,* 108–114.
Malotki, Ekkehart (1983). *Hopi time: A linguistic analysis of temporal concepts in the Hopi language.* Berlin: Mouton.
Mandler, Jean M. (1992). How to build a baby: II. Conceptual primitives. *Psychological Review, 99,* 587–604.
Markman, Arthur B. & C. Miguel Brendl (2005). Constraining theories of embodied cognition. *Psychological Science, 16,* 6–10.
Mayer, Andrew R. & D.S. Kosson (2004). The effects of auditory and visual linguistic distractors on target localization. *Neuropsychology, 18,* 248–257.
McGlone, Matthew S. & Jennifer L. Harding (1998). Back (or forward?) to the future: The role of perspective in temporal language comprehension. *Journal of Experimental Psychology: Learning, Memory, and Cognition, 24,* 1211–1223.

McManus, I. Chris (2002). *Right hand, left hand.* Harvard University Press.
McManus, I. Chris & Nick Humphrey (1973). Turning the left cheek. *Nature, 243,* 271–272.
McNeill, David & Susan D. Duncan (2000). Growth points in thinking-for-speaking. In: McNeill, David (Ed). *Language and gesture.* Cambridge: Cambridge University Press.
McNeill, David (1992). *Hand and mind: What gestures reveal about thought.* Chicago, IL: The University of Chicago Press.
Meier, Brian P. & Michael D. Robinson (2004). Why the sunny side is up: Associations between affect and vertical position. *Psychological Science, 15,* 243–247.
Meier, Brian P. & Michael D. Robinson (2006). Does "feeling down" mean seeing down? Depressive symptoms and vertical selective attention. *Journal of Research in Personality, 40,* 451–461.
Meier, Brian P., Michael D. Robinson & Gerald L. Clore (2004). Why good guys wear white: Automatic inferences about stimulus valence based on brightness. *Psychological Science, 15,* 82–86.
Meier, Brian P., Michael D. Robinson, L. Elizabeth Crawford & Whitney J. Alhvers (2007). When "light" and "dark" thoughts become light and dark responses: Affect biases brightness judgments. *Emotion, 7,* 366–376.
Moore, Kevin E. (2006). Space-to-time mappings and temporal concepts. *Cognitive Linguistics, 17–2,* 199–244.
Murphy, Gregory L. (1996). On metaphoric representation. *Cognition, 60,* 173–204.
Murphy, Gregory L. (1997). Reasons to doubt the present evidence for metaphoric representation. *Cognition, 62,* 99–108.
Nachson, Israel (1981). Cross-cultural differences in directionality. *International Journal of Psychology, 16,* 199–211.
Niedenthal, Paula M., Lawrence W. Barsalou, Piotr Winkielman, Silvia Krauth-Gruber & François Ric (2005). Embodiment in Attitudes, Social Perception, and Emotion. *Personality and Social Psychology Review, 9,* 184–211.
Notebaert, Wim, Wim Gevers, Tom Verguts & Wim Fias (2006). Shared spatial representations for numbers and space: The reversal of the SNARC and the Simon effects. *Journal of Experimental Psychology: Human Perception and Performance, 32,* 1197–1207.
Núñez, Rafael E. & Eve Sweetser (2006). With the future behind them: Convergent evidence from Aymara language and gesture in the cross-linguistic comparison of spatial construals of time. *Cognitive Science, 30,* 1–49.
Núñez, Rafael, Benjamin A. Motz & Ursina Teuscher (2006). Time after Time: The psychological reality of the ego- and time-reference-point distinction in metaphorical construals of time. *Metaphor and Symbol, 21,* 133–146.
Ouellet, Marc, Julio Santiago, María J. Funes & Juan Lupiáñez (2010). Thinking about the future moves attention to the right. *Journal of Experimental Psychology: Human, Perception and Performance, 36,* 17–24.
Ouellet, Marc, Julio Santiago, Ziv Israeli & Shai Gabay (2010). Is the future the right time? *Experimental Psychology, doi: 10.1027/1618–3169/a000036*
Ozçaliskan, Seida (2003). Metaphorical Motion in Crosslinguistic Perspective: A Comparison of English and Turkish. *Metaphor and Symbol, 18,* 189–228.

Pansky, Ainat & Daniel Algom (1999). Stroop and Garner effects in comparative judgement of numerals: The role of attention. *Journal of Experimental Psychology: Human Perception and Performance, 25,* 39–58.
Pansky, Ainat & Daniel Algom (2002). Comparative judgment of numerosity and numerical magnitude: Attention preempts automaticity. *Journal of Experimental Psychology: Learning, Memory, and Cognition, 28,* 259–274.
Pellicano, Antonello, Kim-Phuong L. Vu, Robert W. Proctor, Roberto Nicoletti & Carlo Umiltà (2008) Effects of stimulus-stimulus short-term memory associations in a Simon-like task. *European Journal of Cognitive Psychology, 20,* 893–912.
Piaget, Jean (1927/1969). *The child's conception of time.* New York, NY: Ballantine Books.
Posner, Michael (1980). Orienting of attention. *Quarterly Journal of Experimental Psychology, 32,* 3–25.
Price, Mark C. & Rune A. Mentzoni (2008). Where is January? The month-SNARC effect in sequence-form synaesthetes. *Cortex, 44,* 890–907.
Radden, Gunter (2004). The metaphor TIME AS SPACE across languages. In: N. Baumgarten et al. (Eds.), *Übersetzen, interkulturelle Kommunikation, Spracherwerb und Sprachvermittlung – das Leben mit mehreren Sprachen: Festschrift für Juliane House zum 60. Geburtstag.* Bochum: Aks-verlag.
Rakova, Marina (2002). The philosophy of embodied realism: A high price to pay? *Cognitive Linguistics, 13,* 215–244.
Razpurker-Apfeld, Irene & Asher Koriat (2006). Flexible mental processes in numerical size judgements: The case of Hebrew letters that are used to convey numbers. *Psychonomic Bulletin & Review, 13,* 78–83.
Repp, Bruno H. & Günther Knoblich (2007). Action can affect auditory perception. *Psychological Science, 18,* 6–7.
Richardson, Daniel C., Michael J. Spivey, Lawrence W. Barsalou & Ken McRae (2003). Spatial representations activated during real-time comprehension of verbs. *Cognitive Science, 27,* 767–780.
Rinaldi, M. Cristina & Luigi Pizzamiglio (2006). When space merges into language. *Neuropsychologia, 44,* 556–565.
Ristic, Jelena, Alissa Wright & Alan Kingstone (2006). The number line effect reflects top-down control. *Psychonomic Bulletin & Review, 113,* 862–868.
Rock, Irvin. (1973). *Orientation and form.* New York, NY: Academic Press.
Rusconi, Elena, Bonnie Kwan, Bruno L. Giordano, Carlo Umiltà & Brian Butterworth (2006). Spatial representation of pitch height: The SMARC effect. *Cognition, 99,* 113–129.
Ruz, María & Juan Lupiáñez (2002). A review of attentional capture: On its automaticity and sensitivity to endogenous control. *Psicológica, 23,* 283–309.
Sagiv, Noam, Julia Simner, James Collins, Brian Butterworth & Jamie Ward (2006). What is the relationship between synaesthesia and visuo-spatial number forms? *Cognition, 101,* 114–128.
Santens, Seppe & Wim Gevers (2008). The SNARC effect does not imply a mental number line. *Cognition, 108,* 263–270.

Santiago, Julio, Juan Lupiáñez, Elvira Pérez & María J. Funes (2007). Time (also) flies from left to right. *Psychonomic Bulletin & Review, 14,* 512–516.
Santiago, Julio, Marc Ouellet, Antonio Roman, & Javier Valenzuela (2011). *Attentional factors in conceptual congruency.* Manuscript submitted for publication.
Santiago, Julio, Antonio Román, Marc Ouellet, Nieves Rodríguez & Pilar Pérez-Azor (2008). In hindsight, life flows from left to right. *Psychological Research, 74,* 59–70.
Schubert, Thomas W. (2005). Your highness: Vertical positions as perceptual symbols of power. *Journal of Personality and Social Psychology, 89,* 1–21.
Schubert, Thomas W., Sven Waldzus & Steffen R. Giessner (2009). Control over the association of power and size. *Social Cognition, 27,* 1–19.
Schwarz, Wolfgang & Anja Ischebeck (2003). On the relative speed account of number-size interference in comparative judgements of numerals. *Journal of Experimental Psychology: Human Perception and Performance, 29,* 507–522.
Schwarz, Wolfgang & Inge M. Keus (2004). Moving the eyes along the mental number line: Comparing SNARC effects with saccadic and manual responses. *Perception & Psychophysics, 66,* 651–664.
Seron, Xavier, Mauro Pesenti & Marie-Pascale Noël (1992). Images of numbers, or "When 98 is upper left and 6 sky blue". *Cognition, 44,* 159–196.
Seymour, Philip H.K. (1980). Internal representation of the months. *Psychological Research, 42,* 255–273.
Shaki, Samuel & Martin H. Fischer (2008). Reading space into numbers – a cross-linguistic comparison of the SNARC effect. *Cognition, 108,* 590–599.
Shaki, Samuel, Martin H. Fischer & William M. Petrusic (2009). Reading habits for both words and numbers contribute to the SNARC effect. *Psychonomic Bulletin & Review, 16,* 328–331.
Shank, Roger C. & Robert P. Abelson (1977). *Scripts, plans, goals and understanding.* Hillsdale, NJ: Erlbaum.
Shanon, Benny (1979). Graphological patterns as a function of handedness and culture. *Neuropsychologia, 17,* 457–465.
Shelton, Amy L. & Timothy P. McNamara (2001). Systems of spatial reference in human memory. *Journal of Memory and Language, 43,* 274–310.
Slobin, Dan (1996). From "thought and language" to "thinking for speaking". In: John J. Gumperz & Stephen Levinson (Eds.), *Rethinking linguistic relativity.* Cambridge: Cambridge University Press.
Smilek, Daniel, Alicia Callejas, Mike J. Dixon & Philip M. Merikle (2007). Ovals of time: Time-space associations in synaesthesia. *Consciousness and Cognition, 16,* 507–519.
Smith, Linda B., Susan S. Jones, Barbara Landau, Lisa Gershkoff-Stowe & Larissa Samuelson (2002). Object name learning provides on-the-job training for attention. *Psychological Science, 13,* 13–19.
Spalek, Thomas M. & Sherief Hammad (2005). The left-to-right bias in inhibition of return is due to the direction of reading. *Psychological Science, 16,* 15–18.
Sperber, Dan & Deirdre Wilson (1986). *Relevance.* Harvard University Press.

Stanfield, Robert A. & Rolf A. Zwaan (2001). The effect of implied orientation derived from verbal context on picture recognition. *Psychological Science, 12,* 153–156.
Stoianov, Ivilin, Peter Kramer, Carlo Umiltá & Marco Zorzi (2008). Visuospatial priming of the mental number line. *Cognition, 106,* 770–779.
Sweetser, Eve (1990). *From etymology to pragmatics: Metaphorical and cultural aspects of semantic structure.* Cambridge UK: Cambridge University Press.
Talmy, Leonard (2000). *Toward a Cognitive Semantics. Volume I: Concept Structuring Systems.* Cambridge, MA: MIT Press.
Talmy, Leonard (2003). How language directs attention. Talk presented at the *8th International Cognitive Linguistics Conference*, July 20–25, Logroño, Spain.
Taub, Sarah F. (2000). Iconicity in American sign language: concrete and metaphorical applications. *Spatial Cognition and Computation, 2,* 31–50
Taub, Sarah F. (2001). *Language from the body: Iconicity and metaphor in American Sign Language.* Cambridge: Cambridge University Press.
Taube-Schiff, Marlene & Norman Segalowitz (2005). Linguistic attention control: Attention shifting governed by grammaticized elements of language. *Journal of Experimental Psychology: Learning, Memory, and Cognition, 31,* 508–519.
Teuscher, Ursina, Marguerite McQuire, Jennifer Collins & Seana Coulson (2008). Congruity effects in time and space: Behavioral and ERP measures. *Cognitive Science, 32,* 563–578.
Thagard, Paul (2000). *Coherence in thought and action.* Cambridge, Mass.: MIT Press.
Tops, Mattie & Ritske de Jong (2006). Posing for success: Clenching a fist facilitates approach. *Psychonomic Bulletin & Review, 13,* 229–234.
Torralbo, Ana, Julio Santiago & Juan Lupiáñez (2006). Flexible conceptual projection of time onto spatial frames of reference. *Cognitive Science, 30,* 745–757.
Tversky, Barbara, Sol Kugelmass & Atalia Winter (1991). Cross-cultural and developmental trends in graphic productions. *Cognitive Psychology, 23,* 515–557.
Tse, Chi-Shing & Jeanette Altarriba (2008). Evidence against linguistic relativity in Chinese and English: A case study of spatial and temporal metaphors. *Journal of Cognition and Culture, 8,* 335–357.
Tyler, Andrea & Vyvian Evans (2001). Reconsidering prepositional polysemy networks: The case of *Over. Language, 77,* 724–765.
van Dantzig, Saskia, René Zeelenberg & Diane Pecher (2009). Unconstraining theories of embodied cognition. *Journal of Experimental Social Psychology, 45,* 345–351.
Vallesi, Antonino, Malcolm A. Binns & Tim Shallice (2008). An effect of spatial–temporal association of response codes: Understanding the cognitive representations of time. *Cognition, 107,* 501–527.
Weger, Ulrich, Brian P. Meier, Michael D. Robinson & Albretch W. Inhoff (2007). Things are sounding up: Affective influences on auditory tone perception. *Psychonomic Bulletin & Review, 14,* 517–521.
Weger, Ulrich W. & Jay Pratt (2008). Time flies like an arrow: Space-time compatibility effects suggest the use of a mental time-line. *Psychonomic Bulletin & Review, 15,* 426–430.

Wentura, Dirk, Klaus Rothermund & Peter Bak (2000). Automatic vigilance: The attention-grabbing power of approach- and avoidance-related social information. *Journal of Personality and Social Psychology, 78,* 1024–1037.

Wilson, Paul R. (1968). Perceptual distortion of height as a function of ascribed academic status. *Journal of Social Psychology, 74,* 97–102.

Zebian, Samar (2005). Linkages between number concepts, spatial thinking, and directionality of writing: The SNARC effect and the REVERSED SNARC effect in English, Arabic monoliterates, biliterates, and illiterate Arabic speakers. *Journal of Cognition and Culture, 5,* 165–190.

Zwaan, Rolf A. (2004). The immersed experiencer: Towards an embodied theory of language comprehension. In: B. H. Ross (Ed.), *The Psychology of Learning and Motivation* (*Vol. 44,* pp. 35–62). New York: Academic Press.

Zwaan, Rolf A., Robert A. Stanfield & Richard H. Yaxley (2002). Language comprehenders mentally represent the shape of objects. *Psychological Science, 13,* 168–171.

Estimates of spatial distance:
A Construal Level Theory perspective

Nira Liberman and Jens Förster

Abstract

This chapter examines two hypotheses on the psychological effects of spatial distance, both of which derived from Construal Level Theory of psychological distance (Liberman & Trope, 2008; Liberman, Trope & Stephan, 2007; Trope & Liberman, 2010): that spatial distance affects and is affected by other psychological distances, and that it affects and is affected by level of construal. We present evidence in support of each of these hypotheses, and draw novel predictions that stem from them. We also discuss, from the perspective of CLT, the question of whether spatial distance is more basic than other distances (social distance, temporal distance and hypotheticality).

1. Introduction

In many different languages, people describe social relationships in terms of spatial distance, referring to "close friends" and "distant relatives". We thus map social distance on spatial distance. Similarly, we refer to close versus faraway times, thus mapping temporal distance on spatial distance, and to remote possibilities and "close misses" revealing a similar mapping of high versus low probabilities to near versus distal locations. What is the underlying principle behind these similar mappings? And does it mean that estimations of spatial distance may be affected by social distance, temporal distance and probability? Will a trip to a close relative feel shorter than an objectively equidistant trip to a remote acquaintance?

We examine subjective estimations of spatial distance and effects of spatial distancing within Construal Level Theory of psychological distance (Liberman & Trope, 2008; Liberman, Trope & Stephan, 2007). Specifically, we examine two predictions, both of which derived from CLT – that spatial distance affects and is affected by other psychological distances, and that it affects and is affected by level of construal. For that aim, we first describe CLT and its view of psychological distance. We then describe evidence showing that psychological distances affect each other and that distances affect and are affected by level of construal. We specifically emphasize findings that are related to spatial distance. In doing that, we include suggestions for further research and speculations on other yet untested effects on distance estimates, and attempt to relate them to issues brought up in this volume.

2. Construal level theory of psychological distance

An event is psychologically distant to the extent that it is not part of one's direct experience. We distinguish four dimensions along which an event can be removed from direct experience, and accordingly four dimensions of psychological distance (Liberman & Trope, 2008; Liberman et al., 2007; Trope & Liberman, 2010): an event is more psychologically distant as it takes place farther into the future or the past (temporal distance), as it occurs in more remote locations (spatial distance), as it happens to people whose experience is less like ours (social distance), and as it is less likely to occur (hypotheticality). All the distances are anchored on the same zero point, which is the directly experienced "me, here and now", and they all represent different ways of incrementally diverging from direct experience. Similarly, the experience of the proximal end of all distances coincides – we experience ourselves, here and now simultaneously – and we typically believe that these experiences are real. Two main hypotheses derive from this analysis of psychological distance: that the four dimensions of distance are interrelated and that distancing a stimulus, on any dimension, requires using mental construal to compensate for lack of direct perception.

3. Interrelations among distances

If psychological distance is a common construct that underlies the various distance dimensions, then these distance dimensions should be mentally associated. Bar Anan, Liberman, Trope and Algom (2007) used a picture-word Stroop task (Stroop, 1935) to examine the cognitive interrelations between spatial distance and other psychological distances. Participants viewed landscape photographs containing an arrow that was pointing to either a proximal or a distal point in the landscape. Each arrow contained a word denoting either psychological proximity (e.g., tomorrow, we, sure) or psychological distance (e.g., year, others, maybe; see Figure 1). Participants' task was to respond by pressing one of two keys as quickly and as accurately as possible. In one version of the task, they had to indicate whether the arrow pointed to a proximal or distal location. In another version, they had to identify the word printed in the arrow. In both versions, participants responded faster to distance-congruent stimuli (in which the spatially distant arrow contained a word that denoted temporal distance, social distance, or low likelihood and the spatially proximal arrow contained words that denoted temporal proximity, social proximity, or high likelihood) than to distance-incongruent stimuli (in which spatially distal arrows contained words denoting proximity and spatially proximal arrows contained words denoting distance).

These findings suggest that spatial distance, temporal distance, social distance, and hypotheticality have a common psychological basis, and that people access this common meaning automatically, even when it is not directly related to their current task. We think that the common meaning is psychological distance and that it is automatically assessed because of its important implications for the perceiver. For example, on a rainy day, it matters whether an umbrella one notices belongs to a friend or to a stranger (social distance); in the jungle, it is important whether a tiger is real or imaginary (hypotheticality); in making a financial investment, it is important whether a recession is anticipated in the near or distant future (temporal distance), here or somewhere else (spatial distance). Yet, unlike for example valence, distance is not an inherent aspect of the semantic meaning of objects. Umbrellas, tigers, and recessions are inherently good or bad, but they are not inherently proximal or distal. It is perhaps for this reason that distance has not been included among the basic dimensions of meaning – evaluation, potency, and activity (Osgood, 1956).

The idea that distance dimensions are automatically associated further suggests that the distance of a stimulus on one dimension may affect its perceived distance on other dimensions. Extant research examined this prediction with respect to social distance and hypotheticality. After reviewing that research we move to examining additional implications of that idea for estimations of spatial distance and for the effect of spatial distance on estimations of other distances.

3.1. Social distance

Research by Stephan, Liberman and Trope (in press) has investigated how social distance affects and is affected by spatial distance and temporal distance. This line of research was based on past work showing that polite language signifies and creates interpersonal distance: People address strangers more politely than they address friends, and the use of polite, formal language creates a sense of distance (Brown & Levinson, 1987). Stephan et al. predicted that politeness would thus affect and be affected by other psychological distances. Consistent with this prediction, results showed that the use of normative, polite language rather than colloquial, less polite language led participants to believe that the target of the communication was spatially and temporally more distant. For example, using normative rather than colloquial language to address a person (e.g., "My brother is taking our family car, so the rest of us will stay at home" vs. "... will be stuck at home") led participants to infer that the addressee was in a more remote location and that the conversation referred to an event in the more distant future.

Another set of studies by Stephan et al., (in press) found evidence for the reverse direction of influence, namely, an effect of spatial and temporal distance from the target of communication on the use of polite language. In one study, participants wrote instructions for a person who was expected to read them either in the near future or the distant future (e.g., participants wrote sightseeing suggestions for a tourist that was supposed to arrive on the following day or a year later). The results showed that participants preferred to phrase instructions more politely when they were addressed to the tourist arriving in the distant future than to the tourist that would arrive tomorrow. Similar findings were found with addressing a spatially proximal versus distal stranger. These results indicate that spatial distance and temporal distance affect social distance.

In addition to same level, "horizontal" distance, (e.g., I feel closer to my neighbor than to a polish person in Warsaw), social distance may be also "vertical", namely, apply to status hierarchies (e.g., an assistant professor may feel closer to a full professor than a student does). Smith and Trope (2006) suggested conceptualizing power as a type of social distance. They suggested that social power may engender a sense of distance from others. Indeed, individuals who have power see themselves as less similar to and thus more distant from other people than individuals who have less power (e.g., Hogg, 2001; Hogg & Reid, 2001; Lee & Tiedens, 2001; Snyder & Fromkin, 1980). This perception might be due to the fact that groups, organizations, and societies tend to have fewer individuals occupying high power positions than low power positions. There is therefore greater similarity in the positions held by individuals with low power than individuals with high power: a subordinate is similar to more people around him or her than a boss. If power is a type of social distance, then power should affect and be affected by other distances. For example, figures of power should seem more spatially remote than figures devoid of social power. Figures of power should also bring to mind more remote times and less likely events than figures that are devoid of power. Possibly, considering remote places, times, and highly unlikely events should also induce one with a sense of power. This prediction awaits testing in future research.

3.2. Hypotheticality

Examining the effects of spatial remoteness on the hypotheticality dimension, Wakslak et al. (2008) hypothesized that people would expect unlikely events (which, in terms of CLT are distant on the dimension of hypotheticality), compared to likely events, to occur in situations that are relatively more distant in time, space, and social distance. Consistent with this hypothesis, they found that people expected unlikely events to happen to distal others, in distant places, and at distant time points, whereas they expected likely events to happen to close others, in nearby places, and at proximal time points. For example, a rare cat disease was expected to affect cats in spatially remote rather than nearby places, whereas a common cat disease was expected in a near rather than a remote location. Similarly, when the likelihood of getting a flu infection was low, it was expected to infect people from the outgroup rather than the ingroup, but when the likelihood of the flu was high, the reverse held true. These findings presumably occur because people map probability onto the dimension of social distance, and therefore expect improbable events to happen to distant others and probable events to happen to proximal others.

3.3. Spatial distance

We propose that the propensity to complete the sentence "long time ago, in a ____ place" with "far away" rather than with "nearby" reflects not only a literary convention but also an automatic tendency of the mind. Also, consider the expressions "a long time ago, in a faraway place" and "a little while ago, in a faraway place". We would suggest that "far away" would seem farther away in the former case than in the latter case. We suggest that remote locations broaden our horizons, in that they bring to mind the distant rather than the near future, other people rather than oneself, and unlikely rather than likely events. Perhaps, traveling, or even just planning to travel also broadens people's mental horizons for a similar reason.

The fact that people use spatial metaphors to represent time in everyday language and reasoning (Boroditsky, 2007) is consistent with the notion proposed here that distance dimensions are interrelated (see also Santiago, Román & Ouellet, this volume). The association between spatial distance and social distance is reflected not only in language (in expressions such as "a close friend"), but also in everyday social behavior. In social psychology, for example, spatial distance is often used to measure social distance, such that choosing a more distant seat from another person is taken to reflect social distancing from that person (e.g., Mooney, Cohn & Swift, 1992; Macrae et al. 1994).

According to our approach, the effects of spatial distance should go both ways. Namely, spatial distance would not only affect estimates of temporal distance, social distance and hypotheticality, but should also be affected by them. Indeed, estimates of spatial distance seem to be affected by social categories, such as national borders. Thus, spatial distance that confounds social distance (e.g., includes a border between countries) is judged as larger than a similar distance that does not introduce such confound. For example, a distance between a city in France and a city in Germany would be judged as larger than an objectively similar distance between two cities within France.

Future studies would examine if similar effects would emerge with temporal distance and hypotheticality. For example, would people estimate as larger a spatial distance that involves crossing a time-zone, or a change of a salient temporal boundary, such as midnight? Imagine that a train starts in Amsterdam at 11 pm, and arrived in Groningen at 1:30 am of the next day. Compare it to a situation in which the train leaves Amsterdam at 9 pm and arrives at Groningen at 11:30 pm. Would people judge the distance between the cities as larger in the former case than in the latter case? We are not sure what would constitute a boundary of hypotheticality, but we could predict, for example, that if spatial distancing involves a change in the range of possibilities it would be judged as larger. For example, suppose that California allows for gay marriages, whereas Arizona and Texas do not. Would people judge the distance between a city in California and a city in Arizona as larger than an objectively equal distance between two cities, one in Arizona and the other in Texas?

Another potentially interesting prediction may be derived from CLT in combination with the psychophysical principle of diminished sensitivity, according to which the subjective difference between N and N+X decreases with increasing N. For example, due to diminishing sensitivity, the distance between here and 1 km away would seem larger than the distance between 10 km away and 11 km away (in the same direction). If distances are interchangeable, as CLT suggests, then temporal distancing, social distancing and reduced likelihood (i.e., more distance on the hypotheticality dimension) should diminish estimated distance between two points in space. For example, the distance between here and the neighboring city may seem smaller if we take the perspective of 50 years ago than if we take a contemporary perspective. It may seem smaller from a perspective of a stranger than that of a friend and it may seem smaller if we consider a low likelihood event (traveling on a flying carpet) than a high likelihood event (traveling by car). Future research would test those predictions.

In sum, CLT predicts an association between psychological distances, and also predicts that distancing a stimulus on one dimension would make it seem more distant on other dimensions. Whereas the first hypothesis was examined with spatial distance (Bar-Anan et al., 2007), examination of the second hypothesis concentrated on social distance (Stephan et al., 2008) and hypotheticality (Wakslak & Trope, 2008). We reviewed these findings, and also suggested potentially interesting extension of this prediction to both estimations of spatial distance and to the effect of spatial distance on estimations of other distances.

3.4. Is space a basic dimension of distance?

Some theories propose that some distance dimensions are more basic or influential than others. For example, Boroditsky has recently proposed that spatial distance is primary, and that temporal distance is understood as an analogy to it (Boroditsky, 2000, 2001; Boroditsky & Ramscar, 2002), a view that is shared by some of the authors of chapters in this book (Schubert, Waldzus, & Seibt, this volume; but see Santiago et al., this volume, for a more balanced view). In support of this proposal, Boroditsky showed that thinking about space before answering questions about time influenced the participants' responses, but thinking about time before answering questions about space did not affect participants' responses (Boroditsky, 2000, Experiments 2 & 3). In another series of studies, she presented participants with lines on a computer screen, and showed that judgments of exposure duration were affected by the lines' length whereas judged length was not affected by duration of exposure (Casasanto & Boroditsky, 2008). Perhaps spatial distance is more basic than temporal distance or other distances in that it is more clearly detected, or easier to communicate about. It is also possible, however that other distances are also as basic. For example, the distinction between self and non-self, which, according to object relations theories, the child painfully realizes as the distinction between herself and her caregiver, is learned early in life, and is clear, indispensible for life and is later projected on other constructs and relationships (Winnicott, 1957). In other theories, it is the distinction between reality and imagination, either desired or feared (i.e., the hypotheticality dimension), which underlies the reality principle (Freud, 1923/1949), that is basic and forms the fundament of personality.

Construal Level Theory is silent with respect to the question of which distance dimension is more basic. It suggests, however, the possibility that what underlies all distances is a common core, and that perhaps, the claims about the centrality of different dimensions also share a common core.

Maybe what is learned as basic is the distinction between what is me, here and now, and what is beyond that tangible point, and therefore imposes a fundamentally different way of interacting with it. Grasping a distal object requires a tool or motion, controlling the actions of other people requires communication, bringing about desired hypothetical or future situations and averting negative hypothetical or future situations require planned action. In that general sense, all the distance dimensions are basic in the same way.

4. Distances and level of construal

Construal Level Theory (Liberman et al., 2007; Trope & Liberman, 2003) suggests that more psychologically distal stimuli are represented on a higher level, that is, in a more abstract and general way. For example, "going out with friends to a movie" would be represented more abstractly as "socializing" when it pertains to a more psychologically distant action. Much research within the framework of CLT demonstrated this effect (for recent reviews see Liberman & Trope, 2008; Liberman et al., 2007; Trope, Liberman, & Wakslak, 2007). For example, Liberman and Trope (1998) showed that more distant future actions are represented in more superordinate, "why" terms, rather than in subordinate, "how" terms. Thus, "watching TV" was represented as "getting entertained" when it pertained to the distant future and as "flipping channels" when it pertained to the near future. Furthermore, Liberman, Sagristano and Trope (2002) showed that objects that were intended for more distant future use (e.g., objects that one would take to a trip in the more distant future) were organized in broader, more abstract categories. Conceptually similar findings were shown also for spatial distance (Fujita, Henderson, Eng, Trope, & Liberman, 2006), social distance (Liviatan, Trope & Liberman, 2008; Stephan, Liberman, & Trope, 2007) and likelihood (Wakslak, Trope, Liberman, & Alony, 2006). For example, Fujita et al. (2006) made participants from New York University imagine that they are moving to a new place, either within NYC (proximal spatial distance condition) or the West Coast of the USA (distal spatial condition). Participants then considered different actions that they would perform in the process of moving (e.g., making a list, paying the rent), and chose between a high-level and a low-level description of each action. Participants that imagined moving to a faraway place chose higher-level, more abstract descriptions of the action compared to those who imagined moving within NYC.

Perceptual level of construal is also affected by psychological distance in a similar way. Liberman and Förster (2009) examined the effect of primed distance on global versus local perception, using Navon's (1977) paradigm of composite letters (global letters that are made of local letters). Their studies showed that relative to a control condition, thinking of more distant events, either temporally, spatially, or socially made participants respond faster to global letters and respond slower to local letters. Thinking of more proximal events had the opposite effect.

To appreciate why distance might be related to level of construal, note that high level construals are more likely than low level construals to remain unchanged with increased distance. In our example, "socializing" remains more stable over time, space, social perspectives and alternatives to reality than "going out with friends to a movie". In the distant future, at a distant location, and in a situation very different from the current one, I will probably socialize, but not necessarily by joining friends to a movie. High level features tend to change less also across social perspectives: Most people socialize, but not necessarily by going to movies. Perceptions of global gestalts, likewise, remains more constant over distance and over social and spatial perspectives than perception of local details. The view of individual trees changes more rapidly than the view of the entire forest. According to CLT, then, high level construals may be preferentially used to represent distant objects because increased distance alters low level features of objects more than high level ones, making it advantageous to be able to relate to high level (less variant) aspects of distal objects.

Consider now the reverse direction of influence, namely, the effect of level of construal on distance. Because high level construals afford distancing, they also bring to mind more distal instantiations of objects. For example, "socializing" may bring to mind events in the more distant future and past, in more distant locations, events that include more socially distal others and more yet un-experienced (hypothetical) exemplars than "going with friends to a movie". Another example is that construing a behavior in terms of a personality trait (a high level construct), involves considering past and future behaviors, behaviors in other places and in hypothetical situations. More generally, creating and understanding any abstract construct requires mentally moving beyond the currently experienced object in time and space, it often involves integration of other social perspectives, and a decision rule, implicit or explicit, about hypothetical examples not previously encountered. It is for that reason that higher level constructs prompt one to think about more remote times, persons, locations and alternatives.

According to CLT, the effects of distance on construal and of construal on distance are over-generalized, such that they persist even in the absence of the initial reason that gave rise to the association. That is, remoteness is expected to produce a higher level of construal even when low level details are not particularly likely to change over distance and high level of construal is expected to produce estimations of greater distance even when they do not afford retrieval of particularly distal exemplars. Supporting the notion of an overgeneralized association, Bar Anan, Liberman and Trope (2006) demonstrated automatic associations of construal level with all four psychological distances using an implicit association test (Greenwald et al., 1998). For example, participants more easily paired the words "year", "there", "others" and "maybe" (corresponding to the distal end of temporal, spatial, social and hypothetical distances, respectively) with the word "abstract" and the words "tomorrow", "here", "us" and "sure" (corresponding to the proximal end of the same distances, respectively) with the word "concrete" than vice versa.

To show the effect of construal on estimated temporal distance, Liberman, Sagristano and Trope (2002) instructed participants to provide either a high level, "why" description of an action or a low level, "how" description of the same action (e.g., Ron is considering opening a bank account. Why/how would he do that?). They then estimated how much time later the actor would do the action (e.g., how much time from now would Ron do that?). More distant times were indicated for actions that were construed on a higher level. Stephan (2006) used a similar paradigm to show an effect of level of construal on social distance. Participants first explained either why a person performed an action or how she or he performed it and then indicated how close they felt to the actor. Participants felt more distant from actors whose actions they construed on a higher level. It will be interesting to examine, in future studies, whether similar effects would obtain for spatial distance. For example, would thinking of an event (e.g., the outbreak of swine flu in Mexico) in terms of why it occurred, as opposed to how it occurred, make it seem more spatially distant?

Importantly, the CLT theorizing on psychological distance leads us to predict an effect of construal on distances that are mentally represented as distances from oneself, in the here and now, which we term *egocentric distances*, but not on distances that are represented in other ways, which we term *non-egocentric distances*. This is because high level of construal requires mentally distancing oneself from the object of construal in time, space, social perspective or across counterfactual alternatives, but it does not require distancing that object from other objects. A visual example is that to see the entire forest rather than a tree one needs to assume a spatial distance between oneself and the object of perception. It is not necessary, however, to place that object at a distance from other objects. A conceptual example is that to construe a person's behavior in terms of a personality trait (a high level construct), one needs to consider behaviors in times distant from now, in situations different from the current one, including hypothetical ones. Trait terms also impose a social distance between the perceiver and the actor. Traits do not, however, require assuming that the actor is socially distant from others, or that she is spatially and temporally distant from other points in time and space.

The findings of previous studies are consistent with this prediction, because they examined egocentric distances (i.e., distance in time from here, social distance from the self). These studies, however, did not conceptualize psychological distance as necessarily egocentric, and therefore did not include estimation of non-egocentric distances. Liberman and Förster (in press) predicted and found that level of construal affected estimated egocentric distances but did not affect estimates of temporal distance that are not anchored on now, estimates of spatial distance that are not anchored on here, estimates of social distance that are not anchored on the self, and estimates of probability that are not anchored on the experienced reality but rather on another state of affairs.

Liberman and Förster (in press) used the Navon (1977) paradigm to prime global versus local perception. Specifically, participants were presented with a series of composite letters, which were approximately 2.5×2.5 cm global letters made up of approximately 0.5×0.5 cm local letters. Each horizontal or vertical line making up a global letter was formed from five closely spaced local letters. On each trial, one of eight composite letters was randomly presented, and participants were instructed to press one response key if the stimulus contained the letter L and another response key if the stimulus contained the letter H. They were asked to respond as quickly as possible. The task was set up so that, by random assignment, one third of the participants had to respond always to the global letter (high level construal), one third of the participants had to respond always to the local letter (low level construal), and one third, assigned to the control condition, responded to global letters on half of the trials and to local letters on the other half of the trials.

In the study that examined the effect of construal level priming on estimation of spatial distance participants estimated either the distance in cm between themselves and a sticker on a desk (a self-anchored, egocentric distance), or between the experimenter and a sticker on her desk (a non egocentric distance). As can be seen in Figure 1, level of construal did not affect non egocentric distances, but did affect estimates of egocentric distance, such that compared to the control condition, low level of construal resulted in estimates of the distances as nearer whereas high level of construal resulted in estimates of the distances as farther.

Conceptually similar effects were obtained with egocentric versus non-egocentric estimates of distances within the participants' city, Amsterdam. Perhaps most telling was a study in which participants from Amsterdam estimated the distance between Amsterdam and Groningen (egocentric) or between Groningen and Amsterdam (non egocentric). Again, priming affected the former but not the latter estimates (Figure 2). That is, compared to the control condition, priming of global perception made participants estimate the distance between Amsterdam and Groningen as larger and priming of local perception made them estimate that same distance as smaller. Priming did not affect estimates of distance between Groningen and Amsterdam.

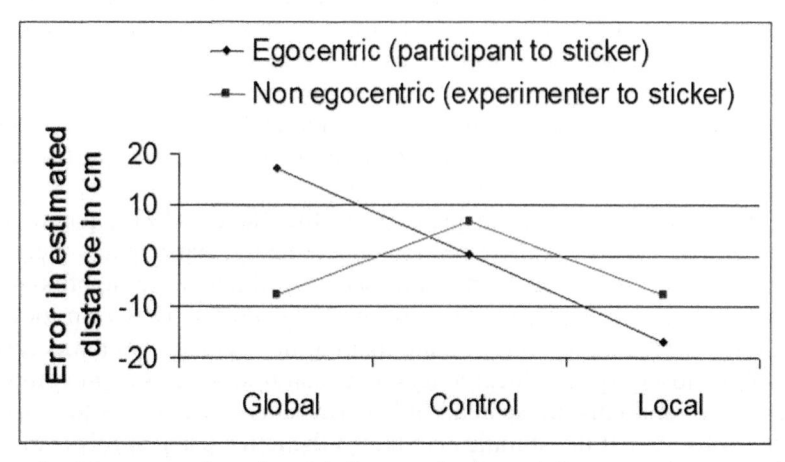

Figure 1. Mean error in estimated distance (estimated distance minus actual distance) to a point in class in cm, by primed processing style and estimate type. Positive values represent overestimation in cm, negative values represent underestimation in cm

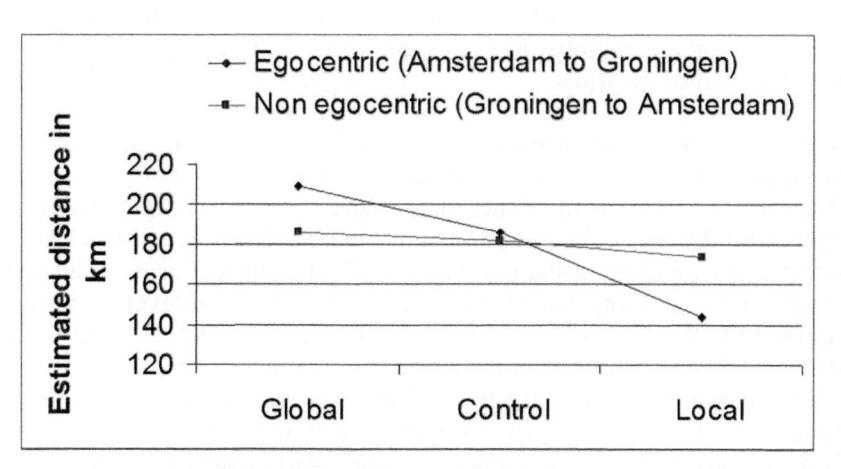

Figure 2. Mean estimated distance in km by participants in Amsterdam, by primed processing style and estimate type.

It is interesting to consider the mechanism behind these results – how does global processing produce estimates of further egocentric distance? One possibility would be that global processing, compared to local processing, makes mental travel faster by increasing the size of one's mental steps. Specifically, it is possible that when estimating egocentric distance, people simulate an actual travel from their current point. If global processing makes one use bigger steps of increment, then this would result in reaching farther within the same number of steps. To accommodate our results, this model will have to assume that estimating non-egocentric distances does not involve such simulation.

This notion is consistent with embodied views of cognition, which assume that in providing estimates people often engage in simulation of a relevant process. For example, Witt and Proffitt (2008) found that participants estimated an object to be spatially closer to them when they held a tool that could potentially help them reach that object. They suggest that this was because in estimating the distance, participants simulated traversing that distance, and used the ease of traversing the distance in the simulation to arrive at the estimate. The tool, according to that view, helped them to simulate reaching the object, hence making it seem closer.

In our results, it is possible that a high level, global construal facilitated a simulation of reaching farther away, thus giving rise to estimates of a larger distance. Perhaps, when estimating non-egocentric distance, which is not represented as distances from one's current point in space, participants did not engage in simulation of travel and hence were not influenced by level of construal.

4.1. Can people shift reference points?

In CLT, psychological distance is egocentric – it is mentally represented as distance from the experienced self, here and now. In principle, non-egocentric distances may be arrived at by mean of egocentric estimates. For example, one can mentally assume another point of view in time or in space, assume a perspective of another person or of a counterfactual state of affairs. For example, to estimate the distance from Groningen to Amsterdam a person might imagine herself in Groningen, and estimate the distance from that point to Amsterdam. As another example, when estimating how much time after returning from a vacation one would go back to work, one could imagine herself as if she gets from vacation now, and estimate how much time later she would go to work. Of course, extant literature suggests that people cannot entirely leave their egocentric stand and fully transport themselves mentally to a different point in time (e.g., Gilbert, Pinel, Wilson, Blumberg, & Wheatley, 1998), assume another person's perspective (Pronin, 2008), or fully consider a counterfactual state of affairs (Epstude & Roese, 2008). They not only lack the necessary knowledge to do that, but also err by failing to abandon the egocentric view (Epley, Keysar, Van Boven, & Gilovich, 2004). Notably, in the Groningen-Amsterdam studies we described above, knowledge was held constant and only the reference point changed – participants in Amsterdam estimated the distance of Amsterdam to Groningen versus Groningen to Amsterdam. Yet, participants in our studies (as in the studies of Codol, 1990) did not simply shift to an egocentric reference point, as was reflected in the fact that the global/local priming manipulation only affected the egocentric estimates. (See also Holyoak & Mah, 1982, for a discussion on how subtle changes in question phrasing may establish different reference points for distance estimates.) Of course, it remains a possibility that participants would be able to shift reference points if they were instructed to do so.

The difficulty of abandoning an egocentric reference point notwithstanding, we may predict that *to the extent* that people represent non-egocentric distances in an egocentric way, the estimates of these distances would be affected by level of construal. In other words, we predict that mentally shifting one's reference point may moderate the effect of level of construal on distance estimates. For example, when reading a narrative (e.g., on a person who plans to travel to another city), participants can identify to different extents with the protagonist. It is possible that the more they identify with the protagonist (in other words, the more they can simulate the experiences and the internal world of the other person, Förster, 2009), the more a high level of construal would make them estimate larger spatial distances in the narrative world (e.g., a higher level of construal would make readers estimate as larger the distance the protagonist would travel). We predict that identifying with a character would make one assume the character's mental horizons, and also to expand and constrict them as a function of applying high level or low level of construal.

4.2. Increased sensitivity around (egocentric) reference points

In a series of studies on the effects of anchors on estimated spatial distances, Holyoak and Mah (1982) showed that distances in the vicinity of the reference point are expanded relative to objectively similar distances far from the point. For example, when rating the closeness of different American cities to the west (versus east) coast, cities near the west coast were rated as more distant from each other, whereas cities near the east coast seemed closer to each other. Interestingly, in addition to the effect of the experimentally provided reference points, an effect of egocentric reference point also emerged, in that participants also over-estimated the distances between cities near Ann Arbor, Michigan, their own geographical location (Holyoak & Mah, 1982, Study 1a).

How are our results related to these findings? Is it possible that in our studies egocentric estimates served as stronger, more habitual reference points than non egocentric estimates, as was found in some studies (e.g., Holyoak & Gordon, 1983; Karylowski, 1990)? Let us first note that in our studies egocentric anchors did not produce estimates of overall larger distance, as would be expected if distances are indeed stretched around the reference point, and if egocentric anchors are more frequently (or more unequivocally) assumed than non egocentric anchors. Rather, this was the case only in the global processing condition, whereas the reverse effect (i.e., smaller estimated distances around the egocentric anchor than around the non-egocentric anchor) occurred in the local processing condition.

Another possibility is that in our studies global versus local processing affected egocentric estimates more than non egocentric estimates simply because people are more sensitive about the former than about the latter. Consistent with the notion of increased sensitivity around the egocentric anchor is the idea that people care more about events that happen to them in the here and now compared to events that happen to others or events that are distant in time and space or are counterfactual. For example, it is possible that participants thought about the distance from Amsterdam to Groningen as "how far *I would need to go* to reach Groningen", whereas they thought about the distance from Groningen to Amsterdam in less self-involving and effort-related terms, as "how far a *person in Groningen would need to go* to reach Amsterdam". The involvement account does not logically follow from CLT, but it would be consistent with its general view that only egocentric distances carry consequences for self regulation and construal. More generally, this view is consistent with the notion that egocentric estimates (but not non-egocentric distances) are embodied, that is, are based on a simulation of an action of traversing that distance (Förster, 2009; Schnall, this volume).

Regardless of its implications for CLT, the idea that global versus local processing mediates or moderates the effect of involvement on estimated distance is testable and potentially interesting. For example, consider the finding that when walking effort is increased due to wearing a heavy backpack, people perceive hills to be steeper and distances to be farther (Bhalla & Proffitt, 1999; Proffitt, Stefanucci, Banton, & Epstein, 2003; Schnall, this volume). Is it possible that this would be the case only in a global processing mode, but not in a local processing mode? If our results were due to more involvement with egocentric (versus non egocentric) anchors, then one would make that prediction. Future studies may test this intriguing possibility.

5. Conclusion

We examined, within the framework of CLT, the antecedents of perceived spatial distance (what may make stimuli seem subjectively farther away versus closer by?) and the consequences of spatial distancing (what are the psychological effects of moving a stimulus farther in space). We showed many implications for these two questions of the two basic principles of CLT: that distances are interrelated (and therefore estimates of spatial distance should affect and be affected by other distances) and that distances are related to level of construal (and therefore estimated spatial distance should affect and be affected by level of construal). We hope that this chapter not only reviewed relevant literature, but also connected to extant theories and findings, and suggested novel, potentially interesting predictions.

References

Anderson, Michael C. & Barbara A. Spellman (1995). On the status of inhibitory mechanisms in cognition: Memory retrieval as a model case. *Psychological Review, 102*, 68–100.

Aron, Arthur, Tracy McLaughlin-Volpe, Debra Mashek, Gary Lewandowski, Stephen C. Wright & Elaine N. Aron (2004). Including others in the self. In Wolfgang Stroebe & Miles Hewstone (Eds), *European review of social psychology (Vol 15.*, pp. 101–132). Hove, England: Psychology Press/Taylor & Francis (UK).

Bar-Anan, Yoav., Liberman, Nira., Trope, Yaacov. (2006). The association between psychological distance and construal level: Evidence from an implicit association test. *Journal of Experimental Psychology: General, 135*, 609–622.

Bar-Anan, Yoav, Nira Liberman, Yaacov Trope & Daniel Algom (2007). The automatic processing of psychological distance: Evidence from a Stroop task. *Journal of Experimental Psychology: General, 136*, 610–622.

Bhalla, Mukul & Dennis R. Proffitt (1999). Visual-motor recalibration in geographical slant perception. *Journal of Experimental Psychology: Human Perception and Performance, 25*, 1076–1096.

Codol, Jean-Paul (1990). Studies on self-centered assimilation processes. In Jean-Paul Caverni, Jean-Marc Fabre & Michel Gonzalez (Eds.), *Cognitive biases* (pp. 387–400). Amsterdam, Netherlands: North-Holland.

Delis, Dean C., Lynn C. Robertson & Robert. Efron (1986). Hemispheric specialization of memory for visual hierarchical stimuli. *Neuropsychologia, 24*, 205–214.

Derryberry, Douglas & Don M. Tucker (1994). Motivating the focus of attention. In Paula M. Niedenthal & Shinobu Kitayama (Eds.), *Heart's eye: Emotional influences in perception and attention* (pp. 167–196). New York: Academic Press.

Epley, Nicholas, Boaz Keysar, Leaf Van Boven & Thomas Gilovich (2004). Perspective taking as egocentric anchoring and adjustment. *Journal of Personality and Social Psychology, 87*, 327–339.

Epstude, Kai & Neil J. Roese (2008). The functional theory of counterfactual thinking. *Personality and Social Psychology Review, 12,* 168–192.

Fink, Gereon R., Peter W. Halligan, John C. Marshall, Chris D. Frith, Richard S. Frackowiak & Raymond J. Dolan (1996). Where in the brain does visual attention select the forest and the trees. *Nature, 382,* 626–628.

Förster, Jens (2009). Opening doors for new research questions: On simulatability. *European Journal of Social Psychology,* 39, 1151–1155.

Förster, Jens, Ronald S. Friedman & Nira Liberman (2004). Temporal construal effects on abstract and concrete thinking: Consequences for insight and creative cognition. *Journal of Personality and Social Psychology, 87,* 177–189.

Förster, Jens, Ronald S. Friedman, Amina Özelsel & Markus Denzler (2006). Enactment of approach and avoidance behavior influences the scope of perceptual and conceptual attention. *Journal of Experimental Social Psychology, 42,* 133–146.

Förster, Jens & E. Tory Higgins (2005). How global versus local perception fits regulatory focus. *Psychological Science, 16,* 631–636.

Förster, Jens, Nira Liberman & Stefanie Kuschel (2008). The effect of global versus local processing styles on assimilation versus contrast in social Judgment. *Journal of Personality and Social Psycholog.* 94, 579–599.

Freud, Sigmund (1923/1949). *The Ego and the Id.* London: Hogarth Press.

Friedman, Ronald S. & Jens Förster (2008). Activation and measurement of motivational states. In A. Elliott (Ed.), *Handbook of approach and avoidance motivation* (pp. 233–246). Mawah, NJ: Lawrence Erlbaum Associates.

Friedman, Ronald S., Ayelet Fishbach, Jens Förster & Lioba Werth (2003). Attentional priming effects on creativity. *Creativity Research Journal, 15,* 277–286.

Fujita, Kentaro, Marlone D. Henderson, J Eng, Yaacov Trope, & Nira Liberman (2006). Spatial distance and mental construal of social events. *Psychological Science, 17,* 278–282.

Fujita, Kentaro F., Yaacov Trope, Nira Liberman & Maya Levin-Sagi (2006). Construal levels and self-control. *Journal of Personality and Social Psychology, 90,* 351–367.

Gasper, Karen & Gerald L. Clore (2002). Attending to the big picture: Mood and global versus local processing of visual information. *Psychological Science, 13,* 34–40.

Gilbert, Daniel T., Elizabeth C. Pinel, Timothy D. Wilson, Stephen J. Blumberg & Thalia P. Wheatley (1998). Immune neglect: A source of durability bias in affective forecasting. *Journal of Personality and Social Psychology, 75,* 617–638.

Greenwald, Anthony G., Debbie E. McGhee & Jordan L.K. Schwartz (1998). Measuring individual differences in implicit cognition: The implicit association test. *Journal of Personality & Social Psychology, 74,* 1464–1480.

Henderson, Marlone, D., Kentaro Fujita, Yaacov Trope, & Nira Liberman (2006). Transcending the "here": The effect of spatial distance on social judgment. *Journal of Personality and Social Psychology, 91,* 845–856.

Holyoak, Keith J. & Peter C. Gordon (1983). Social reference points. *Journal of Personality and Social Psychology, 44,* 881–887.

Holyoak, Keith J. & Wesley A. Mah (1982). Cognitive reference points in judgments of symbolic magnitude. *Cognitive Psychology, 14*, 328–352.
Isen, Alice M. & Kimberly A. Daubman (1984). The influence of affect on categorization. *Journal of Personality and Social Psychology, 47*, 1206–1217.
Kardes, Frank R., Maria L. Cronley & John. Kim (2006). Construal-level effects on preference stability, preference-behavior correspondence, and the suppression of competing brands. *Journal of Consumer Psychology, 16*, 135–144.
Karylowski, Jerzy J. (1990). Social reference points and accessibility of trait-related information in self-other similarity judgments. *Journal of Personality and Social Psychology, 58*, 975–983.
Kühnen, Ulrich & Daphna Oyserman (2002). Thinking about the self influences thinking in general: Cognitive consequences of salient self-concept. *Journal of Experimental Social Psychology, 38*, 492–499.
Lamb, Marvin R. & Lynn C. Robertson (1990). The effect of visual angle on global and local reaction times depends on the set of visual angles presented. *Perception & Psychophysics, 47*, 489–496.
Latane, Bib (1981). The psychology of social impact. *American Psychologist, 36*, 343–356.
Lewin, Kurt (1951). *Field theory in social science: selected theoretical papers* (Edited by Dorwin Cartwright.). Oxford, England, Harpers.
Liberman, Nira & Jens Förster (in press). Expectancy, value and psychological distance: A new look at goal gradients. *Social Cognition.*
Liberman, Nira, Michael D. Sagristano & Yaacov Trope (2002). The effect of temporal distance on level of mental construal. *Journal of Experimental Social Psychology, 38*, 523–534.
Liberman, Nira & Yaacov Trope (1998). The role of feasibility and desirability considerations in near and distant future decisions: A test of temporal construal theory. *Journal of Personality and Social Psychology, 75*, 5–18.
Liberman, Nira & Yaacov Trope (2008). The psychology of transcending the here and now. *Science, 322*, 1201–1205.
Liberman, Nira, Yaacov Trope & Eelena Stephan (2007). Psychological distance. In Arie W. Kruglanski & E. Tory Higgins (Eds.), *Social psychology: Handbook of basic principles* (Vol. 2, pp. 353–383). New York: Guilford Press.
Liviatan, Ido, Yaacov Trope & Nira Liberman (in press). Interpersonal similarity as a social distance dimension: Implications for perception of others' actions. *Journal of Experimental Social Psychology.*
Lord, Charles G. & Mark R. Lepper (1999). Attitude Representation Theory. In Zanna, Mark P. (Ed), *Advances in experimental social psychology, Vol. 31.* (pp. 265–343). San Diego, CA, US: Academic Press.
Macrae, C. Neil & Helen L. Lewis (2002). Do I know you? Processing orientation and face recognition. *Psychological Science, 13*, 194–196.
Mikulincer, Mario, Peri Kedem & Dov. Paz (1990). Anxiety and categorization: 1. The structure and boundaries of mental categories. *Personality and Individual Differences, 11*, 805–814.

Mikulincer, Mario, Dov Paz & Peri. Kedem (1990). Anxiety and categorization: 2. Hierarchical levels of mental categories. *Personality and Individual Differences, 11,* 815–821.

Navon, David (1977). Forest before trees: The precedence of global features in visual perception. *Cognitive Psychology, 9,* 353–383.

Neill, W. Trammell & Richard L. Westberry (1987). Selective attention and the supression of cognitive noise. *Journal of Experimental Psychology: Learning, Memory, and Cognition, 13,* 327–334.

Neumann, Ewald & Brett G. DeSchepper (1992). An inhibition-based fan effect: Evidence for an active suppression mechanism in selective attention. *Canadian Journal of Psychology, 46,* 11–50.

Pennington, Ginger L. & Neal J. Roese (2003). Regulatory focus and temporal distance. *Journal of Experimental Social Psychology, 39,* 563–576.

Posner, Michael I. (1987). Selective attention and cognitive control. *Trends in Neuroscience, 10,* 13–17.

Proffitt, Dennis R., Jeanine Stefanucci, Tom Banton & William Epstein (2003). The role of effort in perceiving distance. *Psychological Science, 14,* 106–112.

Pronin, Emily (2008). How we see ourselves and how we see others. *Science, 320,* 1177–1180.

Santiago, Julio, Antonio Román & Marc Ouellet (this volume). *Flexible foundations of abstract thought: A review and a theory.*

Schnall, Simone (this volume). Embodiment in affective space: Social influences on spatial perception.

Schooler, Jonathan W. (2002). Verbalization produces a transfer inappropriate processing shift. Applied *Cognitive Psychology, 16,* 989–997.

Schubert, Thomas W., Sven Waldzus & Beate Seibt (this volume). More than a metaphor: How the understanding of power is grounded in experience.

Smith, Pamela K. & Yaacov Trope (2006). You focus on the forest when you're in charge of the trees: Power priming and abstract information processing. *Journal of Personality and Social Psychology, 90,* 578–596.

Stapel, Diederik A. & Gün R. Semin (2007). The magic spell of language: Linguistic categories and their perceptual consequences. *Journal of Personality and Social Psychology, 93,* 23–33.

Stephan, Eelena (2006). Social distance and its relations to level of construal, temporal distance and spatial distance. Unpublished Doctoral Dissertation, Tel Aviv University.

Stephan, Elena, Nira Liberman & Yaacov Trope (2007). Politeness and its relation to psychological distancing. *Manuscript submitted for publication.*

Trope, Yaakov & Nira Liberman (2003). Temporal Construal. *Psychological Review, 110,* 403–421.

Trope, Yaakov, Nira Liberman & Cheryl J. Wakslak (2007). Construal levels and psychological distance: Effects on representation, prediction, evaluation, and behavior. *Journal of Consumer Psychology, 12,* 83–97.

Trope, Yaakov & Nira Liberman (2010). Construal-level theory of psychological distance. *Psychological Review, 117,* 440–463.

Tucker, Don M. & Peter A. Williamson (1984). Asymmetric neural control systems in human self-regulation. *Psychological Review, 91,* 185–215.
Vallacher, Robin R. & Daniel M. Wegner (1989). Levels of personal agency: Individual variation in action identification. Journal of Personality and Social Psychology, 57, 660–671.
Wakslak, Cheryl J., Yaacov Trope, Nira Liberman & Rotem Alony (2006). Seeing the forest when entry is unlikely: Probability and the mental representation of events. *Journal of Experimental Psychology: General, 135,* 641–653.
Weinstein, Neil D. (1980). Unrealistic optimism about future life events. *Journal of Personality and Social Psychology, 39,* 806–820.
Winnicott, Donald W. (1957). *Mother and Child. A Primer of First Relationships.*, New York: Basic Books, Inc.
Yovel, Iftah, William Revelle & Susan Mineka (2005). Who sees trees before forest? The obsessive compulsive style of visual attention. *Psychological Science, 16,* 123–129.
Witt, Jessica K. & Dennis R. Proffitt (2008). Action-Specific Influences on Distance Perception: A Role for Motor Simulation. *Journal of Experimental Psychology: Human Perception and Performance, 34,* 1479–1492.

Embodiment in affective space: Social influences on spatial perception

Simone Schnall[1]

Abstract

Unlike social judgments, perceptual judgments are anchored in concrete reality and should not depend on social context. However, recent research suggests that perceptions of physical space can depend on social and emotional considerations. In contrast to theoretical approaches that view visual perception as a low-level process that is entirely independent of situational constraints, many studies support the notion that visual perception takes place in an "embodied" fashion, because people perceive the physical world around them as a function of how they would act in that world. This chapter reviews the influence of social and emotional factors in research involving maps and other conceptual representations of space, and in research involving the perception of distances and inclines. The reviewed findings provide a glimpse of how social factors influence basic cognitive processes previously assumed to be insulated from such influences.

1. Introduction

> We speak of A as a '*close*' friend, B as a '*distant*' sort of person. We keep C at '*arm's length*,' consider E '*aloof*' or '*withdrawn*,' F as '*pushy*' and with some scientific rigor characterize interpersonal relationships in terms of '*social distance*.' (Little, 1965, p. 238, emphasis added).

Metaphors describing social relationships in terms of distance are plentiful (Lakoff & Johnson, 1980, 1999). These metaphors are not arbitrary: People use space in specific ways as a function of social relationships, as shown by *Proxemics*, the study of personal space (Argyle & Dean, 1965; Hall, 1968; Hayduk, 1983). For example, people maintain less distance when they feel "close" to somebody (Patterson, 1977; Willis, 1966), whereas they main-

---

[1] Preparation of this paper was supported by NSF grant BCS 0518835 and ESRC First Grant RES-061-25-0119. Thanks to the Department of Psychology at Harvard University for accommodating the author as a Visiting Scholar during the Spring of 2009 when this paper was prepared.

tain more distance when the other person is disliked, or carries a physical stigma (Kleck, 1968). Further, people maintain an area of personal space around them that is usually not violated by others (Hall, 1968). Thus, social factors often influence how people interact in physical space. Further, recent research has explored the extent to which perceived distance expands or contracts depending on how "close" or "distant" a social relationship is. This chapter will illustrate how social distance is related to perceived distance, and more generally, how social and affective factors influence perception of physical space.

In line with the claim that cognitive processes are embodied and action-driven, spatial perception appears to be constrained by a person's potential to carry out specific actions in a given environment. Recent work by Proffitt and colleagues supports the idea that functional aspects play a critical role in perception. For example, the perception of slants of hills and of distances is influenced by factors such as whether the perceiver is wearing a heavy backpack (Proffitt, Stefanucci, Banton, & Epstein, 2003), is young or old (Bhalla & Proffitt, 1999), is fatigued (Proffitt, Bhalla, Gossweiler, & Midgett, 1995), or has action goals in mind (Witt, Proffitt, & Epstein, 2004). Such factors influence perception because they are relevant to action. For instance, a distance is harder to traverse for an elderly, or a fatigued person, and thus, appears as farther. These studies suggest that visual perception combines aspects of the perceiver with the environment to be perceived. Of primary concern is what Proffitt (2006) calls the *economy of action*. In order to plan and to manage one's physical and mental resources to cope with the world, humans, and indeed all organisms, scale the world in terms of the actions that are afforded by their bodies. According to this view, visual perception provides a mechanism to indicate whether exerting a certain amount of energy is worthwhile, given the potential energetic costs and current resources available: Plans for action are related to their energetic costs, and people are informed about these contingencies through their visual perception, because it reflects, given the current state of the body, how difficult and costly it would be to perform a given action in the environment.

With respect to the two important geometric and psychological parameters that have been studied – slant and extent – it can be argued that social resources may inform perception of the world no less crucially than does the availability of our physical energy. Just as steep hills and great distances require that physical energy be available, they may also require emotional and social resources. The larger idea is that our perception of the physical world, as well as of psychological situations, is constrained by emotional and social factors. All these influences constrain perception, because they are concerned with goals, plans, and resource decisions, or more generally, the anticipation of action. It is because of this motivation to take action that functional demands of a situation make a person literally look at the world differently.

To some extent perceptual estimates of the physical world, namely estimates of distances and of hill slant, might be similar to the kinds of judgments studied by social psychologists, such as ratings of life satisfaction, probability, risk, and so on. The latter kinds of judgments are characterized by two aspects: First, they are "subjective." For example, the same circumstances can result in high ratings of life satisfaction for one person, but low ratings of life satisfaction for another person. Second, judgments depend on various properties of the context in which the judgments are made. Such contextual factors include the framing of the question (Tversky & Kahneman, 1981), the mood of the person being questioned (e.g., Schwarz & Clore, 1983; Schnall, Haidt, Clore & Jordan, 2008), currently accessible cognitive concepts (e.g., Schnall, Benton & Harvey, 2008), and so on. Perceptual estimates may share these two aspects of judgments, and are sensitive to the demands of a given context. However, perceptual estimates differ in one important way from other judgments: They can be more or less accurate. In contrast to judgments of liking, life satisfaction, moral integrity, etc., there is a correct answer when it comes to perceptions of the real world: A 12 cm long line on a piece of paper, such as a map, simply is 12 cm long.

In this chapter research concerning small-scale distance estimates on maps and other visual media will be reviewed first, and how recent work in this domain has started to incorporate social and emotional considerations of the perceiver. Following this, recent developments in cognitive science related to embodied cognition will be discussed. Then research on embodied perception, involving perceptual estimates in the physical environment such as perceptions of hill slant and of distance will be reviewed. The next section will discuss how social and emotional factors inform spatial perception, and parallels between physiological and social resources will be explored. Finally, similarities of subjective and objective judgments within cognitive and social psychology will be considered.

2. Physical and psychological maps

In order to move around in the world individuals need to have an internal representation of the environment to consult for navigation. However, *cognitive distance*, defined as the spatial component of an individual's representations of the environment, differs from actual, or *physical distance* (Golledge, 1987), and can be changed by structural properties of space

(Tversky, 2000). For example, people appear to divide the environment into meaningful categories ("chunks") which subsequently influence spatial judgments, leading to distortions when estimating distances on maps and other visual media. For example, Thorndyke (1981) had participants study maps with city names, and then estimate the distance between pairs of cities. The greater the number of intervening cities between two target cities, the greater was the estimated distance between those two cities. In addition, distances between stimuli that are considered part of a perceptual Gestalt are underestimated compared to stimuli that are outside of that Gestalt (Coren & Girgus, 1980). Thus, when crossing over a boundary, whether physical or conceptual, subjective distance estimates increase.

Additional research has investigated whether subjective psychological feelings associated with crossed borders might also change distance estimates. Indeed, attitudes related to in-groups and out-groups have been shown to influence distance estimates in recent studies (Kerkman, Stea, Norris, & Rice, 2004; Burris & Branscombe, 2005). For instance, Burris and Branscombe (2005) asked university students from Memphis, Tennessee, and Lawrence, Kansas, to estimate distances between cities on a map of the United States. Participants overestimated the distances between a U.S. location and a foreign location relative to a visually equidistant U.S. location. Of primary interest was that this overestimation took place only when the distance estimates involved crossing the U.S. border to a foreign country such as Canada or Mexico, but not when it involved crossing borders between two foreign locations. Burris and Branscombe (2005) interpreted their data as suggesting the effect a "psychological boundary" between relevant space to oneself and one's ingroup, namely one's own country, and nonself-relevant space, namely other countries. Similarly, Carbon and Leder (2005) showed self-involvement as a potential factor for a bias in distance estimation across borders of countries. They found that distances between city pairs that involved crossing the former "Iron Curtain", with one city in East Germany, and the other city in West Germany, were systematically overestimated compared to distances of cities located within the same parts of Germany. Interestingly, this overestimation of distances between regions was especially pronounced for participants who exhibited a negative attitude toward the reunification of Germany.

Bugmann and Schnall (2009) recently showed that experimentally induced negative emotions can also change estimates of distances between cities on a map. Because disgust is considered to be evolutionarily significant in protecting one's physical boundaries (Haidt, Rozin, McCauley & Imada, 1997), Bugmann and Schnall (2009) manipulated disgust by having participants fill out the Disgust Sensitivity Scale (Haidt, McCauley & Rozin, 1994), which involves considering a variety of potentially disgusting situations. After being induced to feel disgust participants systematically gave higher distance estimates between city pairs than participants who were in a neutral emotional state. This finding suggests that an incidental feeling of disgust can establish a psychological boundary involving a desire to remove oneself from an unpleasant source of affect, and as a consequence influences cognitive distance even when the disgust is not relevant to the current situation.

Several recent studies demonstrated that metacognitive factors, such as processing fluency and primed perceptual anchors can change distance estimates. Alter and Oppenheimer (2008) asked participants to consider distances between cities as they were waiting at a train station in New Jersey, and estimated distances to a variety of US cities from their current location. Some of the participants received the questionnaire printed in a font that was easy to read, thus involving a metacognitive state of perceptual fluency (e.g., Winkielman, Schwarz, Fazendeiro, & Reber, 2003), whereas other participants received font that was difficult to read, thus involving perceptual disfluency. When reading the questionnaire was difficult and required effort, participants gave higher distance estimates between the cities than when reading the questionnaire did not require effort. Presumably, the disfluency experienced when reading the item was interpreted to indicate that distances between the cities must be far.

LeBoef and Shafir (2006) asked participants to draw a 3.5 inches long line on a sheet of paper. Half of the participants started with a very short line and had to complete it to make it the required length, whereas the other half of them started with a long line and had to shorten it. Those extending the previously given short line drew significantly shorter lines than those shortening the given long line, suggesting that whatever anchor participants started with determined how long they perceived 3.5 inches to be.

All these findings suggest that rather than being objectively determined by a low-level modular process (Fodor, 1983), visual processes such as estimating small-scale distances on maps are constrained by various contextual factors, which can include mood, processing fluency, and cognitive anchors. The work reviewed above concerned spatial estimates that involved representations of space in the form of maps, or lines on paper. Other research has investigated contextual influences on the perception of physical space to which observers are directly exposed; for example, participants might stand at the bottom of a hill and estimate its slant, or stand in a grassy field and estimate distance to specific targets. Such direct perceptual estimates of physical space are also constrained by contextual factors, which is in line with one of the central tenet of theories of *embodied cognition* that have become prominent in recent years, as will be reviewed next.

3. Embodied cognition

Following researchers in other areas of cognitive science (e.g., Barsalou, 1999; Clark, 1997; Glenberg, 1997; Lakoff & Johnson, 1980, 1999; Varela, Thompson & Rosch, 1991), social psychologists have started to emphasize the benefits of an embodied view of cognition, based on the notion that functioning in the world with bodies fundamentally shapes cognitive processes (e.g., Niedenthal, Barsalou, Winkielman, Krauth-Gruber& Ric, 2005; Smith & Semin, 2004). As in other disciplines, the new focus on embodiment has generated enthusiasm and renewed interest in physical aspects of affective experience.

One of the main assumptions of embodied cognition[2] is that ultimately, the goal of cognitive processes is not to produce mental representations of abstract knowledge, but instead, to facilitate appropriate action in the world. The kinds of actions that are possible, and therefore, the kinds of cognitive structures that follow, are constrained by stable as well as temporary characteristics of the human body. This view is not entirely new (e.g., Gibson, 1979; Merleau-Ponty, 1962); however, traditionally psychologists have tended to treat cognition as taking place entirely "in the head", and the role of the body has been largely underappreciated (for a history of the disembodied mind, see Johnson, 1987; Spellman & Schnall, 2009). To appreciate the excitement following this new perspective, it needs to be clarified what embodiment refers to. The term embodiment has been used by researchers in cognitive science in multiple ways, sometimes without being defined explicitly (Anderson, 2003; Wilson, 2002). Often it has been defined not so much by what it is, but by what it is *not*. For example, it has been noted that the goal of cognitive processes is not simply thinking. Researchers endorsing the embodied approach to cognition have put their perspective in opposition to the assumptions of more traditional approaches to cognition (e.g., Fodor, 1983; Fodor & Pylyshyn, 1988). These research traditions, which have been termed *objectivist* (Lakoff & Johnson, 1999) or *cognitivist* (Clark, 1997; Varela et al., 1991), make very specific claims

---

2   For purposes of simplification, the term "embodied cognition" is used to refer to a cluster of theoretical approaches that share, among other things, a commitment to the physicality of human cognition. It is acknowledged, as cautioned by Barsalou (2008), that the embodied component of such approaches is but one aspect, which downplays the fact that other aspects are necessary and equally important. As a more appropriate and inclusive term Barsalou (2008) suggests "grounded cognition." However, because the term "embodied cognition" has become popular, especially within social psychology, this term was chosen for discussion in the present paper.

about the nature, and the purpose of internal representations. The issue is, to use an often quoted example, how human beings represent the fact that chairs have four legs, a seat, a back, possibly some armrests, and so on. Do people indeed represent objects, ideas, and situations in the form of features or propositions? Traditional theories assume that amodal symbols and properties define conceptual structure, and that cognitive processes correspond to the manipulation of those symbols (e.g., Fodor, 1983; Fodor & Pylyshyn, 1988). The symbols themselves are arbitrary, and are given meaning only by means of how they are combined. This computational metaphor in cognitive science has been influential ever since the cognitive revolution.

In contrast to traditional theories of cognition, according to the embodied approach, the brain evolved not to provide an accurate mirror representation of the world, but rather, to help humans, and non-human animals alike, to successfully act in the world. Because the goal of mental representations is to allow for actions and interactions with the world, representations are the result of interactions with the environment, rather than consisting of arbitrary abstract symbols (Barsalou, 1999; Glenberg, 1997). Such embodied representations maintain the modality of perceptual experience, and concepts are considered to involve simulations of such perceptual processes (Barsalou, 1999).

This general claim is in part based on the notion of *affordance*, coined by Gibson (1979), which describes potential interactions between a person and an object, or an environment. Certain actions are "afforded" by certain objects, whereas others are not: A chair affords sitting on it, but normally does not afford walking on it. However, affordances are not fixed, but depend on specific circumstances. One can easily imagine situations where a chair will not afford sitting, for example, if it is a miniature model in a doll house. Similarly, one can imagine situations in which a chair will afford walking on it, for example when a series of chairs forms a walkable trail out of a flooded house. A critical implication of cognition in the service of action is that specific actions happen in specific contexts.

Importantly, context or situational factors do not simply modify what action, and thus, what cognitive process is appropriate, but rather, they *define* the action. Consider the example of the frog's visual system (Ingle, 1973). Frogs have several neurologically separate visual pathways, such as one pathway to detect prey, another to monitor predators, and yet another to control visually guided locomotion. Thus, frogs do not have a general-purpose visual system that responds differently depending on what input it receives; rather, the input (e.g., prey vs. predator), and the corresponding action associated with the input (catching a fly vs. escaping from a hawk) determines the process of visual perception. The goal of vision is not to see, but to control movements as a response to stimuli in the environment (Milner & Goodale, 1995). By rejecting the notion of "pure" vision (Marr, 1982), or more generally, the notion that perceptual processes are informationally encapsulated (Fodor, 1983) and independent of higher-level cognitive processes, embodied cognition approaches have provided a productive way of studying the interactions of vision and action (e.g., Tucker & Ellis, 1998). One domain of perception for which the embodied view of cognitive processes has become especially relevant is the perception of the physical environment, including distances and slants of hills, as will be reviewed next.

4. Embodied perception: Physiological resources

Judging from their everyday experiences people assume that their visual perceptions accurately reflect the physical world around them. In contrast, inspired by Gibson's (1979) notion of affordance, a view of perception based on the *economy of action* (Proffitt, 2006) proposes that people perceive the space around them relative to how they can act on it. For example, when exhausted due to a long and strenuous run people perceive hills as steeper than when they are not fatigued (Proffitt et al., 1995). Similarly, people who wear heavy backpacks perceive hills to be steeper than do people who are unencumbered (Bhalla & Proffitt, 1999). Such studies have demonstrated an association between spatial perception and factors that are relevant to action: Because climbing a hill is challenging for fatigued or encumbered people, they perceive it be to steeper. Thus, people's perception of the physical world is not simply a function of objective features of the environment such as slant or extent, but is constrained by the perceiver's ability to act on that given space, at a given time. Evidence for the economy of action involved in making perceptual estimates has come from two sources: Studies involving hill slant, and studies involving distance. These will be reviewed in turn.

4.1. Visual slant perception

Various accounts of visual perception propose two distinct functions of vision that appear to be controlled by two anatomically separate visual pathways in the brain (e.g., Milner & Goodale, 1995). The two visual processes relate to action planning and action execution, which are thought to be controlled by the ventral stream, and the dorsal stream of the visual cortex. Studies assessing the perception of hill slants have documented that people give different estimates depending on whether a slant measure taps into one function of vision, or the other (Bhalla & Proffitt, 1999; Proffitt et al., 1995; Schnall et al., 2008): Action planning is captured by a verbal estimate that involves first, having the participant state the slant of a hill in geometric degrees, and second, by asking the participant to engage in visual matching, which involves adjusting a disk to represents the cross-section of the hill. The verbal and visual measures assess people's explicit awareness of slant, and on these measure people tend to dramatically overestimate hill slant. For example, research participants typically estimate a 5° hill to be 20°, or a 10° hill to be 30°. Such overestimation is amplified with experimental manipulations that would make it difficult for a person to climb a hill, such as being encumbered, or fatigued, as noted earlier.

In contrast, action execution is captured by a haptic measure of hill slant, which involves placing the dominant hand on a palmboard that can be adjusted, without sight of the hand, to be parallel to the hill's incline (see Figure 1). This visually-guided action measure is generally accurate and further, is *not* changed by manipulations of physiological state such as whether the person wears a heavy backpack or is fatigued due to previous exercise (Bhalla & Proffitt, 1999). In other words, factors that would make it challenging to ascend a hill lead participants to estimate the hill as more steep on the verbal and visual measures, but do not change how steep they perceive it when using the haptic measure. How can this apparent disconnect

Figure 1. Participant using haptic measure to assess hill slant.

between the two types of measures be explained? Importantly, the haptic palmboard measure is assessed by asking participants to place their hand on the palmboard without looking, and adjust it to be equivalent to the inclination of the hill in front of them. Therefore, there is no visual feedback when performing this task. In contrast, the explicit verbal and visual reports are made by explicitly deciding on the magnitude of hill slant. Thus, one way of thinking of this distinction is to consider the verbal and visual measures as accessible to explicit awareness because they are guided by deliberate manipulation of the measures, and allow the participant to adjust the measure while at the same time looking at the hill, whereas control of the haptic measure relies on visuomotor processes that are not entirely open to conscious consideration (see Witt & Proffitt, 2007, for a detailed discussion).

The overestimation in the measures that relate to action planning is adaptive and is driven by two separate mechanisms (Proffitt, 2006). First, response compression allows for greater sensitivity to small changes in slant for relatively shallow slants, which are the only slants one can walk on and therefore the only slants for which small differences are of any relevance (see Proffitt, 2006, for further detail). Second, because these representations inform decisions about action that need to take into account costs and benefits, anticipating what would be involved in ascending the hill, what resources would be required, and what resources are available, and including this information in explicit perception is adaptive in terms of influencing individuals to be cautious and "on the safe side" when planning future action and energy expenditure. In contrast, for actual navigation and movement within the environment the body needs to act precisely in line with the conditions of the environment: When ascending a steep hill a person needs to lift the foot such that it perfectly accommodates the ground upon which it will be placed and thus factors related to action planning are relatively irrelevant.

Using these convergent measures for which different results are expected has the benefit that effects due to experimental demand characteristics are unlikely, because in that case all measures should show the same pattern of results, which they do not.

4.2. Visual distance perception

Inspired by the initial finding that hills appear steeper when observers wear a heavy backpack relative to when they do not (Bhalla & Proffitt, 1999), follow-up studies tested whether similar effects could be obtained when encumbered observers estimate distance to walkable targets ranging from 1 to 17 meters (Proffitt et al., 2003). In one study, participant stood in a grassy field and estimated how far from them orange traffic cones were that had been placed at varying distances.³ Indeed, participants wearing a heavy backpack estimated the distances to be farther than those who were not, which is consistent with the idea that on some level, perceivers took into account how effortful it would be to walk to specific targets given their current physical state.⁴ Other research had participants throw a heavy or a light ball at targets before estimating the distance to those targets. After throwing a heavy ball participants indicated that distance to the targets was farther than after throwing a light ball (Witt, Proffitt & Epstein, 2004). Presumably, perceived effort when carrying out a specific action, in this case throwing a ball, was interpreted as being diagnostic of the distance to the object relating to that action.

Considerations of how easy or difficult it is to reach a target also influence estimates of distances to closer targets. Witt, Proffitt and Epstein (2005) presented participants with targets that were either just within reach of their arm or outside of arm's reach. Participants were seated in front of a table into which small white circles were projected. When the circle disappeared participants attempted to touch the location in which it had appeared, either using their finger, or using a baton. Targets were estimated as closer when reaching with the baton than when reaching with the finger. However, a follow-up experiment showed that reachability only influenced distance estimates when it was relevant to action, namely when the perceiver had previously formed an intention to reach, but not when merely holding the baton (Witt et al., 2005).

Of particular importance is that studies of embodied perception redefine what might be considered an "accurate", or "rational" response to the questions of "how far is it to get to a target location?" or "how steep is a hill?" On the one hand, if the hill is actually 5 degrees in incline, any deviation from 5 degrees is incorrect. On the other hand, when wearing a backpack the hill becomes functionally steeper, and an answer of 20 degrees might in fact be the appropriate, although factually "irrational" or "incorrect" answer. Overall, studies on embodied perception suggest that even seemingly

---

3   In contrast to the studies on hill slant, these studies involving distance estimates only used "explicit" perceptual estimates in the form of participants giving estimates in feet and inches. No equivalent to the haptic measure was used.
4   In these studies, as in studies involving hill slant described above, experimental instructions to participants leave it ambiguous whether walking to the target (or climbing up the hill) would actually be required after making the perceptual estimates. However, underlying the notion of affordance is the assumption that people automatically perceive the environment with regard to specific actions, without needing an explicit goal to perform such actions.

objective aspects of the physical environment, such as how far is it to get to a target, or how steep is an incline, are constrained by physical considerations of the body that perceives the environment.

4.3. Direct evidence for the economy of action

The economy of action account (Proffitt, 2006) maintains that spatial perceptions depend on the resources necessary to perform actions relative to the resources that a person has available. What kind of resources are required to deal with challenges in the environment? At the most basic level, human beings, like all other animals, are living systems in which energy is necessary to maintain bodily functions such as respiration, digestion, blood circulation and to support any physical activity that goes beyond the resting state. Whenever energy is used, it must be replaced. Carbohydrates supply energy in the form or glucose, which becomes available throughout the body via the bloodstream. Although any physical action requires energy, the precise amount depends on the properties of the environment in which the action takes place. For instance, walking up a 5° hill requires much less energy than walking up a 20° hill. Similarly, walking up a hill while carrying a heavy backpack requires more energy than when unencumbered. If the energetic requirements for an action are high or the available energy is low, then hills will appear steeper than they would otherwise, thereby discouraging an individual from performing energetically suboptimal actions.

The studies reviewed above involving visual slant and distance perception were built on the assumption of the economy of action. However, they did not experimentally manipulate or measure current energetic states of the perceiver. Furthermore, critics have objected that participants might have shown demand characteristics by indicating that the hill is steeper because they knew that they were wearing a backpack or were fatigued.

In recent work, Schnall, Zadra and Proffitt (2010) directly manipulated blood glucose levels, with the expectation that high blood glucose would make hills appear less steep relative to low blood glucose. Under the subterfuge of a taste testing study, participants were given a soft drink that, unbeknownst to them, was sweetened with either sugar, or with artificial sweetener. Thus, some participants were given readily available glucose, whereas the other participants were not. Then participants put on heavy backpacks while performing the same slant estimates as described above, including verbal, visual and haptic reports. Results from two experiments indicate that participants who had consumed a glucose-containing drink perceived the hill's slant to be less steep than did participants who had consumed a drink containing non-caloric sweetener. Because climbing a hill while wearing a heavy backpack poses a metabolic challenge, explicit action planning benefits from the apparent slant of the hill being influenced by one's potential to expend energy. In contrast, visual processes involved in action execution, as measured by the haptic estimates, were unaffected by energetic factors, because the biomechanics of climbing a hill remain unchanged. Schnall et al. (2010) thus argue that a process that is relatively effortless and automatic, namely visual perception, is influenced by glucose levels because visual perception serves as the "fuel gauge" of whether glucose is available or not, and what action in a given physical environment is possible.

5. Embodied perception: Social and emotional factors

In addition to the studies that investigated physiological resources, such as whether a person is rested or fatigued, has high or low levels of blood glucose available, and so on, several studies have started looking into the influence of more psychological processes such as emotion and motivation.

5.1. Emotion and perception of space

Riener, Stefanucci, Proffitt and Clore (2011) tested the influence of *mood* on hill slant perception. Mood was induced by having participants listen to happy music or sad music, or by having participants write about happy or sad life events. Then participants completed slant estimates of a steep hill. Sad participants judged the hill as being steeper than those in the happy condition. As was found previously, the visually guided action measure was unaffected across conditions.

Stefanucci and colleagues have explored the contribution of fear to various perceptual processes. Participants who stood on a skateboard (that was secured to be stationary) at the top of a hill and reported feeling afraid at the prospect of going down the hill perceived it to be steeper than participants who merely stood on a wooden box at the top of the hill (Stefanucci, Proffitt, Clore, & Parekh, 2008). Going beyond perceptual estimates of slant and extent, Stefanucci further developed a new perceptual paradigm by assessing people's perception of height (Stefanucci & Proffitt, 2009). Participants estimated distance either when looking down from a balcony, or when looking up to the balcony. Vertical distance involving the balcony was generally overestimated relative to equivalent horizontal distance. Furthermore, overestimation was particularly pronounced when looking down rather than when looking up, and when looking down from large height rather than small height, presumably because of the potential danger and fear associated with standing exposed on a high balcony. This finding is consistent with earlier work involving hill slant that had shown that hills are perceived as steeper when viewed from the top relative to being viewed from the bottom once their incline makes them too difficult to descend, although it might still be possible to ascend (Proffitt et al., 1995). Further, individuals with pronounced fear of heights overestimate vertical distance from a two-story balcony more than those who do not suffer from fear of heights, thus suggesting that perceptual bias can be symptomatic of underlying emotional processes (Teachman, Stefanucci, Clerkin, Cody, & Proffitt, 2008). In addition to stable individual differences regarding fear of height, components of fear involving arousal have been manipulated experimentally. Stefanucci and Storbeck (2009) first exposed half of their participants to arousing visual images, while the other half of the participants were exposed to non-arousing visual images. Subsequent height estimates of a balcony were significantly higher for participants who previously had seen arousing stimuli, presumably because the arousal from the images intensified the fear associated with looking down from a high balcony. However, in contrast to such vertical distance estimates, high or low arousal did not have any influence on horizontal distance estimates, suggesting that arousal only has an impact when it is functionally relevant to the physical situation under consideration.

Further, testing motivational influences, Balcetis and Dunning (2007) demonstrated that manipulations of *cognitive dissonance* changed the perception of distance and slant. People in high choice conditions estimated slants to be less steep and distances to be less far than those in low choice or control conditions, presumably because they were keen to resolve dissonance.

Such findings involving emotional and motivational factors might be considered intuitive from a social psychologist's perspective; however, they are incompatible with most theories of perception that assume that perception constitutes a modular process that is independent from extraneous factors (Fodor, 1983; Marr, 1982). Instead, these findings are consistent with ecological approaches to perception (e.g., Gibson, 1979; Milner & Goodale, 1995; Proffitt, 2006).

5.2. Social resources and spatial perception

Recent work has further explored whether other people might also be considered valuable resources in a manner that impacts spatial perception, and to some extent lead to effects parallel to the ones obtained on physiological resources. Indeed, the basic finding that social support is a beneficial resource on many levels is well established. Apparently the number and intensity of close social contacts serves as a buffer against life's adverse events (Thoits, 1986) and thereby reduces the risk of stress-related illnesses such as heart disease (Seeman & Syme, 1987) and cancer (Fawzy et al., 1993). Stress responses to threatening situations are dampened when a person is in the presence of a supportive other compared to when being alone (Kamarck et al., 1990), and a similar attenuation of stress reactivity in the presence of conspecifics has been found even in non-human animals, including rats (Davitz & Mason, 1955; Latané, 1969), guinea pigs (Hennessey, O'Leary, Hawke, & Wilson, 2002) and monkeys (Gust, Gordon, Brodie, & McClure, 1994). Overall, social support appears to "lighten the load" of individuals who find themselves in stressful and challenging situations.

If the presence of another person has such benefits, then the perception of challenging spatial environments such as steep hills might be modulated by the presence or absence of supportive others as well. Schnall, Stefanucci, Clore and Proffitt conducted a pilot study to test whether simply verbally invoking a friend's presence would have an effect on people's distance estimates. Participants were graduate students of the Psychology Department at the University of Virginia which is housed in Gilmer Hall. They were asked to complete a two-item survey which they received by email, estimating the distance from Gilmer Hall to the following two locations: The downtown mall, a popular destination approximately 2.3 miles from Gilmer Hall, and Monticello, Thomas Jefferson's former hill-top home, located about 5.8 miles from Gilmer Hall and involving an uphill journey. Half the participants were asked to imagine that they were standing in front of Gilmer Hall and needed to walk to the locations, and estimate how far it was to get there. The other half of the participants, however, was asked to imagine that "you and a friend are standing in front of Gilmer Hall", and needed to walk to the locations, and then give distance estimates. For the short, easily reachable location of the downtown mall mentioning the friend did not make any difference to distance estimate. For the more challenging, long distance to Monticello, however, participants who were asked to imagine walking with a friend found the distance to be significantly shorter than those who imagined walking alone. It seemed that when faced with a difficult situation, having to walk a long distance involving a steep hill, thinking of doing so while a friend was present made it seem less difficult. However, this was only preliminary evidence because it involved imagined or recalled distances, rather than actual spatial features of the environment that one is currently looking at.

Schnall, Harber, Stefanucci and Proffitt (2008) followed up on this suggestive work with more controlled studies involving slant estimates of a steep hill under conditions where social support was either present or absent. In the first study, participants stood at a steep hill while wearing a heavy backpack, and did so either alone, or with a friend standing at their side. Those who were with a friend, compared to those alone, perceived the hill as less steep. Thus, a psychosocial resource, social support, influenced apparent slant in much the same way as do energetic factors. Importantly, being with a friend versus being alone only affected measures related to explicit awareness and planning (verbal and visual estimates), and had no effect on the measure of visually guided action (haptic estimate). This pattern was consistent with earlier findings on energetic resources and slant estimates that implicate two different visual systems (Bhalla & Proffitt, 1999; Proffitt et al., 1995). A second study manipulated social support by having participants first mentally image a positive, neutral, or negative social contact, and then estimate the slant of the hill. Indeed, participants who thought of a positive other estimated the hill to be less steep than participants who had either thought of a neutral or negative other. Again, differences between experimental conditions were only found on the verbal and visual measures, which are related to explicit awareness, but not on the haptic measure, which is related to the visual control of action. Critically, in both studies the quality of the supportive relationship mediated the effect on visual perception. In Study 1, friendship duration was negatively correlated with visual and verbal slant estimates: The longer a friend was known, the less steep the hill appeared. Further, in Study 2, the feelings of closeness to the imaged other were correlated to both the verbal and visual hill slope estimates: The closer participants felt toward their imaged social contacts, the less steep the hill appeared to them. Thus, the critical ingredients that make relationships a powerful psychosocial resource explained why relationships moderate perception.

The studies reviewed above illustrate how perceptions of space can change as a function of supportive others. However, whereas we like to be physically close to people who we feel emotionally "close" to, people prefer to literally maintain a distance to strangers or generally, people who they are not "close" to. More specifically, people maintain an area of personal space around them, and are very sensitive to violations of this personal space (Argyle & Dean, 1965; Hall, 1968). Schnall, Witt, Stefanucci, Augustyn, Clore and Proffitt (2005) conducted a study modeled after field studies in naturalistic settings that involve an invasion of territory (e.g., Sommer, 1959). In contrast to those early studies that measured the person's behavioral response, we measured the person's distance estimate to an object after their personal space was violated. In the invasion condition, participants' space was invaded by an experimenter who casually placed a can of Coke from which she had been drinking immediately in front of them (at a distance of about 10–45 cm). In the control condition, the experimenter retrieved a fresh can of Coke from her briefcase, and placed it in front of the participant, with the words, "This is for you for participating." Thus, the only difference between the two conditions was whether the experimenter had established ownership of the can (as indicated by drinking from it), and thus invaded the participant's personal space, or the participant had ownership of the can (as indicated by the experimenter's comment). Then participants gave a matching estimate of the distance between the Coke can and the edge of the table where they were sitting. Results showed that participants whose space had been invaded estimated the experimenter's can to be significantly closer than participants who had their own can within their personal space. Thus, when personal space was invaded, another person's object was experienced as "too close."

Several mechanisms for the observed effect are possible. First, the effect might be due to the fact that a social norm violation had taken place. Alternatively, it might be that an affective response was created, such as a feeling of disgust toward another person's beverage. Future studies are aimed at differentiating between these possibilities. What is clear, however, is that the perceived distance to an identical object can change dramatically depending on social constructs such as object ownership. Thus, people appear to not only *use* space in specific ways as a function of social relationships, but based on the results obtained in this study, also *perceive* space as a function of social relationships. It further appears that social processes are especially powerful in the action space within reach that has been termed *personal space* (Cutting & Vishton, 1995) because this space coincides to some extent with the *personal space* that has been extensively studied by social psychologists (Argyle & Dean, 1965; Hall, 1968).

All of these studies – whether about physical resources or psychosocial resources – are based on the assumption that perceptual processes depend on a person's resources in the context of navigating the environment. Thus, these studies were conducted from an embodied perspective, because the traditional cognitive model would not make different predictions for a person standing in front of an actual hill, versus sitting at a computer and indicating their response using keyboard presses.

5.3. Subjective vs. objective judgments

As noted earlier, a considerable body of research has demonstrated that subjective judgments of various kinds can be influenced by contextual factors (e.g., Clore et al., 2001). What makes perceptual judgments different, however, is the fact that they are concerned with objective judgments, namely with features of the physical environment such as distances, hill slant or height, for which there is an objectively correct answer. In contrast to judgments of life satisfaction, risk, moral contempt, etc., there is an objective standard that indicates whether the judgment was correct or not. However, although perceptual judgments can be compared to an external standard, as demonstrated in the research reviewed in this chapter, they are nevertheless influenced by a variety of contextual factors relating to both physiological and social resources. Although it might not be that surprising that a hill appears steeper to a person who is wearing a heavy backpack, such a finding is inconsistent with traditional cognitive theories that view visual perception as a low-level process and is only predicted by theories that consider embodied factors within perception. What might be even more surprising, however, is that emotional factors can have a similar effect: A hill appears steeper for a person who is afraid because of standing on a skateboard at the top of a hill. Might this mean that being afraid is functionally similar to wearing a heavy backpack? Or if consuming a sugary drink makes a hill look less steep, and being with a friend also makes a hill look less steep, does this mean that consuming energy in the form of sugar is functionally similar to being supported by a friend? At this point there is not sufficient empirical evidence to provide an answer to whether physiological and social resources might involve the same mechanism in terms of constraining perception of the physical space. However, all this work suggests that such factors are integral to the perceptual situation, and they need to be considered when trying to understand how people metaphorically and literally view the social and physical worlds.

5.4. Spatial perception and spatial metaphors

In their theory of conceptual metaphor, Lakoff and Johnson (1980, 1999) propose that concepts are represented in the form of metaphors that are grounded in basic experiences of how the body interacts with the physical world, for example, how people use resources, or how they move around in physical space. As a directly perceived, immediate concept, *space* can be used as a source of metaphors for various target domains. For instance, the spatial concept of verticality is used when describing positive or negative experiences, for example, when saying "We hit a *peak* last year, but it's been *downhill* ever since." (Lakoff & Johnson, 1980, p. 17). Whereas early work on metaphor theory was conducted within linguistics and consisted of examples of metaphors and how they map onto physical experience, in recent years social psychological studies have confirmed such connections empirically (e.g., Jostmann, Lakens & Schubert, 2009; Landau, Sullivan &

Greenberg, 2009; Meier & Robinson, 2004; Schubert, 2005; Sherman & Clore, 2009; Williams & Bargh, 2008; Zhong, & Leonardelli, 2008). For example, Meier and Robinson (2004) showed that positive words were categorized more quickly when presented in the top half of a computer screen relative to the bottom half of the screen, whereas the opposite was the case for negative words. Such results suggest that conceptual structure might indeed be represented in a form that makes reference to physical space, for example, an upright posture when feeling happy, versus a slumped, "depressed" posture when feeling sad.

The results reviewed above in the context of embodied perception raise an additional possbility of the mutual influence of metaphor and physical space: If being with a friend takes a "load of your shoulders" and makes a steep hill appear less steep, then perhaps the metaphoric representation of friendship and its effect on challenges in life feeds back into how such challenges are literally perceived. The notion of social "support" might indeed mean that somebody is there for you to help with a difficult "load", therefore decreasing the perceived slant of the hill. Similarly, when a target is "within reach" because a tool is available, it appears physically closer. Physical and metaphorical aspects of close vs. far experiences have recently been formalized within the framework of Construal Level Theory (see Liberman & Förster, this volume). Future studies will need to determine the extent to which physical and metaphorical space interact with one another.

6. Summary

Traditionally visual perception has been conceptualized as a low-level process that takes place in a "computationally encapsulated" manner (e.g., Fodor, 1983). Such approaches have assumed that visual perception is a modular process that is invariant to "higher-level" processes such as the perceiver's goals or social context. However, two lines of recent research have challenged this assumption: First, studies involving maps and other conceptual representations of space, and second, studies involving the perception of extent and slant, or in other words, of distances and inclines. Studies on mental maps suggest that people do not represent physical space in a veridical manner, but instead, distort it to be in line with functional considerations, such as whether a map involves a border to another country, or some more abstract boundary. Further, based on Gibson's (1979) notion of affordances, studies on the perception of physical space suggest that people perceive the world around them as a function of how they would act in that world: When their current bodily resources make it difficult in principle to, for example, cover a distance, or climb a hill, such environments are perceived as challenging, with targets appearing far, and hills appearing steep. Although strictly speaking such perceptual processes do not accurately reflect the true geographic properties of space, in a functional way, they are adaptive, because they influence individuals' anticipated action. In other words, although a hill might objectively not be as steep as it looks when the observer wears a heavy backpack, the observer is nonetheless better off by either planning for a challenging ascent, or avoiding it altogether.

In addition to physiological considerations recent research suggest that social and emotional resources might constrain the perception of physical space as well. For example, positive moods can make a hill appear less steep relative to negative moods such as sadness and fear. Further, having a friend nearby can literally and metaphorically provide "support" when ascending a steep hill. Such findings are consistent with recent approaches to embodied cognition, which are based on the premise that cognitive processes follow from interactions of the person in the physical environment. As a consequence, distinctions of modular processes of cognition, perception and action become difficult to maintain; all these aspects of physical and psychological functioning are closely intertwined. Further, bodily metaphors might not only reflect perceptual experience of space, but might indeed feed back into those physical experiences themselves.

References

Alter, Adam L. & Daniel M. Oppenheimer (2008). Effects of fluency on psychological distance and mental construal (or why New York is a large city, but New York is a civilized jungle). *Psychological Science, 19*, 161–167.

Anderson, Michael L. (2003). Embodied cognition: A field guide. *Artificial Intelligence, 149*, 91–130.

Argyle, Michael & Janet Dean (1965). Eye-contact, distance and affiliation. *Sociometry, 28*, 289–304.

Barsalou, Lawrence W. (1999). Perceptual symbol systems. *Behavioral and Brain Sciences, 22*, 577–660.

Barsalou, Lawrence W. (2008). Grounded cognition. *Annual Review of Psychology, 59*, 617–645.

Bhalla, Mukul & Dennis R. Proffitt (1999). Visual-motor recalibration in geographical slant perception. *Journal of Experimental Psychology: Human Perception and Performance, 25*, 1076–1096.

Balcetis, Emily & David Dunning (2007). Cognitive dissonance and the perception of natural environments. *Psychological Science, 18*, 917–921.

Bugmann, Davi & Simone Schnall (2009). *Negative affect and distance estimates on maps*. Manuscript under review.

Burris, Christopher T. & Nyla R. Branscombe (2005). Distorted distance estimation induced by a self-relevant national boundary. *Journal of Experimental Social Psychology, 41*, 305–312.

Carbon, Claus-Christian & Helmut Leder (2005). The wall inside the brain: Overestimation of distances crossing the former Iron Curtain. *Psychonomic Bulletin and Review, 12*, 746–750.

Clark, Andy (1997). *Being there: Putting the brain, body, and world together again*. Cambridge, MA: MIT Press.

Clore, Gerald L., Robert S. Wyer, Bruce Dienes, Karen Gasper, Carol Gohm & Linda Isbell (2001). Affective feelings as feedback: Some cognitive consequences. In Leonard L. Martin & Gerald L. Clore (Eds.), *Theories of mood and cognition: A user's handbook* (pp. 27–62). Mahwah, NJ: Erlbaum.

Coren, Stanley & Joan S. Girgus (1980). Principles of perceptual organization and spatial distortion: The Gestalt illusions. *Journal of Experimental Psychology: Human Perception and Performance, 6*, 404–412.

Cutting, James E. & Peter M. Vishton (1995). Perceiving layout: The integration, relative dominance, and contextual use of different information about depth. In William Epstein & Sheena Rogers (Eds.), *Handbook of Perception and Cognition: Vol. 5: Perception of Space and Motion*. NY: Academic Press.

Davitz, Joel R. & Donald J. Mason (1955). Socially facilitated reduction of a fear response in rats. *Journal of Comparative and Physiological Psychology, 48*, 149–156.

Fodor, Jerry A. (1983). *The modularity of mind*. Cambridge, MA: MIT Press.

Fodor, Jerry A. & Zenon W. Pylyshyn (1988). Connectionism and cognitive architecture: A critical analysis. *Cognition, 28*, 3–71.

Gibson, James J. (1979). *The ecological approach to visual perception*. Boston, MA: Houghton Mifflin.

Glenberg, Arthur M. (1997). What memory is for. *Behavioral and Brain Sciences, 20*, 1–55.

Golledge, Reginald G. (1987). Environmental cognition. In Daniel Stokols, Irwin Altman (Eds). *Handbook of Environmental Psychology* (131–174). John Wiley & Sons.

Gust, Deborah A., Thomas P. Gordon, Anne R. Brodie & Harold M. McClure (1994). Effect of preferred companion in modulating stress in adult female rhesus monkeys. *Physiology and Behavior, 55*, 681–684.

Haidt, Jonathan, Clark McCauley & Paul Rozin (1994). Individual differences in sensitivity to disgust: A scale sampling seven domains of disgust elicitors. *Personality and Individual Differences, 16*, 701–713.

Hall, Edward T. (1968). Proxemics. *Current Anthropology, 9*, 83–95.

Hayduk, Leslie A. (1983). Personal space: Where we now stand. *Psychological Bulletin, 94*, 293–335.

Hennessey, Michael B., Shonagh K. O'Leary, Jesse L. Hawke & Shannon E. Wilson (2002). Social influences on cortisol and behavioral responses of preweaning, periadolescent, and adult guinea pigs. *Physiology and Behavior, 76*, 305–314.

Ingle, David (1973). Two visual systems in the frog, *Science, 181*, 1053–1055.

Johnson, Mark (1987). *The body in the mind: The bodily basis of meaning, imagination, and reason.* Chicago: University of Chicago Press.

Jostmann, Nils B., Daniël Lakens & Thomas W. Schubert (2009). Weight as an embodiment of importance. *Psychological Science, 20,* 1169–1174.

Kamarck, Thomas W., Stephen B. Manuck & J. Richard Jennings (1990). Social support reduces cardiovascular reactivity to psychological challenge: A laboratory model. *Psychosomatic Medicine, 52,* 42–58.

Kerkman, Dennis D., David Stea, Karen Norris & Jennifer L. Rice (2004). Social attitudes predict biases in geographic knowledge. *The Professional Geographer, 56,* 258–269.

Kleck, Robert E. (1968). Effects of stigmatizing conditions on the use of personal space. *Psychological Reports, 32,* 111–118.

Lakoff, George & Mark Johnson (1980). *Metaphors we live by.* Chicago: University of Chicago Press.

Lakoff, George & Mark Johnson (1999). *Philosophy in the flesh: The embodied mind and its challenge to Western thought.* New York: Basic Books.

Landau, Mark J., Daniel Sullivan & Jeff Greenberg (2009). Evidence that self-relevant motivations and metaphoric framing interact to influence political and social issues. *Psychological Science, 20,* 1421–1427.

Latané, Bibb (1969). Gregariousness and fear in laboratory rats. *Journal of Experimental Social Psychology, 5,* 61–69.

LeBoef, Robyn A. & Eldar Shafir (2006). The long and short of it: Physical anchoring effects. *Journal of Behavioral Decision Making, 19,* 393–406

Liberman, Nira & Jens Förster (this volume). Estimates of spatial distance: A Construal Level Theory perspective.

Little, Kenneth B. (1965). Personal space. *Journal of Experimental Social Psychology, 1,* 237–247.

Marr, David (1982). *Vision.* San Francisco: Freeman.

Meier, Brian P. & Michael D. Robinson (2004). Why the sunny side is up: Associations between affect and vertical position. *Psychological Science, 15,* 243–247.

Merleau-Ponty, Maurice (1962). *Phenomenology of perception.* London: Routledge.

Milner, A. David & Melvyn A. Goodale (1995). *The visual brain in action.* Oxford: Oxford University Press.

Niedenthal, Paula M., Lawrence W. Barsalou, Piotr Winkielman, Sylvia Kraut-Gruber & François Ric (2005). Embodiment in attitudes, social perception, and emotion. *Personality and Social Psychology Review, 9,* 184–211.

Patterson, Miles L. (1977). Interpersonal distance, affect, and equilibrium theory. *Journal of Social Psychology, 101,* 205–214.

Proffitt, Dennis R., Mukul Bhalla, Rich Gossweiler & Jonathan Midgett (1995). Perceiving geographical slant. *Psychonomic Bulletin and Review, 2,* 409–428.

Proffitt, Dennis R. (2006). Embodied perception and the economy of action. *Perspectives on Psychological Science, 1,* 110–122.

Proffitt, Dennis R., Jeanine Stefanucci, Tom Banton & William Epstein (2003). The role of effort in perceived distance. *Psychological Science, 14,* 106–112.

Riener, Cedar R., Jeanine K. Stefanucci, Dennis Proffitt & Gerald L. Clore (2011). An effect of mood on the perception of geographical slant. *Cognition and Emotion, 25*, 174–182.

Schnall, Simone, Jennifer Benton & Sophie Harvey (2008). With a clean conscience: Cleanliness reduces the severity of moral judgments. *Psychological Science, 19,* 1219–1222.

Schnall, Simone, Jonathan Haidt, Gerald L. Clore & Alexander H. Jordan (2008). Disgust as embodied moral judgment. *Personality and Social Psychology Bulletin, 34*, 1096–1109.

Schnall, Simone, Kent D. Harber, Jeanine Stefanucci & Dennis R. Proffitt (2008). Social support and the perception of geographical slant. *Journal of Experimental Social Psychology, 44*, 1246–1255.

Schnall, Simone, Jessica K. Witt, Jason Augustyn, Jeanine Stefanucci, Dennis R. Proffitt & Gerald L. Clore (2005). Invasion of personal space influences perception of spatial layout. *Journal of Vision, 5,* 198.

Schnall, Simone, Jonathan R. Zadra & Dennis R. Proffitt (2010). Direct evidence for the economy of action: Glucose and the perception of geographical slant. *Perception , 39, 464–482.*

Schubert, Thomas W. (2005). Your Highness: Vertical positions as perceptual symbols of power. *Journal of Personality and Social Psychology, 89,* 1–21.

Schwarz, Norbert & Gerald L. Clore (1983). Mood, misattribution, and judgments of well-being: Informative and directive functions of affective states. *Journal of Personality and Social Psychology, 45,* 513–523.

Seeman, Teresa E. & S. Leonard Syme (1987). Social networks and coronary artery disease: A comparison of the structure and function of social relations as predictors of disease. *Psychosomatic Medicine, 49,* 341–354.

Sherman, Gary D. & Gerald L. Clore (2009). The color of sin: White and black are perceptual symbols of moral purity and pollution. *Psychological Science, 20,* 1019–1025

Smith, Eliot R. & Gün R. Semin (2004). Socially situated cognition: Cognition in its social context. In M.P. Zanna (Ed.), Advances in Experimental Social Psychology: Academic Press.

Sommer, Robert (1959). Studies in personal space. *Sociometry, 22,* 247–260.

Spellman, Barbara A. & Simone Schnall (2009). Embodied rationality. *Queen's Law Journal , 35, 117–164.*

Stefanucci, Jeanine K. & Dennis R. Proffitt (2009). The roles of altitude and fear in the perception of height. *Journal of Experimental Psychology: Human Perception and Performance, 35,* 424–438.

Stefanucci, Jeanine K., Dennis R. Proffitt, Gerald L. Clore & Nazish Parekh (2008). Skating down a steeper slope: Fear influences the perception of geographical slant. *Perception, 37,* 321–323.

Stefanucci, Jeanine K. & Justin Storbeck (2009). Don't look down: Emotional arousal elevates height perception. *Journal of Experimental Psychology: General, 138,* 131–145.

Teachman, Bethany A., Jeanine K. Stefanucci, Elise M. Clerkin, Meghan W. Cody & Dennis R. Proffitt (2008). A new mode of fear expression: Perceptual bias in height fear. *Emotion, 8,* 296–301.
Thoits, Peggy A. (1986). Social support as coping assistance. *Journal of Consulting and Clinical Psychology, 54,* 416–423.
Thorndyke, Perry W. (1981). Distance estimation from cognitive maps. *Cognitive Psychology, 13,* 526–550.
Tucker, Mike & Rob Ellis (1998). On the relations of seen objects and components of potential actions. *Journal of Experimental Psychology: Human Perception and Performance, 24,* 830–846.
Tversky, Amos & Daniel Kahneman (1981). The framing of decisions and the psychology of choice. *Science, 211,* 453–458.
Tversky, Barbara (2000). Levels and structure of cognitive mapping. In R. Kitchin & S.M. Freundschuh (Eds.). *Cognitive mapping: Past, present and future.* London: Routledge.
Varela, Francisco J., Evan T. Thompson & Eleanor Rosch (1991). *The embodied mind: Cognitive science and human experience.* Cambridge, MA: MIT Press.
Wilson, Margaret (2002). Six views of embodied cognition. *Psychonomic Bulletin and Review, 9,* 625–636.
Williams, Lawrence E. & John A. Bargh (2008). Experiencing physical warmth promotes interpersonal warmth. *Science, 322,* 606–607.
Willis, Frank N. (1966). Initial speaking distance as a function of the speaker's relationship. *Psychonomic Science, 5,* 221–222.
Winkielman, Piotr, Norbert Schwarz, Tedra A. Fazendeiro & Rolf Reber (2003). The hedonic marking of processing fluency: Implications for evaluative judgment. In Jochen Musch & Karl Christoph Klauer (Eds.), *The psychology of evaluation: Affective processes in cognition and emotion* (pp. 189–217). Mahwah, NJ: Erlbaum.
Witt, Jessica K., Dennis R. Proffitt & William Epstein (2004). Perceiving distance: A role of effort and intent. *Perception, 33,* 577–590.
Witt, Jessica K., Dennis R. Proffitt & William Epstein (2005). Tool use affects perceived distance but only when you intend to use it. *Journal of Experimental Psychology: Human Perception and Performance, 31,* 880–888.
Witt, Jessica K. & Dennis R. Proffitt (2007). Perceived slant: A dissociation between perception and action. *Perception, 36,* 249–257.
Zajonc, Robert B. (1968). Attitudinal effects of mere exposure. *Journal of Personality and Social Psychology, 9 (2, Pt. 2),* 1–27.
Zhong, Chen-Bo & Geoffrey J. Leonardelli (2008). Cold and lonely: Does social exclusion literally feel cold? *Psychological Science, 19,* 838–842.

More than a metaphor: How the understanding of power is grounded in experience

Thomas W. Schubert, Sven Waldzus, and Beate Seibt[1]

Abstract

Judgment and thinking about power, a universal form of human sociality, is intimately tied to spatial cues: Nonverbal communication, cultural production of power symbols, and metaphors of power all make use of the vertical spatial dimension. We argue that this overlap is due to a grounding of the concept of power in spatial thought. Evidence confirming this proposition can be found in experiments showing the impact of highly schematized spatial cues on judgments of power. We will discuss how semantic network theories, embodied theories of cognition, and conceptual metaphor theory fare in explaining and predicting the combined evidence on nonverbal behavior, cultural production, and metaphors. In particular, we will ask what role language in the form of metaphors plays for our understanding of power as size and elevation: Whether it is causal, or mainly an outcome of other processes that are not based on language.

1. Introduction

Diverse languages refer to social authority as *power* or *force*. These linguistic practices are more than simply lexical metaphors; they are collective cognitive representations of what [authority ranking] consists of: Authority **is** being above, greater, and more powerful.

A. P. Fiske (2004, p. 100)

---

[1] The preparation of this chapter was supported by a Feodor Lynen Research Fellowship from the Alexander von Humboldt Foundation awarded to Thomas Schubert and a Research Fellowship from the Deutsche Forschungsgemeinschaft awarded to Beate Seibt. We are grateful for the comments provided by Anne Maass, Caterina Suitner, Tomás Palma, and Lotte Thomsen on an earlier version of this chapter, and the inspiring discussion of this chapter in the Relational Models Summer Meetings Group of 2009.

> The most momentous experiences and deepest emotions associated with growing up are crystallized in a scheme of vertical classification.
>
> B. Schwartz (1981, p. 171)

Power is a concept that is important to every human being's social life. From early on, infants have to cope with others' influence over them, and to find ways to gain influence on others' behavior themselves. Finding the right position in authority structures remains an important task throughout life. Accordingly, judging another person's potential for having influence over oneself, and judging one's own potential to influence another person, are spontaneously and efficiently performed daily tasks. Judgments of other people's power use a host of nonverbal cues from the human body and its dynamic movement: face, posture, size, expressiveness, voice (Hall, Coats, & Smith LeBeau, 2005).

Unlike other animals, humans also use cues that go beyond the body, namely elements of the created environment (architecture, furniture, clothes), to judge power. Cues from the human body which are interpreted as indicating power, such as size and elevation, are also interpreted when they appear disconnected from the body in the form of large cars and high towers. In addition, power and status are metaphorically described as spatial relations to such an extent that power and space are intuitively identical. It seems that we are so used to talk of power and status as size and elevation that these have almost come to define the concept of power itself.

It also seems that as potential influence based on bodily strength becomes less important in hierarchically structured societies with institutionalized forms of power, the understanding of power relies more heavily on expressions of size and elevation in cultural artifacts. This tendency to extract cues of power and status from culturally specific artifacts may have been instrumental for developing social hierarchies in larger groups lacking constant face-to-face interaction in the first place (Earle, 2004). It may also be a necessary condition for the constitution of enduring shared representations of power relations, and thereby allow the coordination of actions and complementary role behavior in larger groups (A.P. Fiske, 1991). As larger groups could not be dominated by bodily force alone, legitimacy and consensus became important for the maintenance of power structures. Artifacts emphasizing size and elevation such as crowns and temples enhance both. Consequently, they stabilize societies, but they also make it harder to get rid of despots.

In the current chapter, we explore the complex web of nonverbal cues, cultural production of power symbols, and metaphors of power. The goal is to look at them together instead of separately, and to discuss which theories can explain their commonalities. We first elaborate on the nonverbal cues used for the judgment of power, and then report recent experimental evidence on the impact of their schematized versions. We will then discuss the role of metaphors as underlying our understanding of power and size, and how various theories fare in explaining and predicting the complete picture. In particular, we will ask what role language in the form of metaphors plays for our understanding of power as size and elevation: Whether it is causal, or mainly an outcome of other processes that are not based on language. Our review will be structured by the idea that nonverbal cues to power serve as a template for the use of spatial cues in other modalities – language and artifacts.

In order to allow us a broad overview, throughout this chapter we will simply subsume various related but actually distinct concepts like dominance, power, authority and leadership under the concept of power, in line with other general reviews of the literature (Hall et al., 2005).

2. Size and strength determines influence

For any animal that competes with others for resources (e.g., food or mates), or strives to actually consume other animals as food, bodily strength is a crucial factor of success. Animals are attuned to indices of strength and size, which are very predictive of competitiveness. Freedman (1979, p. 92) summarized this as "throughout nature the rule is the bigger, the more dangerous". Some prey animals have evolved means to create the illusion of body size and thus strength to deter predators.

In humans, we can distinguish two components of the link between power on the one hand and strength because of larger size on the other. First, larger bodily strength allows moving others and coercing them (e.g., the larger toddler hustling a smaller child or taking away a toy from him/her). Second, larger strength frees a person from pressures others try to put on them, and allows them to not yield to others' attempts to influence them (e.g., the larger child resists attempts of a smaller child to push her away). Let us call these two aspects influence and self-determination.

Humans experience the impact of size difference on relative power from very early on. Infants and toddlers have to cope with the bodily strength of their parents and older children when trying to achieve influence, or when trying to resist influence by others. Larger toddlers are more likely to use physical means of social influence: taller, heavier and bulkier children at age 3 have been found to be more aggressive, and body characteristics at this age in fact predict aggression at age 11 (Raine, Reynolds, Venables, Mednick, & Farrington, 1998). Size differences between men and women continue to be a determinant for violence between the genders even at adult age (Felson, 2002).

3. Appraisals of power are tuned to cues of strength and size

Thinking is for doing, and social cognition is for preparing and coordinating social interactions (S.T. Fiske, 1992). Accordingly, one of the most important functions of the processing of nonverbal social signals is to provide a fast appraisal of other individuals upon encounter. Two basic questions seem to be central: Does the other person mean good or harm for me? And, is the person capable of actually having that influence on me? These questions lead to judgments on the two dimensions of trustworthiness and dominance (Oosterhof & Todorov, 2008) or warmth and competence (S.T. Fiske, Cuddy, & Glick, 2007). Abundant evidence shows that dominance judgments are based on nonverbal cues indicating bodily strength. In the following, we will discuss evidence on height, facial features and expressions, posture, and gestures.

3.1. Height

When male strangers approach children of 9–12 months, the height at which the children themselves are determines their affective reaction. Weinraumb and Putney (1978) found that children who are placed lower (89 or 127 cm) react more negatively than children who are placed higher (183 cm) height. Apparently, children are afraid of strangers (at least males) towering over them. In adults, perceiving somebody from below (i.e., looking up to her or him) leads to the perception that this person is more dominant, compared to looking down on him (Giessner, Ryan, & Schubert, 2009; Kraft, 1987).

Height is comparative – somebody is only tall or short in comparison to the others, and to the perceiver. For instance, comparatively taller soccer players are more often considered to have committed a foul than their smaller opponents (van Quakebeke & Giessner, 2010). On average, bodily height is a robust predictor of achieved status and income at least for men (Hensley & Cooper, 1987; Melamed & Bozionelos, 1992; Gawley, Perks, & Curtis, 2009; Mueller & Mazur, 2001; Judge & Cable, 2004).

However, it is possible that height is only a proxy to the more important dimension of muscular strength. Muscular strength, especially of the upper body, is crucial for fighting ability in close combat. Humans are capable to easily and accurately judge fighting ability and muscular strength (Sell et al., 2008).

3.2. Face

Children and women are, on average, shorter and weaker than men. Accordingly, faces that exhibit features of maturity and masculinity are judged to be more dominant than faces that appear to belong to young or female individuals, presumably because both traits signal physical strength (Oosterhof & Todorov, 2008). Indeed, judged dominance and masculinity of men's faces predict their handgrip strength (Fink, Neave, & Seydel, 2007). Furthermore, dominance and masculinity apparent in men's faces may index physiological parameters that are relevant for dominance, such as prenatal testosterone levels (Neave, Laing, Fink, & Manning, 2003), and serve as an honest signal to men's potential to achieve a high status (Mueller & Mazur, 1997). To judge a lack of maturity and masculinity, both the shape of the face as well as features of the face itself are interpreted. Such a lack of maturity and masculinity is called babyishness. Adult men score lowest on this dimension, and babies highest, with adult women falling in between. Features most consistently associated with babyishness are (1) low rather than high vertical placement of facial features, (2) short rather than long features, (3) a small, round, or receding jaw rather than a large jaw, and (4) large or round eyes rather than small eyes (Marsh, Adams, & Kleck, 2005; Zebrowitz & Montepare, 1992). Such features elicit protective responses and caretaking behavior (Berry & McArthur, 1985, 1986).

The association of mature features with dominance extends beyond features of the resting face to facial expressions of emotions. Some facial expressions seem to mimic features of mature vs. immature faces and elicit the associated reactions in observers. The facial expressions of surprise and fear, the function of which is to motivate others to careful and helpful treatment, mimic the face of a baby. The facial expression of anger, in contrast, which entails the motivation to have influence on others and change them, leads to the perception that the expressing person is more dominant, and it does so by mimicking the mature face (Marsh et al., 2005; Zebrowitz, Kikuchi, & Fellous, 2007; Hess, Blairy, & Kleck, 2000; Knutson, 1996; Chiao et al., 2008).

3.3. Posture

Apart from actual body size and height, and their correlates maturity and masculinity, apparent body size and height in the form of extended or constricted postures also influence appraisals of power and dominance. An open body posture is produced by extended arms and legs: composed of open and extended legs, arms away from the body, or behind the head. Such a posture is a valid sign of actual power or dominance in the sense that it is more often shown by dominant or high status individuals, and it is also frequently used as a cue in power judgments (Hall et al., 2005). Note that this tendency extends to behavioral patterns: The size of one's signature increases with social status (Aiken & Zweigenhaft, 1978; Zweigenhaft, 1970). The opposite is a crouched and constricted posture that diminishes apparent body size. Perceiving such postures seems to have effects even without the necessity of a conscious judgment of power. Individuals who interact with a person showing either an expanded or constricted body posture are more likely to adopt the opposite posture than to mimic the perceived posture, leading to compatible postures in terms of an *ad hoc* developing status hierarchy. Furthermore, assuming the compatible instead of the mimicking posture leads to more positive affect (Tiedens & Fragale, 2003). Thus, body postures indicative of power not only influence perceptions and impressions, but directly social behavior.

Just as mature features of the face seem to be mimicked by emotional displays of anger, the extended body posture indicating high status seems to be mimicked by the display of pride. The pride expression typically involves upward extended arms and an elevated head (Tracy & Robins, 2004). It is likely that this posture is biologically innate, as it is also shown by congenitally blind athletes after winning (Tracy & Matsumoto, 2008).[2] The extended body posture might in fact have several different connotations that relate to power. First, it might simply simulate a larger body and thereby larger strength. Second, it might indicate that one's actions are unconstrained by the environment, or self-determined. This would be in line with findings that greater emotional expressiveness is also a valid sign of power (Hall et al., 2005), and that action orientation is perceived as indicating power (Magee, 2009).

The opposite of pride, embarrassment and shame, should then be expressed by a constricted posture. Not surprisingly, then, a bowed head, constricting the body, is part of the appeasement behavior shown by humans when they are embarrassed. Along with the typical shrugged shoulders, it decreases perceived body size. The same behavior is shown by other mammals, such as macaques, baboons, and wolves (Keltner & Buswell, 1997). Darwin (1872) hypothesized that behaviors that reduce apparent body size reduce aggression by others, and this seems indeed to work:

---

2   An alternative explanation could be that blind athletes are systematically reinforced during their career when displaying this kind of posture, or even explicitly taught how to behave when they win.

Playground aggression often stops when the attacked child decreases displayed body size, for instance by crouching down to tie shoes (Ginsburg, Pollman, & Wauson, 1977). In adults, the bowed head induces impressions of submissiveness and inferiority, while a raised head induces impressions of dominance (Mignault & Chaudhuri, 2003).

In sum, we see that a number of nonverbal cues are used to judge power. These cues seem all to be related to strength and thus potential for influence and self-determination. In addition, it becomes apparent that emotional expressions such as those for embarrassment, anger, surprise, fear, or pride, use these same cues to convey dominance/power or submission/powerlessness. It is not yet clear whether all these different indices are proxies for one underlying dimension, such as the ability to prevail in close combat, which seems to be most closely correlated with upper body strength, or whether they developed from different sources. Other sources could include the ability to withstand or withdraw, which might be closely correlated with total body mass, but also with speed and ability to climb, or the motivation to fight, which might be correlated with certain testosterone-markers in the face.

4. Size and strength cues influence power judgments even when schematized and abstracted

We have seen that bodily cues about size and strength are important cues for power appraisals – but how can we explain that architecture and indeed language makes use of the same kinds of cues? Is there a connection in the sense that affordances inherent in the ecology of human bodies shape also the more generalized use of power cues? If so, the same cues need to function even if they are very schematized and abstracted from the human body.

The starting point of schematization may already be the cue of elevation, which is another nonverbal cue that is used in judgments. For instance, when in simple drawings of two persons one is depicted as standing higher (on a pedestal), then that person is judged to be more dominant (Schwartz, Tesser, & Powell, 1982; Spiegel & Machotka, 1974). It is not directly clear how this could indicate bodily strength. One possibility is to assume that there is, on average, an ecological advantage of being higher up when it comes to inner-species fights, as gravity makes throwing, jumping and hitting more effective combat means for those in a higher position. Another, and more convincing, possibility is that the cues associated with power are much more abstract and schematic than the concrete nonverbal cues described above, such as shape of the face and size of the body.

Indeed, it seems that nonverbal cues of power can be schematized to a considerable extent. Simple line drawings featuring diagonal lines and acute angles with downward pointing vertices (see Figure 1) are sufficient to elicit judgments of greater potency, greater activity, and less positivity (Aronoff, Barclay, & Stevenson, 1988). Similarly, diagonal and angular movement patterns convey threat, while round movement patterns convey warmth (Aronoff, Woike, & Hyman, 1992; Aronoff, 2006).

The pictures and movements presented in the studies by Aronoff and colleagues are still very suggestive of the human body; some of them might be interpreted as depicting specific body parts (e.g., eyebrows). Yet, recent evidence shows that the stimuli can be even more abstract and still elicit the same impression. When pictures of faces are presented at the top of the screen, the person is judged to be more powerful than when the same pictures are shown at the bottom of the screen (Meier, Hauser, Robinson, Kelland Friesen, & Schjeldahl, 2007). The same holds when pictures of a powerful animal such as a lion or wolf are shown on a screen: Presentation at the top leads to more respect for the animal than presentation at the bottom (Schubert, 2005). The elevation of pictures has downstream consequences as well: Men judge females depicted at the bottom as more attractive, while women judge males depicted at the top as more attractive (Meier & Dionne, 2009).

In a study by Giessner and Schubert (2007), participants read a short description of a male manager next to a chart depicting the simple organizational structure: the manager, symbolized by a box, and below, connected to him with a vertical line, his five subordinates. Two versions of this organigram were used. They differed only in the length of the vertical line and thus the elevation of the manager above his subordinates. The vertical difference was either about the height of one of the boxes itself, or twice as high. After reviewing the information, participants judged the power this manager had. Those participants who saw the picture with the more elevated manager judged him as more powerful. Thus, even when elevation is perceived without any clear reference to the human body, it is still interpreted as a cue to power.

Figure 1. Acute angles with downward pointing vertices convey potency, negative evaluation, and activity (Aronoff et al., 1988)

These studies already schematize vertical space to a considerable extent. However, one might still wonder whether the pictorial representation of the faces or the organigram elicited some kind of reference to the human body. For instance, it could be that the manager box is somehow interpreted as symbolizing his body. Can the elevation cue be abstracted even further?

One way to explore this question is to use just words that are shown on a computer screen, and to vary their vertical location. Furthermore, instead of looking at the judgment outcome itself, one can investigate the response latency with which it is made. This approach has been used in other domains, for instance to investigate representations of words that are referring to concrete objects: When one has the task to judge whether the word *branch* is semantically associated with *root*, this decision is made more quickly when *branch* is displayed above *root* rather than the other way around (Zwaan & Yaxley, 2003).

Adopting the same approach for studying elevation as a cue for power appraisals has the advantage that the cue is very abstract. A number of studies reported in Schubert (2005) confirm indeed that nevertheless, elevation influences power appraisals. When typical pairs of powerful and powerless groups are shown on the screen (e.g., *master* and *slave*), the powerful group is more quickly identified when it is at the top, and the powerless group is more quickly identified when it is at the bottom. Even when just one group label is shown on the screen, and either at the top or at the bottom, a compatible vertical position speeds up response latencies. Moreover, a visual elevation cue is not even necessary: Categorizing a group label that appears in the middle of the screen as powerful is easier when the up arrow button on the keyboard has to be pressed rather than the down arrow button, and the reverse holds for categorizing powerless groups.

Vertical location on a screen has been found to also influence valence judgments. Positive words such as *ethical* are judged more quickly as positive when they were shown at the top rather than at the bottom of the screen, while the opposite is true for negative words (Meier & Robinson, 2004; Schubert, 2005). Another study showed that the effects for power judgments are independent of the valence of a group label. When judging power, the valence of a group is rather unimportant for facilitation by vertical location. In contrast, when judging valence, the power of a group is rather unimportant. Thus, judging *dictator* as powerful is facilitated when it is shown at the top, but judging *dictator* as bad is facilitated when it is shown at the bottom of the screen (Schubert, 2005).

The group labels used in these studies were well-known powerful or powerless groups. Does the same also hold for power relations among people one has just recently learned about? Recent evidence suggests that the answer is yes (von Hecker, Conway, & Sankaran, 2009). In these studies, participants learned about a hierarchy among four persons. They were then shown the names of two out of the four persons above each other on the screen, either in a manner that was compatible with the hierarchy (powerful on top, powerless at the bottom) or not. They had to identify either the more powerful or the less powerful target by pressing the up vs. down arrow button to indicate whether it was up or down on the screen, respectively. Results showed that targets were more quickly identified when they were in the compatible positions.

As we have seen above, elevation is one nonverbal cue to power judgments, but there is by far more evidence that actual and apparent body size drives power judgments. Thus, the question arises: Is there evidence that schematized and abstracted size cues influence power judgments as well? Such evidence has been reported recently (Schubert, Waldzus, & Giessner, 2009; Schubert, Waldzus, & Seibt, 2008). The paradigm used in these studies is similar to the response latency paradigms by Schubert (2005). Group labels were presented on the screen, but this time always in the middle of it. What varied was the font size; it was either regular or more than twice as large and bold. In one study, participants saw two groups at once, one powerful and one powerless, with the font size either compatible or incompatible, and had to find the more powerful or the less powerful group. In two other studies, participants saw always only one group, and had to categorize it as either powerful or powerless. Response latencies and accuracy were analyzed. The consistent outcome was that if the font size is compatible with the group's power, the judgments are facilitated (i.e., quicker and more accurate).

If we look at this line of evidence, we see that even with more and more schematization, the effects of spatial cues on power judgments persist. The study with the most extreme schematization is perhaps one study also published in Giessner and Schubert (2007). In this study, participants again read about a manager and then judged his power and influence. However, between the information and the judgment, they had to perform an ostensibly unrelated task of repeatedly comparing two lines, a standard and a target line. Participants always had to estimate how much longer the target line was compared to the standard line. Four different groups of participants saw four different versions of this task: The two lines either differed a lot or just slightly, and they were either vertically or horizontally arranged. Judgments of the manager after the line comparison task were influenced by the difference between the lines only when they were vertical. Those who repeatedly saw two vertical lines that differed a lot judged the manager to have more influence over his subordinates than those who repeatedly saw two vertical lines that differed only a little bit. In contrast, the length difference did not matter when the lines were shown horizontally. This suggests that even if a vertical spatial difference is activated completely independently of a social target, it can nevertheless have an influence on power judgments.

Taken together, these findings show that judgments of power take into account spatial cues about elevation or size even when these cues are so schematic and abstract that they do not convey anything about actual strength differences.

More recent evidence shows that the link between space and power might in fact extend beyond perception and influence the expectation of perception – or, in other words, attention. This research used a paradigm developed by Meier and Robinson (2004). In an innovative experiment, they had participants first categorize words that appeared on a screen as either positive or negative, and then identify a letter on the screen as either a *p* or a *q*. The letter was either displayed at the top or at the bottom of the screen. After seeing a negative word, participants could identify the letter more quickly when it appeared at the bottom of the screen rather than at the top. The reverse was true for positive words (albeit not significantly). This experiment suggests that understanding something positive immediately orients attention towards the upper half of the frame of reference. Does this also hold for power stimuli? In a recent paper, van Dantzig and colleagues explored this question (van Dantzig, Boot, Pecher, Giessner, & Schubert, 2008). They repeated Meier and Robinson's experiment, but this time participants categorized group labels presented via headphones as either powerful or powerless before identifying the *p* or *q*. Results confirmed that understanding the label of a powerful or powerless group also orients attention upwards vs. downwards, respectively.

More evidence on how power influences attention has been recently published by Robinson, Moeller, and colleagues. These studies did not investigate the effects of the power attributed to a stimulus, but at the effects of dominance as a personality trait. They showed that individuals who described themselves as more dominant attended more to stimuli in the vertical dimension than individuals who described themselves as less dominant (Moeller, Robinson, & Zabelina, 2008). Other studies show that dominant individuals, but not non-dominant individuals, attend more to stimuli that appear up rather than down (Robinson, Zabelina, Ode, & Moeller, 2008). Even though these results are not perfectly consistent with each other, the results suggest that one's expectations and motivations in social relations constantly influence spatial attention even when no social stimuli are present.

5. The social use of schematized vertical cues

As we just saw, spatial cues about elevation and size enter power judgments even if they are dissociated from the human body, schematized, and abstracted. We argue that it is precisely this fact that allows these cues to be used in human communication about social relations. This starts at a very basic level, as a study by Giessner and Schubert (2007) has shown: In a reversal of the manager study already cited above, participants read descriptions of either a powerful or a less powerful manager of a group of subordinates. They were then asked to illustrate the organizational structure by placing a picture of the manager in a picture where the subordinates were already shown, more or less aligned on a horizontal axis. Those who had read about the powerful manager placed his picture significantly higher than those who had read about the less powerful manager.

This result was found even though no explicit communicative intention was associated with the pictures. We can expect that such effects are even stronger if there is a communicative context present. Because they are indices of power, size and elevation will be used in many different ways to reinforce and perpetuate human hierarchies. A recent review by Alan Page Fiske (2004) concludes that the use of elevation and size to communicate hierarchy is a culturally universal practice. The best evidence comes from systematic anthropological field work in the Pacific region: Solomon Islands (White, 1985), Tikopia (Firth, 1970), Micronesia (Garvin & Riesenberg, 1952; Keating, 2000), and Fiji (Toren, 1999). The practices identified in this field work use both the body and artifacts. First, cultural practices induce bodily behaviors that ritualize postures which elicit appraisals of high or low dominance and power. Bowing as a sign of submission and deference is common. Other prescribed behaviors are sitting vs. standing and walking on knees. Alltogether, vertical positions in the environment are tightly regulated. Second, architecture and furniture is used to create differences in elevation: Kings sit on thrones; houses of people with higher rank are built on platforms (Toren, 1990; Hewes, 1955). These features are nicely illustrated by the description that Garvin and Riesenberg (1952, p. 211) provide of the ceremonials in the communal house of the Ponape in Micronesia:

> The building is arranged with low platforms on the two sides and a higher platform at the front; the Nahnmwarrki, Nahnken [feudal chiefs], their wives, and sometimes other high chiefs ... sit on the high front platform facing the rest of the people on the side platforms and on the central ground-level area; the Nahnmwarrki's position is farthest to the front. No one, with certain exceptions, may sit or stand so that his head is higher than that of the Nahnmwarrki. In passing a man of high rank a commoner must bend low, and he must crawl before a seated chief. If a man wishes to climb a tree near the

house of a man of high title, he must first obtain permission from that man; and he must descend if a chief comes near.

A.P. Fiske (2004) points out that such evidence is available for many other places and times, ranging from ancient Egypt and Rome (Firth, 1970) to Mayans in Chiapas to modern day advertisements (Goffman, 1976). Indeed, a large chair behind a large desk can still prime students to feel and act as if they were powerful (Chen, Lee-Chai, & Bargh, 2001).

6. Cognition and the space-power link: Association, perceptual symbol, or metaphor?

We have seen that size and elevation cues are used to appraise power when they appear as features of the human body. The same is true when the cues are not features of the human body. The latter fact is exploited by cultural practices to communicate and solidify hierarchies. An important question is how the cues in their schematized form can still be understood as denoting power. The remainder of this chapter will evaluate the proposed answers to this question.

This question is crucial in order to explore some effects that we have not mentioned so far. The evidence presented until now concerned effects of spatial and other perceived cues on power judgments. However, there is also evidence for the reversed causal direction. For instance, several studies have shown that judgments about someone else's dominance distort the judged height of that person. Persons who are thought to be more dominant, or have authority, are also judged to be taller (Wilson, 1968; Dannemaier & Thumin, 1964; Higham & Carment, 1992). Similarly, persons who display nonverbal cues of a high status, like an open posture, are judged to be taller (Marsh, Yu, Schechter, & Blair, 2009). This shows that there is a bidirectional link between the concepts of space and power in human mental representation. Together, the persisting impact of schematized cues and the existence of a bidirectional link lead to the question how the power-space link is mentally represented.

There are currently three main approaches that compete for an explanation of this link: semantic network theories, simulation theories, and metaphor theories. All three make different proposals regarding the connection between concrete and abstract cues. Typically, the literature on embodiment pits the simulation account against the semantic network account. In many papers (including our own past work), the simulation account is not differentiated at all from the conceptual metaphor account. However, we hope to show in the remainder of this chapter that it is fruitful to examine all three accounts separately regarding the evidence presented in this chapter.

6.1. Semantic network theories

Semantic network theories propose that learning about the social environment implies the construction of a network in which abstract representations come to stand for perceived stimuli (objects, people, behaviors, events). These formed representations are assumed to be amodal – they have lost the sensory and motor qualities of the original experience of the event (Anderson, 1983, 1993). They are typically depicted as nodes in a network with uni- or bidirectional links. In the depictions, the nodes are labeled, and indeed one can think of these nodes as *quasi verbal*. It is assumed that the activation of one node spreads to other nodes. Because of this spreading activation, the perception of one stimulus can prime other knowledge and thereby influence subsequent thought, feeling and behavior. Such semantic network theories have been inspiring the field of cognition and social cognition for over three decades and let to tremendous advances (Greenwald et al., 2001; Smith, 1998). In particular, they helped to identify and understand automatic effects and overcome the notion that the human mind is governed by conscious, rational thought (Bargh, 1997).

One problem that this form of theorizing is facing is the so-called symbol grounding problem (Harnad, 1990). Put simply, the question is how the nodes in the network acquire their labels, if they always only refer to other nodes. Other, more empirical, challenges have been findings that show rather direct effects of cognition on behavior and of behavior on cognition (Glenberg, 1997; Hommel, Müsseler, Aschersleben, & Prinz, 2001; Barsalou, 2008; Niedenthal, 2007). Some theorists tried to integrate such findings with classic semantic network theories by assuming that in addition to quasi-verbal amodal nodes, the network also includes direct links to perceptual and motor representations (Bargh, Chen, & Burrows, 1996; Dijksterhuis & Bargh, 2001; Mussweiler, 2006).

To explain the link between spatial cues and power with semantic network models, one could assume that the categorization of stimuli as high or big becomes associated over time with their categorization as powerful. This results in a bidirectional link between the nodes for high/big and powerful, and, because of spreading activation, allows for priming of one by the other. To evaluate how such a theory is able to account for the presented findings, the most interesting test cases are the interference paradigm studies (Schubert, 2005; Schubert et al., 2009; von Hecker et al., 2009), because they put most constraints on the theory and rule out conscious processes. How could one explain the finding that a group label presented at the top is more quickly categorized as powerful with semantic network theory? One could argue that perceiving the elevated word triggers the categorization of the spatial location as high, thereby activating a node representing "high," from which activation spreads to the associated node "powerful," which then facilitates the categorization of the presented group label as powerful.

Would this theoretical notion be able to explain the findings? Of course. Indeed, it seems that so far, there is almost no finding that could not be explained by a variant of semantic network theory, especially if one assumes the inclusion of modal content in the network. Some have thus argued that semantic network theory risks being unfalsifiable (note, however, that Machery, 2007, has claimed the same about the embodiment approach). What is more important for us, though, is that semantic network theory would not *a priori* predict the kind of effects presented earlier (Barsalou, 1999), while that is the case for the second category of theories, simulation theories.

6.2. Simulation theories

There are many different theories proposed under the label embodiment, and they often focus on very different assumptions (Wilson, 2002). The assumption that is most relevant for the present purpose is the idea that cognition is *modal*. In Wilson's words, the idea is that "even when decoupled from the environment, the activity of the mind is grounded in mechanisms that evolved for interaction with the environment—that is, mechanisms of sensory processing and motor control" (p. 626). This is what we refer to as simulation.

Perhaps the most frequently used theory of this kind is perceptual symbol systems (PSS) theory. In this theory, Barsalou (1999) implemented the grounding idea by proposing that primary modality-specific perception areas in the brain are not only crucial for perception, but also for a host of higher level cognitive processes such as working memory, long term memory, and conceptual knowledge representation. The key assumption is that these cognitive processes re-activate the modality-specific perception areas that were involved in learning the recalled or simulated content. Each cognitive process consists of simulations that re-activate modality-specific perceptual areas. For instance, working memory processes activate the primary visual cortex when they simulate a visual experience. It is worth noting that PSS includes propositions on how it is implemented in brain functioning. The theory is supported by a large body of evidence with behavioral measures (such as production, recognition, and judgment), as well as with neuropsychological methods (Barsalou, 2008).

Again, how could we explain the findings on the space-power link using this theory? To answer this question, we first have to look at how "powerful" is represented according to PSS. The theory proposes that aspects of experience that are attended to get stored in memory in schematic form. Such a schematized and stored element of experience is called a perceptual symbol. Importantly, re-activation of the perceptual symbol entails activation of the perceptual areas involved in its acquisition. These perceptual symbols can then be combined productively to form propositions. When experiences with powerful others or the self in a powerful position are made, a number of perceptual symbols are likely to be acquired – about bodily strength, height, vertical positions, postures, but also introspective states like emotions. These perceptual symbols are not recordings of the complete situations in which the experience were made. Instead, they are very selective and schematized aspects of the experience. For instance, experiences of moving other's bodies, or being pushed, of perceiving something big, or of looking up will be retained as perceptual symbols. These perceptual symbols get combined and associated with each other. They can then be used to run simulations of powerful others and being in power. Together, the frame of perceptual symbols and the simulations make up our knowledge about power.

Concerning the evidence collected with the interference paradigms, one could argue that in order to judge the power of a group or person (e.g. *master*) whose label is perceived, the power needs to be simulated. Because this simulation will entail the activation of perceptual symbols of vertical positions, the actually perceived information about vertical positions will interfere with or facilitate the simulation and thus influence the response latency of the power judgment.

Simulation theories like PSS can explain the findings on the space-power link just as easily as semantic network theories. In addition, however, they predict these findings *a priori*, and provide a more parsimonious explanation than semantic network models that conceptualize modal and amodal content to be linked in one network. By saying this, we do not claim that these kinds of associative networks do not exist or are not important. On the contrary, assuming a role for both, embodied simulations and associative networks, can help us make more precise predictions regarding the effects of activating the concept "power". Thinking of a group that is powerful should then have different consequences than thinking of an associate of power such as *plug* (Solomon & Barsalou, 2004; Louwerse & Jeuniaux, 2010). Whereas perceiving "generals" should redirect attention upwards, perceiving "plug" should rather redirect it downward. Yet, in a fraction of a second, both concepts might prime "high" through priming "power".

However, perhaps the biggest advantage of simulation theories is that they allow prediction and explanation of the implementation of these processes in the human brain. Recent research started to locate brain regions that are involved in dominance judgments from facial expressions and head postures (Chiao et al., 2008), and the inference of power from more abstract cues such as status insignias (Chiao et al., 2009).

6.3. Conceptual metaphor theory

Conceptual metaphor theory grew out of the work of the cognitive linguists George Lakoff and Mark Johnson on metaphors. In their influential book "Metaphors we live by" (Lakoff & Johnson, 1980), they argued that much of human cognitive processes are grounded in metaphors. Of special importance to our current purposes, they proposed that so-called orientational metaphors that build on spatial orientation organize whole systems of concepts. In particular, they argue that the concepts of *control* and *status* are understood on the basis of orientational metaphors that use the vertical spatial dimension: "HAVING CONTROL OR FORCE IS UP; BEING SUBJECT TO CONTROL OR FORCE IS DOWN," and "HIGH STATUS IS UP; LOW STATUS IS DOWN" (p. 15f).

The central claim of conceptual metaphor theory is that metaphors are not merely vehicles to talk about one thing by referring to something else. Rather, they help to understand and experience one thing in terms of something else: One domain, such as vertical space, acts as the source domain from which knowledge is transferred to the other domain, power. The source domain of a metaphor can thereby bring a certain structure to the target domain, and allow inferences that would not be possible without it. For instance, conceptualizing powerful as up in space can imply that the powerful entity has accumulated potential energy that can be unleashed onto the powerless down at the bottom.

Again, how would this theory explain the interference effects? Actually, conceptual metaphor theory itself does not provide a psychological process model for such effects. However, Boroditsky (2000, 2001) has proposed a process model that builds on conceptual metaphor theory and argues for asymmetric effects: Activation of the source domain should change judgments in the target domain, but activation of the target domain should not change perceptions in the source domain because the target domain depends on the source domain, but not the other way around. This notion can explain well the fact that spatial cues bias power judgments. However, it has problems explaining why power judgments do bias subsequent spatial attention (Zanolie et al., 2010, see also the chapter by Santiago, Román, & Ouellet, this volume).

The relation between the so-called target and source domain thus seems critical for a judgment on whether simulation or metaphor theories provide a more useful account. Simulation theorists acknowledge the role of metaphoric mapping in the elaboration of conceptual representations, but they sometimes argue that metaphors cannot be sufficient to explain the mental representation of abstract concepts. Barsalou (1999, p. 600) for instance stated:

A direct, nonmetaphorical representation of an abstract domain is essential for two reasons: first, it constitutes the most basic understanding of the domain. Knowing only that anger is like liquid exploding from a container hardly constitutes an adequate concept. If this is all that people know, they are far from having an adequate understanding of anger. Second, a direct representation of an abstract domain is necessary to guide the mapping of a concrete domain into it. A concrete domain cannot be mapped systematically into an abstract domain that has no content.

Let us look in more detail at conceptual metaphor theory to evaluate this critique. Lakoff and Johnston (1980) acknowledge that orientational metaphors like CONTROL IS UP arise from "the fact that we have bodies of the sort we have and that they function as they do in our physical environment" (p. 14). In other words, sensory and bodily experience with the natural and the culturally created environment is assumed to give rise to these metaphors. Regarding CONTROL IS UP, the cause is assumed to lie in experiences in which physical size and physical strength correlate, and those in which vertical position and power correlate. This statement reveals that conceptual metaphor theory, just like simulation theories, builds on correlated experiences and their abstraction, at least when it comes to this kind of metaphors.

Furthermore, Lakoff and Johnson (1980) acknowledged that the shortcuts referring to the metaphors, such as "CONTROL IS UP", may be misleading because they suggest an abstractness that goes beyond the abstractness present in the mental representation. For instance, the experiential basis of the metaphor MORE IS UP may differ from that of RATIONAL IS UP in a way that is not captured by the assigned label UP. The two UPs are not identical. This points again to the importance of the actual experience.

Recent formulations of the theory emphasize the grounding of metaphors in concrete experiences even more. Lakoff and Johnson (1999) emphasized the idea that correlations of experiences cause the formation of metaphors by (1) integrating C. Johnson's work on conflation and (2) adopting Grady's notion of primary metaphors (instead of orientational metaphors).

C. Johnson (1999) hypothesized that two concepts joined in a primary metaphor like MORE IS UP or AFFECTION IS WARMTH are for the learning child in the beginning not separated at all, but simply experienced as one, which leads to the creation of strong associations. Only later, the two concepts get cognitively differentiated, but the associations persist.

Grady (1997, 2007, 2005) also emphasized the grounding of conceptual metaphors in correlated experiences. He noted that observing correlations like those between higher and being more as a result of putting liquid into a container or piling things on top of each other "experientially motivates" the formation and use of conceptual metaphors like MORE IS UP:

> Source concepts for primary metaphors include UP, DOWN, HEAVY ..., various simple "force-dynamic" concepts ..., and so on. Corresponding target concepts are such basic building blocks of mental experience as DOMINANT ... These metaphors appear to arise directly from experience ... (Grady, 2007, p. 192f)

Grady (2007) also pointed out that because humans everywhere share the same kind of bodies and thus similar patterns of experience, a large part of the universality of certain metaphors can be explained by universality of correlated experiences.

Surprisingly, however, Grady (2007) also stated that while the source concept is directly experienced, the target concept is not. The examples he cited for this include UP IS DOMINANCE, DOWN IS SAD, HEAVY IS DIFFICULT, BRIGHT IS HAPPY, FORWARD IS SUCCESS, BACKWARD IS THE PAST, SWEET IS APPEALING. For these concepts, he claimed that "the unidirectionality ... is consistent and absolute. In each case, the perceptual concept is the source and is mapped onto the nonperceptual concept" (p. 193). From this assumed asymmetry in perceptual quality, Grady also derived a strong claim about unidirectionality of usage. For instance, he notes that as a result of the unidirectionality of HEAVY IS IMPORTANT, we can communicate that an issue is important by saying it is heavy, but we cannot indicate that a laptop is heavy by saying it is important.

It seems however that there is a logical problem with this analysis: How can an experiential correlation between quantity and height give rise to the metaphor MORE IS UP if more is never experienced directly? It appears that the notions of experiential correlation and conflation contradict the claim that a target and a source concept can be identified in absolute terms. In fact, most of the target concepts listed by Grady appear to have some directly perceivable aspects: Being dominated is experienced when being subject to physical force; happiness, sadness and appeal have clear introspective components independent of the source concepts, etc.[3]

---

3   Let us take another example: the metaphor that TIME IS MOTION IN SPACE. This may be the metaphor with the strongest evidence for asymmetry effects: Reasoning about time and reproduction of time intervals is affected by previously perceived spatial cues, but the reverse is not true (Casasanto & Boroditsky, 2008; Boroditsky, 2000). But even for this clearly asymmetrically used concept, Lakoff and Johnson (1980) note that it is grounded in experiencing "the correlation between an object moving toward us and the time it takes to get to us" (p. 59). Put differently, a rudimentary form of experiencing time (perhaps only short intervals) might exist before correlated experiences give rise to the spatialization of time (Jaynes, 1976) and the development of the proper metaphor, which then enhances the way time can be understood.

In fact, in their early work, Lakoff and Johnson (1980) noted that the apparent asymmetry in metaphor use is not due to physical experiences being more "basic than other kinds of experience, whether emotional, mental, cultural, or whatever" (p. 59). Instead, they argued that what makes physical experiences useful for conceptualizing other kinds of experiences via metaphors is that they are more "clearly delineated" (ibid.). However, a definition of that term is missing.

All things considered, it appears that conceptual metaphor theory and simulation theories are rather compatible when it comes to the processes they assume regarding concepts represented in orientational metaphors (Lakoff & Johnson, 1980) or primary metaphors (Grady, 1997; Lakoff & Johnson, 1999). At least for orientational/primary metaphors, conceptual metaphor theory clearly and consistently states that their formation is driven by correlations between different experiences. Simulation theories assume the same process to be at work when they argue that attention and schematization form modal representations of abstract concepts (Barsalou, 1999). Asymmetry effects between target and source domain, however, need a more precise characterization of the cognitive processes involved in the respective tasks. To our best knowledge, simulation theories are also mute on this point (see also Santiago et al., this volume; Zanolie et al., 2008).

7. Synthesizing embodiment and conceptual metaphor accounts for the embodiment of power

The comparison of semantic network approaches, embodiment and simulation accounts, and conceptual metaphor accounts suggests that simulation theories seem to be best equipped to explain the combined evidence on the effects of bodily and abstracted cues to power. The emerging picture is that a host of experiences in several modalities lead to the formation of perceptual symbols of power. Furthermore, these experiences correlate with each other, and therefore become associated with each other. These will include experiences with bodily force (with the self being both a subject and an object), size, and elevation. In addition, perceptual symbols in other modalities are likely: certain postures such as making a fist (Schubert, 2004; Schubert & Koole, 2009), standing upright (Stepper & Strack, 1993; Roberts & Arefi-Afshar, 2007), and possibly also loudness and a deep voice. Combined, they form a frame that allows the simulation of various aspects of the concept of power.

7.1. Is there an innate proclivity to associate size and spatial relations?

Many of these perceptual symbols can and will arise simply from the way the human body functions when interacting with the physical and social environment. From the invariance of the human body across cultures alone one could predict the similarity of most perceptual symbols across cultures (Lakoff & Johnson, 1980; Clark, 1973): Size is likely to equate power in most cultures as the default, even though this default can be overridden with practice (Schubert et al., 2009).

In addition, it is possible that humans have an innate proclivity to learn at least some of the associations described above, in particular the link between body size, and more generally size, and power. Gorillas, chimpanzees and bonobos establish dominance hierarchies with displays of fighting ability – often in the form of bluffing. In these displays, the large and sharp canines are shown, and the large erectile hair increases apparent body size (Boehm, 1999; Eibl-Eibesfeldt, 1971). Even though humans have lost the innately well-prepared displays and the profuse bristling bodily hair that accompanied those displays, it seems possible that we retained the disposition to associate the perception of such displays with power. It would have been acquired throughout evolution of Homo sapiens and its predecessors in the repeated task of learning these perceptual symbols. A process called Baldwinian selection can select for mechanisms that allow the fast and effortless learning (Richards, 1987). For instance, Baldwinian selection presumably equipped primates with a very efficient mechanism to learn fear of snakes (Öhman & Mineka, 2003). A.P. Fiske (2000, 2004) proposed that Baldwinian selection also supports the association of power and order in vertical space.

The existence of such an innate proclivity to represent dominance hierarchies and to identify them in vertical spatial relations would explain the early onset of this skill. Indeed, recent evidence suggests that children around the age of 1 readily attribute dominance to larger agents even if they have non-human bodies (Thomsen, Frankenhuis, Ingold-Smith, & Carey, 2011). Further, it would account for the overwhelming cultural ubiquity of associations between power and elevation or size (Fiske, 2004).

If such a proclivity exists, it would instantiate another "core system" of human cognition (Carey & Spelke, 1996), along with systems for the representation of objects, agents, numbers, geometry, and us vs. them (Spelke & Kinzler, 2007; Thomsen et al., 2011). These core systems provide a basis for the development of human cognition, and humans share them with many other animals. However, as all infants are also universally and from the beginning of their life confronted with others that are at the same time larger and more powerful, it will be crucial to go beyond showing the early onset of associating power with size.

7.2. Profiting from conceptual metaphor theory

We have seen that the space-power link can be fruitfully understood as the outcome of a learning process that involves modal representations, and that simulation theories are well-equipped to describe this process and predict its outcomes. Does this mean that we do not need conceptual metaphor theory to understand the metaphor that CONTROL IS UP? The answer is complex. On the one hand, the proponents of conceptual metaphor theory themselves propose a learning process based on experiential correlations for primary metaphors such as CONTROL IS UP, and thus come very close to embodiment theories concerning the acquisition process. It seems that understanding the space-power link based on perceptual symbols might allow a better understanding than couching it as primary metaphor.

On the other hand, metaphor theory seems to be better equipped to explain certain aspects of the space-power relation that we did not mention yet: the potential for inferential reasoning, the guiding role of language during schematization, and the usefulness of metaphors to identify perceptual symbols. Let us expand on these points.

Conceptual metaphor theory argues that a metaphor supports inferential reasoning about the target domain by recruiting constraints from and cognitive processes developed for the source domain. Applied to the field of power, this means: Our understanding of power and social status is based on reasoning about space and spatial order, and inferential processes developed for spatial reasoning. We want to give one example of inferences about space that seem to be applied to power (Schubert et al., 2009). Power is inherently *relational* because in addition to pure physical influence, it relies on many aspects that are only defined as a combination of the characteristics of the involved individuals: what is positive and negative for them, their ability to create these positive and negative reinforcements, their perceived legitimacy, etc. Because of this relational quality of power, a situation in which A has power over B and B has power over C does not necessarily imply that A has also power over C. However, if power is understood as size or elevation in space, one might easily commit the error of assuming transitivity because size and elevation, in contrast to power, are comparative, and not relational. Thus, understanding power as size might lead to the erroneous conclusion that A has power over C. Indeed, social hierarchies that use elevation as a crucial index of *status* construct it in a way that implies transitivity (A.P. Fiske, 2004).

Another domain in which a synthesis of metaphor and simulation approaches can contribute to the understanding of the space-power link is language. The linguistic representation of the space-power link in the form of metaphors is the primary interest of metaphor theory. Indeed, metaphors speaking of power as elevation, size and force seem to be used in most languages (Schwartz, 1981; A.P. Fiske, 2004). The simulation account assumes that each individual performs the schematization process anew and from scratch.

Metaphors, however, are transmitted in language; they are socially shared and may exist to a certain degree independent of the original experiential correlation. This explains why they are able to guide which correlations in the environment are picked and used for grounding conceptual representations. For example, "when things get better or easier (for instance, when health improves after illness), for English or German speakers, things go 'uphill'/'bergauf,' for Italians they go 'downhill', they are 'in discesa'" (A. Maass, personal communication, 12.08.2009).[4] Clearly, both metaphors are grounded in experienced correlations, but different ones are used, and language determines to a certain degree which are abstracted (in this example energetic states or opportunities to relax). When we acknowledge that the schematization process assumed by simulation theories works not only on experiences with the natural environment, but also on experiences with the culturally created environment in the form of artifacts such as furniture, and architecture, we see that a similar process might take place also outside of language. Cultures reify the perceptual symbols and metaphors in their environment, and these reifications serve as input for schematization processes of other individuals.

Acknowledging the importance of language for perceptual symbol has another effect. Simulation theories emphasize that language understanding is more than just a transcription of verbal content into a semantic network; in contrast, they hold that perceptual simulations of described scenes are constructed (Fischer & Zwaan, 2008; Zwaan, 2004). If such simulations are constructed during the understanding of space-power metaphors, we see another ecology emerging in which power and space are experienced as correlated. Perceptual content transmitted by metaphors and simulated during language understanding may serve again as input to schematization. This ecology adds to the correlated experiences of space and power in bodily interactions and cultural artifacts.

---

4   The GETTING BETTER IS DOWNWARD metaphor does not extent to power. Gaining social status is associated with upward movement also in Italian, as in "*arrampicatore sociale*" (the "*social climber*") or "*raggiungere la cima*" (reaching the top; M. Bianchi, personal communication, 21.10.2009).

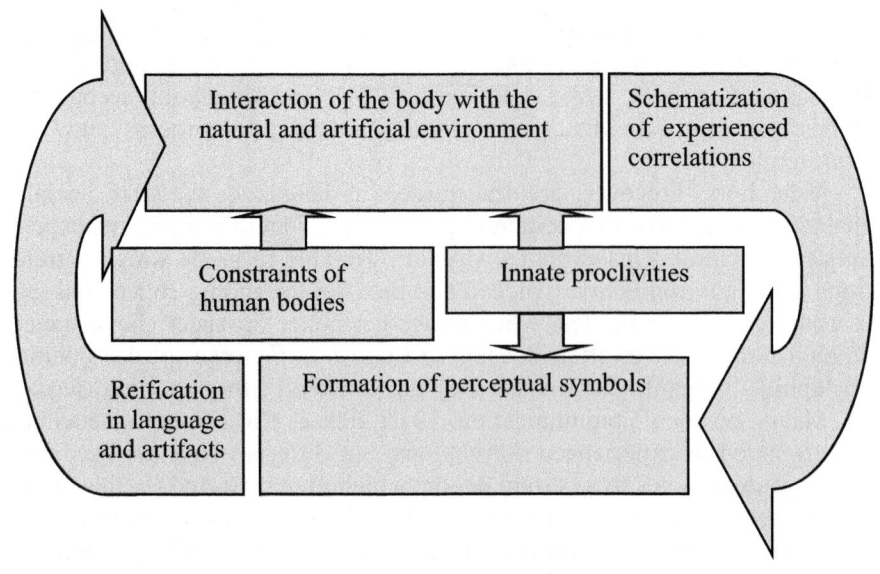

Figure 2. A model of schematization and reification of perceptual symbols, synthesizing individual and cultural processes

When we take these aspects together, we arrive at a model of perceptual symbol processes that takes both individual learning and cultural transmission processes into account. We depict that model in Figure 2. Human bodies constrain the possible interactions with the natural and artificial environment. The experiences made during these interactions are schematized into perceptual symbols. These symbols are themselves again reified in metaphors and artifacts, which serve as content for future interactions and guide further schematizations. Innate proclivities may guide both interactions and schematization processes.

An analysis of space-power metaphors might in fact be fruitful to understand the space-power link in more detail. So far, we have implicitly assumed that the link between up and powerful refers to a rather static situation that simply refers to arrangements in space. Several different spatial prepositions or constructions are used to refer to this link: in English, powerful is denoted as *up*, as *above*, but also as *over*, while powerless is associated with *down*, *below*, but also *under*. Are these terms interchangeable, and do they mean the same? Recent analyses of the use of spatial prepositions for descriptions of concrete situations suggest that these terms actually imply different things, or, in other words, seem to entail different simulations of the described situations (Coventry & Garrod, 2004; Deane, 2009; Vandeloise, 1991). Some spatial prepositions, such as *above/below*, seem to imply primarily geometric information about vertical position. Other spatial prepositions, such as *over/under*, seem to imply primarily functional information that may sometimes override geometric relations. For instance, if a man uses an umbrella against a rainstorm that comes from the front rather than from above, one can still say that the umbrella is *over* the man, even though in a geometric sense it is *in front* of the man – implying protection by and thus a functional relation between the umbrella and the man (Coventry, Prat-Sala, & Richards, 2001).

Given that these spatial prepositions have slightly different meanings when used for concrete situations, it seems likely that they also have different meanings when applied metaphorically. The prepositions *above/below* seem to be used primarily to refer to social status, which is the honor or prestige attached to one's position in society, while metaphorical uses of *over/under* seem to refer primarily to social influence (O'Keefe, 1996). These meanings map very well on the distinction between geometrical and functional meaning of spatial prepositions (Coventry & Garrod, 2004).

We can speculate that in addition to the vertical differences implied in above/below and the potential for influence implied by over/under, a third area of power metaphors may be the direct application of influence. This third aspect is expressed with metaphors like *having somebody in one's grip* (the same metaphor exists in German, *jemanden in der Hand haben*, and Italian, *avere qualcuno in pugno*). In functional terms, this refers to an actually exerted control over the other's location (Coventry & Garrod, 2004). This basically implies a restriction of self-determination. A very similar meaning may be implied by the metaphor of the powerful as *puppet masters* who *pull the strings*.

8. Outlook

We have started with a notion of power as being rooted in direct physical influence. This kind of power is readily judged from various nonverbal cues. We have seen that schematized versions of these cues are appraised as communicating power and reified in cultural artifacts. Finally, we argued that these processes are rooted in schematization and simulation abilities of the human mind, and amplified and communicated by language. We contend that it is this ability for schematizing and abstracting nonverbal cues of power that provides the basis for using space and spatial order for the constitution and conformation of power in authority relations, as described by A.P. Fiske (2004).

In the current chapter, we emphasized the interconnections and similarities between the various levels: bodily cues, nonverbal communication, mental representation, and language. However, the sheer amount of evidence available strongly suggests that *differentiation* may be what is needed in future research. As an outlook, we want to provide two examples for such possible differentiations.

As we have seen before, the aspects of influence and self-determination might require slightly different qualities which could have led to different embodiments in language, metaphors, perceptual symbols and cultural artifacts. It is also possible that the long cultural history of using elevation to denote power has led to differences in the embodiment of force-based, coercive power and hierarchy-based, consensual power. Embodiments for the first kind should include grip, strength, pressure, etc., while those for the latter kind should include elevation, omnipresence, and spatio-temporal extension.

Other perceptual symbols to distinguish are those of status and influence. The concept of power often entails both. Furthermore, power and status are mutually reinforcing (Magee & Galinsky, 2008). Nevertheless, within this field, several different variables can be distinguished that we have used synonymously here, as the field of nonverbal communication typically does (Hall et al., 2005). For instance, leadership and dominance could be both subsumed under the concept of power as we have used it here, but they are clearly different concepts (van Vugt, Hogan, & Kaiser, 2008; van Vugt, 2006). It remains a task for the future to investigate to which extent these concepts have different embodiments and are described with different metaphors and perceptual symbols, such as horizontal movement patterns (Menon, Sim, Fu, Chiu, & Hong, 2010). For instance, it could be that size and force metaphors are more typically used for dominance and social influence, but elevation metaphors are more typically used for status. We believe that a synthesis of conceptual metaphor theory and embodiment theory needs to include a closer analysis of *different* metaphors of power.

References

Aiken, Lewis R. & Richard L. Zweigenhaft (1978). Signature size, sex, and status in Iran. *The Journal of Social Psychology, 106,* 273–274.
Anderson, John R. (1983). *The architecture of cognition.* Cambridge, MA: Harvard University Press.
Anderson, John R. (1993). *Rules of the mind.* Hillsdale, NJ: Erlbaum.
Aronoff, Joel (2006). How we recognize angry and happy emotion in people, places, and things. *Cross-Cultural Research, 40,* 83–105.
Aronoff, Joel, Andrew M. Barclay & Linda A. Stevenson (1988). The recognition of threatening facial stimuli. *Journal of Personality and Social Psychology, 54,* 647–655.

Aronoff, J., Barbara Woike & Lester M. Hyman (1992). Which are the stimuli in facial displays of anger and happiness? Configurational bases of emotion recognition. *Journal of Personality and Social Psychology, 62,* 1050–1066.

Bargh, John A. (1997). The automaticity of everyday life. In Robert S.Wyer (Ed.), *Advances in social cognition: Vol. X* (pp. 1–61). Hillsdale, NJ: Lawrence Erlbaum.

Bargh, John A., Mark Chen & Lara Burrows (1996). Automaticity of social behavior: Direct effects of trait construct and stereotype activation on action. *Journal of Personality and Social Psychology, 71,* 230–244.

Barsalou, Lawrence W. (1999). Perceptual symbol systems. *Behavioral and Brain Sciences, 22,* 577–609.

Barsalou, Lawrence W. (2008). Grounded cognition. *Annual Review of Psychology, 59,* 617–645.

Berry, Diane S. & Leslie Z. McArthur (1985). Some components and consequences of a babyface. *Journal of Personality and Social Psychology, 48,* 312–323.

Berry, Diane S. & Leslie Z. McArthur (1986). Perceiving character in faces: The impact of age-related craniofacial changes on social perception. *Psychological Bulletin, 100,* 3–18.

Boehm, Christopher (1999). *Hierarchy in the forest.* London: Harvard University Press.

Boroditsky, Lera (2000). Metaphoric structuring: understanding time through spatial metaphors. *Cognition, 75,* 1–28.

Boroditsky, Lera (2001). Does language shape thought?: Mandarin and English speakers' conceptions of time. *Cognitive Psychology, 43,* 1–22.

Carey, Susan & Elizabeth Spelke (1996). Science and core knowledge. *Philosophy of Science, 63,* 515–533.

Casasanto, Daniel & Lera Boroditsky (2008). Time in the mind: Using space to think about time. *Cognition, 106,* 579–593.

Chen, Serena, Annette Y. Lee-Chai & John A. Bargh (2001). Relationship orientation as a moderator of the effects of social power. *Journal of Personality and Social Psychology, 80,* 173–187.

Chiao, Joan Y., Reginal B. Jr. Adams, Peter U. Tse, William T. Lowenthal, Jennifer A. Richeson & Nalini Ambady (2008). Knowing who's boss: fMRI and ERP investigations of social dominance perception. *Group Processes & Intergroup Relations, 11,* 201–214.

Chiao, Joan Y., Tokiko Harada, Emily R. Oby, Zhang Li, Todd Parrish & Donna Bridge (2009). Neural representations of social status hierarchy in human inferior parietal cortex. *Neuropsychologia, 47,* 354–363.

Clark, Herbert H. (1973). Space, time, semantics, and the child. In Timothy E. Moore (Ed.), *Cognitive development and the acquisition of language* (pp. 27–297). Oxford, England: Academic Press.

Coventry, Kenny R. & Simon C. Garrod (2004). *Saying, seeing, and acting.* New York: Psychology Press.

Coventry, Kenny R., Mercè Prat-Sala & Lynn Richards (2001). The interplay between geometry and function in the comprehension of *over, under, above,* and *below. Journal of Memory and Language, 44,* 376–398.

Dannemaier, William D. & Fred J. Thumin (1964). Authority status as a factor in perceptual distortion of size. *Journal of Social Psychology, 63,* 361–365.

Darwin, Charles (1872). *The expression of the emotions in man and animals.* New York: D. Appleton and Company.

Deane, Paul D. (2009). Multimodal spatial representation: On the semantic unity of over. In Beate Hampe (Ed.), *From perception to meaning. Image schemas in cognitive linguistics* (pp. 235–282). Berlin, New York: Mouton de Gruyter.

Dijksterhuis, Ap & John A. Bargh (2001). The perception-behavior expressway: Automatic effects of social perception on social behavior. In Mark P. Zanna (Ed.), *Advances in experimental social psychology, Vol. 33* (pp. 1–40). San Diego: Academic Press.

Earle, Timothy (2004). Culture matters in the neolithic transition and emergence of hierarchy in Thy, Denmark: Dinstinguished lecture. *American Anthropologist, 106,* 111–125.

Eibl-Eibesfeldt, Irenäus (1971). *Love and hate: The natural history of behavior patterns.* New York: Holt, Rinehart and Winston.

Felson, Richard B. (2002). *Violence & Gender reexamined.* Washington, DC: American Psychological Association.

Fink, Bernhard, Nick Neave & Hanna Seydel (2007). Male facial appearance signals physical strength to women. *American Journal of Human Biology, 19,* 82–87.

Firth, Raymond (1970). Postures and gestures of respect. In Jean Pouillon & Pierre Maranda (Eds.), *Échanges et communications: Mélanges offerts à Claude Léi-Strauss à l'occasion de son 60éme anniversaire* (pp. 188–209). The Hague: Mouton.

Fischer, Martin H. & Rolf A. Zwaan (2008). Embodied language – A review of the role of the motor system in language comprehension. *Quarterly Journal of Experimental Psychology, 61,* 860–868.

Fiske, Alan P. (1991). *Structures of social life: The four elementary forms of human relations.* New York: Free Press.

Fiske, Alan P. (2000). Complementarity Theory: Why human social capacities evolved to require cultural complements. *Personality and Social Psychology Review, 4,* 76–94.

Fiske, Alan P. (2004). Four modes of constituting relationships: Consubstantial assimilation; space, magnitude, time, and force; concrete procedures; abstract symbolism. In Nick Haslam (Ed.), *Relational Models Theory. A contemporary overview.* (pp. 61–146). Mahwah, NJ: Lawrence Erlbaum Associates.

Fiske, Susan T., Amy J. C. Cuddy & Peter Glick (2007). Universal dimensions of social cognition: warmth and competence. *Trends in Cognitive Science, 11,* 77–83.

Fiske, Susan T. (1992). Thinking is for doing: Portraits of social cognition from Daguerreotype to laserphoto. *Journal of Personality and Social Psychology, 63,* 877–889.

Freedman, Daniel G. (1979). *Human sociobiology.* New York: Free Press.

Garvin, Paul L. & Saul H. Riesenberg (1952). Respect behavior on Panape: An ethnolinguistic study. *American Anthropologist, 54,* 201–220.

Gawley, Tim, Thomas Perks & James Curtis (2009). Height, gender, and authority status at work: Analyses for a national sample of Canadian workers. *Sex Roles, 60,* 208–222.
Giessner, Steffen R., Michelle R. Ryan & Thomas W. Schubert (2009). The power of pictures: Vertical picture angles and power perceptions. Manuscript submitted for publication.
Giessner, Steffen R. & Thomas W. Schubert (2007). High in the hierarchy: How vertical location and judgments of leaders' power are interrelated. *Organizational Behavior and Human Decision Processes, 104,* 30–44.
Ginsburg, Harvey J., Vicki A. Pollman & Mitzi S. Wauson (1977). An ethological analysis of nonverbal inhibitors of aggressive behavior in male elementary school children. *Developmental Psychology, 13,* 417–418.
Glenberg, Arthur M. (1997). What memory is for. *Behavioral and Brain Sciences, 20,* 1–55.
Goffman, Erving (1976). *Gender advertisements.* New York: Harper Colophon.
Grady, Joseph (1997). *Foundations of meaning: Primary metaphors and primary scenes.* Ph.D. dissertation, University of California, Berkeley.
Grady, Joseph (2005). Primary metaphors as inputs to conceptual integration. *Journal of Pragmatics, 37,* 1595–1614.
Grady, Joseph E. (2007). Metaphor. In Dirk Geeraerts & Herbert Cuyckens (Eds.), *The Oxford handbook of cognitive linguistics* (pp. 188–213). New York: Oxford University Press.
Greenwald, Anthony G., Mahzarin R. Banaji, Laurie A. Rudman, Shelly D. Farnham, Brian A. Nosek & Deborah S. Mellott (2002). A unified theory of implicit attitudes, stereotypes, self-esteem, and self-concept. *Psychological Review, 109,* 3–25.
Hall, Judith. A., Erik J. Coats & Lavonia Smith LeBeau (2005). Nonverbal behavior and the vertical dimension of social relations: A meta-analysis. *Psychological Bulletin, 131,* 898–924.
Harnad, Steven (1990). The symbol grounding problem. *Physica D, 42,* 335–346.
Hensley, Wayne E. & Robin Cooper (1987). Height and occupational success: A review and critique. *Psychological Reports, 60,* 843–849.
Hess, Ursula, Sylvie Blairy & Robert E. Kleck (2000). The influence of facial emotion displays, gender, and ethnicity on judgments of dominance and affiliation. *Journal of Nonverbal Behavior, 24,* 265–283.
Hewes, Gordon W. (1955). World distribution of certain postural habits. *American Anthropologist, 57,* 231–244.
Higham, Philip A. & William D. Carment (1992). The rise and fall of politicians: The judged heights of Broadbent, Mulroney and Turner before and after the 1988 Canadian federal election. *Canadian Journal of Behavioral Science, 24,* 404–409.
Hommel, Bernhard, Jochen Müsseler, Gisa Aschersleben & Wolfgang Prinz (2001). The Theory of Event Coding (TEC): A framework for perception and action planning. *Behavioral and Brain Sciences, 24,* 849–937.
Jaynes, Julian (1976). *The origin of consciousness in the breakdown of the bicameral mind.* Boston: Houghton Mifflin Company.

Johnson, Christopher (1999). Metaphor vs. conflation in the acquisition of polysemy: The case of *see*. In Masako Hiraga, Chris Sinha & Sherman Wilcox (Eds.), *Cultural, typological, and psychological perspectives in cognitive linguistics* (pp. 155–169). Amsterdam: John Benjamins.

Judge, Timothy A. & Daniel M. Cable (2004). The effect of physical height on workplace success and income: Preliminary test of a theoretical model. *Journal of Applied Psychology, 89,* 428–441.

Keating, Elizabeth (2000). Moments of hierarchy: Constituting social stratification by means of language, food, space and the body in Pohnpei, Micronesia. *American Anthropologist, 102,* 303–320.

Keltner, Dacher & Brenda N. Buswell (1997). Embarrassment: Its distinct form and appeasement functions. *Psychological Bulletin, 122,* 250–270.

Knutson, Brian (1996). Facial expressions of emotion influence interpersonal trait inferences. *Journal of Nonverbal Behavior, 20,* 165–182.

Kraft, Robert N. (1987). The influence of camera angle on comprehension and retention of pictorial events. *Memory and Cognition, 15,* 291–307.

Lakoff, George & Mark Johnson (1980). *Metaphors we live by*. Chicago and London: The University of Chicago Press.

Lakoff, George & Mark Johnson (1999). *Philosophy in the flesh. The embodied mind and its challenge to Western thought*. New York: Basic Books.

Louwerse, Max M. & Patrick Jeuniaux (2010). The linguistic and embodied nature of conceptual processing. *Cognition, 114, 96–104.*

Machery, Edouard (2007). Concept empiricism: a methodological critique. *Cognition, 104,* 19–46.

Magee, Joe C. (2009). Seeing power in action: The roles of deliberation, implementation, and action in inferences of power. *Journal of Experimental Social Psychology, 45,* 1–14.

Magee, Joe C. & Adam D. Galinsky (2008). Social hierarchy: The self-reinforcing nature of power and status. *The Academy of Management Annals, 2,* 351–398.

Marsh, Abigail A., Reginald B. Jr. Adams & Robert E. Kleck (2005). Why do fear and anger look the way they do? Form and social function in facial expressions. *Personality and Social Psychology Bulletin, 31,* 73–86.

Marsh, Abigail A., Henry H. Yu, Julia C. Schechter & R. J. R. Blair (2009). Larger than life: Humans' nonverbal status cues alter perceived size. *PLoS ONE, 4,* e5707. doi: 10.1371/journal.pone.0005707.

Meier, Brian P. & Sarah Dionne (2009). Downright sexy: Verticality, implicit power, and perceived physical attractiveness. *Social Cognition, 27,* 883–892.

Meier, Brian P., David J. Hauser, Michael D. Robinson, Chris Kelland Friesen & Katie Schjeldahl (2007). What's "up" with god? Vertical space as a representation of the divine. *Journal of Personality and Social Psychology, 93,* 699–710.

Meier, Brian P. & Michael D. Robinson (2004). Why the sunny side is up. *Psychological Science, 15,* 243–247.

Melamed, Tuvia & Nikos Bozionelos (1992). Managerial promotion and height. *Psychological Reports, 71,* 587–593.

Menon, Tanya, Jessica Sim, Jeanne Ho-Ying Fu, Chi-yue Chiu & Ying-yi Hong (2010). Blazing the trail versus trailing the group: Culture and perceptions of the leader's position. *Organizational Behavior and Human Decision Processes, 113,* 51–61.

Mignault, Alain & Avi Chaudhuri (2003). The many faces of a neutral face: Head tilt and perception of dominance and emotion. *Journal of Nonverbal Behavior, 27,* 111–132.

Moeller, Sara K., Michael D. Robinson & Darya L. Zabelina (2008). Personality dominance and preferential use of the vertical dimension of space: Evidence from spatial attention paradigms. *Psychological Science, 19,* 355–361.

Mueller, Ulrich. & Allan Mazur (1997). Facial dominance in *Homo sapiens* as honest signaling of male quality. *Behavioral Ecology, 8,* 569–579.

Mueller, Ulrich & Allan Mazur (2001). Evidence of unconstrained directional selection for male tallness. *Behavioral Ecology and Sociobiology, 50,* 302–311.

Mussweiler, Thomas (2006). Doing is for thinking! Stereotype activation by stereotypic movements. *Psychological Science, 17,* 17–21.

Neave, Nick, Sarah Laing, Bernhard Fink & John T. Manning (2003). Second to fourth digit ratio, testosterone and perceived male dominance. *Proceedings of the Royal Society B, 270,* 2167–2172.

Niedenthal, Paula M. (2007). Embodying emotion. *Science, 316,* 1002–1005.

O'Keefe, John (1996). The spatial prepositions in English, vector grammar and the cognitive map theory. In Paul Bloom, Merrill F. Garrett, Mary A. Peterson & Lynn Nadel (Eds.), *Language and space* (pp. 277–316). Cambridge, MA: MIT Press.

Öhman, Arne & Susan Mineka (2003). The malicious serpent: Snakes as a prototypical stimulus for an evolved module of fear. *Current Directions in Psychological Science, 12,* 1–5.

Oosterhof, Nikolaas N. & Alexander Todorov (2008). The functional basis of face evaluation. *Proceedings of the National Acadamy of Sciences, 105,* 11087–11092.

Raine, Adrian, Chandra Reynolds, Peter H. Venables, Sarnoff A. Mednick & David P. Farrington (1998). Fearlessness, stimulation-seeking, and large body size at age 3 years as early predispositions to childhood aggression at age 11 years. *Archives of General Psychiatry, 55,* 745–751.

Richards, Robert J. (1987). *Darwin and the emergence of evolutionary theories of mind and behavior.* Chicago: University of Chicago Press.

Roberts, Tomi-Ann & Yousef Arefi-Afshar (2007). Not all who stand tall are proud: Gender differences in the proprioceptive effects of upright posture. *Cognition and Emotion, 21,* 714–727.

Robinson, Michael D., Darya L. Zabelina, Scott Ode & Sara K. Moeller (2008). The vertical nature of dominance-submission: Individual differences in vertical attention. *Journal of Research in Personality, 42,* 933–948.

Schubert, Thomas W. (2005). Your Highness: Vertical positions as perceptual symbols of power. *Journal of Personality and Social Psychology, 89,* 1–21.

Schubert, Thomas W. (2004). The power in your hand: Gender differences in bodily feedback from making a fist. *Personality and Social Psychology Bulletin, 30*, 757–769.

Schubert, Thomas W. & Sander L. Koole (2009). The embodied self: Making a fist enhances men's power-related self-conceptions. *Journal of Experimental Social Psychology, 45*, 828–834.

Schubert, Thomas W., Sven Waldzus & Steffen R. Giessner (2009). Control over the association of power and size. *Social Cognition, 27*, 1–19.

Schubert, Thomas W., Sven Waldzus & Beate Seibt (2008). The embodiment of power and communalism in space and bodily contact. In Gün R. Semin & Eliot R. Smith (Eds.), *Embodied Grounding: Social, Cognitive, Affective, And Neuroscientific Approaches* (pp. 160–183). New York: Cambridge University Press.

Schwartz, Barry (1981). *Vertical classification: A study in structuralism and the sociology of knowledge*. Chicago: University of Chicago Press.

Schwartz, Barry, Abraham Tesser & Evan Powell (1982). Dominance cues in nonverbal behavior. *Social Psychology Quarterly, 45*, 114–120.

Sell, Aaron, Leda Cosmides, John Tooby, Daniel Sznycer, Christopher von Rueden, & Michael Gurven (2008). Human adaptations for the visual assessment of strength and fighting ability from the body and face. *Proceedings of the Royal Society B, 276*, 575–584.

Smith, Eliot R. (1998). Mental representation and memory. In D.T.Gilbert & S.T. Fiske (Eds.), *The handbook of social psychology* (pp. 391–445). New York: McGraw-Hill.

Solomon, Karen O. & Lawrence W. Barsalou (2004). Perceptual simulation in property verification. *Memory and Cognition, 32*, 244–259.

Spelke, Elizabeth S. & Katherine D. Kinzler (2007). Core knowledge. *Developmental Science, 10*, 89–96.

Spiegel, John & Pavel Machotka (1974). *Messages of the body*. New York: The Free Press.

Stepper, Sabine & Fritz Strack (1993). Proprioceptive determinants of emotional and nonemotional feelings. *Journal of Personality and Social Psychology, 64*, 211–220.

Thomsen, Lotte, Alan P. Fiske, Jim Sidanius, Miguel Vazques-Larruscain, Simo Køppe, Malin McKinley et al. (2009). *Seeing spatial relations as social relations*. Manuscript submitted for publication.

Thomsen, Lotte, Willem E. Frankenhuis & Susan Carey (2009). *Infants' representation of social dominance among novel agents*. Manuscript submitted for publication.

Tiedens, Larissa Z. & Alison R. Fragale (2003). Power moves: Complementarity in dominant and submissive nonverbal behavior. *Journal of Personality and Social Psychology, 84*, 558–568.

Toren, Christina (1990). *Making sense of hierarchy: Cognition as a social process in Fiji*. London: Athlone Press.

Toren, Christina (1999). *Mind, materiality and history*. London: Routledge.

Tracy, Jessica L. & David Matsumoto (2008). The spontaneous expression of pride and shame: Evidence for biologically innate nonverbal displays. *Proceedings of the National Acadamy of Sciences, 105*, 11655–11660.
Tracy, Jessica L. & Richard W. Robins (2004). Show your pride. Evidence for a discrete emotion expression. *Psychological Science, 15*, 194–197.
van Quakebeke, Nils & Steffen R. Giessner (2010). How embodied cognitions affect judgments: Height-related attribution bias in football foul calls. *Journal of Sports and Exercise Psychology, 32*, 3–22.
van Vugt, Mark (2006). Evolutionary origins of leadership and followership. *Personality and Social Psychology Review, 10*, 354–371.
van Vugt, Mark, Robert Hogan & Robert B. Kaiser (2008). Leadership, followership, and evolution. *American Psychologist, 63*, 182–196.
Vandeloise, Claude (1991). *Spatial prepositions: A case study from French*. Chicago: University of Chicago Press.
von Hecker, Ulrich, Michael Conway & Sindhuja Sankaran (2009). Embodiment of social status: Verticality effects in a newly-learned multi-level hierarchy. Manuscript submitted for publication.
Weinraub, Marsha & Estill Putney (1978). The effect of heigt on infants' social responses to unfamiliar persons. *Child Development, 49*, 598–603.
White, Geoffrey M. (1985). Premises and purposes in a Solomon Islands ethnopsychology. In Geoffrey M. White & John Kirkpatrick (Eds.), *Person, self and experience: Exploring Pacific ethnopsychologies* (pp. 328–366). Los Angeles: University of California Press.
Wilson, Margaret (2002). Six views of embodied cognition. *Psychonomic Bulletin & Review, 9*, 625–636.
Wilson, Paul R. (1968). Perceptual distortion of height as a function of ascribed academic status. *Journal of Social Psychology, 74*, 97–102.
Zanolie, Kiki, Saskia van Dantzig, Inge Boot, Jasper Wijnen, Thomas W. Schubert, Steffen Giessner & Diane Pecher (2010). Mighty metaphors: Behavioral and ERP evidence that power shifts attention on a vertical dimension. Manuscript submitted for publication.
Zebrowitz, Leslie A., Masako Kikuchi & Jean-Marc Fellous (2007). Are effects of emotion expression on trait impressions mediated by babyfaceness? Evidence from connectionist modeling. *Personality and Social Psychology Bulletin, 33*, 648–662.
Zebrowitz, Leslie A. & Joann M. Montepare (1992). Impressions of babyfaced individuals across the life span. *Developmental Psychology, 28*, 1143–1152.
Zwaan, Rolf A. (2004). The immersed experiencer: toward an embodied theory of language comprehension. In B.H. Ross (Ed.), *The psychology of learning and motivation, Vol. 44* (pp. 35–62). New York: Academic Press.
Zwaan, Rolf A. & Richard H. Yaxley (2003). Spatial iconicity affects semantic relatedness judgments. *Psychnomic Bulletin & Review, 10*, 945–958.
Zweigenhaft, Richard L. (1970). Signature size: A key to status awareness. *The Journal of Social Psychology, 81*, 49–54.

Section B
Horizontal asymmetries and social thought

Directional asymmetries in cognition: What is left to write about?

Anjan Chatterjee[1]

Abstract

Humans are surrounded by spatial asymmetries. Surprisingly, spatial asymmetries are not confined to our external environment. They penetrate our mental representations and have subtle but pervasive influences across several cognitive domains. I review evidence for the existence of a spatially asymmetric representation that takes the form of a horizontal directional schema. This schema underlies how we conceptualize actions and events. People in cultures that read and write from left to right conceptualize actions as proceeding from left to right; and they conceptualize agents of actions as being located on the left and recipients of actions as being located on the right. This left to right schema generalizes to memory and aesthetic evaluations. The evidence to date suggests that reading and writing habits influence the specific direction harbored within these schemas. I discuss possible neural instantiations of schemas and further speculate on why such schemas exist. Schemas serve as an intermediate level of abstraction. On the one hand they retain something of the analog structure of perceptual systems, and on the other they contain something of the flexibility of symbolic systems. As such, they are poised between sources of information about the world and our abilities to process and manipulate this information.

---

1 I would like to thank Lisa Santer, Eileen Cardillo, Alex Kranjec and Gwen Schmidt for their helpful comments on an earlier draft of this paper. This work was supported by NIH RO1 HD050199 and RO1 DC008779 and a subcontract under NSF SBE0541957. I am also grateful for discussions with the lively participants of the ESCON Expert Meeting on "Spatial Representation and Social Cognition" held in Venice, June 2008, organized by Drs. Anne Maass and Thomas Schubert.

1. Introduction

We are awash in left-right asymmetries (McManus, 2002). We read and write left-to-right or right-to-left. We drive on the left or on the right side of the road. Even our faucets code hot or cold water with left-right asymmetries. Lateral asymmetries are not confined to conventions of our constructed environment. Even though biological organisms are almost universally organized symmetrically around a principle axis of the body (Palmer, 2004), asymmetries persist within us. Humans are left or right handed. Some of our internal organs are embedded with left-right asymmetries. And while gross anatomic asymmetries of the hemispheres of our brain are subtle, for at least a century and a half we have known that asymmetries in their functional properties are decidedly unsubtle.

Unlike the left-right asymmetries in the environment and in our biology, this chapter addresses a symbolic left-right asymmetry. We are certainly familiar with sinister characters and right-wing politicians. In these cases, the symbolism is made explicit by our use of language. The focus of this inquiry is an asymmetry, which while not explicitly given to awareness, appears pervasively across several cognitive domains. In what follows, I will review the evidence that we represent events with a default directional schema. I will mention ways in which this directional schema generalizes to other cognitive domains. As part of this generalization, I will discuss an example of this schema in visual aesthetics. Then I will how the schema is affected by reading and writing habits, its likely neurobiological underpinnings, before concluding with conjectures about why such directional schemas exist at all.

2. Directional representation of events

Humans in cultures that read and write from left-to-right conceive of events proceeding from left-to-right (Chatterjee, 2001; Chatterjee, Maher, & Heilman, 1995). Within this mental display of events, agents of actions are conceived on the left and the patients or recipients of actions on the right. Evidence for this default representation of the structure of events originated in our clinical observations of a highly educated man with aphasia (Chatterjee, Maher, Gonzales-Rothi, & Heilman, 1995; Maher, Chatterjee, Gonzales-Rothi, & Heilman, 1995). People with brain damage can have remarkably selective language deficits. Some people with brain damage have trouble assigning thematic roles in sentences, or determining who is doing what to whom in semantically reversible sentences, such as "the girl kisses the boy" (Chatterjee & Maher, 2000; Saffran, Schwartz, & Marin, 1980; Schwartz,

Saffran, & Marin, 1980). This sentence is considered reversible because either the girl or the boy could plausibly be the agent of the sentence. Our index patient was a college professor who had significant difficulties in producing and comprehending reversible sentences. However, rather than performing randomly, he used a spatial strategy. In describing pictures, he consistently produced sentences in which the participant on the left of the picture was the agent (Maher et al., 1995). Thus, if a picture showed a circle stick figure on the left kicking a square, he accurately stated that the circle was kicking the square. However, if the picture depicted the circle on the right kicking the square on the left, he would say that the square was kicking the circle. Similarly, in comprehension tasks in which he matched sentences to choices of pictures, he was more likely to match "the circle kicks the square" to pictures with the circle on the left regardless of whether the circle was doing the kicking or receiving the kick (A Chatterjee, Maher, Gonzales-Rothi et al., 1995).

We speculated that the subject's spatial biases reflected a primitive structure of mental representations of events (Chatterjee, 2001; Chatterjee, Maher, Gonzales-Rothi et al., 1995). Hughlings Jackson (1932) in the nineteenth century viewed the nervous system as being organized hierarchically, with higher processes inhibiting lower ones. Jackson thought that dissolution of higher functions released more primitive behaviors. Accordingly, the dissolution of this patient's linguistic abilities by brain damage might have released a primitive prelinguistic representation making explicit an underlying spatial schema that we all might be harboring.

If events are encoded with spatial schemas, then subtle spatial biases might also influence normal subjects' conception of actions and thematic roles. Several subsequent experiments confirmed this prediction (Chatterjee, Maher, & Heilman, 1995; A Chatterjee, Southwood, & Basilico, 1999). Normal U.S. subjects are more likely to draw the circle on the left when asked to draw events like "the circle pushes the square". They also are likely to draw the agent (circle in this example) to the left of where they draw the patient when asked to draw just the circle or just the square on separate cards. They are more likely to depict horizontal actions with trajectories moving from left-to-right than right-to-left. In reaction-time experiments, subject match sentences to pictures more quickly if the agent is on the left than on the right, and if the action proceeds from left-to-right than from right-to-left.

Our original observations have been replicated and extended in Italy by Maass and Russo (2003). The basic finding that events are conceptualized with a left-to-right trajectory is robust in Italian subjects. These subjects also positioned agents to the left of recipients of actions. In tasks matching sentences to pictures their subjects responded more quickly if the action was depicted in a left-to-right direction.

3. Generalization of the directional schema

We have suggested that a directional schema underlies our representation of events and serves as an intermediary between our perceptions of events in the world and our abilities to communicate information about these events. Kant wrote of a "schema of sensuous concepts" that intervenes between sense perceptions and concepts, necessary to make sense of what gets empirically represented and intellectually ordered in the mind (Kant, 1781/1998). More recent theories of intermediary cognitive structures include Johnson's proposal of abstract structures between mental images and logical-propositional structures (Johnson, 1987). He proposes that these structures, while derived from sense percepts, abstract out specific details. Jackendoff suggests that spatial events break down into elements like 'movement', 'path', and 'location' (Jackendoff, 1996). Mandler describes a framework for infant conceptual development in which perceptual-motor aspects are encoded as primitives, which serve as a foundation upon which more complex conceptual structures are built (Mandler, 1996). Schemas are thus conceptualized as primitive structures that abstract perceptual detail away in the interest of providing more flexible cognitive representations.

The flexibility of the directional schema we describe is evident in how it seems to generalize to other cognitive domains. Numbers are conceived as increasing from left-to-right (Dehaene, Bossini, & Giraux, 1993). While time can be viewed as moving from back to front, it is often conceived as proceeding from left-to-right (Santiago, Lupianez, Perez, & Funes, 2007). Even memories are influenced by a left-to-right directionality. Static pictures of actions, such as a jumper in mid-air, are recalled as though the action had proceeded further along than initially depicted (Freyd, 1983). This phenomenon, referred to as "representational momentum," is that these static pictures are represented dynamically. Representational momentum turns out to be more robust if the implied motion is from left-to-right than if it is from right-to-left (Halpern & Kelly, 1993). Finally, even aesthetic judgments are influenced by the direction of implied motion in art, with left-to-right trajectories preferred over right-to-left (Christman, 1995; Freimuth & Wapner, 1979; McLaughlin & Kermisch, 1997; Mead & McLaughlin, 1979).

4. Portrait profiles: A special case

Extending the idea that left-right directional biases influence aesthetic judgments and combining that idea with a left-to-right bias for actions, we proposed the agency hypothesis for a left-right bias in portraits painted within the Western canon (Chatterjee, 2002). Portraits are typically painted at an oblique angle, depicting more or less of one side of the subject's face. However, whether more of the left or the right cheek is depicted is not random (McManus & Humphrey, 1973). Many factors have been postulated for profile asymmetries in portrait paintings, such as mechanical biases (Humphrey & McManus, 1973), perceptual asymmetries (McLaughlin & Murphy, 1994), maternal imprinting (Grusser, Selke, & Zynda, 1988), social distance (Humphrey & McManus, 1973) and emotional expressivity (Nicholls, Clode, Wood, & Wood, 1999) (for an overview see also Suitner & McManus, this volume). However, the agency hypothesis generalizes to virtually all extant observations made of portrait profiles. This hypothesis combines the idea that representations of events have a default schematic structure, and this structure extends to aesthetic considerations. If subjects are biased to think of actions with a left-to-right trajectory, it follows that they tend to think of agents on the left and recipients of actions on the right. A figure on the left of the viewer would display more of their right cheek and a figure on the right would expose more of their left cheek.

1. Gender differences. Painters are more likely to portray the left side of cheeks in general, and this bias is accentuated in portraits of women (McManus & Humphrey, 1973) (Gordon, 1974, 1981). Presumably subjects posing for portraits are in a passive role and consequently artists were biased to paint them with their left cheek exposed. A cultural bias to consider women less as agents then men would result in a greater tendency to depict women with their left cheek exposed. Consistent with this view, the bias to depict women's left cheeks is attenuated in portraits of sovereigns and other powerful women.
2. Historic shifts. The bias to depict the left cheeks of women decreased from the 15th century to the twentieth century. For women, the ratio of left-to-right cheek depictions was about 8 to 1 in the 15th century, and diminished gradually to a ratio of slightly above 1 to 1 in the 20th century (Grusser et al., 1988). This change is likely to reflect a shift in the view of women over the last 6 centuries as more active agents in the world.
3. Self-portraits and social distance. Painters presumably view themselves as agents. In fact, in the process of painting they are explicitly engaged in their productive social role. Consequently they are biased to conceive of themselves with the right cheek exposed.
4. Character attributes. Several da Vinci portraits originally drawn with the right cheek exposed are judged to be more active and potent than those drawn with their left cheek exposed (Benjafield & Segalowitz, 1993). It seems natural that agents as doers of actions would be considered more active and potent. The fact that these faces were judged to be more active and potent even when depicted in mirror-reversed versions

suggests that da Vinci used (implicitly or explicitly) the right cheek exposure as one of several tools at his disposal to depict individuals as active and potent. The other features would still communicate these characteristics in the mirrored versions. Interestingly, the "active" rating diminished slightly when the same portrait was depicted in the mirrored version with the left cheek exposed.

Suitner and Maass (2007) examined a new set of portraits to test the agency hypothesis in portrait profiles. They replicated the original observations of a general bias for artists to paint portraits depicting the left side of the cheek more often than the right. However, they also found that this bias depended on the gender of the artist. The findings obtained on male artists did *not* generalize to women. Female artists, unlike male artists, were not likely to portray women sitters with a left orientation than with a right orientation. The authors suggest that male artists are more likely to select a spatial orientation for their female sitters that reflect their stereotypical view of females as passive, whereas women artists appear less subject to these stereotypic views. They also found that male artists' tendencies to portray themselves with a rightward orientation, and women artists with a leftward orientation, was true only to about the mid eighteen hundreds. In more recent times, gender differences in self-presentation were no longer evident.

5. Cultural influences

An obvious question arising from these observations is whether reading and writing habits produce these directional effects. To address this issue, one of our earlier experiments capitalized on the fact that different verbs convey opposite spatial trajectories (Chatterjee et al., 1999). For example, the verb "push" conveys an action moving away from the agent, whereas the verb "pull" conveys an action moving towards the agent. Normal research participants matched sentences they heard to pictures when pictures depicted the agent on the left and when the action proceeded from left-to-right. The surface structure of English sentences does not easily account for the influence of the direction of action. If these subjects simply mapped the subject-verb-object sentence structure on to the agent-action-patient depiction in pictures, they would not have processed actions from left-to-right more quickly than actions from right-to-left. The advantages of the mapping of subject-verb-object spatial ordering in written language to the same ordering of the pictures would have canceled out the effects of the direction of actions. When the direction of action proceeds from left-to-right, the subject-verb-object sentence sequence maps onto agent-action-patient depictions with "push" verbs, but to patient-action-agent depictions with "pull" verbs. Thus, the left-to-right direction of action seemed to have an influence even when the picture depicted the action with an object-verb-subject layout.

Why should events be represented with a left-to-right schema? We originally proposed that this bias might follow from the left hemisphere's propensity to drive attention with a left-to-right vector (Chatterjee, Maher, & Heilman, 1995) as proposed by Kinsbourne (1987) some years ago. On such an account one would not expect cultural variables to have much of an influence on the direction of the schema. This prediction has since been disconfirmed. Maass and Russo (2003) studied Arab along with Italian participants in several tasks of event representation. The Arab participants displayed directional effects that were the opposite of those in the Italian participants. However, the Arab participants also showed a left-to-right bias with push-pull verbs as did Italian participants. The authors proposed a hybrid model in which the left-to-right directional bias is modifiable by reading habits.

Maass and colleagues (Maass, Pagani, & Berta, 2007) also used action videos to examine the effects of directionality on social ascriptions. Italian subjects rated videos of actions with left-to-right trajectories as faster, more powerful and more beautiful as might be expected from other aesthetics research. However, Arab subjects rated actions going from right-to-left as faster, more powerful and more beautiful. Similar influences of reading habits have also been reported in other domains. For example, Arabic-, Hebrew- or Urdu-reading participants show right-to-left directional biases in perceptual exploration, drawing, decoding of facial affect, number representation and aesthetic preferences (Chokron & De Agostini, 2002; Dehaene et al., 1993; Nachson, Argaman, & Luria, 1999; Padakannaya, Devi, Zaveria, Chengappa, & Vaid, 2002; Tversky, Kugelmass, & Winter, 1991; Vaid, Singh, Sakhuja, & Gupta, 2002). Taken together, the conclusion that reading and writing habits influence the direction of the underlying schema is unavoidable.

As an aside, it is worth pointing out that handedness, one of the most robust asymmetries in humans with pervasive consequences for how individuals act in the world, cannot account for these behavioral observations. For example, for the data on portrait profiles, it is true that right-handed individuals are more likely to draw faces with left facing profiles. However, handedness cannot account for why the bias in depicting facial profiles would change over time or be influenced by the gender or kinship relationship of the subject to the artist. Handedness also cannot account for the modulation and reversal of these directional effects by reading and writing habits.

It is tempting to frame the cross-cultural experiments as testing alternate hypotheses – a biological versus a cultural one. But such a framing of the issue assumes a rigid view of the nervous systems. This dichotomy assumes that cultural factors have effects on human behavior without being mediated by the brain. A better framing of the issues would be investigations into which neuro-cognitive systems are resistant to change, and which are subject to modification based on experience.

6. Neural underpinnings

The biology of the directional schema described here is likely to be part of the neural organization of spatial events (Chatterjee, 2008). This schema lies at the interface of spatial perception and conception, an area of considerable recent research in linguistics, developmental psychology and cognitive neuroscience (Chatterjee, 2001; Gennari, Sloman, Malt, & Fitch, 2002; Hayward & Tarr, 1995; Jackendoff, 1987, 1991, 1996; Kemmerer, 2006; Kemmerer & Tranel, 2000; Mandler, 2004; Regier, 1995; Talmy, 1983, 2000). Three features of these schemas are relevant to its underlying biology. First is motion as related to events. Second is the abstraction and schematic structure of spatial representations. And third, is a directional selectivity that could be modulated by experience.

6.1. Motion

The visual system parses out different attributes of our visual world, including motion. In humans, visual motion areas (MT/MST) respond to simple moving stimuli (Tootell et al., 1995; Treue & Maunsell, 1996) and the posterior superior temporal sulcus (pSTS) responds to biological motion (Grezes et al., 2001; Grossman & Blake, 2002). However, these regions are responsive to more than simple motion. Area MT/MST (located at the posterior part of the inferior temporal gyrus) is activated by implied motion in static pictures (e.g., a picture of a runner) and when semantic judgments of action pictures are made (e.g., someone hopping is judged more similar to someone jumping, than to someone throwing) (Decety et al., 1997; Kable, Lease-Spellmeyer, & Chatterjee, 2002; Martin, Haxby, Lalonde, Wiggs, & Ungerleider, 1995; Martin & Weisberg, 2003). Adjacent areas within the posterior middle temporal gyrus (pMTG) also respond to action words (Kable et al., 2002; Kable, Kan, Wilson, Thompson-Schill, & Chatterjee, 2005). These same areas are involved in segmenting events into discrete units, in what would otherwise be a continuous and unbounded stream of dynamic visual information (Speer, Swallow, & Zacks, 2003; Zacks, Swallow, Vettel, & McAvoy, 2006). Thus, areas within the posterolateral temporal cortex, that traditionally have been implicated in the perceptual processing of motion, are also involved in conceptualizing actions and events (Chatterjee, 2008).

Language highlights another parsing of motion relevant to our conceptual systems. Languages consistently express manners and paths of motion in different constituents (Talmy, 1985). For example, in English, manner of motion is conveyed primarily by verbs. So, *gallop, canter* and *trot* describe different manners of motion. By contrast, path information in English is conveyed primarily by prepositional phrases. So, the horse *gallops across* the meadow or *into* the barn or around the track. If the parsing of motion by language is a clue to its perceptual parsing, the neural processing of manner and paths of motions should segregate. We confirmed this hypothesis in a functional magnetic resonance imaging (fMRI) study demonstrating that manners and paths of motion have distinct neural signatures (Wu, Morganti, & Chatterjee, 2008). Manner more than path activated the pMTG. Path more than manner activated the posterior intraparietal sulcus and posterior middle frontal gyrus.

6.2. Abstraction and schemas

Spatial concepts introduce a level of abstraction to our thinking. Spatial concepts shift cognitive focus away from objects themselves to focus on their relational structures (Gentner & Loewenstein, 2002). Do networks within the postero-lateral temporal cortex that mediate the perception and conception of actions also abstract action representations from the specific actors involved? To address this question, we conducted an fMRI repetition suppression experiment (Kable & Chatterjee, 2006). These experiments capitalized on the physiologic observation that neural responses in specialized circuits diminish when repeatedly processing features for which the circuit is specialized (Grill-Spector & Malach, 2001). By showing subjects action video clips in which the novelty of actors or their actions were systematically manipulated, we showed that area MT/MST, pSTS and the extra-striate body area are part of a distributed network that is sensitive to repeated actions even when performed by different actors. These experiments confirm that the postero-lateral temporal cortex abstracts actions away from the actors themselves performing these actions.

Verbs, in addition to indicating actions, establish thematic roles, such as who is doing what to whom in a sentence. Thus, the verb "push" implies that someone is doing the pushing and that something is being pushed. By coordinating the argument structure of a sentence, verbs organize a set of possible relations being communicated. Similarly, prepositions describe relationships of two or more objects. For example, the preposition "in" implies two objects in a specific spatial configuration. This shift of focus away from concrete perceptual attributes of objects and to their relations delivers considerable cognitive flexibility and generativity (Gentner, 2003). Our index patient, like other aphasics had difficulty comprehending which participant was doing something to another (Berndt, Haendiges, Mitchum, & Sandson, 1997; Caplan, 1995; Caramazza & Miceli, 1991; Miceli, Silveri, Villa, & Caramazza, 1984; Schwartz et al., 1980; Zingeser & Berndt, 1990). The neural bases of these deficits have received scant attention. We found that thematic role deficits were associated more closely with posterolateral temporal lesions (Wu, Waller, & Chatterjee, 2007).

Aphasic patients can also have difficulty comprehending locative prepositions and spatial relationships between objects (Chatterjee & Maher, 2000; Frederici, 1982; Grodzinsky, 1988; Schwartz et al., 1980). Landau and Jackendoff (1993) adapting the what/where visual processing distinction speculated that locative prepositions might be processed within parietal cortices. One PET study found that naming locative relations activated inferior parietal cortices (Damasio et al., 2001), and similar findings have been reported for sign language (Emmorey et al., 2002). Kemmerer, Tranel and Barrash (2001) found that lesions to the left parietal operculum and prefrontal cortices were more likely to produce deficits in knowledge of locative prepositions. We found that deficits in comprehending locative relations in sentences was associated with dorsally located fronto-parietal lesions (Wu et al., 2007).

The schematic representation of events distills essential aspects of actions and spatial relations within a scene (Talmy, 1996). For example, the schema for 'in' may refer to the features denoting containment and control of a figure object by a landmark/enclosing object. Thus, extraneous features like the size, shape, or orientation of the objects are discarded; while schemas are sensitive to analog/topological information (and thus capable of representing continuous gradations, like movement along a path), they do not constitute mental images in the sense of being directly representative of physical experiences. How spatial schemas are represented within the brain has not received much attention. They are likely related to categorical spatial relations first postulated by Kosslyn and colleagues (Kosslyn et al., 1989; Kosslyn & Ochsner, 1994) to be mediated by the left hemisphere. Our preliminary work in a group of patients with focal brain damage suggests that both schematic and categorical spatial knowledge is disrupted with damage to the left posterior parietal and posterior middle frontal gyri (Amorapanth, Widick, & Chatterjee, 2008). These findings are consistent with Tranel and Kemmerer's (2004) findings that deficits in understanding locative prepositions (such as words like "in," "on," and "above") were associated with damage to the left supramarginal gyrus and subjacent white matter as well as the frontal opercula.

To summarize, events are represented within a distributed network that involves the posterolateral temporal cortex, the posterior parietal cortex and probably the prefrontal cortex including posterior middle frontal gyrus and the inferior frontal gyrus. Within this network, the temporal cortex mediates actions and thematic roles and the fronto-parietal cortices probably work in concert to locate these actions in space. The dynamic properties of events are abstracted away from the perceptual features of the participants and objects themselves. Furthermore, they are schematized to make them flexibly available as primitives supporting different cognitive domains. We hypothesize that the directional schema shorn of detailed sensory-motor features of an actual scene would be instantiated in posterolateral temporal motion areas as well as fronto-parietal path areas, more likely in the left than in the right hemisphere. These schemas then interact with higher order representations such as agency, time or number mediated by other structures.

6.3. Directional selectivity

The neural basis underlying the directional selectivity that could be modulated by experience remains an outstanding question. Certainly neurons in area MT and MST (and even in V1 for that matter) respond preferentially to motion in specific directions (Weliky, Bosking, & Fitzpatrick, 1996) and MT/MST as well as the intraparietal culcus is active when subjects are cued to expect motion in a specific direction (Shulman et al., 1999). But these areas are not known to intrinsically harbor more neurons selective for motion in one direction over another. Recent neurophysiological observations suggest a possible mechanism for directional selectivity in motion perception brought about by experience. Visual neurons in ferrets exhibit weak directional biases that lack any spatial coherence. However, training with moving stimuli strengthens the directionally selective responses in individual neurons, induces the emergence of directional selective cortical columns and even reverses the intrinsic bias of some neurons to the trained direction (Li, Van Hooser, Mazurek, White, & Fitzpatrick, 2008). Of course there are many steps between the acquisition of visual motion selectivity in the ferret's visual cortex and the acquisition of directional spatial primitives in humans. The point is simply that neurophysiological mechanisms to induce directional selectivity based on experience exist. The generalization of such basic mechanisms might offer insight into the biology of how experience can influence directional primitives at the interface of perception and conception.

To return to the question of whether schemas are resistant to change or whether they are modifiable by experience, the following functional-anatomic organization for schematic representations seems likely. Simplified directional schemas are localized to networks in the left dorsolateral prefrontal cortex, the posterolateral parietal cortex and the posterolateral temporal cortex. This localization for schemas in general is likely to be "hardwired" and resistant to modification by experience. However, the specific properties of these schematic representations (such as which direction is being coded) are susceptible to modification by experience.

7. Two popular hypotheses unlikely to be relevant

The basic schematic representation of conceptualizing events as proceeding from left-to-right and agents being placed on the left is malleable as evidenced by their reversals in individuals who read from right-to-left. In retrospect, it seems obvious that biases induced by these directional schemas would be malleable. If such a schema, whether left-to-right or right-to-left, were not subject to change, we would ascribe attributes of power or potency to those on one side of our egocentric space, an ascription that would be reversed if we simply walked around them. In the same vein it would make little evolutionary sense to be much better at recognizing actions if they proceeded from left-to-right and thus be better able to respond to a specific threat if it were coming from one direction and not from another (although, see Vallortigara, 2006, for directional biases that might be adaptive in predator-prey population dynamics). This very malleability of the event schema raises the question, why are these directional schemas so pervasive to begin with?

Before offering conjectures about why such schemas exist, I would like to point out two popular explanations that are unlikely to be relevant to the organization of these default schemas for events. The first explanation is that language structures thought, or a neo-Whorfian account. The second explanation is that interactions with the environment structure thought, or an embodied account.

The neo-Whorfian account states that the structure of language affects how we think and perceive the world. Differences in spatial language have been used to support this view (Bowerman & Choi, 2001; Levinson, 1996; Li & Gleitman, 2002; Munnich, Landaub, & Dosher, 2001). The claim that the structure of language affects how we think and perceive the world is controversial (Choi & Bowerman, 1991; Choi, McDonough, Bowerman,

& Mandler, 1999; Gennari et al., 2002; Papafragou, Massey, & Gleitman, 2002). Here, the merit of the claim itself is not the relevant point. Rather, the relevant point is that neo-Whorfian accounts focus on differences in the semantic content of the words in different languages and how these content differences might affect perception and thought. The directional biases related to written language discussed here have nothing to do with the semantic content of language. Rather, it is a consequence of repeatedly engaging with language in its written form. This consequence has more to do with the habit of scanning or moving one's limb from one side to another than with the content of language per se. We would predict that someone working in a factory assembly line, who works on parts moving from a particular direction for hours on end would have a directional bias in conceiving events induced by these movements. Such biases of course would have nothing to do with language, but would be rendered by a visuo-motor habit.

The embodied account states that the structure of our thought is deeply informed by our interactions in the world. Embodied accounts vary in their details and conceptualization (Wilson, 2002). A common version of embodied accounts is that the mental work done in thinking about entities and events in our minds simulates the sensory and motor conditions of our actual interactions with these entities and events (Barsalou, 1999; Glenberg & Kaschak, 2002; Rizzolatti, Fogassi, & Gallese, 2001). For example, athletes often talk about simulating their performance before the actual performance. Basketball players might imagine themselves at a free throw line looking at the basket, preparing and throwing the ball and imagining it going through the basket. As we have reviewed, the schematic directional representations of events are clearly influenced by reading habits, and in that sense they are influenced by interactions in the world. However, they are not simulations of our interactions with actual events as they occur in the world. We perceive events from every possible direction and encounter individuals we might conceive of as agents in any number of locations. Certainly, some stylized events like races on tracks, whether run by humans, horses, dogs or cars, proceed from left-to-right. But most of us do not spend enough time at race-tracks to such events be ingrained as the prototypic direction for actions. Rather, the stylized direction of these events might follow from our underlying schematic representation.

8. Conjectures about the "why" of directional schemas

If these default event schemas are not accounted for by the structure of language or by the structure of simulated events, then why do they exist? Here I offer a conjecture. This conjecture is based on three notions: the mental structuring of space, reasoning with mental models, and processing efficiency.

8.1. Spatial schemas structure space

As mentioned earlier, Talmy (1996) proposes that spatial schemas are "boiled down" features of spatial scenes. For example, "across" refers to a schema that describes a specific path of movement. This path is approximately perpendicular to the principle axis of the reference object, as in across a river or across a plank. When a movement proceeds in parallel to the principle axis of the reference object, then "along" is more appropriate. Both "across" and "along" are abstracted from the actual scene. In these schemas only selective spatial aspects are relevant. Other aspects of the scene, such as whether the referent object is a river or a plank, are not relevant and are not incorporated into the schema. Schemas are topological rather than imagistic. Schemas capture only some of the infinite possible spatial configurations. This property seems to be a precondition of communication, in which a wide array of spatial situations need to be described rapidly. Thus, the constituents of schemas are simple geometric forms such as points, lines and planes rather than containing the rich and infinite possibilities of perception from which they are derived. By virtue of their being categorical spatial representations, shorn of their perceptual richness, these schemas are organized within left hemisphere structures that instantiate abstractions of motion (posterolateral temporal cortex), and locative and path relations (posterolateral parietal and dorsolateral prefrontal cortex).

8.2. Mental models

Our description of spatial schemas bears a striking resemblance to specific aspects of mental models used in reasoning (Johnson-Laird, 1996). There is a long history of the use of mental models in reasoning (Johnson-Laird, 2004). According to Johnson-Laird, perceptions yield models of the world outside of the perceiver, and comprehension of discourse yields models of the world that the speaker describes to the listener. Thinking often involves the manipulation of these mental models in order to anticipate the world and choose among actions (Johnson-Laird, 2006). This may not be the only kind of thinking, but it is a critical one, especially when it comes to thinking about relations.

Mental models are schematic (Johnson-Laird, 2006). They are schematic insofar as their parts and relations correspond to the structure of the situation they represent. They underlie perception but are not identical to perceptions. And mental models represent abstractions, in that they attempt to capture what is common in all the ways a certain situation might occur. This description of the iconic elements in mental models is nearly identical to Talmy's description of spatial schemas. These mental models can be combined with symbolic elements like negation in the process of reasoning. For our purposes, the point is that event schemas form iconic elements for thinking about simple events that can then be manipulated or recombined in more complex reasoning. For such reasoning and manipulations of schemas, the prefrontal cortices are undoubtedly involved. However, at this level of manipulation and complexity, both hemispheres may very well be involved in processing, a hypothesis that remains to be tested in future research.

Thus far, we have argued that events are schematized in a simple form. As discussed earlier, the location of the agent and the patient and the direction of action are important aspects of this schema. Such schematizing is critical to how we conceptualize space and establish elemental particles used in the construction of mental models for reasoning. But why should people pick a specific location for agents, such as on the left, and a specific direction for actions, such as moving from left-to-right?

8.3. Processing efficiency

The convention of assigning a default direction for actions and a default location for agents provides processing efficiency. Such asymmetries of directional behavior are seen even in fish, toads, and birds and may confer efficiencies for both the individual and the population (Vallortigara, 2006). Within the nervous system localization and distribution of function provides the kind of efficiency needed to conduct processing within complex domains. With experience, such as the repeated exposure of reading and writing in specified directions, neuronal clusters within these localized networks can incorporate directional biases. This emergence of directional selectivity is likely to arise from mechanisms similar to the selective neuronal responses to motion direction in the ferret cortex found by Li and colleagues (2008) referred to earlier.

The specific convention chosen (left to right, or right to left) is not nearly as important as the fact that a specific convention is assigned. This point is best made by analogy. There is no logical reason that a society should choose to drive on the left or on the right. However, it is efficient for cultures to choose one or the other convention and adhere to it. Similar observations can be made on busy sidewalks, where norms of where one walks are not established as rigidly as in driving. People may walk on the right or on the left, but when it gets very busy, people organize naturally into streams of movement in ways that maximizes every ones' ability to move. When schematizing events, we need to establish the sources and directions and causes and goals of actions. By analogy with driving or walking conventions, in the constructing mental models, we adopt a default spatial schema that can then be manipulated if there is a lot of mental work to be done. Thus, no mental resources need to be diverted to establishing and remembering the layout of a schematized event, and one can get on with the business of thinking.

9. Conclusions

A simple directional schema underlies several domains of cognition, such as the representations of time and number and these directional schemas can influence memories and aesthetic judgments. We believe this schema is a distilled representation of spatial events that also function as elements in mental models that allow us to think of relations and to reason about situations. The specific direction used in the schema may be arbitrary and modifiable by experience, but that a direction be chosen seems necessary for processing efficiency.

References

Amorapanth, Prin X., Page Widick & Anjan Chatterjee (2008). *The neural underpinnings of spatial schematic representations*. Paper presented at the Cognitive Neuroscience Society: Annual Meeting Program.

Barsalou, Lawrence W. (1999). Perceptual symbol systems. *Behavioral & Brain Sciences, 22*, 577–660.

Benjafield, John & Sidney Segalowitz (1993). Left and right in Leonardo's drawings of faces. *Empirical Studies of the Arts, 11*, 25–32.

Berndt, Rita S., Anne N. Haendiges, Charlotte C. Mitchum & Jennifer Sandson (1997). Verb retrieval in aphasia: 2. Relationship to sentence processing. *Brain and Language, 56*, 107–137.

Bowerman, Melissa & Soonja Choi (2001). Shaping meanings for language: Universal and language-specific in the acquisition of spatial semantic categories. In Melissa Bowerman & Stephen C. Levinson (Eds.), *Language acquisition and conceptual development* (pp. 475–511). UK: Cambridge University Press.

Caplan, David (1995). Issues arising in contemporary studies of disorders of syntactic processing in sentence comprehension in agrammatic patients. *Brain and Language, 50*, 325–338.

Caramazza, Alfonso & Gabriele Miceli (1991). Selective impairment of thematic role assignment in sentence processing. *Brain and Language, 41*, 402–436.

Chatterjee, Anjan (2001). Language and space: some interactions. *Trends in Cognitive Science, 5*, 55–61.

Chatterjee, Anjan (2002). Portrait profiles and the notion of agency. *Empirical Studies of the Arts, 20*, 33–41.

Chatterjee, Anjan (2008). The neural organization of spatial thought and language. *Seminars in Speech and Language, 29*, 226–238.

Chatterjee, Anjan & Lynn Maher (2000). Grammar and agrammatism. In L. Gonzalez Rothi, B. Crosson & S. Nadeau (Eds.), *Aphasia and Language: Theory to Practice* (pp. 133–156): Guilford Publications.

Chatterjee, Anjan, Lynn M. Maher, Leslie J. Gonzales-Rothi & Kenneth M. Heilman (1995). Asyntactic thematic role assignment: the use of a temporal-spatial strategy. *Brain Lang, 49*, 125–139.

Chatterjee, Anjan, Lynn M. Maher & Kenneth M. Heilman (1995). Spatial characteristics of thematic role representation. *Neuropsychologia, 33*, 643–648.

Chatterjee, Anjan, M. Helen Southwood & David Basilico (1999). Verbs, events and spatial representations. *Neuropsychologia*, 395–402.

Choi, Soonja & Melissa Bowerman (1991). Learning to express motion events in English and Korean: The influence of language-specific lexicalization patterns. *Cognition, 41*, 83–121.

Choi, Soonja, Laraine McDonough, Melissa Bowerman & Jean M. Mandler (1999). Early sensitivity to language-specific spatial categories in English and Korean. *Cognitive Development, 14*(2), 241–268.

Chokron, Sylvie & Marie De Agostini (2002). The influence of handedness on profile and line drawing directionality in children, young, and older normal adults. *Brain and Cognition, 48*, 333–336.

Christman, Stephen (1995). The role of weight versus interest versus directionality in aesthetic preferences. *Journal of the International Neuropsychological Society, 1*, 177.

Damasio, Hanna, Thomas J. Grabowski, Daniel Tranel, Laura L. Ponto, Richard D. Hichwa & Antonio R. Damasio (2001). Neural correlates of naming actions and of naming spatial relations. *Neuroimage, 13*(6 Pt 1), 1053–1064.

Decety, Jean, Julie Grezes, Nicolas Costes, Daniela Perani, Marc Jeannerod, Emmanuel Procyk, F. Grassi & Ferruccio Fazio (1997). Brain activity during observation of actions. Influence of action content and subject strategy. *Brain, 120*, 1763–1777.

Dehaene, Stanislas, Serge Bossini & Pascal Giraux (1993). The mental representation of parity and number magnitude. *Journal of Experimental Psychology: General, 122*, 371–396.

Emmorey, Karen, Hanna Damasio, Stephen McCullough, Thomas Grabowski, Laura L. Ponto, Richard D. Hichwa, Ursula Bellugi (2002). Neural systems underlying spatial language in American Sign Language. *Neuroimage, 17*(2), 812–824.

Frederici, Angela (1982). Syntactic and semantic processing in aphasic deficits: the availability of prepositions. *Brain and Language, 15*, 249–258.
Freimuth, Marilyn & Seymour Wapner (1979). The influence of lateral organization on the evaluation of paintings. *British Journal of Psychology, 70*, 211–218.
Freyd, Jennifer (1983). The mental representation of movement when static stimuli are viewed. *Perception and Psychophysics, 33*, 575–581.
Gennari, Silvia, Stephen A. Sloman, Barbara C. Malt & W. Tecumseh Fitch (2002). Motion events in language and cognition. *Cognition, 83*, 49–79.
Gentner, Dedre (2003). Why we're so smart. In Dedre Gentner & Susan Goldin-Meadows (Eds.), *Language in Mind* (pp. 195–235). Cambridge, MA: The MIT Press.
Gentner, Dedre & Jeffrey Loewenstein (2002). Relational language and relational thought. In James Byrnes & Eric Amsel (Eds.), *Language, Literacy, and Cognitive Development* (pp. 87–120). Mahwah, NJ: Erlbaum.
Glenberg, Arthur M. & Michael P. Kaschak (2002). Grounding language in action. *Psychonomic Bulletin & Review, 9*(3), 558–565.
Gordon, Ian. (1974). Left and right in Goya's portraits. *Nature, 249*, 197–198.
Gordon, Ian. (1981). Left and right in art. In David O'Hare (Ed.), *Psychology and the Arts* (pp. 211–241). Sussex: The Harvester Press.
Grezes, Julie, Pierre Fonlupt, Bennett Bertenthal, Chantal Delon-Martin, Christoph Segebarth & Jean Decety (2001). Does perception of biological motion rely on specific brain regions? *Neuroimage, 13*, 775–785.
Grill-Spector, Kalanit & Rafael Malach (2001). fMRI adaptation: a tool for studying the functional properties of human cortical neurons. *Acta Psychologica, 107*, 293–321.
Grodzinsky, Yosef (1988). Syntactic representations in agrammatic aphasia: the case of prepositions. *Language and Speech, 31*, 115–134.
Grossman, Emily D. & Randolph Blake (2002). Brain areas active during visual perception of biological motion. *Neuron, 35*, 1167–1175.
Grusser, Otto-Joachim, Thomas Selke & Barbara Zynda (1988). Cerebral lateralization and some implications for art, aesthetic perception and aristic creativity. In Ingo Rentschler, Barbara Herzberger & David Epstein (Eds.), *Beauty and the Brain. Biological Aspects of Aesthetics* (pp. 257–293). Boston: Birkhauser Verlag.
Halpern, Andrea & Michael Kelly (1993). Memory bias in left versus right implied motion. *Journal of Experimental Psychology: Learning Memory and Cognition, 19*, 471–484.
Hayward, William G. & Michael J. Tarr (1995). Spatial language and spatial representation. *Cognition, 55*, 39–84.
Humphrey, Nick & I. Chris McManus (1973). Status and the left cheek. *New Scientist, 59*, 437–439.
Jackendoff, Ray (1987). On beyond zebra: The relation of linguistic and visual information. *Cognition, 26*, 89–114.
Jackendoff, Ray (1991). Parts and boundaries. *Cognition, 41*, 9–45.

Jackendoff, Ray (1996). The architecture of the linguistic-spatial interface. In Paul Bloom, Mary A. Peterson, Lynn Nadel & Merrill F. Garrett (Eds.), *Language and Space* (pp. 1–30). Cambridge, MA.

Jackson, John (1932). *Selected writings of John Hughlings Jackson*. London: Hodder and Stoughton.

Johnson, Mark (1987). *The body in mind*. Chicago: Chicago University Press.

Johnson-Laird, Philip N. (1996). Space to think. In Paul Bloom, Mary A. Peterson, Lynn Nadel & Merrill F. Garrett (Eds.), *Language and Space* (pp. 437–462). Cambridge, MA: The MIT Press.

Johnson-Laird, Philip N. (2004). The history of mental models. In Ken Manktelow & Man C. Chung (Eds.), *Psychology of Reasoning: Theoretical and Historprical Perspectives* (pp. 179–212). New Yprk: Psychology Press.

Johnson-Laird, Philip N. (2006). *How We Reason*. New York: Oxford University Press.

Kable, Joseph K., Jessica Lease-Spellmeyer & Anjan Chatterjee (2002). Neural substrates of action event knowledge. *Journal of Cognitive Neuroscience, 14*, 795–804.

Kable, Joseph W. & Anjan Chatterjee (2006). The specificity of action representations in lateral occipitotemporal cortex. *Journal of Cognitive Neuroscience, 18*, 1498–1517.

Kable, Joseph W., Irene Kan, Ashley Wilson, Sharon Thompson-Schill & Anjan Chatterjee (2005). Conceptual representations of action in lateral temporal cortex. *Journal of Cognitive Neuroscience, 17*, 1855–1870.

Kant, Immanuel (Ed.). (1781/1998). *The critique of pure reason*. Cambridge: Cambridge University Press.

Kemmerer, David (2006). The semantics of space: Integrating linguistic typology and cognitive neuroscience. *Neuropsychologia, 44*, 1607–1621.

Kemmerer, David & Daniel Tranel (2000). A Double Dissociation Between Linguistic and Perceptual Representations of Spatial Relationships. *Cognitive Neuropsychology, 17*(5), 393–414.

Kemmerer, David, Daniel Tranel & Joseph Barrash (2001). "Patterns of dissociation in the processing of verb meanings in brain-damaged subjects": Addendum. *Language and Cognitive Processes, 16*(4), 461–463.

Kinsbourne, Marcel (1987). Mechanisms of unilateral neglect. In Marc Jeannerod (Ed.), *Neurophysiological and Neuropsychological Aspects of Spatial Neglect* (pp. 69–86). New York: North Holland.

Kosslyn, Stephen, Olivier Koenig, Anna Barrett, Carolyn B. Cave, Joyce Tang & John Gabrielli (1989). Evidence for two types of spatial representations: Hemispheric specialization for categorical and coordinate relations. *Journal of Experimental Psychology: Human Perception and Performance, 15*, 723–735.

Kosslyn, Stephen M. & Kevin N. Ochsner (1994). In search of occipital activation during visual mental imagery. *Trends Neurosci, 17*, 290–292.

Landau, Barbara & Ray Jackendoff (1993). "What" and "where" in spatial language and spatial cognition. *Behavioral and Brain Sciences, 16*, 217–265.

Levinson, Stephen C. (1996). Language and Space. *Annual Review of Anthropology, 25*, 353–382.
Li, Peggy & Lila Gleitman (2002). Turning the tables: language and spatial reasoning. *Cognition, 83*, 265–294.
Li, Ye, Stephen D. Van Hooser, Mark Mazurek, Leonard E. White & David Fitzpatrick (2008). Experience with moving visual stimuli drives the early development of cortical direction selectivity. *Nature, 456*(7224), 952–956.
Maass, Anne, Damiano Pagani & Emanuela Berta (2007). How beautiful is the goal and how violent is the fistfight? Spatial bias in the interpretation of human behavior. *Social Cognition, 25*(6), 833–852.
Maass, Anne & Aurore Russo (2003). Directional bias in the mental representation of spatial events: nature or culture? *Psychological Science, 14*, 296–301.
Maher, Lynn, Anjan Chatterjee, Leslie Gonzales-Rothi & Kenneth Heilman (1995). Agrammatic sentence production: the use of a temporal-spatial strategy. *Brain Lang, 49*, 105–124.
Mandler, Jean M. (1996). Preverbal representation and language. In Paul Bloom, Mary A. Peterson, Lynn Nadel & Merrill F. Garrett (Eds.), *Language and Space* (pp. 365–384). Cambridge, MA: The MIT Press.
Mandler, Jean M. (2004). *The foundations of mind: Origins of conceptual thought.* New York, NY: Oxford University Press.
Martin, Alex, James V. Haxby, Francois M. Lalonde, Cheri L. Wiggs & Leslie G. Ungerleider (1995). Discrete cortical regions associated with knowledge of color and knowledge of action. *Science, 270*, 102–105.
Martin, Alex & Jill Weisberg (2003). Neural foundations for understanding social and mechanical concepts. *Cognitive Neuropsychology, 20*, 575–587.
McLaughlin, John & Julie Kermisch (1997). Salience of compositional cues and the order of presentation in the picture reversal effect. *Empirical Studies of the Arts, 15*, 21–27.
McLaughlin, John & Kimberly Murphy (1994). Preference for profile orientation in portraits. *Empirical Studies in the Arts, 12*, 1–7.
McManus, I. Chris (2002). *Right Hand, Left Hand.* London: Weidenfield & Nicholson.
McManus, I. Chris & Nick Humphrey (1973). Turning the left cheek. *Nature, 243*, 271–272.
Mead, Andrew & John McLaughlin (1979). The role of handedness and stimulus asymmetry in aesthetic preference. *Brain and Cognition, 20*, 300–307.
Miceli, Gabriele, M. Caterina Silveri, Giampiero Villa & Alfonso Caramazza (1984). On the basis for the agrammatics difficulty in producing main verbs. *Cortex, 20*, 207–220.
Munnich, Edward, Barbara Landau & Barbara A. Dosher (2001). Spatial Language and Spatial Representation: a Cross-Linguistic Comparison. *Cognition, 81*(3), 171–207.
Nachson, Israel, Einat Argaman & Assaf Luria (1999). Effects of directional habits and handedness on aesthetic preference for left and right profiles. *Journal of Cross-Cultural Psychology, 30*, 106–114.

Nicholls, Michael E.R., Danielle Clode, Stephen J. Wood & Amanda G. Wood (1999). Laterality of expression in portraiture: putting your best cheek forward. *Proceedings of the Royal Society B: Biological Sciences, 266*(1428), 1517–1522.

Padakannaya, Prakash, M.L. Devi, B. Zaveria, Sanjoo K. Chengappa & Jyotsna Vaid (2002). Directional scanning effect and strength of reading habit in picture naming and recall. *Brain and Cognition, 48*, 404–490.

Palmer, A. Richard (2004). Symmetry Breaking and the Evolution of Development. *Science, 306*(5697), 828–833.

Papafragou, Anna, Christine Massey & Lila Gleitman (2002). Shake, rattle, 'n' roll: the representation of motion in language and cognition. *Cognition, 84*, 189–212.

Regier, Terry (1995). A model of human capacity for categorizing spatial relations. *Cognitive Linguistics, 6*, 63–88.

Rizzolatti, Giacomo, Leonardo Fogassi & Vittorio Gallese (2001). Neurophysiological mechanisms underlying the understanding and imitation of action. *Nature Review Neuroscience, 2*, 661–670.

Saffran, Eleanor M., Myrna F. Schwartz & Oscar S.M. Marin (1980). The word order problem in agrammatism. II. Production. *Brain and Language, 10*, 263–280.

Santiago, Julio, Antonio Román & Marc Ouellet (this volume). *Flexible foundations of abstract thought: A review and a theory.*

Santiago, Julio, Juan Lupianez, Elvira Perez & Maria J. Funes (2007). Time (also) flies from left to right. *Psychonomic Bulletin & Review, 14*, 512–516.

Schwartz, Myrna F., Eleanor M. Saffran & Oscar S.M. Marin (1980). The word order problem in agrammatism. I. Comprehension. *Brain and Language, 10*, 249–262.

Shulman, Gordon, John Ollinger, Erbil Akbudak, Thomas Conturo, Abraham Snyder, Steven Peterson & Maurizio Corbetta (1999). Areas involved in encoding and applying directional expectations to moving objects. *The Journal of Neuroscience, 19*, 9480–9496.

Speer, Nicole K., Khena M. Swallow & Jeffrey M. Zacks (2003). Activation of human motion processing areas during event perception. *Cognitive, Affective & Behavioral Neuroscience, 3*(4), 335–345.

Suitner, Caterina & Anne Maass (2007). Positioning bias in portraits and self-portraits: Do women make different decisions? *Empirical Studies of the Arts, 25*, 71–95.

Suitner, Caterina & I. Chris McManus (this volume). Aesthetic asymmetries, spatial agency, and art history: A social psychological perspective.

Talmy, Leonard (1983). How language structures space. In Herbert Pick & Linda Acredolo (Eds.), *Spatial orientation: theory, research and application.* New York: Plenum Press.

Talmy, Leonard (1985). Lexicalization patterns: Semantic structure in lexical forms. In T. Shopen (Ed.), *Language typology and syntactic description* (pp. 57–149). New York, NY: Cambridge University Press.

Talmy, Leonard (1996). Fictive motion in language and "caption". In Paul Bloom, Mary Peterson, Lynn Nadel & Merrill Garrett (Eds.), *Language and Space* (pp. 211–276). Cambridge, MA: The MIT Press.

Talmy, Leonard (2000). *Towards a cognitive semantics: Concept structuring systems*. Cambridge, MA: The MIT Press.

Tootell, Roger B.H., John B. Reppas, Kenneth K. Kwong, Rafael Malach, Richard T. Born, Thomas J. Bardy, Bruce R. Rosen & John W. Belliveau (1995). Functional analysis of human MT and relating visual cortical areas using magnetic resonance imaging. *The Journal of Neuroscience, 15*, 3215–3230.

Tranel, Daniel & David Kemmerer (2004). Neuroanatomical correlates of locative prepositions. *Cognitive Neuropsychology, 21*, 719–749.

Treue, Stefan & John H.R. Maunsell (1996). Attentional modulation of visual motion processing in cortical areas MT and MST. *Nature, 382*, 539–541.

Tversky, Barbara, Sol Kugelmass & Atalia Winter (1991). Cross-cultural and developmental trends in graphic productions. *Cognitive Psychology, 23*, 515–557.

Vaid, Jyotsna, Maharaj Singh, Tripti Sakhuja & Gian C. Gupta (2002). Stroke direction asymmetry in figure drawing: Influence of handedness and reading/writing habits. *Brain and Cognition, 48*, 597–602.

Vallortigara, Giorgio (2006). The evolutionary psychology of left and right: Costs and benefits of lateralization. *Developmental Psychobiology, 48*, 418–427.

Weliky, Michael, William H. Bosking & David Fitzpatrick (1996). A systematic map of direction preference in primary visual cortex. *Nature, 379*(6567), 725–728.

Wilson, Margaret (2002). Six views of embodied cognition. *Psychonomic Bulletin & Review, 9*(4), 625–636.

Wu, Denise H., Anne Morganti & Anjan Chatterjee (2008). Neural substrates of processing path and manner information of a moving event. *Neuropsychologia, 46*, 704–713.

Wu, Denise H., Sara Waller & Anjan Chatterjee (2007). The functional neuroanatomy of thematic role and locative relational knowledge. *The Journal of Cognitive Neuroscience, 19*, 1542–1555.

Zacks, Jeffrey M., Khena M. Swallow, Jean M. Vettel & Mark P. McAvoy (2006). Visual motion and the neural correlates of event perception. *Brain Research, 1076*(1), 150–162.

Zingeser, Louise B. & Rita S. Berndt (1990). Retrieval of nouns and verbs in agrammatism and anomia. *Brain and Language, 39*, 14–32.

Understanding spatial bias in face perception and memory

Nuala Brady[1]

Abstract

This paper considers a curious spatial bias in the perception of faces, our tendency to see the left half of a face as 'looking more like' or as 'being more representative of' the whole face than is the right half of the face. Although subtle, the phenomenon is robust and a left side bias has also been demonstrated for the perception of emotional expression, gender, age and attractiveness. In considering whether this perceptual bias reflects hemispheric asymmetries in visual processing or a bias in attention that is perhaps related to the convention of reading from left to right, I draw on a literature in psycholinguistics that asks similar questions with respect to word recognition. The conclusion – that perceptual biases in face perception may ultimately reflect the scale of information needed for successful task performance – is considered in light of recent argument that models of word recognition and face perception need consider the problem of interhemispheric integration.

1. Introduction

The human visual system is remarkably sensitive to symmetry, in particular, to mirror symmetry about the vertical axis. Mirror symmetry, which is also known as bilateral symmetry, is defined as self-similarity about a central axis (Weyl, 1952), and is characteristic of many natural and man made forms (Shepard, 1988; McManus, 2002). These forms include the human body and the human face. Although not perfectly symmetrical, bodies and faces are self-similar about the vertical midline so that their right and left halves approximate mirror images of each other. The perceptual salience of

---

[1] I am grateful to Thomas Schubert and Marc Brysbaert for comments on an early draft of this chapter and to Anne Maass and Thomas Schubert for organizing the workshop in Venice.

symmetry may reflect both the prevalence of mirror-symmetric forms in nature and the particular importance of biological forms to social cognition.

For example, since Darwin's early speculations that deviations from 'the law of symmetry' are not inherited, fluctuating asymmetry – the minor, random departures from the ideal of bilateral symmetry – is of great interest to both evolutionary biology and psychology (Palmer & Strobeck, 1986; Thornhill & Gangestad, 1999). Thought to reflect the degree to which an individual has fought disease and toxins during development and growth, facial symmetry may serve as a visual cue to health and reproductive fitness. Evidence from experimental psychology supports this view. For example, images of faces that have been manipulated to increase symmetry by correcting for fluctuating asymmetry are judged to be more attractive than the original faces (Perrett et al., 1999). This evolutionary perspective provides one reason why our visual system is so sensitive to symmetrical form.

The detection of mirror symmetry is fast and seemingly unmediated as shown by Barlow and Reeves (1979) who measured observers' ability to discriminate random dot patterns to which symmetry of varying degrees had been added. This early psychophysical study shows that symmetry detection is versatile, in that observers could detect mirror symmetry when the axis of symmetry was rotated away from the vertical or when a vertical axis of symmetry was displayed to the left or right of the observers' line of sight. But sensitivity was highest for patterns that are symmetrical about a fixated vertical axis, a finding that is perhaps very relevant to understanding face recognition.

Despite, or perhaps because of, its remarkable sensitivity to symmetry, the visual system is, in certain circumstances, insensitive to the perturbation of symmetry (see Wagemans, 1997, for review), a point that is simply demonstrated in Figure 1. Like all human faces, the face of the girl in the top panel shows some degree of asymmetry about the central axis. But this asymmetry is not particularly salient. It is only when two symmetrical versions of the face are made, one from the left half and one from the right half of the face as shown in the lower panel, that the differences between the two sides of the face become evident[2]. This insensitivity to minor asymmetry has been previously described with respect to the perception of shapes and objects; for example, Freyd and Tversky (1984) show that near symmetrical test shapes are judged to be more similar to more symmetrical

---

2   Unless otherwise specified, the terms 'left (and right) half of the face' are used throughout this paper to refer to the left and right side of the face from the perspective of the viewer.

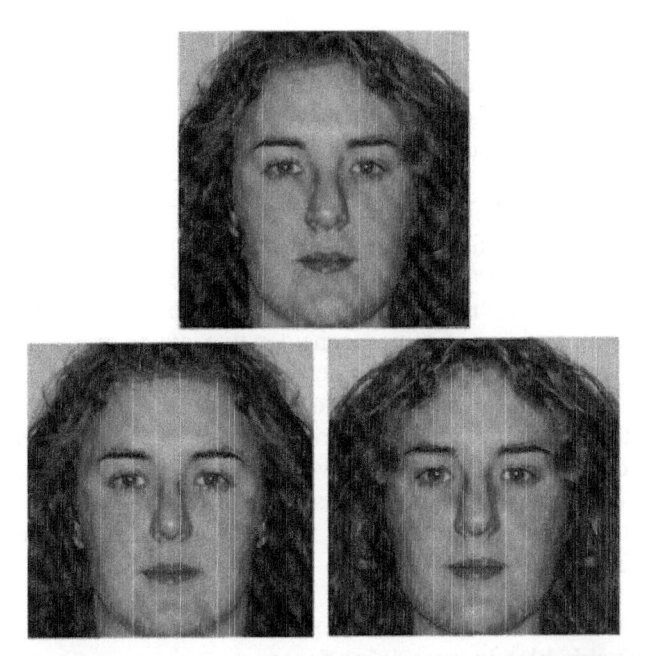

Figure 1. Asymmetry is often overlooked in near symmetrical forms. The differences between the left and right halves of the girl's face are clear when we compare the left-left (bottom left panel) and right-right (bottom right panel) composites but are less obvious when we view the original, left-right face (top panel).

than to less symmetrical standards. An analogous result is reported for faces. Tjan and Liu (2005) measured observers' ability to discriminate pairs of faces differing only in the degree of symmetry and found that discrimination was less easy when the comparison was between a perfectly symmetrical face and a less symmetrical one than when it was between two asymmetrical faces. They conclude that the presence of symmetry impedes the discrimination of minor asymmetry.

This tendency to see symmetry in near symmetrical forms was well known to the Gestalt psychologists for whom symmetry was an example of 'good form'. Attneave (1954), for whom 'good form' implied predictability, saw symmetry as one of the many forms of redundancy in pattern and shape which the visual system might exploit in providing an economical description of the world. Similarly, Barlow and Reeves (1979) suggest that the perceptual salience of symmetry might reflect this potential for economical description rather than the prevalence or importance of symmetry in natural forms. They note that, in the case of mirror symmetry, the visual system need only represent one half of the form.

Obviously, the fact that we perceive asymmetry in faces – and this perception underlies judgments of facial attractiveness – shows that at some level of visual coding, both halves of the face are represented. But perhaps there are circumstances in which the redundancy of bilateral symmetry may be used to advantage? Looking again at Figure 1, the reader may perceive the left-left composite image in the lower panel to look more like the original face in the top panel than does the right-right composite. Our perception appears dominated by one half of a near symmetrical form. Below I review experimental evidence for this left side bias in face perception and memory and consider two major explanations for the effect, that the spatial bias reflects hemispheric asymmetries in visual processing, or a bias in attention to the left side of the face. As this same debate occurs in the literature on word recognition – where there is a well-documented spatial bias in fixating words to the left of centre during reading – I also consider how recent research in psycholinguistics might inform discussion about the relative roles of lateralization and scanning biases in perceptual asymmetries.

2. The left side bias in perceiving faces

Chimeric faces, including those where one half of a photograph is combined with a mirror reversed copy of itself, are central to the study of the perception of facial identity (Wolff, 1933; Gilbert & Bakan, 1973; Rhodes, 1985; Luh, Redl, & Levy, 1994; Chen, German, & Zaidel, 1997). A typical experiment involves a matching task as illustrated in Figure 1. When asked whether a left-left or right-right composite face looks more like the original (left-right) face, a majority of people choose the left-left composite which corresponds to the half face that lies in their left visual field when viewing the original photograph.

This bias was attributed to the physical characteristics of the face itself in early studies of the effect, with the right side of the face (which lies to the viewer's left) said to be more expressive of its owner's character and personality (Wolff, 1933; see McManus, 2002). However, with regard to the portrayal of emotion at least, it is the left side of the face (which lies to the viewer's right) that is perceived to be the more expressive (Moscovitch & Olds, 1982). In a review of forty-nine experiments that measured asymmetry in both posed and spontaneous expressions, Borod et al. (1998) report that when spatial asymmetries are observed they are mainly left-sided (right-sided from the viewer's perspective). If asymmetry of expression is a factor determining the spatial bias in perceiving faces, then this bias should be the opposite of what it is.

Gilbert and Bakan (1973) proposed and investigated an alternative explanation that the perceptual bias reflects a lateralization of function in the viewer's brain. In their study, participants who were originally shown a true (left-right) image of a face chose the left-left composite as being more like it, whereas those shown the mirror-reversed (left^M-right^M) image chose the left^M-left^M composite for a perceptual match (see Figure 2 for terminology). Perceptual judgments, then, are biased toward the half-face that lies in the viewer's left visual field and seem to have little to do with physiognomy.

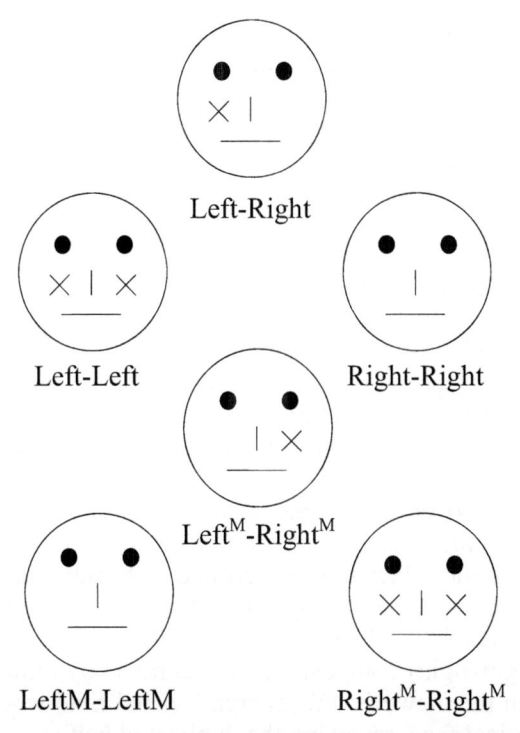

Figure 2. Gilbert and Bakan (1973) introduced a novel variant of the chimeric faces task by presenting some participants with an original (left-right) face (top panel) and others with a mirror-reversed (left^M-right^M) original (bottom panel). Those presented with the left-right face were biased toward choosing the left-left composite as looking more like it, whereas those presented with the left^M-right^M face were biased toward choosing the left^M-left^M composite. A left-right face refers to an image of a face in the true, original or photographed orientation. The left and right halves of the face correspond to those that fall in the viewer's left and right visual fields respectively when centering their gaze on the face. A left^M-right^M face is a mirror-reversed version of this face where the left and right halves are switched.

The left side bias in chimeric face perception is robust and has been demonstrated for the perception of gender and age, attractiveness and emotional expression (Burt & Perrett, 1997; Chen et al., 1997; Vaid & Singh, 1989; See Vaid, this volume, for a review of the literature on emotional expression). The experimental setup is different in these studies and involves presenting a pair of composite images, which differ in whether the characteristic of interest (e.g., beauty, masculinity) is presented to the right or to the left side. Particularly striking are the computer generated chimeras made by Burt and Perrett (1997) by blending the right and left sides of composite images which represent the 'average face' from a particular population (e.g., young females, attractive males). As these averaged images are free of symmetrical skin blemishes, idiosyncratic hairstyles and the central seam often visible in badly made chimeras, they are arguably suited to the study of eye movement patterns generated when viewing faces (Butler et al., 2005; Butler and Harvey, 2006). As discussed below, the left-side bias in perception is also seen with these chimeras.

3. The left side bias and memory

My research, in collaboration with colleagues at University College Dublin, shows that the spatial bias in the perception of facial identity is retained in memory for faces that are highly familiar to us and this is illustrated here for the specific case of friends' faces (Brady, Campbell, & Flaherty, 2004, 2005).

Our study employed both a memory task and a matching task. In the memory task, 99 participants were each presented with two composite images of a close friend's face – a left-left and right-right composite image – and were asked to choose the composite which looked most like their friend based on their memory of their friend's face. As shown in Figures 1 and 2, a left-left (or right-right) composite image is made by duplicating the half-face that falls in the viewer's left (or right) visual field when centring their gaze on the original face, reversing the duplicated half and stitching the two halves together to form a symmetrical image. Participants were not shown the original face in this memory task, only a pair of symmetrical composites such as the two images in the lower panel of Figure 1. In our study, about 68% of participants choose the left-left composite to be a better likeness to their friend as remembered, suggesting that the left side bias is retained in our memory for highly familiar faces. This percentage is significantly different from the 50% expected if there were no spatial bias in memory.

The matching task was identical to that used by Gilbert and Balkan (1973), except that we used highly familiar friends' faces whereas they used faces that were unfamiliar to participants. Approximately half of the participants (52/99) were presented with an image of their friend's face shown in the familiar, photographed (left-right) orientation and were asked to choose whether a left-left or right-composite image looked most like the image of their friend. This task is illustrated in the upper panel of Figure 2. The rest of the participants (47/99) were presented with an image of their friend's face shown in the unfamiliar, mirror-reversed (left^M-right^M) orientation and were asked to choose whether a left^M-left^M or right^M-right^M composite image looked most like the image of their friend. This task is illustrated in the lower panel of Figure 2.

The data for the matching task concur with the results of the memory task in showing a left side spatial bias. When matching to a photograph of a friend presented in the familiar (left-right) orientation, a large majority (42/52, ~81%) chose a left-left composite match, a value much higher than reported previously in matching tasks with unfamiliar faces (Gilbert & Bakan, 1973; Rhodes, 1985; Chen et al., 1997). This value is highly significant, $p < 0.001$, one-sided binomial test [42,52,1/2]. By comparison, when matching to an unfamiliar mirror image of a friend (left^M-right^M), the number that chose a left^M-left^M composite match was much smaller, (29/47, ~62%), and this value did not reach significance at conventional levels, $p = 0.072$, one-sided binomial test [29,47,1/2]. The difference in these percentages (81% and 62%) was significant, and this contrast in performance when matching to a true or mirror image was not seen in our control experiment employing participants who were unfamiliar with the faces or in previous research with unfamiliar faces, see Brady et al. (2005) for details. We suggest that the very high percentage of left-left matches in the case of matching to a true (left-right) original reflects a coincidence of bias that exists both in perception and in memory. By comparison, when matching to a face presented in the unfamiliar, mirror reversed (left^M-right^M) orientation, the left-side bias of perception (which induces people to choose a left^M-left^M composite) conflicts with a memory bias to choose a left-left composite as looking most like one's friend. Note that the left-left composite is identical to the rightM-rightM composite in Figure 2.

In summary, it appears that the left side bias in the perception of faces gets translated into a left side memory bias in the case of highly familiar faces, reinforcing the notion of right hemisphere dominance in face processing.

4. Hemispheric asymmetry or scanning bias?

Although the spatial bias in the perception of faces has been studied for a long time, its neurological basis is still unclear. As information from the left visual field projects to the right hemisphere of the brain, the bias is normally assumed to reflect the dominance of the right hemisphere in face processing (Gilbert & Bakan, 1973). This is consistent with neurological findings that prosopagnosia normally involves damage to the right brain (De Renzi et al., 1994), that patients with right brain damage fail to show a left visual field bias in matching chimeric faces (Kolb, Milner, & Taylor, 1983), and with experimental studies which show a left visual field or right hemisphere advantage in normal processing of faces (Rizzolatti, Umiltà, & Berlucchi, 1971). But the effect has also been attributed to a bias of attention to the left side of the face, and here the story is complicated by the different ways in which an attentional bias might operate. The effect could reflect the specialized role of the right parietal cortex in the control of spatial attention, which may bias eye movements and attention toward the left side of visual space (Burt & Perrett, 1997). Or, following the ideas of Kinsbourne (1970), the attentional bias to the left of the face might be induced by the 'preponderant activation' of the dominant right hemisphere. Finally, as first studied by Gilbert and Bakan (1973), the left side bias in the perception of facial identity may reflect a scanning pattern that is related to the convention of reading from left to right.

The notion that reading – a taught skill that requires extensive practice in childhood before adult fluency is reached – influences a seemingly effortless and early developing skill like face perception is, at first pass, a curious one. But reading practice may induce a bias in scanning that influences visuospatial processing outside the verbal domain, and scanning biases have been shown, at least in part, to underlie spatial biases in line bisection (Chokron & Imbert, 1993), the mental representation of action events (Maass & Russo, 2003; but see also Chatterjee, 2001), and judgments of facial affect (Vaid & Singh, 1998). Kazandjian and Chokron (2008) provide a recent summary.

Gilbert and Bakan (1973) investigated the idea that a scanning bias underlies the left side bias normally seen in matching chimeric faces by comparing the performance of American and Israeli participants, the latter being experienced in reading Hebrew, a script that is read from right to left. The strong leftward bias shown by the American group was reduced, although still present, for the Israeli group. Using chimeras in which either the right or left half face was smiling, Vaid and Singh (1989) measured spatial bias in the perception of expression for different groups of participants, including right-handed readers of Hindi (read left to right), and right-handed readers of Arabic and Urdu (both read right to left, but with Urdu readers, who were also experienced in reading Hindi, considered as bidirectional readers). As predicted, the Hindi readers showed a greater leftward spatial bias than the other two groups. In turn, the rightward bias shown by readers of Arabic was more pronounced than that shown by the bidirectional readers in the Urdu group, although this difference did not reach significance. As the left to right and right to left readers' biases did not mirror each other, the authors conclude that the overall pattern of bias likely reflects a bias due to the lateralization of perceptual functioning that is modulated by habitual reading direction.

Although scanning direction whilst viewing faces has not been formally compared for readers of different scripts, a number of studies provide information on how we scan faces. Particularly relevant are two recent studies in which eye movements were recorded while participants made judgments of gender of chimeric faces (Butler et al., 2005; Butler & Harvey, 2006). In the first of these, the faces were presented for 2 seconds each, and participants showed the expected left side perceptual bias in judging gender. Consistent with other reports of a bias to the left of centre in the initial fixation of faces (Phillips & David, 1997; Leonards & Scott-Samuel, 2005; Barton et al., 2006), this study reports that 75% of initial fixations were to the left of centre. However, this bias was seemingly unrelated to performance on the task; on trials where participants showed the expected left-side bias, 77.1% of initial fixations were to the left and on trials where participants showed a right-side perceptual bias, 71% of initial fixations were to the left. An analysis of subsequent fixations provided some support for the idea that a bias in scanning underlies the bias in perception, in that participants made significantly more fixations to the left than to the right on trials in which perception was biased to the left side (62.8% of all trials). However, there was no difference in the number or duration of fixations to the left or right for trials on which participants showed a right-side perceptual bias (37.2% of all trials).

In a follow-up study, Butler and Harvey (2006) show that the left perceptual bias persists when faces are presented centrally for 100 milliseconds, a time too brief to allow for a saccade and new fixation. The authors conclude that the perceptual bias likely reflects the dominance of the right hemisphere in face perception, and speculate that, with longer viewing times, it is the increased salience of the left side of the face during the initial fixation (due to the dominance of the right hemisphere) that drives eye movements leftward. To clarify, the initial central fixation is enforced by the experimental design so that what is referred to above as the 'initial saccade' (of which 75% were leftward) is in fact the first free saccade made from a centrally fixated starting point.

A recent study of the role of eye-movements in face recognition by Hsiao and Cottrel (2009) distinguishes itself from those reviewed above by a simple but important difference in methods. In investigating the minimum number of fixations needed for face recognition, the authors also asked whether there is a 'preferred landing position' in viewing faces analogous to that documented in the literature on reading. Participants were presented with novel faces in the learning phase of the experiment and were asked to distinguish these from foils in a later test phase. They fixated a centrally placed mark at the start of each trial, and the faces were then presented either to the upper or lower half of the display, thus allowing an analysis of where people initially fixate when not forced to fixate centrally. In addition to showing that two fixations suffice for recognition of recently learned faces, the data also show something remarkable about the initial saccades made to the face. The distribution of the first fixation, particularly in the test phase, is tightly tied to the central midline of the face, the mean position showing but a slight bias to the left of centre of the nose. This suggests that in viewing faces, at least for the purpose of recognition, there is a 'preferred landing position' close to the centre of the face. The result is reminiscent of that reported by Barlow and Reeves (1979) in their study of the detection of mirror symmetry about the vertical midline; detection is most efficient for centrally fixated patterns (see also Herbert & Humphrey, 1996).

To conclude this section, while both lateralization of visual processing and attentional biases have been proposed to underlie the left side bias in face perception, the bulk of the evidence appears to favor the former explanation. First, while there is some evidence that a habitual pattern of right to left scanning during reading may lessen the leftward bias in face perception, the way in which this modulates underlying hemispheric asymmetries is poorly understood. Research on how right-to-left readers scan faces is needed, and in particular, whether they show characteristically different scan-paths to left-to-right readers. Secondly, the leftward bias is seen for briefly presented and centrally fixated stimuli, showing that a scanning bias is not necessary for the effect to occur. Finally, while a number of studies have shown a leftward bias in the initial saccade to images of faces, this 'initial saccade' is usually from a centrally positioned fixation point preset by the experimenter. Under more naturalistic viewing conditions we appear to centre our initial gaze when looking at faces, at least when our task is to decide whether we have seen the face before (Hsiao & Cottrel, 2009). Assuming that the time course of the 'chimeric faces effect' is rapid, it may predominantly reflect the dominance of the right hemisphere in face perception and recognition. This raises the important question of what it is that is special about the right hemisphere and faces.

5. What is special about the right hemisphere?

Face recognition is often described as 'special' where this term is used to imply a form of representation that is unique to faces (Farah, Wilson, Drain, & Tanaka, 1998). Although both facial features and facial shape are important in recognizing faces, it is generally accepted that our expertise in distinguishing faces relies to a large extent on a representation of shape or configuration (Leopold, O'Toole, Vetter, & Blanz, 2001; Leopold, Bondar, & Giese, 2006). Face recognition is lateralized in early infancy (de Schonen & Mathivet, 1990), and it is now known that the development of expertise in configural face processing is dependent on visual input to the right hemisphere during infancy (LeGrand, Mondloch, Maurer, & Brent, 2003).

LeGrand et al. (2003) showed that adults who had suffered early deprivation of input to the right hemisphere due to cataract in the left eye (in infancy, visual input to either eye projects predominantly to the contralateral hemisphere) were impaired in discriminating faces on the basis of configuration but were unimpaired in discriminating faces on the basis of features. In comparison, adults who had suffered early deprivation of input to the left hemisphere showed comparable performance to normally developed controls on both tasks. The study shows that 'the two hemispheres are not created equal' (LeGrand et al., 2003; p. 1110). Normal input to the left hemisphere alone is insufficient for the development of expert configural processing whereas the right hemisphere seems predisposed to develop this expertise. The authors' suggestions, that neural networks in the right hemisphere are predisposed to respond to faces or to respond to the low spatial frequency information that describes facial configuration, are reminiscent of early ideas on the relative roles of the two hemispheres in face perception.

One idea is that opposite hemispheres of the brain process perceptual information at different scales with the right hemisphere biased toward the analysis of relatively global information and the left hemisphere toward the analysis of local detail (Sergent, 1985; Ivry & Robertson, 1998). In early versions of this proposal, the terms 'local' and 'global' are often used in analogy with the Gestalt terms 'parts' and 'wholes'. For example, our perception of a face depends not just on the presence of local parts or features (the eyes, nose and mouth), but also on the specific spatial arrangement of these features. This arrangement constitutes the global form. Later versions of this account borrow from the language of Fourier analysis, which describes how complex spatial patterns such as faces may be described as a composite of simple, sinusoidal gratings of different frequencies (cycles of light and dark grating bands), orientations and phases. Here the terms 'local' and 'global' are used to refer to relatively high and low spatial frequencies respectively. For example, a middle range of spatial frequencies, around 8–16 cycles per face, is noted as important for the identification of faces (Costen, Parker, & Craw, 1996).

Since the seminal work of Campbell and Robson (1968) proposing that the visual system performs a local, spatial frequency analysis of the visual scene, there is a wealth of evidence that neurons in primary visual cortex may be modeled as local filters tuned to the scale and orientation of luminance and color contrast (for review, see Lennie & Movshon, 2005). As there is no evidence for differences in the spatial frequency tuning of individual neurons in the right and left visual cortices, scale based processing is proposed to operate at the level of 'attentional filtering' in Ivry and Robertson's account, i.e., the right and left hemispheres are said to differentially amplify information at different spatial scales. A recent model by Hsiao, Shieh and Cottrel (2008) assumes hardwired differences in the scale of processing between the hemispheres at the level of neural networks. By both these accounts the right hemisphere is 'special' in the sense of allowing a representation of configuration at a scale that is particularly important for face recognition. This may account for the predominance of right hemisphere damage in prosopagnosia (De Renzi et al., 1994), and for the left visual field (right hemisphere) advantages in speed and accuracy seen in normal processing of faces (Rizzolatti, Umiltà, & Berlucchi, 1971).

To summarize, if we accept that the left-side bias in perceiving faces predominantly reflects differences in how the left and right hemispheres process spatial information, then we must specify what these differences are. The idea that the left and right hemispheres represent relatively 'local' and 'global' information, respectively, is strengthened by evidence for scale-based processing in early vision. It is also supported by recent reports of a hardwired (or early developing) division of labor between the hemispheres in the representation of features and configural information for faces (LeGrand et al., 2003).

However, this is not to suggest that our perception of and memory for faces is determined exclusively by right hemisphere processing. First, spatial biases in face perception are relative rather than absolute as expected from models that assume considerable overlap in the scale of information represented by the hemispheres (Ivry & Robertson, 1998; Hsiao, Shieh & Cottrel, 2008). Secondly, while some perceptual tasks (recognition and discrimination of faces) may rely on a relatively global analysis, others (recognition of emotional expression) may rely on a more local analysis (Xu, Dayan, Lipkin, & Qian, 2008). Thirdly, as discussed in the next section on word recognition, there is evidence for a foveal split in early visual processing such that information from the right and left visual fields are represented independently. How this information is brought together for a unified, conscious percept is poorly understood. However, the effect of its initial separation on conscious perception is dramatically illustrated in a recent case study of 'unilateral left prosopometamorphopsia'. Here, following recovery from a lesion to her left occipital cortex, a women perceived the left side of peoples' faces (right side from her perspective) to appear distorted (Trojano, Conson, Salzano, Manzo, & Grossi, 2009).

6. Hemispheric asymmetry and word recognition

Models of word recognition often implicitly assume that the central visual field, which is characterized by high visual acuity, is represented bilaterally (Brysbaert, 2004). However, there is little evidence to support this assumption. Instead, results from brain imaging studies, from studies of visual processing in the split brain, and from behavioral studies using the Poffenberger paradigm all suggest that the foveal representation is split (Brysbaert, 2004; Lavidor & Walsh, 2004). Information from the right visual field projects to the left hemisphere of the brain and information from the left visual field projects to the right hemisphere of the brain with minimal or no overlapping representation of the midline. As transfer of information across the corpus callosum is estimated to take ~10 ms for letter-like stimuli (Murray et al., 2001), Brysbaert (2004) argues that models of word recognition need to consider how information from the two visual fields is integrated.

Word recognition, like face perception, has a well-studied spatial bias. There is a 'preferred landing position' in reading text such that when fixating a word, readers position that initial fixation somewhere between the start and the middle of the word. They rarely fixate the middle as would be expected if the goal were to centre the word on the fovea. This 'preferred landing position' in fluid reading is close to the 'optimal viewing position', which is defined as the position associated with the shortest recognition times for words viewed in isolation (O'Regan & Jacobs, 1992; see Rayner, 1998, for a review). As reviewed in this chapter, the left side bias in face perception has been attributed to three different factors; these include differences in the informational content of the two sides of the face (i.e., the very old idea that one half of the face is more expressive than the other), a scanning bias related to the convention of reading from left to right, and to lateralization of perceptual function. These same three factors have been put forward to explain the sensorimotor bias in fixating words to the left of centre (see, for example, Nazir et al., 2004, for an account of the effect of reading habits on the 'optimal viewing position' for character recognition).

Research by Marc Brysbaert and colleagues (Brysbaert, 1994; Hunter, Brysbaert, & Knecht, 2007) makes a strong case that the spatial bias in fixating a word reflects the normal superiority of the left hemisphere in language processing. The idea is that the leftward bias in fixation shifts the bulk of the word into the right visual field, which is processed by the language-dominant left hemisphere. By this reasoning, the effect should be diminished or absent in people with atypical lateralization of language (right hemisphere or bilateral representation). Their studies confirm this expectation, showing that for participants with left lateralization of language, fixations to the first or second letter of a word produce the fastest recognition times whereas fixations to the last letter produce the longest latencies. The effect is reversed for participants with atypical language lateralization in the case of short (3 letter) words and absent or inconsistent in the case of longer words. Notably, the other two explanations of the left fixation bias in word recognition – that it reflects a bias in scanning or that it reflects a difference in the information content between the start and the end of a typical word – do not predict these results.

Returning to face perception, and accepting that the right hemisphere is dominant for this task, findings of a leftward bias in scanning now seem counterintuitive (Butler et al., 2005). In scanning to the left of centre, the bulk of the face is shifted to the right visual field and so to the less dominant left hemisphere. If eye movements during reading operate to facilitate word processing by the dominant hemisphere, why do they seem to operate in a less than facilitatory manner when viewing faces? A closer look at the eye movement data is revealing. First, as noted above, studies reporting a leftward bias in the 'initial saccade' to a face often utilize a paradigm in which participants' first view is actually of a centrally fixated face. Secondly, Butler et al. (2005) show that over a 2 second viewing period, the left side bias in the number of saccades is slight and non-significant, 55% to the left and 45% to the right. The distribution of saccades collected across participants for both whole faces and for chimeric faces, shown in their Figure 1 (Butler et al., 2005, p. 56), seem well centered on the face and it is possible that the slight bias to the left reflects the normal phenomenon of pseudo-neglect, i.e., the usual slight leftward bias in spatial attention. Thirdly, when saccade distributions are measured over a shorter time period, one that, however, is sufficient for efficient face recognition, they are closely centered on the midline of the face (Hsiao & Cottrel, 2009).

Recognition of facial identity, gender and age rely on configural processing, i.e., on perceiving the 'second order spatial relations' or geometric arrangement of the features within a face. Given that the external contour of the face is important to the perception of configuration (Kemp, McManus, & Pigott, 1990; Balas & Sinha, 2007) a central fixation may be optimal in maximizing the information available in these tasks. Half of the face – a largely symmetrical and therefore redundant stimulus – is positioned in the left visual field with the features located on or close to the visual midline and with the contour of the face in the near periphery.

7. Conclusions

Our tendency to see the left half of a face as 'looking more like' the whole face is well documented in experimental psychology, and this spatial bias extends to the perception of age, gender, attractiveness and emotional expression. For highly familiar faces the perceptual bias manifests itself as a memory bias. This asymmetry in perception appears to predominantly reflect an asymmetry in visual processing, and to reveal the seemingly inbuilt facility of the right hemisphere to represent configural information at a scale that is most useful for face recognition and discrimination. Others have similarly emphasized brain lateralization as the main determinant of a well-studied sensorimotor bias in word recognition whereby performance peaks for words fixed to the left of centre. This bias to saccade to the left of centre is argued to optimize word recognition by shifting the bulk of the word to the language dominant left hemisphere.

While there is evidence that the leftward spatial bias in face perception is lessened in readers of right-to-left scripts, there is, at present, a lack of information as to whether readers of different scripts scan faces differently. Indeed, the idea that we scan faces with a directional bias that reflects a cultural requirement to read from left-to-right or from right-to-left may ultimately be quite misguided. Face discrimination is estimated to occur within 150ms of stimulus onset (Jacques & Rossion, 2006), which suggests that the positioning of the very first saccade is the crucial one. Recent evidence that this initial saccade is centered near the midline of the face (Hsiao & Cottrel, 2009) is perhaps not surprising, given that faces are highly symmetrical about the vertical midline. An older literature shows that the detection and discrimination of mirror symmetry in dot patterns is best about a fixated vertical axis (Barlow & Reeves, 1979).

The dominance of the right hemisphere in face and visuo-spatial processing may help explain a paradox in symmetry perception, that is, despite our extraordinary sensitivity to symmetrical form we are sometimes insensitive to minor perturbations of symmetry (Wagemans, 1997). Finally, evidence for a foveal split in visual processing raises the interesting question of how visual information is brought together for a unified, conscious percept (Lavidor & Walsh, 2004), and disorders such as unilateral prosopometamorphopsia (Trojano et al., 2006) highlight the initially independent input of the right and left hemispheres to the perception of facial shape. Models of symmetry detection, particularly those that emphasize connectivity via the corpus callosum, may ultimately help our understanding face perception (Herbert & Humphrey, 1996).

References

Attneave, Fred (1954). Some informational aspects of visual perception. *Psychological Review, 61*, 183–193.

Balas, Benjamin & Pawan Sinha (2007) Portraits and perception: configural information in creating and recognizing face images. *Spatial Vision, 21*, 119–135.

Barlow, Horace & B.C. Reeves (1979). The versatility and absolute efficiency of detecting mirror symmetry in random dot displays. *Vision Research, 19*, 783–793.

Barton, Jason, Nathan Radcliffe, Mariya Cherkasova, Jay Edelman & James Intriligator (2006). Information processing during face recognition: The effects of familiarity, inversion, and morphing on scanning fixations. *Perception, 35*, 1089–1105.

Borod, Joan, Elissa Koff, Sandra Yecker, Cornelia Santschi & Michael Schmidt (1998). Facial asymmetry during emotional expression: Gender, valence, and measurement technique. *Neuropsychologia, 36*, 1209–1215.

Brady, Nuala, Mark Campbell & Mary Flaherty (2004). My left brain and me: a dissociation in the perception of self and others. *Neuropsychologia, 42*, 1156–1161.

Brady, Nuala, Mark Campbell & Mary Flaherty (2005). Perceptual asymmetries are preserved in memory for highly familiar faces of self and friend. *Brain & Cognition, 58*, 334–342.

Brysbaert, Marc (1994). Interhemispheric transfer and the processing of foveally presented stimuli. *Behavioural Brain Research, 64*, 151–161.

Brysbaert, Marc (2004). The importance of interhemispheric transfer for foveal vision: A factor that has been overlooked in theories of visual word recognition and object perception. *Brain and Language, 88*, 259–267.

Burt, Michael & David Perrett (1997). Perceptual asymmetries in judgements of facial attractiveness, age, gender, speech and expression. *Neuropsychologia, 35*, 685–693.

Butler, Stephen, Iain Gilchrist, Michael Burt, David Perrett, Elisa Jones & Monika Harvey (2005). Are the perceptual biases found in chimeric face processing reflected in eye-movement patterns? *Neuropsychologia, 43*, 52–59.

Butler, Stephen & Monika Harvey (2006). Perceptual biases in chimeric face processing: Eye-movement patterns cannot explain it all. *Brain Research, 1124*, 96–99.

Campbell, Fergus & John Robson (1968). Application of Fourier analysis to the visibility of gratings. *Journal of Physiology (London), 197*, 551–566.

Chatterjee, Anjan (2001) Language and space: Some interactions. *Trends in Cognitive Sciences, 5*, 55–61

Chen, Audrey, Craig German & Dahlia Zaidel (1997). Brain asymmetry and facial attractiveness: Facial beauty is not simply in the eye of the beholder. *Neuropsychologia, 35*, 471–476.

Chokron, Sylvie & Michel Imbert (1993). Influence of reading habits on line bisection. *Cognitive Brain Research, 1*, 219–222.

Costen, Nicholas, Denis Parker, & Denis, Craw (1996) Effects of high-pass and low-pass spatial filtering on face recognition. *Perception & Psychophysics, 58*, 602–612.

De Renzi, Ennio, Daniela Perani, Giovani Carlesimo, Caterina Silveri & Ferruccio Fazio (1994). Prosopagnosia can be associated with damage confined to the right-hemisphere: an MRI and PET study and a review of the literature. *Neuropsychologia, 32*, 893–902.

De Schonen, Scania & Eric Mathivet (1990). Hemispheric asymmetry in a face discrimination task in infants. *Child Development, 61*, 1192–1205.

Farah, Martha, Kevein Wilson, Maxwell Drain & James Tanaka (1998). What is "special" about face perception? *Psychological Review, 105*, 482–498.

Freyd, Jennifer & Barbara Tversky (1984). Force of symmetry in form perception. *American Journal of Psychology, 97*, 109–126.

Gilbert, Christopher & Paul Bakan (1973). Visual asymmetry in perception of faces. *Neuropsychologia, 11*, 355–362.

Herbert, Andrew & Keith Humphrey (1996). Bilateral symmetry detection: testing a 'callosal' hypothesis. *Perception, 25*, 463–480.

Hsiao, Janet & Garrison Cottrel (2009). Two fixations suffice in face recognition. *Psychological Science, 19*, 998–1005.

Hsiao, Janet, Danke Shieh & Garrison Cottrel (2008). Convergence of the visual field split: hemispheric modeling of face and object recognition. *Journal of Cognitive Neuroscience, 20*, 2298–2307.

Hunter, Zoë, Marc Brysbaert & Stefan Knecht (2007) Foveal word reading requires interhemispheric communication. *Journal of Cognitive Neuroscience, 19*, 1373–1387.

Ivry, Richard & Lynn Robertson (1998). The two sides of perception. MIT Press, Cambridge, Massachusetts.

Jacques, Corentin & Bruno Rossion (2006) The speed of individual face categorization. *Psychological Science, 17*, 485–492.

Kazandjian, Seta & Sylvie Chokron (2008). Paying attention to reading direction. *Nature Reviews Neuroscience, 9*, 965.

Kemp, Richard, Chris McManus & Tara Pigott (1990). Sensitivity to the displacement of facial features in negative and inverted images. *Perception, 19*, 531–543.

Kinsbourne, Marcel (1970). The cerebral basis of lateral asymmetries in attention. *Acta Psychologica, 33*, 193–201.

Kolb, Bryan, Brenda Milner & Laughlin Taylor (1983). Perception of faces by patients with localized cortical excisions. *Canadian Journal of Psychology, 37*, 8–18.

Lavidor, Michal & Vincent. Walsh (2004). The nature of foveal representation. *Nature Reviews Neuroscience, 5*, 729–735.

LeGrand, Richard, Catherine Mondloch, Daphne Maurer & Henry Brent (2003). Expert face processing requires visual input to the right hemisphere during infancy. *Nature Neuroscience, 6*, 1108–1112.

Lennie, Peter & Anthony Movshon (2005). Coding of color and form in the geniculostriate visual pathway. *Journal of the Optical Society of America A, 22*, 2013–2033.

Leonards, Ute & Nicholas Scott-Samuel (2005). Idiosyncratic initiation of saccadic face exploration in humans. *Vision Research, 45*, 2677–2684.

Leopold, David, Igor Bondar & Martin Giese (2006). Norm-based face encoding by single neurons in monkey inferotemporal cortex. *Nature, 442*, 572–575.

Leopold, David, Alice O'Toole, Thomas Vetter & Volker Blanz (2001). Prototype-referenced shape encoding revealed by high-level after-effects. *Nature Neuroscience, 4*, 89–94.

Luh, Karen, Julie Redl & Jerre Levy (1994). Left- and right-handers see people differently: free-vision perceptual asymmetries for chimeric stimuli. *Brain & Cognition, 25*, 141–160.

Maass, Anne & Aurore Russo (2003). Directional bias in the mental representation of spatial events: Nature or Culture? *Psychological Science, 14*, 269–301.

McManus, Chris (2002). Right hand, left hand: The origins of asymmety in brains, bodies, atoms and cultures. London: Weidenfeld & Nicolson.

Moscovitch, Morris & Janet Olds (1982). Asymmetries in spontaneous facial expression and their possible relation to hemispheric specialization. *Neuropsychologia, 20*, 71–82.

Murray, Micah, John Foxe, Beth Higgins, Daniel Javitt & Charles Schroeder (2001) Visuo-spatial neural response interactions in early cortical processing during a simple reaction time task: a high-density electrical mapping study. *Neuropsychologia, 39*, 828–844.

Nazir, Tatjana, Nadia Ben-Boutayab, Nathalie Decoppet, Avital Deutsch & Ram Frost (2004) Reading habits, perceptual learning, and recognition of printed words. *Brain and Language, 88*, 294–311.

O'Regan, Kevin & Arthur Jacobs (1992). Optimal viewing effect in word recognition: A challenge to current theory. *Journal of Experimental Psychology: Human Perception & Performance, 18*, 185–197.

Palmer, Richard & Curtis Strobeck (1986). Fluctuating asymmetry: Measurement, analysis, patterns. *Annual Review of Ecology & Systematics, 17*, 391–421.

Perrett, David, Michael Burt, Ian Penton-Voak, Kieran Lee, Duncan Rowland & Rachel Edwards (1999). Symmetry and human facial attractiveness. *Evolution & Human Behavior, 20*, 295–307.

Phillips, Mary & Anthony David (1997). Viewing strategies for simple and chimeric faces: an investigation of perceptual bias in normals and schizophrenic patients using visual scan paths. *Brain & Cognition, 35*, 225–238.

Rayner, Keith (1998). Eye movements in reading and information processing: 20 years of research. *Psychological Bulletin, 124*, 372–422.

Rhodes, Gillian (1985). Perceptual asymmetries in face recognition. *Brain & Cognition, 4*, 197–218.

Rizzolatti, Giacomo, Carlo Umiltà & Giovanni Berlucchi (1971). Opposite superiorities of the right and left cerebral hemispheres in discriminative reaction time to physiognomical and alphabetical material. *Brain, 94*, 431–442.

Sergent, Justine (1985). Influence of input and task factors in hemispheric involvement in face processing. *Journal of Experimental Psychology: Human Perception and Performance, 11*, 846–861.

Shepard, Roger (1988). The role of transformations in spatial cognition. In J. Stiles-Davis, M. Kritchevsky & U. Bellugi (Eds.), *Spatial Cognition: Brain Bases and Development.* Hillsdale, NJ: Lawrence Erlbaum Associates.

Thornhill, Randy & Steven Gangestad (1999). Facial attractiveness. *Trends in Cognitive Sciences*, *3*, 452–460.

Tjan, Bosco & Zili Liu (2005). Symmetry impedes symmetry discrimination. *Journal of Vision, 5*, 888–900.

Trojano, Luigi, Massimiliano Conson, Sara Salzano, Valentino Manzo, & Dario Grossi, (2009) Unilateral left prosopometamorphopsia: a neuropsychological case study. *Neuropsychologia, 47*, 942–948.

Vaid, Jyotsna (this volume). *Asymmetries in representational drawing: Alternatives to a laterality account.*

Vaid, Jyotsna & Maharaj Singh (1989). Asymmetries in the perception of facial affect: Is there an influence of reading habits? *Neuropsychologia, 27*, 1277–1287.

Wagemans, Johan (1997). Characteristics and models of human symmetry detection. *Trends in Cognitive Sciences, 1*, 346–352.

Weyl, Hermann (1952). Symmetry. Princeton, NJ: Princeton University Press.

Wolff, Werner (1933). The experimental study of forms of expression. *Character and Personality, 2*, 168–173.

Xu, Hong, Peter Dayan, Richard Lipkin & Ning Qian (2008) Adaptation across the cortical hierarchy: Low level curve adaptation affects high-level facial-expression judgments. *Journal of Neuroscience, 28*, 3374–3383.

Asymmetries in representational drawing: Alternatives to a laterality account

Jyotsna Vaid[1]

Abstract

When drawing familiar objects there is a bias in starting location, stroke direction, and object orientation or facing. Directional biases are also apparent in the speed and accuracy with which rightward vs. leftward facing objects are recognized and in aesthetic preference. Two different explanatory principles have been offered for directionality effects, one based on attentional/representational asymmetries arising from cerebral hemispheric specialization, and the other based on motoric factors influenced by biomechanical and/or cultural variables. These two accounts lead to differing predictions about the nature and strength of directionality effects in right vs. left-handed users and in users of left-to-right vs. right-to-left scripts. The available evidence suggests that a motoric rather than a laterality account is a more parsimonious explanation of directionality effects.

1. Introduction

"An unpremeditated profile drawing, if done by a right-handed draftsman, will be represented looking to the left as, if it is the work of a left-handed draftsman, it will certainly look to the right" (Wilson, 1885, cited in Alter, 1989).

---

1 In the interest of space and because there are other interpretive issues arising from the normal developmental and clinical neuropsychological literature on drawing directionality, the focus of this review is on studies of directionality in normal adults. Further, I have chosen to focus predominantly on representational drawings, rather than on the many studies of symbol copying or geometric drawings.
I am grateful to Hsin Chin Chen, Chaitra Rao, and Rebecca Rhodes for assistance in the preparation of this manuscript. This work was supported by a Faculty Fellowship awarded to the author by the Melbern G. Glasscock Center for Humanities Research, Texas A&M University.

"S[ubject]s from other cultures who read and write from right to left should be included in the study ... before final interpretations are justifiable." (Ross, 1951, cited in Jensen, 1951, p. 80).

As ancient cave paintings of horses, lions, and human figures attest, representational drawing is an activity that humans have engaged in for at least 30,000 years. An apparently universal human activity and one that emerges early in life, drawing has attracted the interest of researchers from a variety of perspectives, including developmental psychology, motor perception, and cognitive neuroscience (e.g., Trojano, Grossi, & Flash, 2009). Representations of common figures typically show directionality effects in perception, production, preference, and recognition. The focus of the present review is on mechanisms underlying asymmetries in the processing of depictions of objects as a function of semantic category (e.g., animate/inanimate, stationary/moving, graspable/not-graspable) and execution parameters (starting location, stroke sequencing, facing).

There are differing views as to the source of directionality effects in object perception and production (e.g., Chokron, 2002). A prevailing view, particularly among neuropsychologists, is that directionality effects arise from representational and/or attentional asymmetries in cerebral hemispheric functioning. According to this view, which we will call *the laterality account*, directional tendencies are predominantly biological in origin. An alternative to the laterality account regards asymmetries in drawing preference and production as arising from directional biases associated with reading and writing direction. In this view, which we will call *the script directionality account*, individuals favor a particular side of space or direction of movement depending on their reading/writing direction. A third view, which we will call *the biomechanical or chiral account*, maintains that directionality effects reflect neuromuscular principles affecting the ease of execution of inward vs. outward-directed hand or limb movements. In this view, biomechanical constraints arising from the anatomical structure of the hands, arms and nervous system are thought to influence the preferred direction of stroke production by adults (see Van Sommers, 1984). A fourth view, *the chiral/scriptal account,* suggests that reading/writing habits constitute a form of motoric influence and interact with biomechanical variables to affect drawing directionality.

In reviewing the available studies of drawing directionality, we will conclude that a chiral/scriptal view appears to be able to account for more of the findings than the other views.

2. Hemisphere/attentional accounts of asymmetries in perception and/or production

Numerous studies with neurologically intact individuals conducted since the 1960s have shown that when words are briefly presented to the right visual half field participants are more accurate in identifying them than when the same items are presented to the left visual half field. This right visual field superiority was interpreted as support for a left cerebral hemisphere representational and/or attentional bias for language (Kinsbourne, 1970).

However, as Bryden and Mondor (1991, p. 428) pointed out in a review of the laterality literature, "[d]espite this predilection for interpreting visual field effects in terms of functional cerebral asymmetries, there have been regular cautionary reminders that the procedure may not be so simple to interpret." Among the numerous factors besides cerebral specialization that also appear to influence the magnitude and direction of visual field asymmetries is that of scanning biases arising from experience in reading or writing from left to right (see, e.g., Nazir, Ben-Boutayab, Decoppet, Deutsch, & Frost, 2004). In acknowledging that scanning effects offer a potential alternative account of visual field asymmetries one is not necessarily arguing that visual field asymmetries in perception or production have nothing to do with cerebral functional asymmetries, but simply that it is incumbent on researchers to consider whether asymmetries can be accommodated more parsimoniously in other ways. In what follows we evaluate laterality vs. non-laterality accounts of asymmetries in directionality.

Heron (1957) noted that there are two kinds of scanning effects associated with reading and writing: one involves scanning to the beginning of a text (i.e., to the left in left-to-right readers) and the other involves scanning from one word to the next in a line of text (i.e., from left to right in English readers). Thus, under bilateral viewing conditions readers of English would be expected to orient their attention first to the left side of space whereas under unilateral presentation conditions they would more easily scan from the center to the right side of space, and thereby show a right field advantage in word recognition. A right field superiority in these participants, therefore, need not relate to hemispheric functional asymmetry at all.

Proponents of a laterality account have acknowledged the possibility of a scanning artifact but have tended to discount it. Attempts to test for scanning biases in laterality studies by using readers of Hebrew, a language ostensibly written from right to left, have been inconclusive. However, the lack of definitive findings from studies of Hebrew readers may in part be due to the fact that typical participants in these studies also know English and thus are more properly characterized as bidirectional readers. Further, Hebrew itself may be considered bidirectional given that individual letters, numbers and musical notes are written from left to right although words are read from right to left.

Fortunately, some studies have been conducted with readers of other languages, such as Urdu, that are more consistently right to left in their script directionality. Vaid, Rao and Chen (2011) compared visual field asymmetries for Urdu vs. Hindi among readers of both scripts in north India (see also Rao, 2010). These languages are identical in phonology and grammar but differ primarily in orthography and script directionality. In Hindi word recognition, participants showed a strong right visual field advantage; when tested in Urdu, a comparable right visual field advantage was obtained (see also Vaid, 1988, who reported an equivalent right visual field asymmetry in native Hindi and native Urdu readers, and Adamson & Hellige, 2006, who reported a right field advantage in Urdu-English skilled readers). These findings suggest that a laterality account may indeed be a viable explanation of observed asymmetries in word recognition since even readers of right-to-left scripts show a right visual field superiority.

However, if a laterality account may serve to explain visual field asymmetries in verbal processing in left-to-right and right-to-left readers alike, it remains to be determined if it also provides a sufficient account of visual field asymmetries in nonverbal tasks or whether reading/writing habits affect performance on such tasks and offer an alternative explanation to a right hemisphere/left hemispatial bias account.

To address this issue let us consider studies bearing on two ostensibly nonlinguistic tasks – facial affect judgments and aesthetic preferences – both of which have been mainly interpreted within a laterality framework.

2.1. Face perception directionality

In the free viewing version of the chimeric faces task (Levy, Heller, Banich, & Burton, 1983), participants are shown pairs of chimeric faces in which either the left or the right half of the face from the viewer's perspective is smiling. On this task a left field bias is typically observed; that is, participants favor the face in which the smile is in the viewer's left field as the more expressive, "happier" face. This effect has been replicated across several studies. It is noteworthy that all of the replications of the chimeric faces effect by Levy and her colleagues were done on users of left to right languages. The standard interpretation of the left field bias has been in terms of right hemisphere specialization for facial affect judgments.

Vaid and Singh (1989) administered the chimeric faces task to adult readers of Hindi, Urdu-Hindi biliterates, and illiterate speakers of Urdu/Hindi and found a significant left field bias only in the Hindi readers, that is, the left-to-right readers. Three subsequent studies have replicated and extended Vaid and Singh's (1989) finding. Sakhuja, Gupta, Singh and Vaid (1996) found that the left field bias was reduced in Urdu as compared to Hindi right handers as well as in left handed readers in each group. Eviatar (1997) found a reduced left field bias in native Hebrew readers as compared to native English readers. Heath, Rouhana and Ghanem (2005), who administered the chimeric faces task to a large sample of Arabic readers in Lebanon using photographed faces from the local population, showed that a left side bias was strongest in the subgroups that had the most exposure to English. Indeed, the association between right-to-left reading/writing experience and a reduced left field preference on the chimeric faces task was confirmed by Eviatar (1997) in a meta-analysis of chimeric faces studies, supporting the script directionality view over the laterality view of the left bias.

A scanning interpretation is consistent with findings from three recent studies, all with left-to-right readers. One found that participants initially look to the left when viewing centrally presented (non-chimeric) faces (Hsaio & Cottrell, 2009). Another noted that, when viewing a face, viewers first look to the side of space that is contralateral to their dominant eye; thus, right eye-dominant individuals initially look to the left side of a face (Hernandez, Metzger, Magne, Bonnet-Brilhault, Roux, Barthelemy, & Martineau, 2009). A third study showed a left attentional bias when viewing scenes, with better spatial memory for objects on the left side (Dickinson & Intraub, 2009). Of course, in the absence of data from right to left readers on these tasks one cannot definitively conclude that a script direction effect underlies the observed biases noted in these studies; however, given that studies of chimeric face viewing with right to left readers showed opposite effects to those of left to right readers (Eviatar, 1997), one can predict that right-to-left readers would show a right field initial gaze preference in viewing centrally presented non-chimeric faces as well.

2.2. Aesthetic response as a function of directionality

Another domain in which a right hemisphere account has been prevalent is in studies of aesthetic response to rightward vs. leftward facing photographs, drawings or portraits (e.g., Levy, 1976; McLaughlin, 1986; McLaughlin & Murphy, 1992). In these studies, a typical effect is that viewers prefer right-facing figures over left-facing ones, and/or figures in which there is some focal element on the right side of the painting rather than on the left side. It is not clear if this effect is moderated by the viewer's (or the artist's) handedness. Very few studies of aesthetic preference have included sufficient numbers of left handers to allow definitive conclusions about how this variable may affect performance but even where left handers have been included in studies of aesthetic judgments, the results have been inconclusive, (e.g., Mead & McLaughlin, 1992).

Turning to studies of aesthetic preference, one study examined aesthetic response to spatial placement of mirror-reversed objects shown in a rectangular frame (Palmer, Gardner, & Wickens, 2008). Viewers preferred right-facing objects over their left-facing counterparts; they also preferred objects that faced towards the center rather than towards the edge of the frame (Palmer et al., 2008). Importantly, these same preferences were also found under unconstrained response conditions: three objects – a steam iron, a tape dispenser, and a teapot – were individually placed on a turntable and participants were allowed to rotate the object to whatever orientation they preferred before photographing it. Over 80% of the participants rotated the objects to face rightward (Palmer et al., 2008, Exp. 4).

A number of studies of aesthetic response have examined the effect of implied direction of movement in a painting. Implied movement in Western works of art was commented on by early art theorists, such as Gaffron (1950), who proposed that viewers enter a painting by scanning it from the lower left and proceeding in an upward rightward arc. Asymmetry in paintings, these early theorists suggested, lends an aesthetic dimension of movement in graphic art; the particular preference for an asymmetry to be located on the right side may in turn reflect the fact that "[m]ovement from left to right in a painting is easier and faster while movement from right to left is slower and perceived as having to overcome resistance" (Gross & Bernstein, 1978, p 36).

Freimuth and Wapner (1979) reported that participants preferred paintings in which the implied motion was from left to right rather than from right to left. Banich, Heller and Levy (1989) reported that paintings in which the salient element was located on the viewer's right side and where the implied movement was thus from right to center were preferred (by right-handers only) over those with a left-biased salient element. Banich et al. proposed that having the more important figure on the right side offsets a right-hemisphere-mediated left hemispace attentional bias and creates balance, which is judged pleasing. However, Beaumont (1985) enlisted eye movement data to support his claim that in making aesthetic judgments participants' gaze is first drawn to the left hemispace and then moves rightward towards the asymmetric dimension of interest (see also Mead & McLaughlin, 1992).

If, as Gaffron (cited in Gross & Bernstein, 1978, p. 36) noted, "we 'read' a picture in a certain way just as we read a page of a book," one may well ask whether those who read from right to left would show a leftward preference in their aesthetic response. Whereas Gross and Bernstein provide anecdotal examples in support of this idea, four empirical studies bear on this issue.

Chokron and de Agostini (2000) tested 81 right-handed, monolingual readers of French (including 41 Grade 3 children and 40 adults) and 81 right-handed readers of Hebrew from Israel (including 40 Grade 3 children and 41 adults). Stimuli were 30 pairs of mirror reversed line drawings of objects presented one above the other; participants were asked to judge which member of the pair was more aesthetically pleasing or interesting. The stimulus pairs included ten static (e.g., a statue) and ten mobile, directional objects (e.g., a truck) in which one member of the pair faced leftward and the other faced rightward. In addition, ten pairs of asymmetric landscape pictures were presented in which the salient element was located on the right or on the left side. Chokron and de Agostini (2000) reported that left to right readers preferred pictures that faced rightward, whereas right to left readers preferred pictures that faced leftward. They concluded that these results support a non-laterality, reading-habit-based account of aesthetic preference, since, "[t]here is neither experimental nor clinical argument for a reverse pattern of cerebral lateralization in subjects with opposite reading habits" (Chokron & de Agostini, 2000, p. 48). However, given the fact that landscapes showed a tendency (significant in the Israeli adults) for a right-side preference, they suggested that a hemisphere-based interpretation might also be at work.

Christman and Rally (2000), cited in Heath, Mahmasanni, Rouhanna and Nassif (2005) tested aesthetic preferences in a sample of left-to-right (English) readers, biliterate (left to right and right-to-left) readers of Arabic and English, and top-to-bottom readers (of Japanese), using geometric stimuli differing in direction of implied movement, weight and interest. They reported a significantly stronger right-movement-directed preference in the left to right group compared to the other two groups. Further, degree of rightward preference in the biliterate and top-bottom readers was correlated with years of exposure to English.

Heath, Mahmasanni, Rouhana and Nassif (2005) also examined aesthetic preferences using geometric stimuli. Their participants included 65 English readers tested in the U.S., 58 native Arabic-only readers, 326 biliterate readers of Arabic and English, and 118 illiterate adults who were speakers of Arabic. All except the first group were tested in Lebanon. Participants ranged in age from 17 to 75. The test items, presented in booklet form, consisted of 44 different permutations of three geometric elements configured to represent four levels each of weight and interest (right, on left, balanced, or absent), and two levels of implied movement direction (left to right or right to left). Mirror images of the stimulus arrays were presented in pairs placed one above the other, and participants were to indicate which array was more appealing. As only the 13 pairs that contained movement directionality cues showed a significant bias, analyses were done only on those. A significant group difference interacting with the other factors showed that English use was associated with more rightward preference; further, in the English-only participants, a rightward movement bias was enhanced when the "interest" element was placed to the left rather than to the right. By contrast, the Arabic- only readers showed a leftward movement bias when the interest element was placed to the right. Biliterates and illiterates did not show interpretable effects. It is difficult to know how participants were actually evaluating the fairly abstract geometric stimuli used in this study and, in particular, whether the experimenter-designated labeling of the elements conveying interest, weight or directionality in fact matched participants own perceptions of the stimuli. Nevertheless, script direction appears to have differentially influenced preference judgments.

Whereas the studies of aesthetic responses of right to left readers reviewed thus far looked only at right handers, one study reviewed below included left handers as well. Nachshon, Argaman and Luria (1999) presented participants with left-facing and right-facing profiles of human faces and bodies taken from art books. Stimuli were presented side by side in mirror image pairs with the members facing outward or inward. Participants were normal adult readers of Arabic (28 right-handed, 17 left-handed), Hebrew (54 R, 8L), and Russian (16R, 15L), all tested in Israel. They were to indicate whether the left or the right member of the pair was the more beautiful. It was found that Russian readers preferred right-directed profiles whereas Hebrew readers showed a significant preference for left-directed profiles; Arabic readers' preferences, though showing a tendency for a left-directed preference, did not differ from chance. A handedness by stimulus direction interaction indicated that, across groups, right handers preferred left-directed profiles, whether in outward- or inward-directed pairs of faces or bodies, whereas left handers showed a right-directed preference for all conditions except for inward-directed facial profiles. A near significant handedness by language group interaction suggested that differences between right and left handers were most pronounced in the Russian readers, with Russian left handers showing the strongest right-directed preference. The authors concluded that "stimuli with directional dynamics (such as profiles) that correspond to the participant's direction of scan are judged as being more beautiful than those with directional dynamics that oppose the direction of scan, thus demonstrating a link between aesthetic preference and reading/writing habits" (Nachshon et al., 1999, pp. 111–112). This study clearly suggests that reading/writing habits influence aesthetic judgments; however, replications of this study in which the stimuli are presented one above the other rather than side by side would strengthen the argument.

Taken together, we have seen that in the case of two nonlinguistic domains – facial affect judgments and aesthetic judgments – the predominant outcome of a left hemispatial bias in the former case and a right facing bias in the latter was restricted to readers of scripts that proceed from left to right. In users of right to left or bidirectional scripts the effect was much weaker or even reversed, suggesting that reading/writing habits provide a sufficient alternative account of directional asymmetries in perceptual tasks without the need for invoking laterality differences.

2.3. Directional asymmetries in drawing directionality

Directionality in drawing may arise at planning or execution stages of drawing and may be revealed in a tendency to start a drawing on a particular quadrant of the page, on a particular side of the object to be drawn, in stroke direction, and/or in the orientation or facing of the object (Van Sommers, 1984). For each of these parameters a clear asymmetry has been observed. Aymmetries have also been observed in the identification of objects that face left vs. right (Viggiano & Vannucci, 2002), and in the accuracy of recall or recognition of right- vs. left-facing objects (Martin & Jones, 1999).

2.4. Accounts of the origin of directionality effects in drawing

There is a longstanding association between damage to the right hemisphere and visual neglect of the left side of space (see Bartolomeo, 2007, for a review). When drawing common objects from memory or when copying drawings of objects, neglect patients tend to omit left side details. The availability of visual feedback appears to exacerbate left neglect, as drawing with eyes closed results in more complete drawings in left neglect patients (Chokron, Colliot, & Bartolomeo, 2004). That drawing recruits more right hemisphere regions was suggested by a recent fMRI study of neurologically intact individuals which reported a stronger activation of a region in the right frontal cortex (BA 44/45) when participants were asked to imagine drawing as compared to a condition where they were to imagine writing (Farias et al., 2006, Exp. 2). Findings such as these support the view that processes involved in spatial attention and object perception more generally are associated with right hemisphere functioning.

Drawing orientation or the right- vs. left-facing of objects with an intrinsic front appears to vary by handedness. Some researchers have wondered whether this association of drawing directionality with handedness may signal that drawing directionality is lateralized. Thus, for example, Levy and

Reid (1978) included a profile drawing task in a series of laterality tests administered to right- and left-handed adults "to see if profile orientation might prove an additional behavioral measure indicating cerebral dominance" (p. 126). Alter (1989, p. 563) administered a drawing task to a large sample of individuals varying in handedness and proposed a way of quantifying the assessment of drawing directionality and relating it to measures of cerebral laterality, noting that "[t]he case will be made that 'directionality' – or the tendency to a stable perceptuo-motor bias – is cerebrally lateralized." Alter claimed that the tendency for leftward facing, which is especially pronounced in right handers, was associated with a stronger right visual field preference on verbal laterality tasks (Alter, Rein, & Toro, 1989).

A rather different conceptualization of handedness was proposed by Martin and Jones (1999), who argued that handedness exerts a direct, motoric effect in the recognition and production of objects facing rightward vs. leftward. Right and left handers, in this view, differ in their performance on a range of cognitive tasks not because of differences in cerebral lateralization but because of differences in motoric activation associated with left vs. right hand use. For example, it is well established that tensor movements, or movements directed away from the body midline, are performed more smoothly and rapidly than flexor movements, or movements directed towards the body (Brown, Knauft, & Rosenbaum, 1948). This would lead to different outcomes in drawing directionality depending on whether the right or the left hand is used to draw.

3. Different predictions of biomechanical/chiral and laterality accounts of drawing directionality

According to the biomechanical account, right handers using their dominant hand should be more likely to draw profiles facing left whereas left handers using their dominant hand should draw profiles facing right, simply because of the greater motoric ease in each case of making outward rather than inward movements. By the same token, right handers should be better at remembering left-facing than right-facing objects, and should misremember right-facing objects as left-facing, reflecting a left-looking memory schema. A biomechanical/chiral account would also predict that the way one normally interacts manually with an object should affect its ease of identification as well as how it is depicted in drawing. Thus, manipulable objects should be drawn or pictured oriented in a way that reflects usage – so, for example, handles of saucepans should be aligned to the same side of space as the hand used to draw them (i.e., to the right side in right handers and to the left in left handers).

To the extent that handedness in the laterality account is seen as an indirect marker of lateralization, directionality effects observed in left handers should be in the same direction, but not as strong in their magnitude, as those observed in right handers. By contrast, the biomechanical/chiral view would predict that right and left handers should show equally strong but opposite directionality effects, reflecting the different neuromuscular factors underlying graphic production depending on hand used. Furthermore, whereas the variable of handedness (or preferred hand) is emphasized in the laterality account, the biomechanical account emphasizes hand used, regardless of hand dominance, as the variable of interest (e.g., Braswell & Rosengren, 2002).

Finally, a chiral view can, in principle, accommodate differences associated with writing habits or script directionality. It would predict that directionality effects represent an interaction of biomechanical and cultural influences on hand movement biases. Thus, when script direction is congruent with hand movement-related directional preferences directionality effects should be strong (as when left to right readers perform a drawing task with their right hand or right to left readers perform the task with their left hand) Directionality effects should be weaker when biomechanical variables counter script directionality effects, as when left to right readers perform a drawing task with their left hand (script directionality would favor left to right movement whereas biomechanical variables would favor right to left movements) or when right to left readers perform a drawing task using their right hand (a right to left script-based movement preference would go against a left to right biomechanical movement preference). The relative strength of script direction vs. biomechanical variables in any given task becomes an empirical issue. A laterality account is silent on the issue of script direction and its potential interaction with hand used.

4. Drawing directionality effects in right- vs. left-handed users of left to right scripts

We now review findings that bear on these predictions, with particular attention to studies of the drawing of horizontal lines, human profiles, animals, and objects that convey movement (e.g., vehicles), and/or are graspable (e.g., have handles).

4.1. Drawing horizontal lines

The biomechanical principle of tensor movements being executed more easily than flexor movements would lead to a prediction that right handers will tend to draw horizontal lines from left to right when using their dominant hand, whereas left handers will draw them from right to left when using their dominant hand. Scheirs (1990) compared right-handed and left-handed 4-to12-year old children on a series of actions including using a hammer, drawing circles, tracing a circle in the air, boring into wood with a tool, drawing a human profile, and drawing horizontal lines. He found that the latter task was the only one on which consistent differences were observed between right and left handers.

Braswell and Rosengren (2002) tested 67 4–6 year olds and 15 adult right handers on a figure copying task to be performed repeatedly over six trials by each hand. On the figure with horizontal components (a cross), they found opposite movements in the adults as a function of hand used: when using their right hand, participants mainly produced horizontal lines in a left to right direction whereas when using their left hand, they mainly produced the lines in a right to left direction.

Several other studies have replicated this effect in comparisons of right- vs. left handed children and adults: right handers consistently produce lines in a left to right direction whereas left handers do so from right to left (see de Agostini & Chokron, 2002; Dreman, 1974; Glenn, 1995; Lehman & Goodnow, 1975; Reed & Smith, 1961; Shanon, 1979; Von Sommers, 1984). The size of the effect is equally strong in right and left handers, supporting the predictions of the motoric view.

A similar outcome is found on other graphic production tasks involving horizontal movements, such as when participants have to rapidly place dots in a horizontal array of boxes; performance by right handers is significantly faster when proceeding in a left to right direction whereas that by left handers is significantly faster in a right to left direction (Vaid, 1998). Singh, Vaid and Sakhuja (2000) found that lines drawn to approximate a target line by right handed left to right readers of Hindi were closer to the target in actual length when drawn from left to right, whereas lines drawn by individuals with bidirectional writing experience (Hindi/ Urdu) were equally accurate whether drawn from left to right or from right to left.

4.2. Drawing human facial profiles

Painted portraits tend to look towards the observer's left (Humprey & McManus, 1973), as do school yearbook pictures, and photographs of celebrities. This tendency for leftward orientation of human faces is also consistently observed when people – particularly right-handers- are asked to draw profiles of faces (see Richardson, 1992; Van Sommers, 1984, pp. 6–8,

120–122). One of the earliest and most extensive studies of profile drawing directionality was that by Jensen (1952) who examined this effect in a number of different groups. Jensen found that 64% of a sample of 355 American right handed children showed a left facing bias as compared to 42% of a much smaller sample of left handed children (n=33). A left bias was also observed in 84% of right handed American college students (n=88), and 88% of right-handed art students (n=16), and was replicated in a sample of Norwegians (Jensen, 1952).

Crovitz (1962) investigated the relationship between handedness and profile drawing directionality in a group of 375 American college students. Like Jensen, he found a left facing bias among right handers, which was significantly different from that of left handers. Levy and Reid (1978) examined profile drawing orientation in 24 right-handed and 48 left- handed adults, the latter further subdivided as a function of hand posture while writing (inverted vs. non-inverted). The vast majority (83.3%) of right handers showed a left-facing bias, as compared to 33.3% of the non-inverted left-handers and 25% of the inverted left handers. Shanon (1979) similarly reported a left facing preference for human profiles in 77.5% of right handed adults (n=40) as compared to 47.5% of left handers (n=40).

Vaid (1995) reported a left facing bias in profile drawing among 89.1% of Hindi right handers (n=55). Martin and Jones (1999) reported a left facing bias for human profiles in 57.4% of right handed adults (n=166) as compared to 38.5% of left handers (n=110). De Agostini and Chokron (2002) reported that in young adults a left facing bias was evident in 75% of right handers vs. 50% of left handers (n=20, each); among older adults, a left facing bias was evident in 89% of right handers (n=37) but only 20% of left handers (n=5). Karev (1990) found that 92.4% of right handers (n=264) showed a left-facing bias, as compared to 70.7% of left handers (n=270).

4.3. Drawing animals, vehicles, and objects

Vaid (1995, Study 1) reported a strong left bias in the facing of bicycles (90.9%) and elephants (92.7%) in a sample of 55 right-handed Hindi speaking adults. In a follow-up study investigating 16 right- and 16 left-handed Hindi users between the ages of 9–13 who were asked to draw a fish, an arrow, and a flag, right handers were significantly more left-facing than left handers (Vaid, 1995).

Alter (1989) tested 212 right handers and 42 left handers ranging in age from 11 to 72 years in a drawing task involving six objects: a bicycle, a dog walking, a bus, a facial profile, an airplane, and a pitcher. Data were not presented separately per drawing. Alter (1989) found that right handers were significantly left-directed whereas left handers were right-directed in their drawings. Importantly, right-and left handers did not differ in their degree of directional bias. Further, of those who oriented the drawings to the left, the vast majority (83%) were right-handed (only 3% were left-handed); among right-directed participants, handedness was evenly represented across right, left and mixed handers.

Using the same items as Alter (1989), Karev (1999) tested 264 right handed adults and 270 left handers, as well as a sample of mixed handers. Left-facing directionality was observed across groups but was significantly greater in right handers. Further, the frequency of right-directed drawings was greatest in left handers.

Animacy

Vaid and Chen (2009, Exp. 1) examined differences in drawing directionality in a sample of 284 right handed and 145 left handed native English speakers on the following items: fish, arrow, profile, elephant, bicycle, and flag. Handedness differences were observed for all three animate items – profile, fish, and elephant – in the direction of a greater left facing bias among the right handers. There were no handedness differences for the inanimate items (arrow, bicycle, flag). Martin and Jones (1999) similarly reported significant handedness difference in drawing directionality for profiles but not for the drawing of bicycles. However, the apparent conclusion from these two studies that directionality differences between right and left handers are restricted to animate objects is not a consistent finding across other studies.

Movement

Viggiano and Vannucci (2002, Exp. 1) administered a drawing test to 115 right handed and 75 left handed participants between the ages of 18 and 30. Participants were to draw 60 animals, 31 vegetables and 155 nonliving objects (vehicles, tools, furniture) with their preferred hand in two separate sessions. Percent frontward, leftward, and rightward facing was analyzed. No handedness or orientation differences were observed for vegetables, tools, or furniture. However, significant differences were obtained in the facing of animals and vehicles: 71% of right handers drew animals facing leftward while 65% of left handers showed a rightward orientation. For vehicles, 58% of right handers oriented them to the left whereas 66% of left-handers oriented them to the right.

Object graspability

Karev (1999) reported that the facing of a jug depended on participants' handedness: there was a clear preference for drawing the handle in the same side of space as the dominant hand: i.e., to the right in the case of right handers and to the left in the case of left handers. A similar effect was noted by Vaid and Chen (2009) in the drawing of a teacup. These findings demonstrate that graspable objects are drawn in the direction of the hand with which they are likely to be grasped.

de'Sperati and Stucchi (1997) showed 15 right handers and 15 left handers between the ages of 20 and 46 years a computer animation of a screwdriver in different orientations moving in a righward or leftward motion. Participants were asked to judge the direction of motion. In another condition, they were to imagine holding the screwdriver with either their dominant or nondominant hand and then decide on the motion. Participants' ability to recognize the motion of the screwdriver was affected by its orientation, such that the farther away the handle was positioned from the observer, the longer the response latency. Only right handers showed a preference for the screwdriver orientation in which the handle was to the right. In the imagined holding condition, both right and left handers imagining holding the screwdriver with the right hand showed a preference for rightward orientations whereas there was no orientation preference for imagined left hand holding. These results were taken as support for the spontaneous use of motor imagery for internally simulating movements of the preferred hand resulting in different response times depending on the graspability of the visual stimulus (see also Symes, Ellis & Tucker, 2007).

Dominant vs. non-dominant hand used

Five studies of left to right readers examined the effects of drawing with the dominant vs. the non-dominant hand. The earliest study to examine this variable was that of Crovitz (1962), which proposed that differences in drawing orientation "may be related to a simple peripheral sensory-motor variable; viz., whether the pencil is held in the left vs. the right hand" (Crovitz, 1962, p. 196). Eleven right handers were asked to draw a profile using their right hand, and 11 other right handers did so using their left hand. Crovitz found that those using the right hand drew significantly more left-facing than right-facing profiles, whereas those using the left hand drew more right-facing than left-facing ones.

Examination of the detailed movements made in drawing a figure may clarify why the drawings end up facing as they do. The relative ease of drawing a left-facing figure when using the right vs. the left hand, Crovitz (1962) suggested, may relate to different movement patterns; in the right hand, "[t]he elbow is close to the body, the ulnar surface of the hand is in contact with the writing surface, the hand is in line with the arm, the pencil point is on an extension of this line, and the first pencil stroke is laid down by a wrist flexion. This counterclockwise pencil stroke lays down the forehead of a left-facing figure. When the pencil is held in the left hand, precisely the same movement pattern lays down the forehead of a right-facing figure" (Crovitz, 1962, p. 196).

An additional variable here may be that when using the right hand lateral movements are easier to make in a left to right direction. Taguchi and Noma (2005) studied 20 right-handed Japanese adults on a fish drawing and circle drawing task performed with each hand. They found an overall left facing bias which was stronger when the right hand was used; further, a relationship was found between left-facing of the fish and the use of a clockwise movement in circle drawing, but only when the right hand was used. Thus, tendency to draw circles in a clockwise movement (which involves a left to right movement direction) was correlated with a tendency to face fish to the left, suggesting that the fish were drawn from left to right as well, starting with the head (see also van Sommers, 1984).

Alter (1989) asked right- and left-handed participants to draw one of six objects using their non-dominant hand as well as their dominant hand. She found that switching hands generally did not change drawing orientation; in the few instances where it did, this was more likely for left-handers than right handers. Given that the actual object to be drawn with each hand differed across participants, it is hard to know how to interpret Alter's (1989) findings on the effects of hand used on drawing directionality. Nevertheless, it is noteworthy that where drawing orientation shifted by hand used, this was more likely to be the case for left handers than right handers.

Vaid and Chen (2009, Exp. 2) tested 161 right handers and 64 left handers on a profile drawing task with each hand, with hand order counterbalanced. They found a main effect of hand order which indicated a stronger overall leftward facing bias when the dominant hand was used first. A main effect of hand used was also found, as was a hand used by handedness interaction. The interaction indicated that right handers showed the same pattern of facing whether they used their right or their left hand; left handers, by contrast, showed a stronger leftward facing bias when using their right hand than when using their left hand. In other words, the direction of writing was a stronger influence than biomechanical factors for right handers.

4.4. Identifying objects

Viggiano and Vannucci (2002, Exp. 2) hypothesized that right and left handers should show differences in the ease of identification of objects facing leftward vs. rightward, respectively. Participants (37 right handers and 23 left handers) were shown 84 line drawings of objects (40 animals, 8 vehicles, 14 items of furniture, and 22 tools) in fragmented versions at the center of a screen for 100 ms in a sequence of three levels of fragmentation, keeping the direction of facing of the objects across levels.

Viggiano and Vannucci (2002) found a three way interaction of handedness, directionality and object mobility. No handedness differences were observed for immobile objects (furniture, tools); for mobile objects (animals, vehicles) right handers named leftward facing objects faster than rightward facing ones; the converse was found for left handers. Moreover, right handers identified leftward facing animals at lower threshold levels than they identified rightward facing ones, while left handers showed no threshold differences. The authors interpreted their results as supporting the motor imagery theory of Martin and Jones (1999) which proposes an isomorphism between the structure of a movement and the structure of the image or mental representation. According to this theory, one should expect the same pattern of findings from tasks that require the manipulation, identification or recognition of the same visual object, indicating that the mental representation involved in motoric acts such as drawing, and in visual processes such as object identification, contain a description of the directionality of the object.

4.5. Recognizing object orientation

Three studies have examined the accuracy of orientation memory for figures. Takala (1951) found that when asked to reproduce an array of geometric figures presented in specific orientations, right handers were better at remembering the position of left-facing than right-facing figures. This effect was also observed by McKelvie (2001), who tested incidental recognition memory for facial orientation in 241 adults across three experiments. He found that faces that looked to the left elicited better orientation memory accuracy than those that looked to the right, suggesting that people have a schema that faces generally look to the left. Martin and Jones (1999) found that memory for coins, faces of famous figures, and other faces was generally better for leftward facing profiles for right handers but for rightward facing profiles by left handers.

5. Drawing directionality effects in right- vs. left-handers as a function of script directionality

5.1. Developmental studies of drawing directionality

Many developmental studies have compared readers of left to right scripts (English) with readers of right to left scripts (Hebrew) on symbol copying tasks that involve horizontal or circular movements (see Nachshon, 1981). However, as with the studies of perceptual asymmetries, the findings from drawing directionality do not provide a clear picture of script directionality influences. For reasons already noted, Hebrew may not be a particularly good candidate to test claims about directionality effects. When English is introduced in school Israeli school children show a sharp shift in their directionality effects, presumably reflecting the influence of exposure to a left to right script. Importantly, this shift does not occur in children who were taught both Hebrew and English scripts at the same time (Nachshon, 1983). Interestingly, children who learned scripts with opposing directionality from the start show directionality effects that are different from those of either monoliterate group (Nachshon, 1983).

5.2. Estimating length of lines produced from left to right vs. right to left

Singh, Vaid, and Sakhuja (2000) compared left- and right-handed schoolchildren with unidirectional left-to-right (Hindi) or bidirectional (Hindi and Urdu) reading/writing experience on a line length judgment task. Participants were asked to draw 3 cm lines from left to right or from right to left with each hand. Regardless of hand used, lines drawn from left to right were closer in length to the target than those drawn from right to left in right handed unidirectional readers. Bidirectional readers showed no directional effect. Furthermore, bidirectional readers produced lines that were closer in length to the target line than were unidirectional readers. These results support a greater influence of script-related directional scanning effects than handedness on the task of line length estimation.

5.3. Speeded dot filling of horizontal arrays

Vaid (1998) tested readers of Arabic vs. English on a task requiring participants to place a dot in a row of boxes from left to right or from right to left as quickly as possible, using the right or the left hand. A biomechanical account would predict faster performance in an outward direction (i.e., left to right with the right hand, right to left with the left hand) than in an inward direction. This was supported except when biomechanical movement patterns conflicted with the preferred (right to left) writing direction of the users, in which case script direction influenced movement speed (Vaid, 1998).

5.4. Drawing human facial profiles

As already noted, the majority of studies of human facial profile drawing directionality that have been conducted with readers of left to right languages have shown a strong leftward facing bias, which is stronger in right- than in left-handers. With right to left readers one might expect a tendency for a rightward bias. In one of the earliest studies to include a sample of right to left readers, Jensen (1952) reported that, of 90 Grade 3–8 right handed Arabic schoolchildren tested in Egypt, only 34% drew profiles facing rightward. This effect did not differ from that of right-handed American children. However, Jensen did not include left-handed users of Arabic. Shanon (1979) compared profile drawing in right vs. left handed adult users of Hebrew and found a right-facing tendency in 15% of the right handers but in 60% of the left handers (n=40 per group).

Vaid (1995) found a nonsignificant right-facing tendency in 54.8% of right handed Arabic readers (n=82) as compared to a significant left-facing bias (86.8%) in right handed Urdu-Hindi readers (n=38) and Hindi readers (89.1%, n=55); left handers were not tested on this task. Vaid and Chen (2009, Exp. 3) examined Arabic vs. Hindi right-handers' facing of profiles as a function of hand used. They found a significantly greater right-facing bias in right-handed Arabic readers (n=50) as compared to Hindi readers (n=30), regardless of whether they used their right or their left hand to draw: Arabic – right hand=64%, left hand=66%, Hindi – right hand=13.3%, left hand=16.7%.

5.5. Drawing animals, vehicles, other objects, and scenes

Vaid (1995) reported a significant rightward facing of bicycles (65.9%) and elephants (63.3%) in right-handed Arabic readers (n=82), whereas right handed Hindi readers showed a strong left facing bias for these objects. Vaid and Chen (2009, Exp. 3) compared drawing orientation in Arabic and Hindi readers as a function of hand used and found that, regardless of hand used, a significantly greater rightward facing bias characterized Arabic vs. Hindi readers in the drawing of an elephant (58% vs. 16.1%), a bicycle (68.7% vs. 16.1%), a shoe (62.2% vs. 8%), and a cup (29.8% vs. 3.2%).

The variable of hand used was significant only for the item, cup: the handle was placed on the right when the right hand was used to draw; this effect was considerably reduced when the left hand was used to draw. There was a tendency for an interaction of hand used with group, suggesting that Hindi readers were much less likely to show a change in orientation as a function of a switch in hands, suggesting that script direction had a greater influence than hand movement bias due to biomechanical variables.

To date, no studies of object naming, object perception, or memory for object orientation have been done in right to left readers. Finally, a recent study an effect of script directionally on drawing a scene containing a near house and a far house: Whereas 75% of right-handed English readers placed the near house to the left of the far house, only 44.4% of native Arabic readers did, suggesting rightward placement preference in this group (Vaid, Rhodes, Tosun, & Eslami, in press). Importantly, there was no effect of handeness on this task.

6. Concluding remarks

An overview of existing studies suggests that the available evidence on drawing directionality is more compatible with a motoric account (which includes an influence of script directionality) than with a strictly laterality-based account (which makes no predictions about opposite effects as a function of hand used, or script direction).

Further research on directionality effects would do well to address certain methodological weaknesses. In all but one study of drawing directionality (Viggiano & Vannucci, 2002), fewer than 10 stimuli have been used. When only a few items are used, and particularly when the items differ in how they are produced (e.g., for some items, such as a fish or a profile of a face, the directional element tends to be drawn first whereas for others, e.g., the tip of an arrow, or the handle of a teacup, it is drawn last) and thus in how they may end up being faced, it is important to analyze facing orientation separately by object. To reduce variance across studies, it would be important to standardize such aspects of the procedure as whether the drawings are to be made on separate sheets of paper or on a single sheet containing a grid, whether the paper is positioned upright or allowed to be tilted to the right or left, whether the drawing is to be made within a frame, and whether the frame is symmetrical (e.g., square or circle) or not (e.g., rectangular or ellipse), and whether the drawing is to be done in two or three dimensions. More fine-grained analyses are needed to investigate starting position in the drawing of human faces by right vs. left hand users varying in their preferred writing direction. To separate out visual-attentional from motoric inflences on drawing directionality, drawing tasks could be studied under conditions where visual feedback is available vs. not available (see Chokron et al., 2004). Finally, more studies should use within-subjects designs to examine the degree of consistency in directionality effects across production, perception, preference, and memory tasks.

A number of studies have accumulated demonstrating the influence of reading/writing habits on performance on spatial tasks used in studies of hemispheric asymmetry. Directional biases have also been suggested to underlie other domains as well, such as representational momentum (Halpern & Kelly, 1993; Spalek & Hammad, 2005), line bisection (Zivotovsky, 2004), and the perception of numerical magnitude (Shaki, Fischer, & Petrusic, 2009). In many of these cases the interactive effects of script direction-related motoric habits and tensor/flexor-related hand movement biases have not been sufficiently tested. What is sufficiently evident, though, is that motor imagery affects the way we interact with objects in perception, production, and memory and, thus, that the variable of hand movement needs to be foregrounded in models of spatial cognition for its implications for embodiment approaches to cognition (e.g., Fischer & Zwaan, 2008).

References

Adamson, Maheen & Joseph Hellige (2006). Hemispheric differences for identification of words and nonwords in Urdu-English bilinguals. *Neuropsychology, 20*, 232–248.
Alter, Isabelle (1989). A cerebral origin for "directionality". *Neuropsychologia, 27*, 563–573.
Alter, Isabelle, Stephanie Rein & Alfredo Toro (1989). A directional bias for studies of laterality. *Neuropsychologia, 27*, 251–257.
Banich, Marie, Wendy Heller & Jerre Levy (1989). Aesthetic preference and picture asymmetries. *Cortex, 25*, 187–195.
Bartolomeo, Paolo (2007). Visual neglect. *Current Opinion in Neurology, 20*, 381–386.
Beaumont, J. Graham (1985). Lateral organization and aesthetic preference: The importance of peripheral visual asymmetries. *Neuropsychologia, 23*, 103–113.
Braswell, Gregory S. & Karl S. Rosengren (2002). The role of handedness in graphic production: Interactions between biomechanical and cognitive factors in drawing development. *British Journal of Developmental Psychology, 20*, 581–600.
Brown, Judson S., K.B. Knauft & G. Rosenbaum (1948). The accuracy of positioning movements as a function of their direction and extent. *American Journal of Psychology, 61*, 167–182.
Chokron, Sylvie (2002). On the origin of free-viewing perceptual asymmetries. *Cortex, 38*, 109–112.

Chokron, Sylvie, Pascale Colliot & Paolo Bartolomeo (2004). The role of vision in spatial representation. *Cortex, 40,* 281–290.
Chokron, Sylvie & Maria De Agostini (2000). Reading habits influence aesthetic preference. *Cognitive Brain Research, 10,* 45–49.
Crovitz, Herbert F. (1962). On direction in drawing a person. *Journal of Consulting Psychology, 26,* 196.
deAgostini, Maria & Sylvie Chokron (2002). The influence of handedness on profile and line drawing directionality in children, young, and older normal adults. *Brain and Cognition, 48(2–3),* 333–336.
De'Sperati, C. & N. Stucchi (1997). Recognizing the motion of a graspable object is guided by handedness. *NeuroReport, 8,* 2761–2765.
Dickinson, C. & H. Intaub (2009). Spatial asymmetries in viewing and remembering scenes: Consequences of an attentional bias? *Attention, Perception & Psychophysics, 71,* 1251–1262.
Dobel, Christian, Gil Diesendruck & Jens Bolte (2007). How writing system and age influence spatial representations of actions. *Psychological Science, 18(6),* 487–491.
Dreman, S.B. (1974). Directionality trends as a function of handedness and of reading and writing habits. *American Psychologist, 37,* 247–254.
Eviatar, Zohar (1997). Language experience and right hemisphere tasks: The effects of scanning habits and multilingualism. *Brain and Language, 58,* 157–173.
Farias, D., C. Davis & G. Harrington (2006). Drawing: Its contribution to naming in aphasia. *Brain and Language, 97,* 53–63.
Fischer, Martin & Rolf Zwaan (2008). Embodied language: A review of the role of the motor system in language comprehension. *The Quarterly Journal of Experimental Psychology, 61,* 825–850.
Freimuth, Marilyn & Seymour Wapner (1979). The influence of lateral organization on the evaluation of paintings. *British Journal of Psychology, 70,* 211–218.
Gaffron, M. (1950). Left and right in pictures. *Art Quarterly, 13,* 312–331.
Glenn, S.M. (1995). Handedness and the development of direction and sequencing in children's drawings of people. *Educational Psychology, 15,* 11–21.
Gross, Charles G. & Marc H. Bornstein (1978). Left and right in science and art. *Leonardo, 11,* 29–38.
Halpern, Andrea & Michael Kelly (1993). Memory biases in left vs. right implied motion. *Journal of Experimental Psychology: Learning, Memory and Cognition, 19,* 471–484.
Heath, Robin L., Oula Mahmasanni, Aida Rouhana, Nader Nassif (2005). Comparison of aesthetic preferences among Roman and Arabic script readers. *Laterality, 10,* 399–411.
Heath, Robin L., Aida Rouhana & Dana Abi Ghanem (2005). Asymmetric bias in perception of facial affect among Roman and Arabic script readers. *Laterality, 10,* 52–64.
Hernandez, N., A. Metzger, R. Magne, F. Bonnet-Brilhault, S. Roux, C. Barthelmy & J. Martineau (2009). Exploration of core features of a human face by healthy and autistic adults analyzed by visual scanning. *Neuropsychologia, 47,* 1004–1012.

Heron, Woody (1957). Perception as a function of retinal locus and attention. *American Journal of Psychology, 70*, 38–48.

Hsiao, Janet H. & Garrison Cottrell (2009). Two fixations suffice in face recognition. *Psychological Science, 19*, 998–1006.

Jensen, B. (1952). Left-right orientation in profile drawing. *Perceptual and Motor Skills, 65*, 80–83.

Karev, George (1999). Directionality in right, mixed and left handers. *Cortex, 35*, 423–431.

Kinsbourne, Marcel (1970). The cerebral basis of lateral asymmetries in attention. *Acta Psychologica, 33*, 193–201.

Lehman, Elyse B. & Jacqueline Goodnow (1975). Directionality in copying: Memory, handedness, and alignment effects. *Perceptual and Motor Skills, 41*, 863–872.

Levy, Jerre (1976). Lateral dominance and aesthetic preference. *Neuropsychologia, 14*, 431–445.

Levy, Jerre, Wendy Heller, Marie T. Banich & L. Burton (1983). Asymmetry of perception in free viewing of chimeric faces. *Brain and Cognition, 2*, 404–419.

Levy, Jerre & M. Reid (1978). Variations in cerebral organization as a function of handedness, hand posture in writing, and sex. *Journal of Experimental Psychology: General, 107*, 119–144.

Maass, Anne & A. Russo (2003). Directional bias in the mental representation of spatial events: Nature or culture? *Psychological Science*, 14, 296–301.

Martin, Marian & G. Jones (1999). Motor imagery theory of a contralateral handedness effect in recognition memory: Toward a chiral psychology of cognition. *Journal of Experimental Psychology: General, 128*, 265–282.

Mead, Andrew M. & John P. McLaughlin (1992). The roles of handedness and stimulus asymmetry in aesthetic preference. *Brain and Cognition, 20*, 300–307.

McKelvie, Stuart (2001). Is memory for head orientation based on a left-looking schema? *The Journal of General Psychology, 12*, 209–225.

McLaughlin, John P. & Kimberly E. Murphy (1992). Preference for profile orientation in portraits. *Empirical Studies of the Arts, 12*, 1–7.

McLaughlin, John (1986). Aesthetic preference and lateral preferences. *Neuropsychologia, 24*, 587–590.

Nachshon, Israel (1981). Cross-cultural differences in directionality. *International Journal of Psychology, 16*, 199–211.

Nachshon, Israel (1983). Directional preferences of bilingual children. *Perceptual and Motor Skills, 56*, 747–750.

Nachson, Israel, Einat Argaman & Assaf Luria (1999). Effects of directional habits and handedness on aesthetic preference for left and right profiles. *Journal of Cross Cultural Psychology, 30*, 106–114.

Nazir, Tatjana A., Nadia Ben-Boutayab, Nathalie Decoppet, Avital Deutsch, Ram Frost (2004). Reading habits, perceptual learning, and recognition of printed words. *Brain & Language, 88*, 294–312.

Padakannaya, Prakash, M.L. Devi, B. Zaveria, Shyamala K. Chengappa & Jyotsna Vaid (2002). Directional scanning effect and strength of reading habit in picture naming and recall. *Brain and Cognition, 48*, 484–490.

Palmer, Stephen, Jonathan Gardner & Thomas Wickens (2008). Aesthetic issues in spatial composition: effects of position and direction on framing single objects. *Spatial Vision, 21*, 421–449.

Rao, Chaitra (2010). *Morphology in word recognition: Hindi and Urdu*. Unpublished doctoral dissertation, Texas A&M University.

Reed, G. & A.C. Smith (1961). Laterality and directional preference in a simple perceptual motor task. *Quarterly Journal of Experimental Psychology, 13*, 122–124.

Sakhuja, Tripti, Gyan C. Gupta, Maharaj Singh & Jyotsna Vaid (1996). Reading habits affect asymmetries in facial affect judgments: A replication. *Brain and Cognition, 32,* 162–165.

Scheirs, J.G. (1990). Relationships between the direction of movements and handedness in children. *Neuropsychologia, 28(7)*, 743–748.

Shaki, Samuel, Michael Fischer & William Petrusic (2009). Reading habits for both words and numbers contribute to the SNARC effect. *Psychonomic Bulletin & Review, 16,* 328–331.

Singh, Maharaj, Jyotsna Vaid & Tripti Sakhuja (2000). Reading/writing vs. handedness influences on line length estimation. *Brain and Cognition, 43(1–3)*, 398–402.

Spalek, Thomas & Sherief Hammad (2005). The left-to-right bias in inhibition of return is due to the direction of reading. *Psychological Science, 16(1)*, 15–18.

Symes, Ed, Rob Ellis & Michael Tucker (2007). Visual object affordances: Object orientation. *Acta Psychologica, 124*, 238–255.

Taguchi, Masanori & Yutaka Noma (2005). Relationships between directionality and orientation in drawings by young children and adults. *Perceptual & Motor Skills, 101(1)*, 90–94.

Takala, Martti (1951). *Asymmetries of the visual space*, 1–175, Helsinki.

Trojano, Luigi, Dario Grossi & Tamar Flash (2009). Cognitive neuroscience of drawing: Contributions of neuropsychological, experimental and neurofunctional studies. *Cortex, 45*, 269–277.

Vaid, Jyotsna (1988). Asymmetries in tachistoscopic word recognition: Scanning effects re-examined. *International Journal of Neuroscience*, 253–258.

Vaid, Jyotsna (1995). Script directionality affects nonlinguistic performance: Evidence from Hindi and Urdu. In Insup Taylor and David Olson (Eds.), *Scripts and literacy* (pp. 295–310). Kluwer.

Vaid, Jyotsna (1998). Cultural vs. biomechanical influences on a graphic production task. *Brain and Cognition, 37(1)*, 75–78.

Vaid, Jyotsna & Hsin-Chin Chen (2009). *Drawing directionality as a function of handedness, hand used and script directionality*. Unpublished manuscript, Texas A&M University.

Vaid, Jyotsna, Chaitra Rao & Hsin-Chin Chen (2011). *Right visual advantage characterizes lexical decision in rightward and leftward scripts: Evidence from Hindi/Urdu*. Unpublished manuscript, Texas A&M University.

Vaid, Jyotsna, Rebecca Rhodes, Sumeyra Tosun & Zohra Eslami (in press). Script directionality affects depiction of depth in representational drawings. *Social Psychology*.

Vaid, Jyotsna & Maharaj Singh (1989). Asymmetries in the perception of facial affect: Is there an influence of reading habits? *Neuropsychologia, 27*, 1277–1287

Vaid, Jyotsna, Maharaj Singh, Tripti Sakhuja & Gyan C. Gupta (2002). Stroke direction asymmetry in figure drawing: Influence of handedness and reading/writing habits. *Brain and Cognition*, 597–602.

Viggiano, Maria P. & Manila Vannucci (2002). Drawing and identifying objects in relation to semantic category and handedness. *Neuropsychologia, 40*, 1482–1487.

Van Sommers, Peter (1984). *Drawing and cognition: Descriptive and experimental studies of graphic production processes.* Cambridge: Cambridge University Press.

Zivotofsky, Ari Z. (2004). Choosing sides: lateralization in line trisection and quadrisection as a function of reading direction and handedness. *Cognitive Brain Research, 20,* 206–211.

Cultural and biological interaction in visuospatial organization

Sylvie Chokron, Seta Kazandjian, and Maria De Agostini

Abstract

A growing literature on perceptual bias has investigated the factors that determine normal performance in simple visuospatial tasks, such as line bisection, aesthetic preference, and egocentric reference. Patterns of performance seen among healthy, right-handed left-to-right readers have been attributed to the hemispheric activation hypothesis. The leftward bias seen in these early studies was explained by an activation of the right hemisphere during visuospatial tasks. However, imposed scanning direction and stimuli saliency have also been used to explain these spatial asymmetries. One example of scanning direction is that which is well-trained as a result of reading direction. Here we present studies that target the role of reading direction on three different nonverbal tasks: line bisection, aesthetic preference, and straight-ahead pointing by comparing left-to-right and right-to-left readers. The findings are discussed regarding the interaction between cultural factors, such as reading habits, and biological factors, such as cerebral lateralization, in visual and proprioceptive perception.

1. Introduction

It is by now well established that the right and left cerebral hemispheres of healthy humans differ in the psychological functions they subserve. Clinical and experimental evidence converge on the conclusion that in the great majority of right-handers, the left hemisphere is specialized for a number of language-related functions, while the right hemisphere is specialized for a number of spatial abilities (Kimura, 1961; White, 1972; Witelson, 1976; Young, 1983). This lateralized view of cognitive functioning has led to the development of a hemispheric specialization framework to interpret functional asymmetries. In recent years the rigid lateralized view of cognitive functioning has become more flexible as studies began to show right hemisphere activation for some verbal, language-based tasks (see Lindell, 2006 for review). However, functional asymmetry in verbal and non-verbal visual perception tasks, for the most part, continue to be interpreted in terms of a hemispheric specialization framework. This is particularly the case for perceptual biases that have been described in normal participants. Based on this framework, the commonly seen leftward bias among healthy normal participants when performing tasks such as bisecting a line, determining preference of lateralized graphic representations, or in proprioceptive reaching has been attributed to the right hemisphere's attentional pull to the contralateral side of the body or visual field.

However, this framework is neither the only one available nor the one that was initially considered in early studies of visual hemifield presentation of words. Interestingly, the original interpretation of visual field asymmetries was in terms of post-exposure directional scanning tendencies arising from reading and writing experience (Heron, 1957). In this view, visual field asymmetries predominantly reflect a tendency to scan information in the direction in which one reads. Thus, a reader of English, who is fixating at center, will show a right visual field advantage for unilaterally presented words and a left visual field advantage for bilaterally presented words.

Indeed, the suggestion has been raised that directional bias arising from reading direction may even generalize to non-verbal material in the visual modality (Corballis, 1994) or even in the auditory modality (Bertelson, 1972). It is reasonable to expect that features of the languages used in a culture may affect various aspects of behavior of the members of that culture. Given that the majority of studies conducted on perceptual biases have been performed in Western laboratories using participants whose dominant language uses a left-to-right written script, it is not surprising that the research seems to largely agree in terms of the perceptual biases seen, which are consistent with the view of a right hemisphere preference for nonverbal tasks and left hemisphere preference for verbal tasks.

The question of culture has been revisited over the past decades in the attempt to clarify whether there is a universal, biological functional asymmetry of non-verbal perceptual biases, if there are cultural differences, or, more likely, if there is an interaction between biology (hemispheric specialization) and culture. Frith (1998), discussing the possibility of an influence of culture on brain anatomy, asked: "Is it possible that learning to read has an effect on processes underlying visual perception and thinking?"

This chapter will present our research that specifically looked at three types of nonverbal visuoperceptual and proprioceptive tasks among right-to-left readers. We will present studies that have investigated the influence of reading direction (left-to-right versus right-to-left) on line bisection, aesthetic preference, and egocentric reference. Through a comparative look at the results from these studies with the existing hypotheses of perceptual bias in visuospatial tasks, the goal of this chapter is to bring forward the question of whether there is an interaction between culture and biology when performing visuospatial tasks.

1.1. Effect of reading direction on lateral bias: Position of the problem

Reading is a complex cognitive process that plays a significant role in daily functioning for a large portion of the world's population. There are different levels of literacy and individual differences in reading ability and speed. There are also cultural differences in the reading process. All these factors can effect how readers transfer their well-learned reading process onto nonverbal tasks that require the use of the same underlying basic processes.

The reading process requires two basic cognitive functions: visual perception and eye movement. Research has indicated that skilled English readers scan text in a left-to-right direction with an effective visual field of 3–4 characters to the left and about 14–15 characters to the right, an average saccade length of 7–9 character spaces, and an average fixation duration of 200–250 ms (see Rayner, 1998 for review). A consensus as to the underlying processes for the perceptual span and fixation patterns seen in reading has not been reached. Whereas some researchers consider the perceptual span and scanning direction to be due to a function of visual acuity needs (foveal visual field) and the visual properties of the text (e.g., spaces between words), others propose a higher-level cognitive processing at play which particularly influences fixation duration (see Starr and Rayner, 2001 for review). In addition, the asymmetric perceptual span to the right (i.e., greater attention to the right visual field) and left-to-right scan direction has been attributed to the left hemisphere's specialized role in language and reading. At the cortical level, several left hemisphere regions have been implicated in the reading process (Price, Wise, Watson, Patterson, & Frackowiak, 1994).

Yet, when comparing different orthographic systems (such as left-to-right reading versus right-to-left reading direction), significant differences are seen in the scanning process based on the language or orthographic system. In terms of perceptual span, among Hebrew readers who read right-to-left, an asymmetric perceptual span to the left is seen (with 14–15 characters to the left and 3–4 characters to the right) (Pollatsek, Bolozky, Well, and Rayner, 1981) as opposed to the rightward span seen in left-to-right readers.

The scanning of text may be considered to be a low-level cognitive process that is reliant on the visual information presented. If a bilingual reader confronts Hebrew text, he/she will scan from right-to left and attend to an effective visual field that is asymmetric to the left. The same individual, when confronted with English text, will scan from left-to-right and attend to an effective visual field that is asymmetric to the right. The question then arises: which pattern of scanning and perceptual span would a Hebrew, Arabic or Urdu reader, for example, use when confronted with nonverbal stimuli, such as a visual scene, an image, a graph, or even a straight, horizontal line? Do left-to-right readers and right-to-left readers differ in this regard?

An effect of reading direction on perceptual skills has been described both for school children (Abed, 1991; Braine, 1968; Kugelmass & Lieblich, 1970) and pre-school children (Shannon, 1978) who exhibited scanning of non-directional visual material related to reading direction before learning how to read. Some studies have emphasized the fact that children as young as four years old have the ability to produce graphics which exhibit some of the characteristics of writing, such as directionality: from left to right for French pre-school children (Gombert & Fayol, 1992) and from right to left for Israeli pre-school children (Tolchinsky-Landsman & Levine, 1985). This effect of reading direction on space perception and exploration has thus challenged the well-known link between cerebral lateralization and bias described both in normal and brain-damaged patients.

In respect to spatial asymmetry, reading direction has been proven to be influential on perceptual exploration within the normal population (Kugelmass & Lieblich, 1970). The effect of reading direction on directional preferences in reproducing visual stimuli has also been shown by various authors, corroborating other findings concerning the environmental influences on the regulation of perceptual scanning (Shannon, 1978).

The initial scanning direction was found to have a significant influence on the position of the subjective middle in line bisection (Brodie & Pettigrew, 1994). In fact, the bias displayed by normal right-handed participants when bisecting a visually presented line, was found to be a function of the hand and of the initial scan strategy used to perform the task. Using the left hand, or initially scanning from the left, will result in a significant leftward deviation, whereas initially scanning from the right with the right hand will normally result in no significant deviation from the objective midpoint. We subsequently replicated this finding in a proprioceptive straight ahead pointing task in normal and brain-damaged patients suffering from left neglect, in which we demonstrated that the direction of the motor exploration significantly affects the position of the subjective middle (Chokron & Bartolomeo, 1997). These results indicate the role of scanning direction on visuospatial organization and reveal how the position of the subjective middle in space may depend upon the scanning direction used to reach it. The experiments we present below were designed to thoroughly study these effects.

2. Effect of reading direction on spatial asymmetry: an experimental approach

2.1. Line bisection

The use of bisection protocols with normal participants has demonstrated an asymmetric perception of space. The line bisection task involves the presentation of a series of straight, horizontal lines of varying lengths, of which the participant is asked to mark the center (or bisect it with a hatch mark) (Manning, Halligan, & Marshall, 1990). Judging the center of horizontally oriented linear stimuli, either in the visual or tactile modality, is a task that has been used widely to explore lateralization of perceptual and attention factors in normal participants (for a review, see Brodie & Pettigrew, 1996). Numerous authors have described the tendency of healthy participants to place the subjective middle of the line (or a rod) to the left of the objective center (Bowers & Heilman, 1980; Bradshaw, Bradshaw, Nathan, Nettleton, & Wilson, 1987; Bradshaw, Nathan, Nettleton, Wilson, & Pierson, 1987; Manning, Halligan, & Marshall, 1990; Sampaio & Chokron, 1992; Sampaio & Philip, 1991). This phenomenon has been interchangeably termed pseudoneglect or Left Side Underestimation (LSU), because the direction of the deviation (to the left of the objective middle) opposes that which is presented by left unilateral neglect patients. Left unilateral neglect patients tend to place the subjective middle to the right of the objective center. In fact, line bisection is often used as a screening tool for hemispatial neglect. The shift of the objective center seen among normal participants has led to a debate regarding its cause. Is the shift a result of hemispheric imbalance and/or is it dependent on other factors, such as scanning or attention?

Certain authors have suggested that because of the spatial nature of the bisection task, the leftward bias seen among healthy participants might be related to a preferential activation of the right hemisphere (Bowers & Heilman, 1980; Bradshaw, Nathan, Nettleton, Wilson, & Pierson, 1987). According to this *hemispheric activation theory*, preferential activation of the right hemisphere effectively leads to an overestimation of the left hemispace and therefore to a displacement of the subjective center to the left of the objective center of the line. This theory is a corollary of Kinsbourne's activation theory, which states that the distribution of attention in space is biased in the direction contralateral to the more activated hemisphere (Kinsbourne, 1970). Regarding this hypothesis, during line bisection, normal dextrals should deviate to the left of the objective middle and this leftward bias should be more important when using the left hand or looking to the left (activation of the right hemisphere).

However, a review of the literature reveals that bias in visuo-motor line bisection cannot be explained only in terms of hemispheric activation (for a review, see Jewell & McCourt, 2000). For example, in several studies, no significant difference between left and right hand use was reported (Delatollas, Vanluchene, & Coutin, 1996; Harvey, Milner, & Roberts, 1995; Mefferd, Wieland, & Dufiho, 1969). Gaze deviation to one side did not induce a deviation of the subjective middle to the same side, as the activation hypothesis predicts (Chokron, Bartolomeo, Colliot, & Auclair, 2002; Chokron & Imbert, 1993a). Finally, the majority of studies examining the influence of sex (that could affect cerebral lateralization) on line bisection performance report non-significant effects (Jewell and McCourt, 2000).

Taking these findings into consideration, Nicholls and Roberts (2002) hypothesized that perceptual-attention bias may be reflecting an asymmetry in the neural mechanisms that control attention, rather than reflecting a hemispheric asymmetry driven by unilateral activation. According to the *perceptual-attention hypothesis*, various factors that can increase saliency of the right side of the line leads to an underestimation of the left side of an object or the line, and thus a shift of the objective center to the left, also termed LSU.

In a series of studies conducted with children and adults with opposing reading direction modes, we aimed at measuring the extent to which reading direction may affect the position of the subjective middle in line bisection (Chokron & De Agostini, 1995; Chokron & Imbert, 1993b). According to the *activation hypothesis*, dextrals regardless of directional habits, should bisect lines on the left of the true center (due to the activation of the RH), whereas according to the *perceptual-attention hypothesis* the direction of reading could bias the scanning of the to-be-bisected line and might thus orient attention specifically during line bisection in left-to-right and right-to-left readers leading to opposite biases.

Exclusively left-to-right reading, French monolinguals and right-to-left reading, Israeli monolinguals were tested with the line bisection task. Although our Israeli participants were born and raised in Israel and identified themselves as monolingual Hebrew speakers, it is probable that they had been exposed to some left-to-right directional material over the course of their education, e.g., math and music, their daily exposure to English language road signs and bulletin boards, and, most possibly, English language courses. However, comparing the two groups, we were able to demonstrate that the participants' reading direction modes may influence the position of the subjective middle in line bisection, with a leftward deviation for left-to-right adults and a rightward one for right-to-left (Figure 1).

Visuospatial organization

Deviation (in cm)

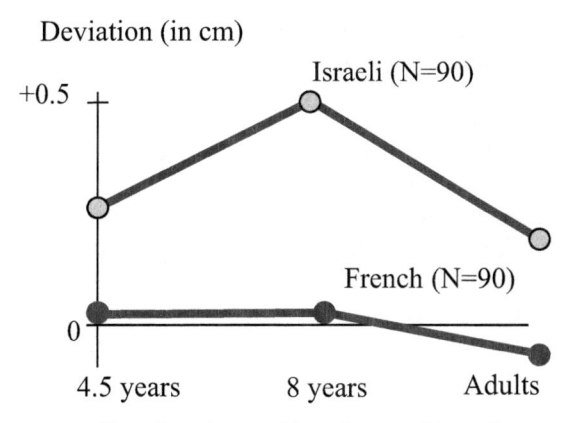

Figure 1. Effect of reading direction on bisection. In this task, a score of 0 defines the objective center, therefore, leftward deviation is defined as any score below 0 (negative scores), and rightward deviation is defined by scores above 0 (positive scores).

The greatest effect was seen between the Israeli and French 8 year olds, followed by the adults. Notably, a significant difference was also seen between the French and Israeli pre-school children (i.e., 4.5 years old), who had not yet received formal reading instruction. The high sensitivity of this task results in significant leftward or rightward deviation following only a few millimeters deviation to either side.

In another experiment (Chokron, Bernard & Imbert, 1997), we confirmed our previous findings showing that there is also an effect of reading direction on the performance on a line extension task, where the participants had to construct the missing half of a line from a given one (left or right). In the first part of this research, 45 French (left-to-right readers) and 30 Israeli (right-to-left readers) normal dextrals were given half a line and requested to construct the missing other with the same length (either the left one or the right one). Using this line extension task, a significant effect of reading habits on the performance was found, with no significant bias for Israeli subjects, and a significant underconstruction when building the left half from the right one for French subjects. In the second part, two patients with opposite reading habits (one French, one Israeli) suffering from left unilateral neglect were submitted to the same protocol. Both patients were found to under-construct the right half of the line from the left given half, and to over-construct the left half from the right given one, hence reproducing the well-known line bisection bias. Results, thus, confirmed that perceptual asymmetries among normal as well as in brain-damaged adults are not only due to cerebral activation but may depend on the direction of visual scanning and, in this way, of reading habits.

While some authors have postulated that the deviation in bisection occurs in the hemispace contralateral to the most activated hemisphere (Bradshaw, Bradshaw, Nathan, Nettleton, & Wilson, 1986; Bradshaw et al., 1987), our results show an opposite pattern between French and Israeli participants and suggest an opposite cerebral organization relative to the opposing reading direction. Rather than reasoning in terms of level of hemispheric activation, one can imagine that the scanning direction of the line, relative to reading direction may influence the orientation of attention along the line and, in this way, the length representation and the position of the bisection.

2.2. Aesthetic preference

Another task that has been previously attributed to cerebral activation and hemispheric dominance is aesthetic preference judgments (Beaumont, 1985). Chemtob (1979) and Van Houten, Chemtob and Hersh (1981), using tachistoscopic presentation, found that healthy participants reported greater preference for images presented to their left visual field (LVF) compared with images presented to their right visual field (RVF). Using mirror-image pairs of landscape photographs and paintings, studies have confirmed that right-handed adults exhibit systematic preferences for the images that had the center of interest oriented to the right over its mirror-image, while left-handed adults did not exhibit a significant preference (Levy, 1976; McLaughlin, 1986; Mead & McLaughlin, 1992). Beaumont (1985) suggests that the rightward preference of the center of interest would attract the subject's gaze thus leaving most of the picture in the left visual field allowing the right hemisphere to analyze the pictorial information. Levy (1976), however, proposed that "... in viewing pictures, the right visuospatially specialized hemisphere is selectively activated producing a bias of attention toward and a psychological waiting of the left side of space. Pictures which correct for this imbalance by having their more important content or greater heaviness on the right are considered [...] to be more pleasing."

Levy's hypothesis fits Gaffron's (1950) phenomenological work which revealed the scanpath that individuals from Western cultures use when looking at paintings. They start in the lower left foreground and sweep up and to the right in the picture space. This left-to-right scanpath of pictures may, in fact, reflect the viewer's reading habits rather than his/her neural organization.

(a) Lateralized Landscape (b) Directional Static (c) Directional Mobile

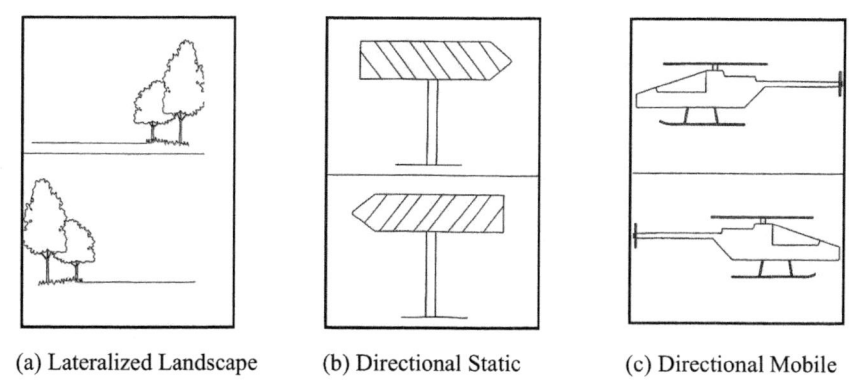

Figure 2. Sample aesthetic preference images

We sought to determine the extent to which aesthetic preferences of images may be determined by reading direction. Chokron and De Agostini (2000) compared French (left-to-right readers) and Israeli (right-to-left readers) healthy adults on an aesthetic preference judgment task. Participants were presented with pairs of images, one being the mirror-image of the other (i.e., a cat facing to the right and then to the left), and were asked for their aesthetic preference. The images consisted of landscape images with salient elements lateralized to the left or the right side of the page (Figure 2a), directional static images (i.e., a road sign or statue pointing either to the left or the right; Figure 2b), and directional mobile images (i.e., a helicopter or cat; Figure 2c).

A significant effect of reading direction was found with left-to-right readers showing a preference for stimuli depicting objects with a rightward directionality (the helicopter facing right), while right-to-left readers preferred stimuli depicting objects with a leftward directionality (the helicopter facing left). For the landscape images, however, both groups showed a rightward directionality preference (trees lateralized to the right of the page), with the Israeli participants showing a stronger preference than the French participants. See Figure 3.

While individuals preferred object pictures consistent with the directionality of their reading script, all participants reported a preference for the rightward oriented landscape images. This difference in preferences based on image characteristics suggests an interaction between reading direction (culture) and hemispheric specialization in right-handed participants.

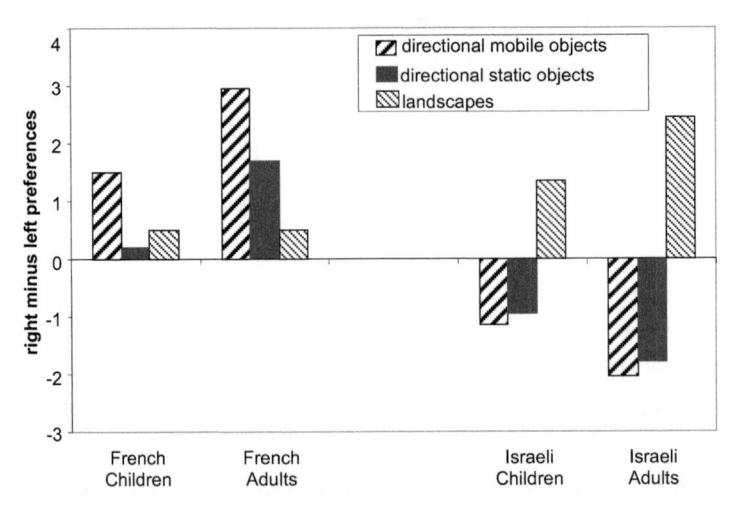

Figure 3. Effect of reading direction on aesthetic preference. Results are expressed as left minus right preferences with 'left' preference corresponding to a preference for a picture with a right-to-left directionality whereas 'right' preference corresponds to a picture with a left-to right directionality.

2.3. Egocentric reference

In a recent study we aimed to test if reading habits could influence spatial organization, not only in the visual modality, but also in the proprioceptive modality (Kazandjian, Dupierrix, Gaash, Love, Zivotofsky, De Agostini, & Chokron, 2009). Egocentric Reference (ER), the perceived direction of the body's sagittal axis, has been proposed to act as an anchor for movements in extracorporeal space (Jeannerod and Biguer, 1989). A common way of testing the direction of the ER is with a proprioceptive straight-ahead pointing task, by asking participants to point straight ahead while blindfolded and to record this subjective position (Bartolomeo and Chokron, 1999; Chokron, Colliot, Atzeni, Bartolomeo, and Ohlmann, 2004; Chokron and Imbert, 1995; Jeannerod and Biguer, 1989; Richard, Rousseaux, Saj, & Honoré, 2004;Werner, Wapner, and Bruell, 1953). ER is considered to result from the permanent integration of incoming sensory (visual, vestibular, neck, and proprioceptive) and motor-related signals (Biguer et al., 1988; Jeannerod and Biguer, 1989; Karnath, Sievering and Fetter, 1994; Ventre, Flandrin, and Jeannerod, 1984). As originally proposed, in normal conditions ER lies on the sagittal axis due to symmetrical functioning of the multiple neural structures which process sensory information, thus splitting personal and extra-personal space into two equal halves.

In support of this theoretical framework, the perturbation of this usual symmetry by unilateral sensorimotor stimulation or a unilateral cerebral lesion has shown to directly modulate the construction of the ER. Such a link between on-going sensorimotor integration and ER was evidenced by the influence of directional exploration of space (either visual or proprioceptive) in straight-ahead judgment among healthy adults and brain-damaged patients (for review see Chokron, 2003). By imposing a starting point that is to the right or left of the objective midline (0°), the participant must find or return to midline by scanning space either from left-to-right (LR) or from right-to-left (RL). According to these studies, when the arm is positioned to the left of the objective 0°, healthy LR-reading adults tend to present an ER shift that is to the left of the objective 0°. Conversely, when scanning from right-to-left, a shift to the right is observed.

Using a straight-ahead pointing task to assess egocentric reference (Figure 4), unidirectional left-to-right readers (Uni-LR) were compared with three groups of bidirectional readers (who differed in the reading direction of their native language and/or the level of their second language literacy): low-English literate, native right-to-left, bidirectional readers (Lo-Bi-RL), high-English literate, native right-to-left, bidirectional readers (Hi-Bi-RL), and native left-to-right, bidirectional readers (Bi-LR). Participants were asked to point straight-ahead while blindfolded using either a left-to-right or a right-to-left scanning direction to approach the subjective sagittal midline.

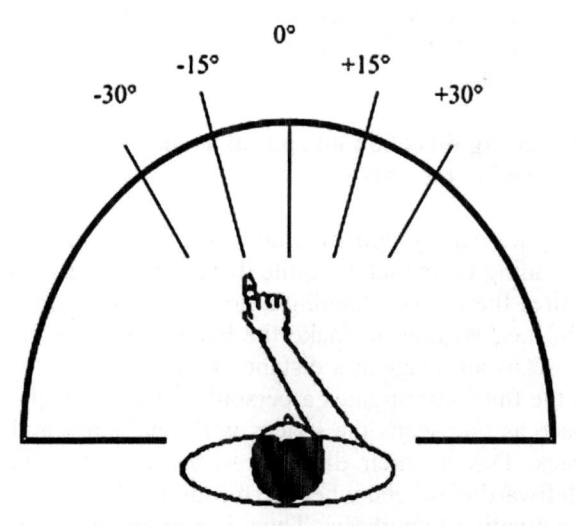

Figure 4. Straight-ahead Pointing Task: By imposing a starting point that is to the right or left of the objective midline (0°), the participant must find or return to midline by scanning space either from left-to-right (LR) or from right-to-left (RL).

Uni-LRs showed left-side significant spatial bias when scanning left-to-right and right-side bias during right-to-left scanning, Bi-LRs and Lo-Bi-RLs (i.e., intermediate level or less in their second language) demonstrated the opposite pattern, and Hi-Bi-RLs showed significant left-side spatial bias regardless of scanning direction. To summarize, we found that reading direction (either only from left-to-right) or both (from left-to-right and from right-to-left) significantly influences the perception of the subjective sagittal middle during a proprioceptive straight ahead pointing task.

The present results obtained in monolinguals and bilinguals confirmed the effect of reading directionality on spatial exploration. Interestingly, bidirectional literacy appears to play a role in non-visual, proprioceptive spatial perception. Unidirectional, left-to-right readers were consistent in their ability to find the objective center (or their egocentric reference) and showed an ipsilateral spatial bias dependent upon the direction of scanning. In contrast, bidirectional readers (regardless of native language) were inconsistent and demonstrated a variable pattern in proprioceptive straight-ahead pointing. Overall, these findings suggest that bidirectional readers, regardless of reading proficiency or native language, demonstrate a different pattern in estimating straight-ahead compared to unidirectional LR readers. This study provided additional supporting data for the hypothesis that reading direction habit can influence non-visual spatial performance, including proprioceptive measures of egocentric reference. This is of importance, because it demonstrates that a visual task (reading) may affect non-visual performance (proprioceptive straight-ahead) not only in monolingual participants but also in bilinguals (English-Hebrew readers).

3. Effect of reading direction on spatial asymmetry: Discussion and perspectives

Line bisection, aesthetic judgments, and straight-ahead pointing are three non-verbal scanning tasks that are quite different from each other. Whereas one task requires the use of scanning a horizontal line and induces a well-learned action, i.e., writing, to make the hatch mark, the second task taps into how one scans an image at a distance without use of any sensorimotor activity, and the third investigates a person's sense of corporeal and extra-corporeal space as one scans the spaces with one's arm and hand without visual feedback. Despite their differences, early studies had, at first, attributed the leftward bias seen when performing either of these tasks to the hemispheric activation hypothesis. Thus, it was hypothesized that the non-verbal nature of these tasks activated the right hemisphere, which in turn led to a scanning in a left-to-right direction or even an attentional pull toward the left side of the visual field. Later, this hypothesis was amended to include the role of attention. The perceptual-attention hypothesis suggested that in a nonverbal task, specifically line bisection, a salient feature or a scanning direction, not activation of the right hemisphere per se, will pull our attention to the left or the right side of the visual field.

If scanning direction can influence our performance of certain nonverbal tasks, then a well-learned scanning habit, such as reading direction, is also likely to influence performance. The studies presented in this chapter clearly demonstrated that this is in fact the case. Reading direction appears to play a significant role in the perceptual biases seen when performing not only line bisection tasks, but also during directional preference judgments of images, and in determining the subjective midline in a blind-folded, straight-ahead pointing task.

These studies show that bisection is dependent upon reading direction with a leftward deviation of the subjective middle for left-to-right readers, and a rightward deviation for right-to-left readers. This difference in perceptual bias is seen even among pre-schoolers who have not yet formally learned to read. Looking at three age groups that were compared in this study, an effect of level of exposure to reading was seen. Although both the adult and the 8-year old groups showed greater differences in perceptual bias compared to the pre-schoolers, the greatest difference overall was seen among the 8 year olds. Given that the 8 year olds were in the process of learning to read, and that the Israeli 8 year olds had not yet been taught to read English (as the Israeli adults had), this elevation in effect may be attributed to a greater level of exposure to one reading direction versus the other.

In terms of aesthetic preference judgments as well, left-to-right readers showed a preference for images with rightward directionality (thus consistent with a left-to-right scanpath) and the right-to-left readers showed a preference for images with leftward directionality (thus consistent with a right-to-left scanpath). Yet, images that were lateralized to one visual hemispace or the other did not seem to be affected by reading direction. Rather, regardless of viewer's reading direction mode, landscape images that were lateralized to the right of the visual hemispace were preferred. This dissociation in image type and preference suggests not only a role of reading direction, but also a role of hemispheric activation. These results lead us to propose that mobile objects or objects that can move in a given direction are associated to a preferred visual directionality that may correspond to the viewer's reading direction. On the contrary, perceiving a static object in a given hemispace seems to rely on hemispheric contingencies instead of cultural, directional effects. This proposition should be further investigated by combining the stimulus nature (static or mobile) to the visual field of presentation.

Finally, on the proprioceptive task of straight-ahead pointing, a more complex pattern is revealed. In this study, the participants were monolingual left-to-right readers compared with bidirectional readers varying in level of their left-to-right reading skills. The results of this study provided greatest support for our hypothesis that there is an interaction between biology (in terms of hemispheric specialization) and culture (reading direction). The monolingual or unidirectional left-to-right readers demonstrated a consistent pattern of estimating straight-ahead, both in accuracy and spatial bias, while the bidirectional readers, regardless of native language or left-to-right reading skill, were inconsistent. In particular, balanced bidirectional readers (those with high level of reading skill in both Hebrew and English) would underestimate midline when scanning from left-to-right (a pattern similar to that of unidirectional left-to-right readers), but overestimate the center when scanning from right-to-left (similar to unidirectional right-to-left readers). This result can be interpreted as an ability of balanced bilinguals to switch between languages, including in terms of reading direction mode, based on task demands. Overall, these results provide supporting evidence that sensorimotor cues and over-trained habits can work in tandem. Through the comparison of readers of opposing reading directions, past findings are partially confirmed on the role of sensorimotor exploration in both personal and extracorporeal space. Proprioceptive feedback received from the hands versus the trunk combined with the position of the arms (starting point) has been well-demonstrated to influence spatial scanning tasks, such as line bisection (Berberovic & Mattingley, 2003; Brodie & Dunn, 2005; Brodie & Pettigrew, 1996; Colliot, Ohlmann, & Chokron, 2001; Jewell & McCourt, 2000).

There is thus mounting evidence of an interaction between reading direction and brain function and a cultural hypothesis has been proposed. According to this hypothesis, although there are proven functional hemispheric specializations, well-trained behaviours based on culture can either reinforce these biases or influence them. Reading may have this reinforcing role due to the specific scanning bias associated with each language.

Interestingly some free-viewing asymmetries cannot be explained in terms of reading direction effects. Abed (1991) was able to demonstrate that when exploring non-directional visual stimuli patterns, Western, East Asian, and Middle Eastern participants fixate more often on the top and left of the visual display independent of their reading direction mode. Chokron and De Agostini (2000) found that the normal population, independent of their reading modes (from left to right or from right to left), prefer pictures where a landscape is represented on the right part of the page, compared to its mirror-image. Nicholls and Roberts (2002) showed that the leftward bias in the grey scale task seems to be unaffected by the participant's reading mode. These dissociations favor the view of an interaction between culture and brain function (Paulesu, McCrory, Fazio, Menoncello, Brunswick, Cappa, et al., 2000). As Eviatar (1997) pointed out, the finding that a cognitive skill related to language (reading scanning direction) can affect performance asymmetry for non-language tasks believed to be subserved by the right hemisphere (Chokron & De Agostini, 1995, 2000; Chokron & Imbert, 1993a, 1993b; Vaid & Singh, 1989) might possibly reflect large scale interactions between cognitive functions and hemispheric asymmetries which are not covered by a general model.

Heron (1957) proposed that scanning habits are comprised of two distinct mechanisms. The first is the scan in the direction in which the language is read (e.g., to the right in English and many other languages, to the left in Hebrew or Arabic). The second is the scan for the first element of the text (i.e., to the left in English, to the right in Hebrew or Arabic). Regarding this hypothesis, when the task requires a visual exploration, such as in line bisection, an effect of the direction of reading (rightward orientation for left-to-right readers and lefward orientation of attention for right to left readers) would affect the performance. Interestingly, the effect of reading direction on visuospatial performance might be simulated just by reversing the subject's scanning direction (Chokron et al., 1993). On the other hand, Eviatar (1995) has shown that the second mechanism (the scan for the first element to read) seems to bias movement of covert attention of left-to-right readers to the left side, and right-to-left readers to the right side. Along those lines, in terms of the orientation of attention, when begining a task or a visual search, left-to-right readers should be biased to the left (origin or reading exploration) and right-to-left readers should be biased towards the opposite right hemispace. This suggests quicker visual detection in the left rather than in the right visual field for left-to-right readers and the reverse for right-to-left readers. However, such attentional bias has never been demonstrated in normal participants who show no significant spatial bias in visual detection. Regarding Heron's two-stage model and Eviatar's hypothesis, it may be useful to delimit the conditions under which reading scanning directions will affect performance asymmetries in non-language tasks, and the factors (i.e., hemispheric specialization for the task, presentation of attentional cues, and unilateral or bilateral hemifield presentation) which modulate these effects to disentangle between the effect of initial visual fixation on covert attention and the effect of scanning direction on spatial exploration and representation.

Future research is now needed to understand the consequence of such findings. If the position of the egocentric reference depends on reading habits, one could propose that a multitude of spatial processing can be affected by acquired directional or non-directional abilities. There is mounting psychophysical and neuropsychological evidence that the spatial asymmetries seen in performance and preference are not due solely to symmetrical hemispheric specialization but rather are a function of reading direction habits (Kazandjian and Chokron, 2008). Recently, Han and Northoff (2008), in a review of transcultural neuroimaging studies, noted cultural differences in neural activations for perceptual processing, attention, and mental calculation. These findings argue in favor of a close interaction between cultural and biological factors in spatial organization. This influence of reading direction on spatial processing is clear even if neuroanatomical substrates have not been investigated as yet. For this, not only do we need to pay closer attention to cultural differences and linguistic factors on a variety of cognitive tasks in both neuropsychological assessments and psychophysical studies, but we must also shift toward the use of neuroimaging to provide further evidence of the influence on reading direction habits on attentional and spatial processing.

Considering the estimated number of right-to-left readers is more than 300 million in the world, (e.g., Arabic, Urdu, Hebrew) the discussion and further investigation of the cognitive and neural functional differences compared to Roman script readers is overdue and necessary. Furthermore, with the widespread, worldwide accessibility of computers and the internet, bilingualism and bidirectional reading have become more common, suggesting further inquiry into the neural correlates of bidirectional readers as well.

References

Abed, Farough (1991). Cultural influences on visual scanning patterns. *Journal of Cultural Psychology, 22,* 525–534.

Bartolomeo, Paolo & Sylvie Chokron (1999). Egocentric frame of reference: its role in spatial bias after right hemisphere lesions. *Neuropsychologia, 37*(8), 881–894.

Beaumont, J. Graham (1985). Lateral organization and aesthetic preference: The importance of peripheral visual asymmetries. *Neuropsychologia, 23,* 103–113.

Berberovic, Nadja & Jason Mattingley (2003). Effects of prismatic adaptation on judgements of spatial extent in peripersonal and extrapersonal space. *Neuropsychologia, 41*(4), 493–503.

Bertelson, Paul (1972). Listening from left to right versus right to left. *Perception, 1,* 161–165.

Biguer, Benjamin, Iain M. Donaldson, Alan Hein & Marc Jeannerod (1988). Neck muscle vibration modifies the representation of visual motion and direction in man. *Brain, 111,* 1405–1424.

Bowers, Dawn & Kenneth M. Heilman (1980). Pseudoneglect: effects of hemispace on a tactile line bisection task. *Neuropsychologia, 18*(4–5), 491–498.

Bradshaw, John L., Judy A. Bradshaw, Greg Nathan, Norman C. Nettleton & Lyn Wilson (1986). Leftward error in bisecting the gap between two points: stimulus quality and hand effects. *Neuropsychologia, 24*, 849–855.

Bradshaw, John L., Greg Nathan, Norman C. Nettleton, Lyn Wilson & Jane Pierson (1987). Why is there a left side underestimation in rod bisection? *Neuropsychologia, 25*, 735–738.

Braine, Lila G. (1968). Asymmetry of pattern perception observed in Israelis. *Neuropsychologia, 6*, 73–88.

Brodie, Eric E. & Emma M. Dunn (2005). Visual line bisection in sinistrals and dextrals as a function of hemispace, hand, and scan direction. *Brain and Cognition, 58*(2), 149–156.

Brodie, Eric E. & Laura E.L. Pettigrew (1996). Is left always right? Directional deviations in visual line bisection as a function of hand and initial scanning direction. *Neuropsychologia, 34*(5), 467–470.

Chemtob, Claude M. (1979). Paradoxical complementarity in the esthetic preferences of the cerebral hemispheres: an exploratory study. *Perceptual & Motor Skills, 48*(3 Pt 1), 799–806.

Chokron, Sylvie (2003). Right parietal lesions, unilateral spatial neglect, and the egocentric frame of reference. *NeuroImage, 20*, S75–S81.

Chokron, Sylvie & Paulo Bartolomeo (1997). Patterns of dissociation between left hemineglect and deviation of the egocentric reference. *Neuropsychologia, 35*, 1503–1508.

Chokron, Sylvie, Paolo Bartolomeo, Pascale Colliot & Laurent Auclair (2002). Effect of gaze direction on tactilo-kinesthetic perception. *Brain and Cognition, 48*, 312–317.

Chokron, Sylvie, Jean Marc Bernard & Michel Imbert (1997). Length representation in normal and neglect subjects with opposite reading habits studied through a line extension task. *Cortex, 33*, 47–64.

Chokron, Sylvie, Pascale Colliot, Thierry Atzeni, Paolo Bartolomeo & Théophile Ohlmann (2004). Active versus passive proprioceptive straight-ahead pointing in normal subjects. *Brain and Cognition, 55*(2), 290–294.

Chokron, Sylvie & Maria De Agostini (1995). Reading habits and line bisection: a developmental approach. *Cognitive Brain Research, 3*, 51–58.

Chokron, Sylvie & Maria De Agostini (2000). Reading habits influence aesthetic preference. *Cognitive Brain Research, 10*, 45–49.

Chokron, Sylvie & Michel Imbert (1993a). Egocentric reference and asymetric perception of space. *Neuropsychologia, 31*, 267–275.

Chokron, Sylvie & Michel Imbert (1993b). Influence of reading habits on line bisection. *Cognitive Brain Research, 1*, 219–222.

Chokron, Sylvie & Michel Imbert (1995). Variations of the egocentric reference among normal subjects and a patient with unilateral neglect. *Neuropsychologia, 33*(6), 703–711.

Colliot, Pascale, Théophile Ohlmann & Sylvie Chokron (2001). Position of the egocentric reference and performance in line bisection and subjective vertical estimation tasks. *Brain and Cognition, 46*(1–2), 82–86.

Corballis, Michael C. (1994). Neuropsychology of perceptual functions. In Dahlia W. Zaidel (Eds.), *Neuropsychology*, (pp. 83–104). San Diego, CA: Academic Press, Inc.

Dellatolas, George, Jerome Vanluchene & Thierry Coutin (1996). Visual and motor components in simple line bisection: An investigation in normal adults. *Cognitive Brain Research, 4*, 49–56.

Eviatar, Zohar (1995). Reading direction and attention: Effects of lateralized ignoring. *Brain and Cognition, 29*, 137–150.

Eviatar, Zohar (1997). Language experience and right-hemisphere tasks: The effect of scanning habits and multi-lingualism. *Brain and Language, 58*, 157–173.

Frith, Uta (1998). Literally changing the brain. *Brain, 121*, 1011–1012.

Gaffron, Mercedes (1950). Right and left in pictures. *Art Quarterly, 13*, 312–321.

Gibson, James J. (1966). The problem of temporal order in stimulation and perception. *Journal of Psychology, 62*, 141–149.

Gombert, Jean Emile & Michel Fayol (1992). Writing in pre-literate children. *Learning and Instruction, 2*, 23–41.

Han, Shihui & Georg Northoff (2008). Culture-sensitive neural substrates of human cognition: a ranscultural neuroimaging approach. *Nature Review Neuroscience, 9*(8), 646–654.

Harvey, Monika, A. David Milner & Robert C. Roberts (1995). An investigation of hemispatial neglect using the landmark task. *Brain and Cognition, 27*, 59–78.

Heron, Woodburn (1957). Perception as a function of retinal locus and attention. *American Journal of Psychology, 70*, 38–48.

Jeannerod, Marc & Benjamin Biguer (1989). Egocentric reference and represented space. *Revue Neurologique (Paris), 145*(8–9), 635–639.

Jewell, George & Mark E. McCourt (2000). Pseudoneglect: A review and meta-analysis of performance factors in line bisection tasks. *Neuropsychologia, 38*, 93–110.

Karnath, Hans-Otto, D. Sievering & Michael Fetter (1994). The interactive contribution of neck muscle proprioception and vestibular stimulation to subjective "straight ahead" orientation in man. *Experimental Brain Research, 101*(1), 140–146.

Kazandjian, Seta & Sylvie Chokron (2008). Paying attention to reading direction. *Nature Review Neuroscience, 9*(12), 965.

Kazandjian, Seta, Eve Dupierrix, Esther Gaash, Itamar Y. Love, Ari Z. Zivotofsky, Maria De Agostini & Sylvie Chokron (2009). Egocentric reference in bidirectional readers as measured by the straight-ahead pointing task. *Brain Research, 1247*, 133–141.

Kimura, Doreen (1961). Cerebral dominance and the perception of verbal stimuli. *Canadian Journal of Psychology, 15*, 166–171.

Kinsbourne, Marcel (1970). The cerebral basis of lateral asymmetries in attention. *Acta Psychologica, 33*, 193–201.

Kugelmass, Sol & Israel Lieblich (1970). Perceptual exploration in Israeli children. *Child Development, 41*, 1125–1131.

Levy, Jerre (1976). Lateral dominance and aesthetic preference. *Neuropsychologia, 14*(4), 431–445.

Lindell, Annukka K. (2006). In your right mind: right hemisphere contributions to language processing and production. *Neuropsycholy Review, 16*(3), 131–148.
Manning, Lilianne, Peter W. Halligan & John C. Marshall (1990). Individual variation in line bisection: a study of normal subjects with application to the interpretation of visual neglect. *Neuropsychologia, 28*(7), 647–655.
McLaughlin, John P. (1986). Aesthetic preference and lateral preferences. *Neuropsychologia, 24*(4), 587–590.
Mead, Andrew M. & John P. McLaughlin (1992). The roles of handedness and stimulus asymmetry in aesthetic preference. *Brain and Cognition, 20*(2), 300–307.
Mefferd, Roy B. Jr., Betty A. Wieland & L. Paul Dufilho (1969). Systematic alterations of the apparent centers of lines. *Perceptual and Motor Skills, 28,* 803–825.
Nicholls, Michael E.R. & Georgina R. Roberts (2002). Can free-viewing perceptual asymmetries be explained by scanning, pre-motor or attentional biases? *Cortex, 38,* 113–36.
Oscar-Berman, Marlene, Lucio Rehbein, Alan Porfest & Harold Goodglass (1978). Dichaptic hand-order effects with verbal and non verbal tactile stimulation. *Brain and Language, 6,* 323–333.
Perez-Arce, Patricia (1999). The influence of culture on cognition. *Archives of Clinical Neuropsychology, 14,* 581–592.
Paulesu, Eraldo, Eamon McCrory, Ferruccio Fazio, L. Menoncello, Nicola Brunswick, Stefano F. Cappa et al., (2000). A cultural effect on brain function. *Nature Neuroscience, 3,* 91–96.
Pollatsek, Alexander, Shmuel. Bolozky, Arnold D. Well & Keith Rayner (1981). Asymmetries in the perceptual span for Israeli readers. *Brain and Language, 14*(1), 174–180.
Price, Cathy J., Richard J. Wise, John D.G. Watson, Karalyn Patterson, David Howard & Richard S. Frackowiak (1994). Brain activity during reading. The effects of exposure duration and task. *Brain, 117 (Pt 6),* 1255–1269.
Rayner, Keith (1998). Eye movements in reading and information processing: 20 years of research. *Psycholical Bulletin, 124*(3), 372–422.
Rayner, Keith, Alexander Pollatsek & Katherine S. Binder (1998). Phonological codes and eye movements in reading. *Journal of Experimental Psychology: Learning, Memory, and Cognition, 24*(2), 476–497.
Richard, Christelle, Marc Rousseaux, Arnaud Saj & Jacques Honore (2004). Straight ahead in spatial neglect: evidence that space is shifted, not rotated. *Neurology, 63*(11), 2136–2138.
Sampaio, Eliana & Sylvie Chokron (1992). Pseudoneglect and reversed pseudoneglect among left-handers and right-handers. *Neuropsychologia, 30*(9), 797–805.
Sampaio, Eliana & Jean Philip (1991). Sensory and motor aspects of pseudoneglect, hemifield, and hemispace in the tactile modality. *Brain and Cognition, 16*(1), 74–82.
Shannon Lael (1978). Left-right sequencing in unschooled children: a function of learning or maturation. *Perceptual and Motor Skills, 47,* 971–976.
Starr, Matthew S. & Keith Rayner (2001). Eye movements during reading: some current controversies. *Trends in Cognitive Sciences, 5*(4), 156–163.

Tolchinsky-Landsman, Liliana & Iris Levine (1985). Writing in preschoolers: An age-related analysis. *Applied Psycholinguistics, 6,* 319–339.
Vaid, Jyotsna & Maharaj Singh (1989). Asymmetries in the perception of facial affect: Is there an influence of reading habits? *Neuropsychologia, 27,* 1277–1287.
van Houten, Weicher H., Claude M. Chemtob & S.I. Hersh (1981). Hemispheric lateralization and aesthetic judgement. *Cortex, 17*(4), 477–489.
Ventre, Jocelyne, Jean Marc Flandrin & Marc Jeannerod (1984). In search for the egocentric reference. A neurophysiological hypothesis. *Neuropsychologia, 22*(6), 797–806.
Werner, Heinz, Seymour Wapner & Jan H. Bruell (1953). Experiments on sensory-tonic field theory of perception. VI. Effect of position of head, eyes, and of object on position of the apparent median plane. *Journal of Experimental Psychology, 46*(4), 293–299.
White, Murray J. (1972). Hemispheric asymmetries in tachistoscopic information processing. *British Journal of Psychology, 63,* 497–508.
Witelson, Sandra F. (1976). Sex and single hemisphere: Specialization of the right hemisphere for spatial processing. *Science, 193,* 425–427.
Young, Andrew W. (1983). The development of right hemisphere abilities. In Andrew W. Young (Ed.), *Functions of the right cerebral hemisphere* (pp. 147–169). London: Academic Press Inc.

Aesthetic asymmetries, spatial agency, and art history: A social psychological perspective

Caterina Suitner and Chris McManus

Abstract

The analysis of works of art provides a fertile meeting point between the arts and the sciences. In this chapter we focus on the statistical regularities that can be identified in large series of paintings, and we discuss possible explanations for such regularities, particularly assessing the extent to which spatial arrangement is used strategically in portrait paintings, and how this is related to Spatial Agency Bias. The availability of large corpuses of artistic images provides fertile ground both for generating and testing such theories. Spatial regularities in artworks can be explained in terms of embodiment theory, as a consequence of cultural determinants such as the direction of writing and reading, as well as being a consequence of social group membership of both observers and those being portrayed, invoking social psychological processes such as stereotyping and inter-group processes.

1. Introduction

"Space is the breath of art." – Frank Lloyd Wright

Artistic production provides a remarkable field for investigation by psychologists, not only by providing an enormous set of rich and complex data to be analyzed in detail, but because it also represents a fertile meeting point between the arts and the sciences, providing the possibilities of a place where art becomes scientifically valid and science confronts beauty.

The arts, as with all areas of human expertise, provide a wealth of information both about human performance and its limitations and constraints. Great artists in some ways are similar to elite sportsmen, whose record-breaking performances in competition occur after years of extensive training which considers and reflects on every nuance of bodily action. Such sportsmen can tell psychologists and social scientists about the trainability of the human motor system, the extremes of which it is possible, and its physical and psychological limits. The master works of great artists have likewise been thought through in vast detail, a host of alternative configurations and components having been considered and mostly rejected. The eventual work is therefore some form of optimum, solving a host of problems concerning form, composition, symbolic meaning, and, of course, the communication of its central ideas. All of this is to ensure that in the final result, the viewers obtain as much as possible of the richness of meaning that the artist intended.

Inevitably any painted work of art has multiple levels at which it can be interpreted – the richness, harmony and appropriateness of colours, the accuracy of representation, the nature of technique, the spatial composition and balance of visual forms, and the symbols and their inter-relationships. All of these contribute to the dual impact of the art object, both as social communication, and as a thing of beauty (and beauty and communicative effect necessarily support and reinforce each other). For all those reasons, works of art extend their meanings across time, and contemporary relevance can often be seen in them. In the present chapter we focus on paintings, and specifically on portraits, as they offer the opportunity to study their spatial orientation from a clear point of view, namely the point of view of the observer. Pre-twentieth century paintings in particular are an important database for study, as not only are the objects themselves fixed and unchanging, and well recorded, and hence they provide a database on the psychology of past ages, but also, in ages such as the Renaissance when there was a relatively fixed range of themes which were being represented, such as the Madonna and Child or the Crucifixion, the images are available in sufficiently large quantities for statistical analysis, and hence the testing of hypotheses against empirical evidence is possible. We will argue here that what we can call archival research, the studies of large corpuses of paintings or other artistic images, can be of great help to psychologists. Such a meeting place of the arts and the sciences will inevitably inform and benefit both disciplines.

Artists are in many ways similar to sportsmen in that although they have remarkable intuitions about performance and the expression of their ideas and intentions, they are often also not good either at explaining, or even understanding, the effects of their own actions. In part that is because so much of the determination of each action is probably unconscious (as is generally true with much of human behaviour, particularly when action, as with every kick of a ball or touch of a brush, is 'hot', being carried out in real time under a wealth of only partially articulated constraints). For such tasks the bigger picture, the patterns and constraints, often only appear when the scientist stands back and looks for larger patterns, the statistical regularities that appear when many objects are studied. One of us (Chris McManus) was lucky, at the beginning of his career, to recognise such a regularity. The most superficial of visits to any great art gallery will show that humans particularly like portraying other humans in their paintings, and that a sizeable proportion consists of pictures of individual humans – portraits. We are a social animal, and faces are complex biological structures comprising bones, eyebrows, eyes, facial muscles, facial hair, lips and mouth, which attract our visual attention, providing information about identity, intentions, and probably also personality and attitudes. It is not surprising either that people are interested in faces, or that art galleries are full of representations of them. Nor is it unexpected that most portraits are not full-face, but instead are three-quarter poses, looking slightly to right or left, for that is the canonical view which allows a more accurate reconstruction of the three-dimensional structure of the head and face.

Suddenly, though, at that point an artist has an apparently arbitrary choice – should the subject of the portrait turn slightly to their left or right (or as we will say here, show their left or right cheek to the world, and hence as they turn to their right, show their left cheek and look to the left side of the viewer's space)? At that point, biological theory says nothing. The world is broadly symmetric, people have two cheeks, they are roughly equivalent, and so what does it matter which cheek is shown? Just as physicists assumed that the laws of the physical world are symmetric (wrongly as it happens, as Yang and Lee were to show in 1957 in the case of the weak force – see McManus, 2002), so an immediate and obvious assumption would be that right and left cheeks are equally represented in art galleries. It is an easy hypothesis to test, although Chris McManus had no intention of doing that when, in 1971 as part of a project aimed at a different question on the shape of paintings, he coded information into a computer about several hundred Elizabethan and Jacobean portraits (Strong, 1969). The 'null hypothesis' in statistical terms, the position of no interest as it were, is that half the paintings would show their left cheek and half their right. They didn't though, and there were significantly more left than right cheeks. A visit to the National Portrait Gallery in London, with its larger and more representative collection, rapidly confirmed the basic finding – of 1474 paintings, 891 (60.4%) showed their left cheek, and only 583 (39.6%) showed their right cheek. The odds of 1.53:1 for a left cheek rather than a right cheek is very different from the 'evens' that a simple chance hypothesis would expect (McManus & Humphrey, 1973). Some force has to be at work to produce such a regularity.

Finding statistical regularities is one thing. Explaining them – and particularly their subtleties, such as why more male subjects in portraits showed their left cheeks than did female subjects – is another matter. The data of the original study were confirmed by other researchers in other contexts, but a good explanation of them was not available. As so often happens in science, evidence from two other fields eventually converged into a possible explanation. Initially the Spatial Agency Bias was developed within neuropsychology to account for deficits seen in some patients with brain lesions, and then it was adopted also to account for observations within social psychology. Spatial Agency Bias was originally a theory to account for cognitive strategies in thematic role representation in the field of neuropsychology (Chatterjee, Maher, & Heilman, 1995; Maher, Chatterjee, & Rothi, 1995), associating the left position with an agent and the right position to the recipient of an action. Subsequently the same principle was applied to understanding the spatial representation of social targets, with a particular emphasis on gender differences (Maass, Suitner, Favaretto, & Cignacchi, 2009; Suitner & Maass, 2007). The present chapter will outline how the Spatial Agency Bias was discovered, in part by looking at portrait paintings, and how that finding then stimulated further research. After defining Spatial Agency Bias, we will discuss the strategic use of space both in portraits of people, and in artworks with religious themes. It is suggested that the social membership of individuals in a work of art (the *'targets'*) affects the spatial organisation and biases of an image, because of the attribution of agency to targets, often being influenced by stereotypes. In addition, the social membership of *observers* of art works, is evaluated as a possible influence in activating social or group processes (such as ingroup favouritism) in the choice of spatial representations of ingroup members. Finally, the cultural origins of spatial biases are discussed from the perspective of embodiment theory.

2. The Spatial Agency Bias

Spatial Agency Bias describes the tendency to associate targets (the individuals in paintings) to specific spatial features in a visual representation according to the agency they express. Agency is defined from a cognitive point of view as the role of being the agent of an action and from a social point of view as the potential to act socially, often measured in terms of power or social status. In particular, the more a given target is characterized by agency, the more they are likely to be associated with the agentic spatial representation, namely to the left acting toward the right. The Spatial Agency Bias originated in observations of portraits produced in Western art, but has been later studied with a variety of methods, from archival research to laboratory studies, focusing on different dependent variables. Commonly used dependent variables in studies are:

- The direction of profile direction in portraits (leftward or rightward facing, from the observer point of view, both in lab drawing tasks and archival research.
- The relative spatial allocation in the visual field of two targets (one to left and the other to the right) in lab drawing tasks and archival research.
- The choice in thematic role assignment (e.g., "who is the agent?") of two targets presented in the visual field, one to the left and the other to the right.
- Reaction times in thematic role recognition assignment (e.g., "who is the agent?") of two targets presented in the visual field one to the left and the other to the right.
- Evaluation (such as, "how much do you like it?") of visual targets characterized in terms of spatial directionality (e.g., facing rightward or leftward).

In the following section, we will discuss the strategic use of space by artists for emphasising the role or nature of the individuals they are portraying.

2.1. Space as a communication tool in artistic production

The spatial layout of paintings does not occur due to chance, but rather it results from systematic and meaningful strategies. Painters are often not directly aware of their strategic use of spatial features, but it can be observed that they employ spatial layouts in systematic ways. According to Poseq, artists such as Leonardo, Ingres and Michelangelo exploited in their artworks the conventional direction of observation from left to right, also producing mirror versions of their paintings in order to convey specific meanings that can be read in line with the given sequence of protagonists (Poseq, 1999, 2001). Left-to-right scanning has been identified as the standard direction of gaze movements in observing artwork both by art historians (Arnheim, 1986; Gaffron, 1950; Oppe, 1944) and also by psychologists (Elkind & Weiss, 1967; Heron, 1957). For example, in a representation of "Oedipus and the Sphinx" Ingres produced at first a painting in which Oedipus was placed to the right of the Sphinx (Ingres, *Oediphus and Sphinx*, 1808, Paris, Louvre) and about sixty years later he reversed the composition, placing Oedipus to the left (Ingres, *Oediphus and Sphinx*, 1864, Baltimore, Walters Art Gallery). According to Poseq (2001), the two versions differ sensibly in the message they communicate. In the first version Oedipus is on the right and observed by the viewer after seeing the Sphinx (according to the left-to-right scanning bias). That position would suggest the lack of agency of Oedipus and anticipates the tragedy that he is going to face (i.e., killing his father Laius and having an incestuous relation with his mother Jocasta). In the second version, Oedipus is placed in the agentic position (i.e., on the left), emphasizing another aspect of the myth, namely the success of Oedipus in solving the Sphinx' riddle. In such a case the spatial layout of the painting suggests different interpretations of its meaning, with Ingres probably using the practice of inversion not as a mere pictorial technique but as a specific tool to alter the impression given to the observer. In another example described by Poseq (2001), Ingres used inversion to create suspense, moving the protagonist, Stratonice, from the left position in the first version of *Antiochus and Stratonice* (Ingres, 1834–40, Chantilly, Musée Condé) to the right position in the later version of the same painting (1866, Montpellier, Musée Fabre). In the second version the protagonist is the last element perceived by the observer, which creates a sense of suspense in the observation of the artwork. Although these effects are highly subjective as they strongly depend on the interpretation of the viewer, it seems clear that direction has meaning only when defined from an observer's point of view. Left and right are irrelevant issues unless there is a viewer able to relate the difference between left and right to her- or himself.

Flipped images are sometimes used with particular attention to the observer's point of view, an extreme example being the mirror-reversed sign "ƎƆNAJUBMA" on the front of ambulances, since it presumes it is usually being seen in a driver's rear-view mirror (Soresen, 2000). Such reasoning accords with the hypothesis that inversion often has a communicative aim, the same picture changing its meaning when its orientation is changed (Arnheim, 1974), there being "a dynamic vector leading from the left to the right of the visual field" (p. 33). For example, "Viewed from the right side,):), is a happy face, viewed from the left, it is a sad face" (Soresen, 2000). The importance of the observer's point of view is emphasised within the semiotics of art, particular attention being paid to the interpretation and understanding by those who view the art work (Bal & Bryson, 1991). "Semiotics is centrally concerned with reception" (*ibidem*, p. 184). Consistent with such a viewpoint, the terms right and left are used throughout this chapter to refer to the observer's point of view, and hence are interpreted as communication tools. In the next section, evidence is presented on spatial asymmetries in portrait paintings, and interpreted according to the agency hypothesis.

2.2. The Spatial Agency Bias in portraits

The strategic use of space in paintings has been the subjects of several systematic studies, particularly concerning left and right orientations in large collections of painted portraits. Much of this work dates back to the study of McManus and Humphrey (1973). Most portraits show three-quarter profiles, as this provides a better sense of three-dimensionality, as compared either with a full-face pose or a complete profile. In profiles of any sort, the sitter's gaze can either look toward right or left. Although it might be expected that half would be to the right and half to the left, as already mentioned, McManus and Humphrey (1973) found a clear excess of left facing profiles from the sixteenth to the twentieth centuries.

That leftward bias was subsequently confirmed by Gordon (1974) in a sample of 295 portraits by Goya. Grüsser et al. (1988) and Suitner and Maass (2007, Study 1) also found the effect in 933 portrait paintings and 298 painted portraits, respectively. Conesa and his colleagues also confirmed the leftward bias in a sample of 4180 single-subject portraits of various media (Conesa, Brunold-Conesa, & Miron, 1995). This leftward bias is in line with the general claim that the leftward direction is associated with a lack of agency. Specifically, Chatterjee (2002) interpreted the findings in art history as evidence for his Agency Hypothesis, according to which action is associated with a rightward direction that develops from an agent positioned on the left to a recipient positioned on the right of the visual field. Given that the sitters portrayed in artworks are typically posing in a still and passive fashion, it would be expected that they are characterized by an absence of agency that is emphasized by the leftward direction of their profile.

The idea of Spatial Agency Bias originated in observations of an aphasic patient who developed the strategy of assigning the agentic role to the target presented to the left side and the recipient role to the target presented to the right side. For example whenever the target X was represented to the left, X was indicated as the agent of the action relating X with Y, even when X was receiving the action. As part of the analysis, the study then tested if this spatial bias in the conceptualization of thematic roles also occurred in the general population, and indeed it did. In this case the dependent variable was the relative position (in terms of right and left) assigned to the recipient and the agentic target. For instance, when control individuals without neurological lesions were asked visually to represent a sentence such as, "the circle pushes the square", they also were more likely to draw the circle to the left of the square (Maher et al., 1995). Similar findings were also found in studies involving other thematic roles. When asked to draw pairs of interacting persons, the agent tends to be positioned to the left (Chatterjee et al., 1995; Maass & Russo, 2003). Similar results were found analysing participants' reaction time in a recognition task. They were asked to recognize the agentic target among interacting targets represented in the visual field. The agent was recognized more easily when positioned to the left of the recipient with action going from left toward right (Chatterjee, Southwood, & Basilico, 1999). Additionally, Chatterjee and colleagues (Chatterjee et al., 1999) showed that actions are better processed when evolving from left toward right rather than vice versa, and Maass and colleagues found that rightward trajectories are evaluated as more beautiful, faster and stronger than are leftward ones (Maass, Pagani, & Berta, 2007).

The Spatial Agency Bias is not always present (Coles, 1974, Suitner & Maass, 2007, Study 2) and sometimes appears to be reversed (Coles, 1974; Latto, 1996; ten Cate, 2002; Uhrbrock, 1973). Coles (1974), for instance, found no leftward bias studying the profile direction of Rembrandt's portraits, but a more detailed analysis suggests that the positioning bias in Rembrandt's portraits and self-portraits varies systematically as a function of the social distance between painter and sitter (Humphrey & McManus, 1973), with the rightward bias falling off progressively from self-portraits, through male kin, male non-kin, female kin, and female non-kin. The spatial bias seemed therefore to vary with gender and kinship. The analyses of such inconsistencies led social psychologists to interpret spatial representation as a way of representing social differentiation, varying both with the represented target and with social characteristics such as gender. Gender differences had been reported by McManus and Humphrey (1973), the leftward bias being greater when the portrayed sitters were women. Gordon (1974) replicated that finding in his study of Goya, and further support came from the study of Grüsser, Selke and Zynda (1988). Last, the gender-linked leftward bias was confirmed in a study of portraits of leading figures in academia, in spite of the small number of women in the sample containing only 7 female and 1124 male professors portraits (ten Cate, 2002). So the question that spontaneously arises is why male and female targets are differently represented in term of profile direction. Before answering this question it is important to note that asymmetries are present also in representations of other targets, such as in religious paintings.

2.3. The Spatial Agency Bias in other portrayals of people

In the Italian Renaissance, portraits were relatively rare paintings (although they do show the same patterns of an excess of left cheeks, particularly in male subjects, as elsewhere – see McManus, 1979) and far more common are paintings on the great religious themes of the Catholic Church. The large-scale catalogues of such paintings by Bernard Berenson (1957, 1963, 1967, 1968) provide a superb archival resource for analysing compositional asymmetries, and have been described in detail in chapter 13 of McManus (1979). Here we will briefly look at three types of images.

The Crucifixion. All but one of the 147 portrayals of the Crucifixion in Berenson show Christ's left cheek (i.e., the leftward profile), indicating the non-agentic role of the dying man. There are potentially many other explanations for this asymmetry, particularly in the symbolism of right and left within Christian theology, but agency is also a good explanation.

The Annunciation. The Annunciation, in which the Angel Gabriel announces to Mary that she is to conceive a child by the Holy Ghost, who would be the son of God, has two individuals, one of whom, the Angel is clearly the agent. It is therefore no surprise that in 202 of the 209 Annunciations in Berenson, the Angel enters from the left side, showing his right profile, whereas Mary, who is non-agentic, shows the left profile.

The Madonna and Child. This was perhaps the most frequent of all images in the Renaissance, particularly later in the Renaissance as the Cult of the Virgin Mary took hold (Carroll, 1986). The young mother, Mary, holds the Christ Child, typically to one side, and there is potential for several asymmetries – is Mary or the Child to be to the left, and do Mary and the Child show their left and right profiles. The answer is complicated, although a typical early Renaissance painting shows the child to the right of the picture (i.e. held on Mary's left arm), with the Madonna showing the right profile and the Child the left profile. Mary is, in some sense, the agent responsible for creating the child, and she is in the dominant, powerful position compared with the weak, vulnerable young child. The pattern however shows large historical changes (see McManus 1979 for details), so that by the end of the Renaissance the child is held on the viewer's left (Mary's right), and both Mary and the Child show their left cheeks. Explaining such a pattern in terms of agency is not straightforward, and at present provides somewhat of a challenge to the theory. There are also other approaches to the problem, not least because of the broader tendency of human mothers, irrespective of handedness, to hold babies on their left side (see e.g. Harris, in press, for a comprehensive review, and Harris, Cardenas, Michael, Spradlin, & Almerigi, in press, for a demonstration that adults prefer paintings in which the child is held on the mother's left (the viewer's right)).

Taken overall, these three different types of images, with their portrayal of one person, and then two individuals interacting, exist in very large numbers and therefore provide excellent archival data for testing the details of theories of spatial agency, and indeed can do so within the context of perceptions that are changing in history, as with the Cult of the Virgin Mary.

2.4. A note of caution or a confirmation?

Uhrbrock (1973) had noted that Queen Elizabeth II, as with all monarchs on British postal stamps, is represented facing to the left. Conversely, American presidents are usually represented facing right on stamps. Interestingly, although monarchs are always portrayed facing to the left on British stamps (and it must be remembered that stamps are usually stuck in the top right-hand corner of an envelope, so the monarch faces inwards), on British coins the monarchs have alternated to right and left since the time of Charles II (see "Coins of the pound sterling", 2009) (and in some sense, Charles II, in facing right, was symbolically distancing himself from Oliver Cromwell, who had faced left). At one level, the use of such conventions (always to the left for stamp, alternating for coins) suggests that spatial agency bias is not relevant to interpreting the particular objects, while at a higher, more general level, the conventions themselves are perhaps necessary as without them there would be a risk of a portrait erroneously being perceived as agentic or non-agentic, and thereby conveying an implicit message of weakness or strength, so that the use of conventions over-rides any such agentic interpretation.

In the next two sections, the spatial agency is discussed from a social psychological perspective, namely as the result of the attribution of agency to the target, according to the social stereotype. First, we will present the case of gender and then of other social groups.

3. A social psychological perspective: The case of gender

Although originally proposed in the context of neuropsychology (Chatterjee, 2002), the Spatial Agency Hypothesis has been recently applied more broadly within social psychology (Maass et al., 2009; Suitner & Maass, 2007). Agency, and its counterpart, communion, are addressed in many social-psychological models as the key dimensions of stereotypes about social targets (Conway & Vartanian, 2000; Fiske, Cuddy, & Glick, 2007; Fiske, Cuddy, Glick, & Xu, 2002; Judd, James-Hawkins, Yzerbyt, & Kashima, 2005). Although there are many terms used in the literature to address the concept of agency (e.g., masculinity by Bem 1974; competence by Fiske, Cuddy, & Glick, 2007; agency by Abele, 2003, Bakan, 1966 and Eagly & Kite, 1987), a bi-dimensional model for defining social groups is widely accepted. Moreover, the overlap in terms of items between the different theories (Suitner & Maass, 2008) makes us believe that we can, at least in the present context, assimilate them into a major broad differentiation between the agentic and the non agentic groups (see Abele &

Wojciszke, 2007). Males are one social group that is consistently characterized by agency, being stereotypically perceived as more agentic (i.e., powerful and assertive) than females (e.g., Abele, 2003; Diekman, 2005). For example, Heilman, Block and Martell (1995) showed that women are perceived as less agentic than men, and this is the case even when women have a masculine role, such as women managers. The stereotype is so pervasive that it is not only descriptive but even prescriptive, that is, women not only are thought to be less agentic than males, but they also have to be (Heilman, 2001). This difference in agency has been interpreted as the cause of the different representations in visual fields (Chatterjee, 2002; Maass et al., 2009; Suitner & Maass, 2007). Given that women are usually associated with high communality but low agency (Best & Williams, 1993), it is not surprising that women are represented in the less agentic position, namely facing leftward. At a theoretical level, stereotypes are relevant in the hermeneutic coding of art at a semantic level (Bal & Bryson, 1991). To simplify, social stereotypes are used to understand the meaning of an artwork, for example identifying the identity of the represented target (male vs. female, young vs. old). At an empirical level, the importance of stereotypes has been supported in relation to spatial representation of male and female targets, and in particular to their relative position in the visual field in terms of right and left. Archival research on the representation of couples showed the male partner is mainly positioned to left of the female partner (Maass et al., 2009, Study 1a; see Suitner & Maass, this volume, for a detailed description); this bias is furthermore defined by the stronger agency ascribed to the male partner of the couple (Maass et al., 2009, Study 1b). Empirical research has additionally confirmed the importance of target gender in the spatial representation showing that participants tend to draw male targets to the left and female targets to the right especially when they hold stereotypic beliefs about gender (Maass et al., 2009; Suitner & Maass, 2007, Study 2).

An additional effect found in several studies is a subtle change in gender bias over time when analysing the direction in which portraits face. Grüsser and his colleagues (1988) were the first to note that "[...] the gender difference for head position of portrayed subject becomes more evident when the quotient of left and right position is plotted as a function of historical time" and "with the gradual social emancipation of women over the last three centuries, the L/R-quotient in head position decreased considerably" (Grüsser et al., 1988, p. 281). Several years later, in 1996, Latto replicated these results on a sample of 47 self-portraits, and again, the positioning bias (that this time was rightward oriented) was found decreasing with time. Recently, ten Cate (2002) analysed the effect of time in their study on portraits of professors and found that the rightward bias in the portraits of scientists present before 1820 turned into a leftward bias after 1900. All of these shifts over time can be accounted for by a change of stereotype content. This hypothesis was further supported by Suitner and Maass (2007, Study 2), who compared the representation of males and females over a wide time period, from 1370 to 1958, and found a clear decline over time in the leftward representation of females (and a partial fading of rightward male profiles), which is consistent with increasing female emancipation.

Laboratory studies have also examined the relationship between spatial features and the characteristics of the person being portrayed. In such studies participants are generally asked to evaluate either the represented target and to indicate how positive, potent, active (Benjafield & Segalowitz, 1993) or attractive (Zaidel & Fitzgerald, 1994) is the person in the image or the painting itself. In some cases participants are asked which of two mirror versions of the same artwork they prefer (McLaughlin & Murphy, 1994) or how much do they like the artwork (Zaidel & Fitzgerald, 1994) or how much Evaluation, Dynamism and Spirituality the artwork expresses (McManus, 1979). Benjafield and Segalowitz (1993) asked participants to rate eight portrait drawings by Leonardo da Vinci (4 of women, 4 of men, half showing the left cheek and half showing the right cheek) and also mirror reversals of the images on the three semantic differential dimensions of Evaluation, Potency and Activity. Images showing the right cheek, be it in the original or the reversed versions, were seen as more active and potent, but not different on evaluation. Female faces were also judged as less potent and more positive than those of men. McLaughlin and Murphy (1994), however, found somewhat different results in a study in which participants judged 48 portraits, painted from the fifteenth to the twentieth centuries, as well as their mirror-reversals. The 55 participants were asked which version of each portrait they preferred, and right-cheek versions (original or not) were preferred by the majority of participants, although there was no effect of sitter's gender, apart from a higher proportion of male participants preferring the right cheek version. Another study was conducted by Zaidel and Fitzgerald (1994) on 48 portraits from European museums (27 left facing, 19 women, 8 men, and 21 right facing, 6 women, 15 men). Participants rated their overall liking for the portrait, as well as the attractiveness of the sitter. Both judgements suggested that women showing their right cheek in the original version of the painting were judged more favourably, whereas spatial orientation did not affect the rating of men's portraits. Finally, it is perhaps worth mentioning the two unpublished studies in chapter 14 of the unpublished PhD thesis of McManus (1979). In Study 1, 20 subjects judged 16 portraits on a semantic differential task, and in Study 2, 4 subjects rated 106 portraits, pictures in each study being shown both in the original or a mirror-imaged orientation in a between-subjects design. Three factors were identified, labelled Evaluation, Dynamism and Spirituality, and while there was no difference in judgements according to the cheek presented to the subject, there was a significant tendency for paintings originally showing the right cheek to be evaluated more positively (although there was no difference on Dynamism or Spirituality). Taking all these results together, there is some, albeit not always consistent, support for the social stereotype that males are more agentic than females and with Chatterjee's hypothesis (2002) according to which positively evaluated agentic targets are more likely to be represented facing right compared with less agentic targets. This interpretation found further experimental evidence in the studies described below.

Schirillo (2000) analysed the viewer perception of 40 Rembrandt portraits (and of their mirror images for twenty of these paintings). Participants rated these paintings on 24 personality and emotional trait pairs, and judged leftward female portraits as less socially appealing than rightward ones, and rightward male portraits as more socially appealing than either leftward male or leftward and rightward female portrait. The results were independent of whether the original or mirror-image version of the image was shown suggesting that the actual direction observed by participants is central to conveying agency and not the original one. In a subsequent study by Schirillo, participants were asked to indicate the extent to which they would approach the sitter in 373 portraits by Rembrandt. Female sitters were judged as likely to be approached more when leftward oriented, whereas male sitters were judged as likely to be approached when rightward oriented, although the effect was stronger in the female sample (Schirillo, 2007). Finally, ten Cate (2002, Study 2) asked 86 participants to rate 36 images of portraits with respect to how "scientific" the sitter appeared. Right-cheeked portraits were perceived as more scientific than left-cheeked ones, an effect that was due to the original orientation and not to viewing orientation.

Nicholls, Clode, Wood, and Wood (1999) shifted the point of analysis from viewer to sitter of portraits. They asked half of their participants to pose for a family portrait revealing their "warm hearted and affectionate" emotions and the other half to pose for the Royal Society, the premier scientific society in the UK, and to appear impassive and cool-headed. Participants presented their left cheek in the family portrait and turned their right cheek in the impassive, scientist portrait. This happened to the same degree for both female and male participants. Therefore, participants presented their left cheek when asked to pose for a family portrait revealing their "warm hearted and affectionate" emotions and turned their right cheek when asked to pose for the Royal Society and to appear impassive and cool-headed (Nicholls et al., 1999). In other words, subjects showed the right half face to communicate agency.

Another open question regards the application of the Spatial Agency Bias to groups other than gender, such as social status or age. For example, although Grüsser et al. (1988) did not carry out any statistical analyses about this issue, they noted that portraits of female sitters depicted with the right half of their face exposed were generally official paintings of sovereignty or someone of similarly high social rank. The social status had also been mentioned in a completely different study by Costa, Menzani, and Ricci Bitti (2001) who found an effect of social status on the posture of figures represented in painting. Although these authors analysed the posture in term of "head canting" it is interesting to note that they found a systematic variation of "head canting" along three social categories: artists, professionals, and nobility, with nobility showing the least, artists the strongest head canting, and professionals occupying an intermediate position. The role of social status in determining spatial position does therefore remain an open question. However there is evidence of differential representation of age groups, Suitner and Maass (2007, Study 2) reporting a curvilinear relation between sitter's age and spatial representation, such that younger and older sitters are mainly represented facing left, but adult sitters facing right. This effect is consistent with the commonsense idea that agency, influence and power typically reach a peak in adulthood, but are considerably lower in childhood and in old age. The spatial bias in age groups has also been confirmed in a laboratory study by Maass et al. (2009) who found that that young targets are positioned to the left of older targets, mirroring the spatial bias found in gender representations.

Although the majority of these studies found greater appeal and potency associated with a rightward position, the studies are somewhat inconsistent. Given the results of Maass et al. (2009) on stereotype endorsement, a possibility is that participants were not always holding a traditional view of gender roles and that stereotypic beliefs are a key factor in the appearance of the bias. In fact, in all those studies in which the agency attribution was directly addressed, the spatial bias was clearly defined by the association of rightward direction (and/or left position) and high agency.

In the following section, the activation of group processes such as ingroup favouritism is proposed as a possible factor affecting the choice of the spatial representation of a given target.

3.1. A social psychological perspective: Group processes

There are diverse findings in research on large corpuses of paintings that point to the possible use of spatial features to favour either the self or the ingroup. This hypothesis finds theoretical grounding in McManus's theory regarding the representation of targets that are (or are not) assimilated to the self (McManus, 1979, 2005). According to this perspective the rightward profile is an expression of similarity to the self, therefore accounting for the prevalence of rightward orientation in self-portraits and in paintings of others that are close to the self. Because agency is a characteristic that is generally desirable for the self (Abele, 2007), we can hypothesize that a like-self representation is somewhat an agentic representation. In line with this assumption, Humphrey and McManus's (1973) recorded a high frequency of right facing profiles in Rembrandt's self-portraits, a finding consistent with Landauer's observation that 183 out of 302 of self-portraits showed the right cheek (Landauer, personal communication to Chris McManus – see Humphrey and McManus, 1973). A rightward bias in self-portraits was also observed by Latto (1996) on 47 self-portraits of 44 European authors from 1630 to 1904 and by Suitner and Maass (2007) on 362 self-portraits covering more than five centuries. These results suggest that artists may deliberately choose the rightward profile for self-presentations in order to communicate their own agency. This self-presentation bias however has not yet been confirmed with experimental methods.

A similar bias may be hypothesized at the group level. The already described study by Humphrey and McManus' (1973) can be interpreted as a first indirect evidence for this idea. The progressively decrease off frequency of right cheek exposure in portraits across the sitter's categories of male kin, male non-kin, female kin, female non-kin, can be interpreted as an ingroup bias, in terms of stronger ascription of agency to one's own group (gender and kin). However, such an effect was not replicated in other artists. For instance, Gordon (1974) studied the relationship between artist and sitter in 295 Goya portraits but found a very different pattern of results, with Goya seeming not to be affected by kinship in positioning the sitters in his paintings. It is possible that some of the effects found are due to idiosyncratic differences between artists, and their own personal perceptions of the world. Thus McManus (1979) reported how although both van Gogh and Dante Gabriel Rosetti painted their self-portraits showing the right cheek, they differed in other ways, van Gogh showing that in male portraits, while middle-classes were portrayed showing the left cheek, peasants were shown primarily with the right cheek; in contrast, for Rosetti, the main influence was once more of sex, but in a reversal of the standard findings, males showed a stronger left cheek excess than did females, implying that perhaps females were more agentic to Rosetti.

In line with the idea of an ingroup bias, Suitner and Maass (2007, Study 2) found that the leftward bias in representations of female sitters was present only among male artists, whereas it was absent among female artists, who represented female sitters mainly facing right. Thus, both male and female artists prefer to present their own gender group with the more agentic orientation, namely rightward-facing. Together, archival research, although not entirely consistent (especially with respect to kinship), does provide preliminary evidence for an ingroup bias according to which artists prefer to portray members of their own group in the more agentic position. At the experimental level, only one unpublished study has until now addressed the issue, showing that participants identify rightward oriented groups (i.e., groups whose members' profile are mainly rightward facing) with their own political affiliation when ingroup membership is made salient (Suitner, 2009). Hence, the role of favouritism in spatial representations, initially identified in the realm of artwork, remains at the moment an open issue.

A final issue that requires explanation is the origins of the bias. Until now we have proposed the rightward direction as the direction that conveys agency. Why should it be the rightward direction rather than the leftward direction? In the following section the direction of writing is proposed as a possible origin.

3.2. A possible explanation: The cultural hypothesis

Although more than one explanation has been put forward to account for the spatial bias in portraits (for recent reviews see Chatterjee, 2002, and Powell & Schirillo, 2009), the cultural hypothesis is particularly relevant from the perspective of psycholinguistics. According to this hypothesis, the rightward direction is particularly striking because it matches the writing direction. In fact, all the results discussed until now involve artistic production in Western cultures, where languages are written in a left-to-right direction (e.g., as with English, Italian, German, and so forth). This vector is therefore prominent because writing and reading are very common actions in people's everyday lives (at least nowadays and among educated people in the past). In line with the theory of grounded cognition, a frequently experienced action shapes our cognition and grounds it in the bodily states involved in the action (Barsalou, 2008; Boroditsky, 2000; Gallese & Lakoff, 2005; Lakoff, 1992; Rohrer, 2006; Semin & Smith, 2008). An example of the embodied effect of reading in cognition is that people's judgments of difficulty are influenced by the reading ease of a text-instruction, such that instructions written with a "*difficult*" font (i.e., Brush) lead participants to evaluate the described task as more difficult to do (Song & Schwarz, 2008). The fluency in reading is therefore transposed into a dimension that is completely unrelated to it, namely the difficulty of a task. A similar line of reasoning can be found in discourse about art hermeneutics, where the interpretation of artwork is thought to be embedded in the chain of signifiers pre-existing the given piece of art. The artwork is contextualized in the social system of communication, and the observer recalls the symbolic order of visual patterns to organize the visual experience (Bal & Bryson, 1991). Therefore the scanning order is meaningful both to the observer and to the artist who consistently use this information in their communication.

From such a perspective, the fluency of a trajectory may be used to represent characteristics of the subject of a portrait, such as their agency. The rightward trajectory of writing or reading can therefore itself determine the direction of agency. This point of view is consistent with the Spatial Agency Bias, in which a rightward direction conveys agency. For such a theory, though, the representation of agency should be reversed, and hence leftward, in cultures whose languages are written from right to left, as the hermeneutic code is embedded in the cultural background of the perceiver. "Interpretants are new meanings resulting from the signs on the basis of one's *habit*. And habits, precisely, are formed in social life. [...] Thus, not only is experience a legitimate basis of interpretation, it is the only possible one." (Bal & Bryson, 1991, p. 202). A dynamic view of art signs is congruent with the cultural hypothesis and the claim that visual tools such as direction are used in context-specific ways. Although the cultural hypothesis has been widely studied in the field of cognition (Chokron & De Agostini, 2000; Maass et al., 2007; Maass & Russo, 2003; Maass et al., 2009; Israel Nachson, Argaman, & Luria, 1999), it has mostly been neglected in the field of the psychology of art, although Heath, Mahmasanni, Rouhana, and Nassif (2005) did find, with abstract stimuli that right-to-left readers showed reversed patterns of preference to left-to-right readers. At a theoretical level it is acknowledged that the convention for a left to right scanning of artwork is valid in Western cultures where languages are written from left-to-right and that it reverses in those countries in which writing implies a right-to-left motion, with a congruent change in the spatial arrangement of pictorial work (Gaffron, 1956). However, to our knowledge, the only study is that of Iranian and Western photography carried out by Carmen Pérez González (2007), who discusses the role of writing direction in the spatial layout of artwork, arguing that the convention to explore artwork with a left-to-right trajectory (Gaffron, 1950) reflects the predominant writing direction within the Western world. According to Pérez González, when language is written from right to left, as with Farsi, there should also be a mirror reversal of the spatial layout of artwork, and she supports that suggestion with examples of family photographs where, for instance, family portraits are organized by age. While in Western examples, the youngest child is placed to the left and the oldest to the right, suggesting a growing pattern from left to right, in the Iranian example, the pattern is reversed, the youngest child being on the right and the oldest on the left, in a right-to-left trajectory (see Figure 1). Consistent with the cultural hypothesis is also the observation that Eastern painters sign their artwork in the left, Western artists in the right corner of the painting (Haack, 1938, as cited in Uhrbock, 1973).

This chapter has proposed that artwork may serve as a starting point for laboratory studies of psychology. However, in the case of the cultural hypothesis, we observe a lack of systematic investigations in the field of art history, in contrast to a large corpus of psychological research comparing left-to-right readers (e.g. English, Italian or French participant) with right-to-left readers (e.g. Hebrew, Arabic, or Urdu participant), which has provided strong evidence for the role of reading habits in spatial biases. Patterns of spatial bias congruent with the direction of written language are evident in a wide range of tasks, from symbolic representations (Zebian, 2005) to attentional shifts (Spalek & Hammad, 2005).

Most pertinent to the topic of the present chapter is the extensive work by Vaid and her collaborators (see also Vaid, this volume) providing cross-cultural evidence for the role of writing habits in spatial biases, comparing Hindi, Urdu and Arabic readers, groups which are in many ways comparable in terms of culture. In particular Urdu and Hindi participants are very similar in terms of spoken language, which are both North Indian languages, and have similar phonology, semantics and syntactics, but differ primarily in writing direction, Urdu being written from right to left in a script related to Arabic, whereas Hindi is written from left to right (and for the historical background to this, see Vaid, 1995). In one these studies, Hindi, Urdu and Arabic speakers were compared in a chimeric facial affect judgement task (Vaid, 1989). Participants were shown composite faces consisting of either two left hemifaces (the original left plus its mirror) or two right hemifaces. The results are consistent with the cultural hypothesis, namely when asked to choose the happier face, Hindi participants preferred the chimeric face in which the smile was in the left hemiface, whereas Urdu and Arabic speakers preferred the chimeric face with the smile in the right hemiface. This study was later replicated with similar results adding an illiterate control group that was characterized by an absence of a spatial bias (Sakhuja, Gupta, Singh, & Vaid, 1996), supporting the thesis that the visuo-motor action involved in reading/writing is relevant to the spatial bias. Vaid also found opposite drawing order patterns in Hindi and Urdu participants, who commenced the drawing task at the top left vs. the top right, and used a left to right vs. a right to left drawing sequence, with Arabic participants performing similarly to Urdu participants, consistently with the common writing direction (Singh & Vaid, 1987, reported in Vaid, 1995). Similarly, participants drew objects (e.g. an arrow, a pen, a fish) with a direction that was consistent with their writing habits (rightward for Hindu and leftward for Urdu participants (Vaid, Singh, Sakhuja, & Gupta, 2002), an effect that is similar to the one reported by Nachson, 1985), whereas Arabic and Hebrew readers drew stimuli from right to left and English readers from left to right.

Together, these findings support the hypothesis that the writing system plays an essential role in the spatial bias. However, such an explanation is one of several possible explanations, and does not necessarily contradict with explanations based on handedness or hemispheric specialization. Rather, culture is proposed as an additional factor contributing to the analyses of spatial bias. To summarise, although fairly well investigated in cognitive psychology, the cultural hypothesis needs further investigations within art history as only tentative evidence has been reported until now.

4. Conclusion and open issues

The Spatial Agency Bias, although only developed relatively recently, finds support in both analyses of artworks and laboratory studies, and also provides an explanation for some of the various effects found in different types of art work. A social psychological perspective proposes that space is used as a communicative tool, both in ordinary discourse, and also by artists. In particular, horizontal differences are used to represent abstract concepts related to action and agency. Such differences are specifically defined by left and right positions, and rightward and leftward directions, as seen from the observer's perspective and are related to the embodied actions of writing. A rightward direction is used to represent agency in those cultures where the writing is from left to right, and, vice-versa, the leftward direction representing agency in cultures where writing is from right to left. Although the convergence between writing direction and spatial biases has been shown in laboratory studies, this requires further demonstration with archival research, which would allow stronger theorising about the importance of culturally situated spatial communication. Of course the type of spatial biases described here not only apply to fine art, but also to a range of popular social communications, and further investigation is needed of web sites, advertisements and other visual materials. A second issue concerns the consequences of such biases for communication. Would a social communication (such as a painting or an advertisement) be as effective if presented with a spatial layout that is not consistent with writing direction? A third key matter concerns the social consequences of spatial choices. It seems clear that social membership plays a role in the spatial biases. If we consider art as a tool for status quo maintenance or change, do the aesthetic asymmetries observed in artworks play a role in it?

Figure 1. Left picture: Reza Akasbashi, The Daughters of Nasset-al-Doulet, 1866. Credit: Golestan Palace Library, Tehran. Album Nr. 133, photo Nr. 91. Right picture: Ignac Scháchtl, Untitled, before 1901, silver-bromide glass negative, 18 × 24 cm. Credit: Photo-Museum of Tábor, Czech Republic.

Throughout this chapter, works of art have been proposed as providing evidence for analysing psychological processes, in this case focussing specifically on the nature of Spatial Agency and its social communicative function. The potential for analysing large corpora of painted images, research that is archival in approach, to test psychological theories, is well shown here, and is effective, both in practical terms, because art historians in particular have already assembled large collections of images, and because artists act as elite observers whose sensitivities provides clues to underlying psychological processes. Although there is often supposed to be a gap between art and science, here instead there is a convergence of evidence between the two different approaches. Having said that, the great art historian, Bernard Berenson, was sceptical about the sort of statistical approach we have used, saying at one point, "The most meagre adept may make elaborate statistics of the number of times in the art of the middle ages our Lord blesses with three fingers, how many times with two and a half, and how many times with two only; or how frequently St. Catherine has her wheel, or St. Andrew his cross, to right or again to left" (Berenson, 1950). We however, would prefer to follow the approach adopted by the great landscape artist, John Constable, who stated that, *"Painting is a science and should be pursued as an inquiry into the laws of nature. Why, then, may not a landscape* [or indeed any painting] *be considered as a branch of natural philosophy, of which pictures are but experiments?"* *(Beckett, 1970).*

References

Abele, Andrea E. (2003). The dynamics of masculine-agentic and feminine-communal traits: Findings from a prospective study. *Journal of Personality and Social Psychology, 85,* 768–776.

Abele, Andrea E. & Bogdan Wojciszke (2007). Agency and communion from the perspective of self versus others. *Journal of Personality and Social Psychology, 93,* 751–763.

Arnheim, Rudolf (1974). *Art and visual perception: A psychology of the creative eye, The new version.* Berkely, CA: University of California Press.

Arnheim, Rudolf (1986). *New essays on the psychology of art.* Berkeley: University of California Press.

Bakan, David (1966). *The duality of human existence. An essay on psychology and religion.* Chicago: Rand McNally.

Bal, Mieke & Norman Bryson (1991). Semiotics and art history. *The Art Bulletin, 73,* 174–208.

Barsalou, Laurence W. (2008). Grounded cognition. *Annual Review of Psychology, 59,* 617–645.

Beckett, Ronald B. (Ed.). (1970). *The history of landscape painting, fourth lecture, Royal Institution (1836-06-16), from John Constable's Discourses.*

Bem, Sandra L. (1974). The measurement of psychological androgyny. *Journal of Consulting and Clinical Psychology, 42,* 155–162.

Benjafield, John & Sidney J. Segalowitz (1993). Left and right in Leonardo's drawings of faces. *Empirical Studies of the Arts, 11,* 25–32.

Berenson, Bernard (1950). *Aesthetics and history.* London: Constable.

Berenson, Bernard (1957). *Italian pictures of the Renaissance: Venetian school.* London: Phaidon.

Berenson, Bernard (1963). *Italian pictures of the Renaissance: Florentine school (two volumes)* London: Phaidon.

Berenson, Bernard (1967). *The Italian painters of the Renaissance.* London: Phaidon.

Berenson, Bernard (1968). *Italian pictures of the Renaissance: Central and North Italian schools.* London: Phaidon.

Best, Debora L. & John E. Williams (1993). A cross-cultural view-point. In Robert J. Sternberg, Anne Beall (Eds.), *The psychology of gender* (pp. 215–248). New York: Guilford Press.

Boroditsky, Lera (2000). Metaphoric structuring: understanding time through spatial metaphors. *Cognition, 75,* 1–28.

Carroll, Michael P. (1986). *The cult of the Virgin Mary.* Princeton: University Press.

Chatterjee, Anjan (2002). Portrait profiles and the notion of agency. *Empirical Studies of the Arts, 20,* 33–41.

Chatterjee, Anjan, Lynn M. Maher & Kenneth M. Heilman (1995). Spatial characteristics of thematic role representation. *Neuropsychologia, 33,* 643–648.

Chatterjee, Anjan, M. Helen. Southwood & David Basilico (1999). Verbs, events and spatial representations. *Neuropsychologia, 37,* 395–402.

Chokron, Sylvie & Maria De Agostini (2000). Reading habits influence aesthetic preference. *Cognitive Brain Research, 10*, 45–49.

Coins of the pound, Wikipedia: The free encyclopedia. (2009, October, 12). FL: Wikimedia Foundation, Inc. Retrieved November 14, 2009, from en.wikipedia.org/wiki/British_coinage

Coles, Peter R. (1974). Profile orientation and social distance in portrait painting. *Perception, 3*, 303–308.

Conesa, Jorge, Cynthia Brunold-Conesa & Maria Miron (1995). Incidence of the half-left profile pose in single-subject portraits. *Perceptual and Motor Skills, 81*, 920–922.

Conway, Michael & Lenny R. Vartanian (2000). A status account of gender stereotypes: Beyond communality and agency. *Sex Roles, 43*, 181–199.

Costa, Marco, Marzia Menzani & Pio E. Ricci Bitti (2001). Head canting in paintings: An historical study. *Journal of Nonverbal Behavior, 25*, 63–72.

Diekman, Amanda B. (2005). Dynamic stereotypes about women and men in latin america and the united states. *Journal of Cross-Cultural Psychology, 36*, 209–226

Eagly, Alice H. & Mary E. Kite (1987). Are stereotypes of nationalities applied to both women and men? *Journal of Personality and Social Psychology, 53*, 451–462.

Elkind, David & Jutta Weiss (1967). Studies in perceptual development, III: Perceptual exploration. *Child Development, 38*, 553–561.

Fiske, Susan T., Amy J.C. Cuddy & Peter Glick (2007). Universal dimensions of social cognition: Warmth and competence. *Trends in Cognitive Sciences, 11*, 77–83.

Fiske, Susan T., Amy J.C. Cuddy, Peter Glick & Jun Xu (2002). A model of (often mixed) stereotype content: Competence and warmth respectively follow from perceived status and competition. *Journal of Personality and Social Psychology, 82*, 878–902.

Gaffron, Mercedes (1950). Right and Left in Pictures. *Art Quarterly, 13*, 312–331.

Gaffron, Mercedes (1956). Some new dimensions in the Phenomenal Analysis of Visual Experience. *Journal of Personality and Social Psychology, 24*, 285–307.

Gallese, Vittorio & George Lakoff (2005). The Brain's concepts: the role of the Sensory-motor system in conceptual knowledge. *Cognitive Neuropsychology, 22*, 455–479.

Gordon, Ian (1974). Left and right in Goya's portraits. *Nature, 294*, 197–198.

Grüsser, Otto J., Thomas Selke & Barbara Zynca (1988). Cerebral lateralization and some implications for art, aesthetic perception and artistic creativity. In Ingo Rentschler, Barbara Herzberg & David Epstein (Eds.), *Beauty and the brain: Biological aspects of aesthetics* (pp. 257–293). Boston: Birkhauser.

Harris, Lauren J., Rodrigo A. Cardenas, Michael P. Spradlin & Jason B. Almerigi (2009). Adults' preferences for side-of-hold as portrayed in paintings of the Madonna and Child. *Laterality*, 14, 590–617.

Harris, Lauren J. (2010). Side biases for holding and carrying infants: Reports from the past and possible lessons for today. *Laterality*, 15, 56–135.

Heath, Robin. L., Oula Mahmasanni, Aida Rouhana & Nader Nassif (2005). Comparison of aesthetic preferences among Roman and Arabic script readers. *Laterality: Asymmetries of Body, Brain and Cognition, 10*, 399 – 411.

Heilman, Madeline E. (2001). Description and prescription: How gender stereotypes prevent women's ascent up the organizational ladder. *Journal of Social Issues, 57*, 657– 674.

Heilman, Madeline E., Caryn. J. Block & Richard F. Martel (1995). Sex stereotypes: Do they influence perceptions of managers? *Journal of Social Behaviour and Personality, 10*, 237–252.

Heron, Woodburn (1957). Perception as a function of retinal locus and attention. *American Journal of Psychology, 70*, 38–48.

Humphrey, Nicholas K. & I. Christopher McManus (1973). Status and the left cheek. *New Scientist, 59*, 437–439.

Judd, Charles M., Laurie J. James-Hawkins, Vincent Yzerbyt & Yoshihisa Kashima (2005). Fundamental dimensions of social judgment: Understanding the relations between judgments of competence and warmth. *Journal of Personality and Social Psychology 89*, 899–913.

Lakoff, George (1992). The contemporary theory of metaphor. In A. Ortony (Ed.), *Metaphor and Thought (2nd edition)*. Cambridge: University Press.

Latto, Richard (1996). Turning the other cheek: Profile direction in self-portraiture. *Empirical Studies of the Arts, 14*, 89–98.

Maass, Anne & Aurore Russo (2003). Directional bias in the mental representation of spatial events: Nature or culture? *Psychological Science, 14*, 296–301.

Maass, Anne, Damiano Pagani & Emanuela Berta (2007). How beautiful is the goal and how violent is the fistfight? Spatial bias in the interpretation of human behavior. *Social Cognition, 26*, 833–852.

Maass, Anne, Caterina Suitner, Xenia Favaretto & Marina Cignacchi (2009). Groups in space: Stereotypes and the spatial agency bias. *Journal of Experimental Social Psychology, 45*, 496–504.

Maher, Lynn M., Anjan Chatterjee & Leslie J. Rothi (1995). Agrammatic sentence production: The use of a temporal-spatial strategy. *Brain and Language, 48*, 105–124.

McLaughlin, John P. & Kimberly Murphy (1994). Preference for profile orientation in portraits. *Empirical Studies of the Arts, 12*, 1–7.

McManus, I. Christopher (1979). *Determinants of human laterality*. Unpublished PhD Thesis, University of Cambridge. Retrieved November, 14, 2009 from http://www.ucl.ac.uk/medical-education/publications/phd.

McManus, I. Christopher (2002). *Right hand, left hand: The origins of asymmety in brains, bodies, atoms and cultures*. London: Weidenfeld and Nicolson.

McManus, I. Christopher (2005). Symmetry and asymmetry in aesthetics and the arts. *European Review, 13*, 157–180.

McManus, I. Christopher & Nicholas Humphrey (1973). Turning the left cheek. *Nature, 243*, 271–272.

Nachson, Israel (1985). Directional preferences in perception of visual stimuli. *International Journal of Neuroscience, 25*, 161–174.

Nachson, Israel, Einat Argaman & Assaf Luria (1999). Effects of directional habits and handedness on aesthetic preference for left and right profiles. *Journal of Cross Cultural Psychology, 30*, 106–114.

Nicholls, Michael E.R., Danielle Clode, Stephen J. Wood & Amanda G. Wood (1999). Laterality of expression in portraiture: Putting your best cheek forward. *Proceedings of the Royal Society B, 266, 1517–1522*.

Oppe, Adolph P. (1944). Right and left in Raphael's cartoons. *Journal of the Warburg and Courtauld Institutes, 7*, 82–94.

Pérez González, Carmen (2007). Defining a model of representation for 19th century Iranian Portrait Photography. *Photoresearcher, 10*, 17–22.

Poseq, Avigdor W.G. (1999). Aspects of laterality in Michelangelo. *Artibus et Historiae, 20*, 89–112.

Poseq, Avigdor W.G. (2001). Lateral inversions and introversion in Ingres. *Laterality, 6*, 1–20.

Powell, W. Ryan & James A. Schirillo (2009). Asymmetrical facial expressions in portraits and hemispheric laterality: A literature review. *Laterality, 13*, 1–28.

Rohrer, Tim (2006). The body in space: Dimensions of embodiment. In Tom Ziemke, Jordan Zlatev & Roslyn M. Frank (Eds.), *Body, Language and Mind* (Vol. 1, pp. 339–377). Berlin: Mouton de Gruyter.

Sakhuja, Tripti, Gyan G. Gupta, Maharai Singh & Jyotsna Vaid (1996). Reading habits affect asymmetries in facial affect judgements: A replication. *Brain and Cognition, 32*, 162–164.

Schirillo, James A. (2000). Hemispheric asymmetries and gender influence Rembrandt's portrait orientations. *Neuropsychologia, 38*, 1593–1606.

Schirillo, James A. (2007). Gender's effect on the hemispheric laterality of Rembrandt's portraits *Spatial Vision, 21*, 19–26.

Semin, Gun S. & Eliot R. Smith (Eds.). (2008). *Embodied Grounding*. Cambridge: University Press.

Song, Hyunjin & Norbert Schwarz (2008). If it's hard to read, it's hard to do. *Psychological Science, 19*, 986–988.

Soresen, Roy (2000). The aesthetics of mirror reversal. *Philosophical Studies: An International Journal for Philosophy in the Analytic Tradition, 100*, 175–191.

Spalek, Thomas M. & Sherief Hammad (2005). The left-to-right bias in inhibition of return is due to the direction of reading. *Psychological Science, 16*, 15–18.

Strong, Roy (1969). *The English icon: Elizabethan and Jacobean portraiture*. Routledge, Kegan and Paul: London.

Suitner, Caterina (2009). *Where to place social targets? Stereotyping and Spatial Agency Bias*. Doctoral Thesis, University of Padova.

Suitner, Caterina & Anne Maass (2007). Positioning bias in portraits and self-portraits: Do female artists make different choices? *Empirical Studies of the Arts, 25*, 71–95.

Suitner, Caterina & Anne Maass (this volume). *Writing direction, agency and gender stereotyping: An embodied connection*.

ten Cate, Carel (2002). Posing as professor: Laterality in posing orientation for portraits of scientists. *Journal of Nonverbal Behavior, 26*, 175–192.

Uhrbrock, Richard S. (1973). Laterality in art. *The Journal of Aestetics and Art Criticism, 32*, 27–35.
Vaid, Jyotsna (1989). Asymmetries in the perception of facial affect: Is there a influence of reading habits? *Neuropsychologia, 27*, 1277–1287.
Vaid, Jyotsna (1995). Script directionality affects nonlinguitsic performance: Evidence from Hindi and Urdu. In I. Taylor & D. Olson (Eds.), *Scripts and literacy* (pp. 295–310). Dordrecht: Kluwer Academic.
Vaid, Jyotsna (this volume). Asymmetries in representational drawing: Alternatives to a laterality account.
Vaid, Jyotsna, Maharaj Singh, Tripti Sakhuja & Gyan C. Gupta (2002). Stroke direction asymmetry in figure drawing: Influence of handedness and reading/writing habits. *Brain and Cognition, 48*, 597–602.
Zaidel, Dahlia W. & Peter Fitzgerald (1994). Sex of the face in Western art: Left and right in portraits. *Empirical study of the Arts, 12*, 9–18.
Zebian, Samar (2005). Linkages between Number Concepts, Spatial Thinking, and Directionality of Writing: The SNARC Effect and the REVERSE SNARC Effect in English and Arabic Monoliterates, Biliterates, and Illiterate Arabic Speakers. *Journal of Cognition and Culture, 5*, 166–190.

Writing direction, agency and gender stereotyping: An embodied connection

Caterina Suitner and Anne Maass

Abstract

Writing direction has surprising effects on social cognition. Such effects are addressed with a specific focus on languages written from left-to-right and right-to-left. The horizontal trajectory in which a language is written is related to cognitive spatial biases and to the representation of social targets. Specifically, social targets such as males and females are differently envisaged in space (Spatial Agency Bias), with representations of agentic targets (for example males) being more strongly associated with the writing trajectory (e.g., showing the rightward profiles in languages written rightwards). In line with the embodiment perspective, this effect is interpreted as the result of a simulation of the writing/reading actions while mentally representing an agentic target. The bias is shown to pervade different stages, including on-line and off-line cognition, encoding and decoding processes. It is moderated by people's beliefs, but it also affects such beliefs, suggesting a bi-directional link between attitudes and spatial arrangements.

1. Introduction

Psycholinguists have investigated different aspects of language, including phonetics and phonology, morphology, orthography, syntax, and semantics. By comparison, relatively little attention has been given to the way in which languages are written (and read). Writing systems differ greatly in the cognitive units represented by each symbol. There are at least three large categories of traditional writing systems. In logographic writing, such as Chinese, each character represents a semantic concept (word or morpheme) although the large majority of logograms also contain phonological information. In syllabic writing systems, such as Cherokee, each written symbol represents a syllable (typically a small sequence of consonants and vowels). In alphabetic writing systems, letters roughly correspond to phonemes although the degree of correspondence between writing and pronunciation varies greatly from language to language, as does the explication of vowels (which may be comparable to consonants, reduced to diacritics, or missing altogether).

Important to our argument, writing systems also differ in spatial arrangements. For instance, among logographic scripts, Chinese is written top-down (with columns arranged from right to left), whereas Mayan logograms are mostly represented in columns of two glyphs each, with each column read left to right. Similarly, some alphabetic languages, including all European languages, are written from left to right, others are written in a right to left fashion (with lines organized top-down in both cases). The latter group includes Hebrew and Arabic, as well as modified versions of the Perso-Arabic script, in particular Urdu and Farsi. Importantly, there is no intrinsic correspondence between language and writing system. The same language may be written with different writing systems, as in the case of Hindi and Urdu that are practically identical languages, except for the fact that Hindi is written from left-to-right, whereas Urdu is written from right-to-left (Vaid, this volume). Similarly, Farsi is written with a leftward Perso-Arabic script in Iran, but with a rightward Cyrillic script in Tajikistan. The same is true for the Kurdish language which, depending on country, is written from right to left or from left to right.

The question addressed in this chapter is whether the spatial arrangements of different writing systems have effects on human cognition, including social cognition, above and beyond tasks that are directly related to writing. In doing so, we will focus on the horizontal vector, comparing left-to-right (LR) vs. right-to-left (RL) writing systems. Cognitive psychologists, especially those interested in cross-cultural psychology, have long argued that scanning habits due to writing and reading affect people's thoughts in a variety of tasks unrelated to writing and reading. To cite only few examples, Gaffron (1956) suggested that the tendency of people to explore art work with a glance curve evolving from left to right is typical of Western cultures and that this behavior is acquired after reading habits; along the same line, people tend to draw pictures (Vaid, Singh, Sakhuja, & Gupta, 2002) and graphs (Tversky, Kugelmass, & Winter, 1991) along the direction of their written language. Moreover, aesthetic preferences (Nachson, Argaman, & Luria, 1999; Chokron & De Agostini, 2000) and memory for pictures (Padakannaya, Devi, Zaveria, Chengappa, & Vaid, 2002) match participants' writing direction, with LR preferences in North America and Europe and RL preferences in populations whose native language is Arabic, Hebrew, or Urdu (see also the Chapter of Chokron et al. in the present volume). People also tend to imagine human interactions (e.g., *A pushes B*) such that the vector of the action corresponds to the direction of written language (Chatterjee, Southwood, & Basilico, 1999; Maass & Russo, 2003). Similarly, research on numeric cognition shows that individuals in LR writing cultures envisage the number line spatially such that small numbers are located to the left, large numbers to the right, whereas individuals in RL writing cultures show the opposite tendency, with bicultural or illiterate individuals falling in between (Dehaene, Bossini, & Giraux, 1993; Zebian, 2005). Interestingly, even very basic attentional processes such as inhibition of return (i.e., the tendency to orient attention to novel locations rather than to return to previously attended locations, Spalek & Hammad, 2005) and apparent motion (Morikawa & McBeath, 1992) follow a culture-specific pattern with both effects being stronger when the implied trajectory matches the predominant scanning habit of a given culture.

2. Extension to the social domain: Spatial bias and gender stereotyping

Most phenomena mentioned above (exploration of art work, number line, inhibition of return, representational momentum etc.) belong to the world of inanimate objects, so one may wonder whether the spatial asymmetry also extends to the social realm. One can easily envisage ways in which spatial information pervades social-cognitive processes. For instance, spatial arrangements may become critical when trying to guess the temporal order of events (*who started the quarrel?*), when trying to understand the causes of events (*how did the situation come about?*), or when assigning responsibility for such events (*who is responsible of the crime?*).

A less obvious way in which spatial information may intrude social cognition is by affecting the way we process social categories. It has long been known that some groups are perceived as more agentic, more influential, and more dominant than others. For instance, a long research tradition on gender stereotypes reveals that men are perceived as agentic, women as communal (Abele, 2003; Conway, Pizzamiglio, & Mount, 1996; Else-Quest, Hyde, Goldsmith, & Van Hulle, 2006; Spence, Helmreich, & Stapp, 1974; Spence & Helmreich, 1978 for an overview). In other words, men are stereotypically perceived as more assertive, powerful, and active than women. If men are perceived as the "doers" and women as the "receivers" of action, then one may advance the hypothesis that this will also be reflected spatially, given that spatial layout speaks about the targets' role in the interaction.

This hypothesis was first proposed by Chatterjee (2002, see also Chatterjee, this volume) who asserts that certain spatial representations are distinctly associated with the perception of agency, with left positions being more strongly linked with agency than right positions. This hypothesis finds its origins in the observation of an aphasic patient who was unable to transfer the grammatical role of subject and object in a sentence into the thematic roles of, respectively, agent and recipient of the described action. The patient developed an interesting strategy, namely the assignment of the agentic role to the target presented on the left side and the recipient role to the target presented on the right side of the scene (Maher, Chatterjee, & Rothi, 1995). Consistent with Chatterjee's model, subsequent research has shown that the same spatial schema is present also in the general population. When participants are asked to draw pairs of interacting persons, the agent tends to be positioned to the left (Chatterjee, Maher, & Heilman, 1995; Maass & Russo, 2003). Similarly, the agent is recognized more easily when positioned to the left of the recipient with action going from left toward right (Chatterjee et al., 1999).

The idea that males and females are differently represented in space has been tested in diverse lines of research using different methodologies. First evidence for the link between gender and spatial representation comes from studies on portrait orientation showing a pervasive leftward bias (from the observer's perspective) such that the sitter's leftward profile is exposed above chance (Conesa, Brunold-Conesa, & Miron, 1995; Gordon, 1974; Grüsser, Selke, & Zynca, 1988; McManus & Humphrey, 1973). Considering that the role of sitters is, by definition, passive this is quite in line with Chatterjee's hypothesis. Importantly for our argument, this leftward bias in portraits is enhanced when the portrayed sitter is a woman, but greatly reduced for men (Gordon, 1974; Humphrey & McManus, 1973; ten Cate, 2002), presumably reflecting distinct gender stereotypes. In line with this interpretation is also the fact that only male painters show the bias (Suitner & Maass, 2007). Also, given that the status of women has undergone considerable changes over history, it may not surprise that also the gender-related spatial bias has decreased over the centuries, in all likelihood due to women's emancipation (Grüsser et al., 1988; Suitner & Maass, 2007; ten Cate, 2002).

But do these systematic differences in spatial orientation really affect the observer? There is suggestive evidence that observers are sensitive to spatial information when interpreting paintings, considering that right-oriented portraits are considered more "potent" and more "active" (Benjafield & Segalowitz, 1993), terms that are easily interpreted as sub-dimensions of agency. Together, these analyses of existing artwork (summarized in greater detail in Suitner and McManus, this volume) confirm Chatterjee's hypothesis that (male) artists choose spatial layouts so as to portray male sitters (as well as women in power) with a more agentic orientation than female sitters.

Different from these analyses of existing representations of men and women in the arts, our own research relies mainly on experimental methods to investigate spatial representations of men and women. In the following parts of this chapter, we will present recent experimental evidence from our lab testing the hypothesis that males are envisaged to the left of females in left-to-right writing languages such as Italian (the language spoken by the participants of all of our studies) and that this bias pervades different stages, including on-line and off-line cognition, encoding and decoding processes. In line with this idea, we will first focus on the moment of production of visual images, thus asking how people envisage male-female pairs to be co-located in space. We will then focus on categorization and ask whether people will identify males and females with greater ease when their spatial orientation matches common stereotypes (rightward for stereotypically agentic males and leftward for stereotypically not agentic females). Subsequently, we will report preliminary findings on the consequences of spatial bias for the maintenance and change of gender stereotypes and, finally, address the question of the underlying processes driving spatial bias.

2.1. Producing spatial images of females and males

Different from the above analyses of portrait orientation of single targets, our own research on mental imaging has focused mainly on the spatial arrangement of male-female pairs. The first question addressed was whether people would indeed represent male-female pairs so as to position the more agentic person to the left of the less agentic one (see Maass, Suitner, Favaretto, & Cignacchi, 2009). This was first tested in two content analyses using a Google images search. In the first research, the targets Adam and Eve were investigated, counterbalancing the word order of the two names as research key-words. The results fully support the hypothesized positioning of the male partner to the left of the female partner, with 62% of the images portraying Adam left of Eve. Although the order of Adam and Eve was counterbalanced, we cannot exclude a word order effect in any definite way considering that "Adam and Eve" is the standard order in which the two are generally mentioned. To overcome this limit, in the second Google image research, we therefore used family names as key words, namely "The Simpsons", "The Addams" and "The Flintstones". Note that the three couples were chosen so as to vary in terms of their relative agency. In fact, a pretest confirmed that the Addams family is perceived as largely corresponding to traditional sex roles, whereas in the case of the Simpsons, the male - Homer – does not match the idea of a highly agentic male partner, with the Flintstone falling in between these two extremes. This difference in relative agency was reflected in the spatial positing of male and female across couples. In the case of the Addams family, there was an overwhelming tendency to represent the male to the left of the female (82% of all images), whereas the distribution in the case of the Simpsons and the Flintstones was practically random.

We then tested the same hypothesis experimentally, asking participants to draw scenes of teams, composed of females or males, competing with each other in different sport competitions such as volleyball, ping-pong, or chess. Importantly, we also assessed people's endorsement of gender stereotypes. The results showed that those who held traditional gender stereotypes did, indeed, draw the male team to the left of the female team in 70% of all drawings. Those who considered males and females equally agentic showed no bias. Interestingly, there was also a minority of participants who thought that females were, on the average, more agentic than males. In the majority of their drawings (62%) it was the female team that appeared to the left. Together, these studies suggest that there is a small but reliable tendency to represent males to the left of females and that this spatial bias is systematically linked to gender stereotyping. The bias does not emerge for male-female pairs that do not conform to traditional stereotypes (as in the case of Homer and Marge of the Simpsons family) and it does not emerge in participants that reject traditional gender roles.

2.2. Processing males and females profiles

The previous set of studies demonstrates that people tend to create visual images of male-female pairs that reflect their gender stereotypes. The question then arises whether they also use spatial information when decoding information. For instance, when asked to decide as quickly as possible whether a target is male or female, will observers make use of spatial coordinates to reach the decision? Although space is logically irrelevant to the task at hand, we suspect that people will rely on spatial information especially when the stimulus is ambiguous or when the task is difficult for other reasons. The assumption underlying this prediction is that reading and writing is so pervasive in every day life and the resulting scanning habit so strong that the promoted direction is processed even in tasks where its processing is not only irrelevant to the task, but even disturbing (Borkenau & Mauer, 2006; Halpern & Kelly, 1993; Hubbard, 2005; Meier & Robinson, 2004). The automatic processing of information often experienced together provides the basis for the hypothesized relation between gender categorization and writing direction. Specifically, given that agency is related to the rightward trajectory that is constantly activated by reading/writing in Western cultures, and given the relation between agency and maleness that is a central part of well-learned gender stereotypes, we expected that also the association between spatial direction and gender would emerge in an automatic fashion.

In order to explore this hypothesis, we asked participants to guess which of two mirror photographs of a male or of a female target was the original picture (Suitner, 2009). The target was portrayed in the original photo as either facing right or left, whereas the mirror image showed the same target facing in the opposite direction. Participants observed the images and selected for each pair the image that, in their opinion, was the original one. Unsurprisingly, participants were not able to correctly identify the original photo, however, they did not responded randomly. Rather, they used a spatial strategy to make their decision by mainly indicating the rightward image as the original. Even more interestingly, they varied their strategy according to the gender of the represented target. When the target was a male, the rightward photo was believed to be the original one in 57% of all cases, however, this rightward bias was almost absent in the evaluations of female targets (52%). This result is in line with the hypothesis that male targets are distinctly associated with the rightward direction and that this association emerges even in tasks in which the processing of spatial direction is not only irrelevant, but even harmful to task performance. However, one may argue that profile direction was the only information that participants could rely on in differentiating the stimuli.

This is a sensible argumentation, that was addressed in a subsequent study (Suitner, 2009), in which the direction was, again, irrelevant to the completion of the task, but it was not the only information available to the participants. We explored these issues by asking participants to indicate whether a key word (namely MALE vs. FEMALE) correctly predicted the subsequent picture (namely the profile of a male vs. a female target). Half of the males' and of the females' profiles in the pictures were rightward (and half leftward). The results provide a clear answer regarding the automaticity of the use of spatial information that is completely irrelevant to the categorization task, in fact participants were more accurate in categorizing rightward male profiles and leftward female profiles compared to leftward male profiles and rightward female profiles. Apparently, participants found it easier to correctly identify males when shown with a rightward profile and females when shown with a leftward profile, suggesting that they inadvertently used spatial information to perform the task. We therefore conclude that the association between spatial direction and gender stereotypes emerges both at the encoding and decoding level, and it does so regardless of whether direction is relevant or irrelevant to the task.

2.3. Consequences for attitude maintenance and change

At this point, a central question remains unanswered, namely if the spatial bias may have consequences for the maintenance or change of existing stereotypes. To provide a first answer to this question, we had included two additional conditions in the previously described study. In fact, the ratio of rightward and leftward profiles presented was manipulated in three experimental conditions. In the Control Condition, the ratio was equal, as previously described. In the so-called Stereotypic Condition, 80% of male targets' profiles were rightward oriented (with the remaining 20% leftward oriented) and 80% of female targets' profile were leftward oriented (with the remaining 20% rightward oriented). In what can be defined the Counter-Stereotypic Condition, 80% of female targets' profile were rightward oriented (and 20% leftward oriented) and 80% of male targets' profile were leftward oriented (and 20% rightward oriented). Participants were also asked to complete a questionnaire measuring gender stereotype endorsement and ambivalent attitudes toward males and females before and after the categorization task.

In the stereotypic condition (in which the majority of males were presented as facing right-, the majority of females as facing leftward) the pattern of results was very similar to the previously described findings in the control condition, showing that males were recognized more easily when rightward-, women when leftward-oriented. Interestingly, in the counter-stereotypical condition, in which the majority of males faced toward left and the majority of females toward right, accuracy rates reversed, attesting to the fact that the Spatial Bias is sensitive to context effects.

Another important result regards the implication of the Spatial Bias for gender stereotype endorsement and ambivalent attitudes toward males and females. Stereotype endorsement prior to the experiment had little effect on the use participants made of spatial information when performing the categorization task. However, the performance on the categorization task affected participants' subsequent gender stereotype endorsement. The more participants showed a Spatial Agency Bias, associating males with rightward and females with leftward direction, the more they subsequently attributed stereotypic characteristics to males and females and the more ambivalent their attitudes were toward males and females. This relation remained significant even after controlling for pre-experimental attitudes, suggesting that the Spatial Agency Bias plays an important role in strengthening gender stereotypes.

Together, these results suggest that spatial information is automatically decoded in order to facilitate the categorization of social targets. In the absence of other concurrent factors, the scanning habits, presumably derived from language directionality, constitute the most accessible direction, and this information is used to categorize male vs. female targets. Moreover, our results show that the association between direction and gender has important consequences for maintaining gender stereotypes. Finally, this experiment suggests that spatial information is used in a flexible way and that it can be altered through the selective exposure to directed images. This specific issue is further addressed in the following sections, in which we will investigate the role of scanning habits, due to writing and reading, in producing the Spatial Agency Bias. We will first discuss writing direction as one possible mechanism underlying spatial bias and examine its relation to hemispheric specialization. In a brief digression into the history of language we will ask why most but not all languages are written from L to R. In the final section we will ask whether the effects of habitual scanning habits can be altered by short-lived experiences with a scanning direction opposite to one's writing/reading habits. We will argue that the standard writing direction functions as the distal cause of spatial bias, whereas the momentary exposure to directionality (congruent or incongruent with the standard writing direction) is seen as a proximal, transient cause affecting spatial bias.

2.4. Mechanisms underlying spatial bias: Scanning habits due to writing and reading

What is driving the Spatial Agency Bias? Given that both visual scanning and motor activity are involved in writing, the culture-specific asymmetries reported above may derive from visual or motor habits, or from a combination of the two. People in developed countries spend a considerable amount of their time reading and writing and, as a consequence, do habitually direct attention in correspondence to their writing direction (for a provocative hypothesis of how scanning habits may translate into asymmetrical directional selectivity at the neural level see Chatterjee, this volume). By extention, while processing stimuli that have real or implied motion, they may experience a subjective feeling of fluency when the direction of the movement corresponds to the predominant scanning habit. This interpretation is also roughly in line with recent approaches of embodied cognition according to which cognition is shaped by visuo-motor experiences, including the organism's *habitual* interaction with its environment (Barsalou, 1999; Rohrer, 2006). Note that habitual embodiment is conceptually distinct from embodiment as sensorimotor simulations. According to the latter point of view, the exposure to an object or concept activates the perceptual modality related to it. For instance, the mere exposure to the verb "kick" or "smile" is linked to a particular fMRI or facial EMG pattern usually activated while actually performing the action (see Foroni & Semin, in press; Tettamanti et al., 2005). In contrast, habitual scanning habits represent a more general case of embodiment, that is likely to exert a broad (but comparably weak) influence on attention and imaging.

Our own model attributes the Spatial Agency Bias to the joint influence of two processes, namely, on one side, the asymmetrical physical activity of writing and reading and, on the other side, the temporal order in which grammatical subjects and grammatical objects are mentioned in standard active sentences. In most languages, the sentence subject generally precedes the object.[1] In active sentences, arguably the majority of phrases in everyday discourse, this implies that the actor is mentioned before the patient, possibly reflecting the intuition that the execution of an action (cause) precedes its impact (effect), rather than vice versa. The temporal ordering of actor and patient is reflected in a corresponding spatial ordering which, depending on writing direction, implies that the actor occurs to the left (English, Italian, etc.) or to the right (Arabic, Hebrew, Farsi, Urdu) of the patient. Thus, we argue that it is the *combined* effect of word order and writing direction that will produce a general scheme for action that is either LR or RL oriented. Not surprisingly, Italians tend to envisage simple descriptions such as "*X pushes Y*" with the actor to the left and the patient to the right, whereas Arabic speakers show an opposite tendency (Maass & Russo, 2003). Thus, spatial bias may result from two independent features of language, on one side the direction in which language is written and read, on the other side the order in which actor and patient are typically mentioned, resulting in a conventional schema for action (see also Chatterjee, this volume).

But what aspects of our cognitive functioning should be affected by writing direction? We believe that writing direction has at least three implications. First, reading direction should affect what people will attend to first and what attracts their *attention* most. There is indeed evidence that LR readers are particularly attracted by information in their left, but RL readers by information in their right visual hemifield, as illustrated by studies on chimeric faces. In chimeric face tasks, participants are presented with pairs of faces, each composed of two half faces, typically a smiling and a neutral hemiface. The smile is positioned either in the left or in the right hemiface of each pair. Participants are asked to indicate which face of each pair looks happier. While English speakers usually exhibit a left visual field bias, indicating the face with the smile to the left as the happier face, Hebrew and Arabic readers do not exhibit this bias (Eviatar, 1997, Study 2, but also Vaid, 1989; see also Vaid's and Brady's chapters in the present volume). This left hemifield advantage is in line with the starting point of scanning promoted by language direction, considering that the left side of the visual field is the starting point of scanning in languages such as English. Consistently, English readers prefer stimuli in which the main information (the smile) is placed to the left.

---

1   There are only few languages communities, all of small size, in which the sentence object precedes the subject, including Fijian, Malagasy, Xavante, Hixkaryana, Dyrbal (see Maass, Suitner, Favaretto, & Cignacchi, 2009).

Besides directing initial attention, writing habits are likely to affect the subjective *fluency* with which motion is experienced. Motion that coincides with our scanning habits is likely to be perceived as easier or more "natural". In fact, subjective fluency is related to past experience and the more frequent, prolonged, and recent the experience is, the greater the likelihood that a feeling of fluency arises (for a recent review on the concept of fluency see Oppenheimer, 2008). Surely the trajectory involved in writing and reading is experienced very often and the exposure duration is as long as the time we have been living after learning it. In line with this idea of fluency, writing-coherent motion is perceived as faster and as more impactful (Maass, Pagani, & Berta, 2007). For instance, soccer goals are perceived as faster, more powerful, and more beautiful by Italian observers when they evolve in a LR fashion, but by Arabic speakers when they evolve in the opposite direction.

Third, and most important for the aims of this chapter, we believe that writing direction, in conjunction with subject-object order, will create a *schema for action* that generalizes to non-linguistic tasks, explaining why "doers" are positioned before "recipients". For the same reasons more agentic individuals or groups are envisaged as acting in the direction of one's dominant scanning habit. Whereas asymmetric attention and subjective fluency can be accounted for by writing habits alone, we believe that the development of an asymmetrical schema for action (in which the doer is on the left of the receiver in LR writing cultures) derives from the joint influence of writing and subject-object order in language. In summary, we believe that language direction plays a key role in spatial biases, promoting an asymmetrical perception of human action.

3. The origins of writing direction

But where does directionality of written language come from and why is the majority of today's languages written from R to L? According to Lars Marius Garshol, the RL direction has been used for 20, the LR direction for 44 scripts throughout history (Garshol, n.d.), showing a clear predominance of LR writing systems. What is the reason for this asymmetry?

An obvious answer to this question is based on mere motor functions. It simply is easier to pull than to push a writing utensil across pergament or paper and since the majority of people worldwide are right-handed, this may easily account for the fact that the "default" writing direction is from left to right. However, this does not explain why there are exceptions to the rule.

An alternative explanation was offered by de Kerckhove (1988a, 1988b) who takes a neuro-science point of view by considering hemispheric specialization as a key factor for the prevalence of a given direction in writing (see also Reuter-Lorenz, Kinsbourne, & Moscovitch, 1990). From this perspective, the visuo-spatial function of the right hemisphere plays an important role in defining the supremacy of the left visual field for pictorial information. This hemisphere is specialized in face recognition and attentional monitoring (Gazzaniga, 2000). Moreover, it is involved in the identification of coordinate properties for locating objects (Kosslyn et al., 1989) and in the exploration of novel stimuli (see Novelty Routinization Theory, Goldberg, 2001). In contrast, the left hemisphere is mainly implicated in linguistic functions, in problem solving, and in understanding categorical properties that define a specific object. Since the specialization of the two hemispheres creates a mirror asymmetry in the two visual fields, this implies that the left visual field is the perfect candidate to start the visual exploration and to locate a stimulus. Subsequently, a shift of attention towards the right visual field enables the perceiver to analyze the characteristics of the object in relation to previously known categories. This hypothetical cognitive/physical path may be responsible for a left-to-right bias suggesting a preference for information starting to the left and evolving toward the right side of the visual field, thus accounting for the preference for a left-to-right scanning path in written language (see de Kerckhove, 1988a).

The hypothesis that hemispheric specialization is responsible for the fact that most languages are written from left to right is intriguing and opens the scenario for a second question, namely why some languages are written from right-to left and others from left-to-right. In other words, if the LR trajectory is advantageous for reading, why have opposite writing systems survived over time? A brief digression into the history of writing may help to understand this issue. Written language history has recently been interpreted as the result of an evolutionary process that started around 3500 B.C. in Mesopotamia with the Sumerian script, although there were probably other writing systems in other areas such as China at about the same time (Aaron & Malatesha, 2006). According to Aaron & Malatesha (2006), the evolution can be traced along a general pattern that starts with pictograms (such as in simple symbolic drawings), then develops into ideograms and later into rebus writing, such as in Egyptian Hieroglyphics in which the drawing may represent the name of the object and not only the object itself. The syllabic writing is the major step toward the two modern writing systems, namely consonantal writing and alphabetic writing. This progression is accompanied by a parallel development of a consistent writing direction. Before consonantal writing systems were developed, direction was not a consistent feature of writing systems. It was only with the invention of consonantal writing systems, that there was a passage from a multi directional style to a consistent leftward direction (see Watt, 1988). The development of an alphabetic vocal system is ascribed to the Ancient Greeks who, between 800 and 500 B.C., borrowed the consonantal Phoenician alphabet and added vowels (Watt, 1988). Adding the vowels, the Greeks changed the nature of writing from a context- to a sequence-based process (de Kerckhove, 1988a). Interestingly, they also changed the writing direction, from the original leftward direction of the Phoenician writing to the rightward direction of Ancient Greek. Why? According to de Kerckhove (1988b), the differential preference for rightward vs. leftward writing systems derives from the different type of relations that exist among the individual characters in rightward and leftward texts. Languages written from right to left (e.g., Hebrew and Arabic) are characterized by consonantal alphabets that imply a contextual relationship between the letters. That is, the missing vowels, and hence, the meaning of the word have to be guessed from the context. Rightward languages (like English or Italian), on the contrary, have vocalic alphabets in which letters are sequentially related by contiguity. Taylor (1988) has argued that there is a match between hemispheric specialization and writing systems, such that the characteristics of writing systems mirror the feature of the hemisphere mainly involved in the processing of the given writing system. In line with this idea de Kerckhove (1988a) surmises that the left hemisphere, specialized in sequential and analytic processing, promotes the rightward direction for vocalic alphabets in which the sequence is the key feature. In contrast, the right hemisphere, specialized in holistic processes, promotes a leftward direction for consonantal alphabets requiring more complex pattern recognition.[2]

Together, there are reasons to believe that writing direction is not arbitrary. Alphabetical writing systems, containing vowels, tend to be written from left to right, whereas consonantal systems in which vowels must be inferred from context tend to be written from right to left. According to authors such as de Kerckhove (1988 a&b) and Taylor (1988) this may reflect the different demands that the two writing systems put on the left vs. right hemisphere, specialized, respectively, in sequential vs. global processing.

---

2   Naturally, the entire debate can be reversed if we interpret brain asymmetries as the result, rather than as cause, of cultural processes. According to Vallortigara and Rogers (2005), the asymmetries in a population can be conceptualized as the result of social interactions. In fact, whereas at the individual level there is no evolutionary advantage in a same-side lateralization, at the population level the alignment in the direction of lateralization facilitates a coordinated behaviour, and it is therefore socially promoted. In line with this point of view, Eviatar (2000) proposes writing direction as a learned behaviour in which the alignment of the reading direction is highly adaptive at the population level.

4. Distal and proximal causes of spatial bias

We have argued above that language is the key factor in spatial bias, promoting an advantage for the trajectory that corresponds to the direction in which language is written/read even on tasks that are unrelated to writing or reading. In line with this idea, we found that Arabic speaking students attending an Italian university placed male teams to the right (rather than to the left) of female teams when drawing inter-gender sports competitions (Maass et al., 2009, Exp. 3). Although these students were highly familiar with right-to-left writing languages and, indeed, used Italian language on a daily basis when studying text books, reading newspapers, or writing homework, they still showed a spatial bias that was in line with the first language they had learned to write and to read, namely Arabic. Apparently, early-acquired scanning habits have lasting effects on spatial schemata. However, in this and many other studies, all the instructions were given in the participants' native language (either Italian or Arabic), so that language direction not only represented a well-learned habit, but was also primed locally, in the context of the experiment.

It is therefore unclear whether the writing direction of one's primary language exerts a chronic and invariable influence or whether momentary, situational primes play a role in spatial bias. Depending on the direction, such momentary experiences may either bolster the culturally given spatial bias or they may promote a different trajectory, for example when people are exposed to visual stimuli that move in a direction opposite to their usual scanning habits or when they perform writing exercises that run counter to their normal writing direction. Specifically we investigated whether a counter-directional writing exercise was sufficient to reduce the strength of the spatial bias associated with the standard writing direction (Suitner, 2009). We therefore asked adult Italian participants to perform a writing simulation similar to the pre-writing exercises that children perform in k-grade, by repeatedly writing letters such as *eeeee* or *gggg* between two lines. Half of our participants performed the exercise in a rightward direction, the other in a leftward direction. After the exercise, participants evaluated pairs of mirror images of target persons moving rightward or leftward indicating, for each pair, which target appeared more masculine. The results illustrate the malleability of the writing direction. After performing a rightward exercise that corresponded to normal writing, participants showed a reliable spatial bias, selecting the rightward running target as more masculine. Again, this bias was related to agency beliefs, such that the more participants endorsed the gender stereotype according to which males are more agentic than females, the more they indicated the rightward moving target as more masculine. Most importantly, the spatial bias disappeared after performing a leftward writing exercise that runs counter to the participants' normal writing direction. Thus, the effect of scanning habits can be reduced or nullified when temporary experiences with the opposite trajectory come into play, attesting to the malleability of the Spatial Agency Bias.

5. Conclusion

The brief review of our research on the Spatial Agency Bias suggests a non-obvious link between writing direction and gender stereotyping. In people's minds, women and men are not randomly distributed in space, but occupy positions that, we believe, reflect their roles in society: men to the left and women to the right, men oriented towards the right and women towards the left. This is not the first time that gender has been linked to space. For instance, we know that men are more likely to strategically occupy the head place at a table, suggesting that men deliberately select spatial positions that convey power and that are conducive to leadership (Jackson, Engstrom, & Emmers-Sommer, 2007). They also tend to keep greater distance from others and are more annoyed by invasions of their personal space (e.g., Barnard & Bell, 1982), suggesting that they claim more space. These findings, however, refer to *actual* spatial behaviors of women and men, not to images in our minds.

That spatial images and spatial behaviors are, in part, independent of each other is easily illustrated by the fact that mixed-sex couples, when walking side by side, generally arrange themselves so that females walk on the males' preferred, dominant side more often than would be expected by chance (Borden & Homleid, 1978). Since the majority of people are right-handed, this means that men tend to walk to the left of the female, a tendency generally interpreted as a sign of spatial dominance.[3] In real life, we are therefore likely to encounter more couples, in which – from our perspective as observers – the male is on the right (rather than left) side of the woman. The same is true when one analyzes images from the Internet of wedding photos in which couples tend to arrange so that, from the observer's perspective, the male appears to the right of the female more than would be expected by chance (approximately 60%). Despite this fact we

---

3 Most people prefer to have others walk on the side of their dominant hand. Since the majority of humans is right-handed, this potentially creates a conflict which is usually resolved in favour of the more dominant person. In male-female pairs, it is generally the male claiming the favourite position to the left of the female, whereas in adult-child interactions, it is usually the adult walking to the left of the child.

imagine the male to the left of the woman as our research shows. Apparently then, reality constraints are weak in this case and our imagination is guided by factors other than our actual experiences with men and women's spatial behavior.

In many spatial biases, one such factor involves metaphoric thinking. In fact, it has long been argued that our thinking is, in large part, channeled by spatial metaphors (Lakoff & Johnson, 1980, see also Chapter by Tversky, this volume). For instance, as Schubert's research on the vertical axis shows, we envisage dominant groups above dominated groups, a bias that is reflected in numerous metaphors such as "looking up to somebody", "your highness", "top manager", etc. (Schubert, 2005; see also Schubert, Waldzus, & Seibt, this volume). Ultimately, this bias derives from our experiences with the physical world, in particular the fact that larger entities (e.g. parents) tend to exert power over smaller ones (e.g., children) and that, thanks to gravity, physical force is generally exerted top-down rather than bottom-up. Thus, in the case of verticality, our spatial experience with gravity is transposed to the social level through linguistic metaphors that are shared within a given language community.

In the case of the horizontal bias described in this chapter, there are no linguistic metaphors that would link the left-to-right vector to agency, suggesting that the underlying process driving vertical and horizontal bias are quite different. Our interpretation is that horizontal bias is linked to a habitual activity, writing and reading, that, combined with the standard ordering of subject and object in active sentences, produces a generalized schema for action that corresponds to the trajectory with which a given language is written, with the "doer" envisaged to the left of the "patient" in LR writing cultures. By the same token, influential, active, and dominant social groups are envisaged to the left of more passive ones. Thus, horizontal bias is believed to derive from a habitual physical activity, independent of linguistic metaphors.

The presence vs. absence of metaphors is not the only reason why vertical biases such as those demonstrated by Schubert (see Schubert et al., this volume) are more pervasive and robust than the comparably weak and malleable horizontal biases investigated in our own research. Another difference lies in the frequency with which we experience vertical vs. horizontal asymmetries in the real world. Whereas gravity is ever present in our lives and has pervaded our language and thinking, horizontal directionality is more flexible. People in industrialized countries spend considerable time reading and writing, and written language pervades practically all areas of our daily lives (including teaching devices, books, magazines, advertisements, product labels, street signs, documents, operating instructions, emergency and way-finding devices, contracts, cell-phones, agendas, etc.), yet, the world is not rigidly organized in a unidirectional way. For instance, we may observe cars, trains, animals, and human beings moving leftward, wind-shaken trees bending towards the left, or light signals on a highway suggesting a right-to-left motion. Or we may perform right-to-left movements, for instance when throwing a dart or a ball. As our own research shows, such temporary exposures to the opposite trajectory are sufficient to override our "preferred" trajectory.

Thus, although the Spatial Agency Bias pervades different facets of thought, including imaging, categorization, and interpretation of ambiguous stimuli, and operates both on-line and off-line, the bias is generally rather small and malleable. Our research suggests that cultural factors, in particular writing direction, predisposes us to perceive action as evolving either from left to right or from right to left. However, this general readiness to perceive action, time, and (probably) cause in line with one's scanning habit can easily be overridden by temporary experiences, such as momentary primes of alternative trajectories, turning the Spatial Agency Bias into a flexible and highly adaptive cognitive tool.

References

Aaron, P. Gnanaolivu & R. Malatesha Joshi (2006). Written language is as natural as spoken language: A biolinguistic perspective. *Reading Psychology, 27*, 263–311.

Abele, Andrea E. (2003). The dynamics of masculine-agentic and feminine-communal traits: Findings from a prospective study. *Journal of Personality and Social Psychology, 85*, 768–776.

Barsalou, Laurence W. (1999). Perceptual symbol systems. *Behavioral and Brain Sciences, 22*, 577–660.

Barnard, William A. & Paul A. Bell (1982). An unobtrusive apparatus for measuring interpersonal distances. *Journal of General Psychology, 107*, 85–90.

Benjafield, John & Sidney J. Segalowitz (1993). Left and right in Leonardo's drawings of faces. *Empirical Studies of the Arts, 11*, 25–32.

Borden, Richard J. & Gorden M. Homleid (1978). Handedness and lateral positioning in heterosexual couples: Are men still strong-arming women? *Sex-Roles, 4*, 67–73.

Borkenau, Peter & Nadine Mauer (2006). Processing of pleasant, unpleasant, and neutral words in a lateralised emotional Stroop task. *Cognition and Emotion, 20*, 866–877.

Chatterjee, Anjan (2002). Portrait profiles and the notion of agency. *Empirical Studies of the Arts, 20*, 33–41.

Chatterjee, Anjan (this volume). *Directional asymmetries in cognition: What is left to write about?*

Chatterjee, Anjan, Lynn M. Maher & Kenneth M. Heilman (1995). Spatial characteristics of thematic role representation. *Neuropsychologia, 33*, 643–648.

Chatterjee, Anjan, M. Helen Southwood & David Basilico (1999). Verbs, events and spatial representations. *Neuropsychologia, 37*, 395–402.

Chokron, Sylvie & Maria De Agostini (2000). Reading habits influence aesthetic preference. *Cognitive Brain Research, 10*, 45–49.

Conesa, Jorge, Cynthia Brunold-Conesa & Maria Miron (1995). Incidence of the half-left profile pose in single-subject portraits. *Perceptual and Motor Skills, 81*, 920–922.

Conway, Michael, M. Teresa Pizzamiglio & Lauren Mount (1996). Status, communality, and agency: Implications for stereotypes of gender and other groups. *Journal of Personality and Social Psychology, 71*, 25–38.

de Kerckhove, Derrick (1988a). Critical brain processes involved in deciphering the Greek alphabet. In Derrick de Kerckhove & Charles J. Lumsden (Eds.), *The Alphabet and the brain*. Berlin: Springer.

de Kerckhove, Derrick (1988b). Logical principles underlying the layout of Greek orthography. In Derrick de Kerckhove & Charles J. Lumsden (Eds.), *The Alphabet and the brain* (pp. 153–172). Berlin: Springer.

Dehaene, Stanislas, Serge Bossini & Pascal Giraux (1993). The mental representation of parity and number magnitude. *Journal of Experimental Psychology: General, 122*, 371–396.

Else-Quest, Nicole M., Janet S. Hyde, H. Hill Goldsmith & Carol Van Hulle (2006). Gender differences in temperament: A meta-analysis. *Psychological Bulletin, 132*, 33–72.

Eviatar, Zohar (1997). Language experience and right hemisphere tasks: The effects of scanning habits and multilingualism. *Brain and Language, 58*, 157–173.

Eviatar, Zohar (2000). Culture and brain organization. *Brain and Cognition, 42*, 50–52.

Foroni, Francesco & Gün R. Semin (in press). Language that puts you in touch with your bodily feelings: The Multimodal Responsiveness of Affective Expressions. *Psychological Science*.

Gaffron, Mercedes (1956). Some new dimensions in the Phenomenal Analysis of Visual Experience. *Journal of Personality and Social Psychology, 24*, 285–307.

Garshol, Lars M. (n.d.). Writing direction. Retrieved 1° September 2009, from http://www.ontopia.net/i18n/directions.jsp

Gazzaniga, Michael S. (2000). Cerebral specialization and interhemispheric communication. Does the corpus callosum enable the human condition? *Brain, 123*, 1293–1326.

Goldberg, Elkhonon (2001). *The executive brain: Frontal lobes and the civilized mind.* New York: Oxford University Press.

Gordon, Ian (1974). Left and right in Goya's portraits. *Nature, 294*, 197–198.

Grüsser, Otto J., Thomas Selke & Barbara Zynca (1988). Cerebral lateralization and some implications for art, aesthetic perception and artistic creativity. In Ingo Rentschler, Barbara Herzberg & David Epstein (Eds.), *Beauty and the brain: Biological aspects of aesthetics* (pp. 257–293). Boston: Birkhauser.

Halpern, Andrea R. & Michael H. Kelly (1993). Memory biases in left versus right implied motion. *Journal of Experimental Psychology: Learning, Memory and Cognition, 19*, 471–484.

Hubbard, Timothy (2005). Representational momentum and related displacements in spatial memory: A review of the findings. *Psychonomic Bulletin & Review, 12*, 822–851.

Humphrey, Nick K. & I. Christopher McManus (1973). Status and the left cheek. *New Scientist, 59*, 437–439.

Jackson, Danielle, Erika Engstrom & Tara Emmers-Sommer (2007). Think leader, think male and female: Sex vs. seating arrangement as leadership cues. *Sex Roles, 56*, 713–723.

Kosslyn, Stephen M., Olivier Koenig, Anna Barrett, Carolyn B. Cave, Joyce Tang & John D. E. Gabrieli (1989). Evidence for two types of spatial representations: Hemispheric specialization for categorical and coordinate relations. *Journal of Experimental Psychology: Human Perception and Performance, 15*, 723–735.

Lakoff, George & Mark Johnson (1980). *Metaphors we live by.* Chicago: University of Chicago Press.

Maass, Anne & Aurore Russo (2003). Directional bias in the mental representation of spatial events: Nature or culture? *Psychological Science, 14*, 296–301.

Maass, Anne, Damiano Pagani & Emanuela Berta (2007). How beautiful is the goal and how violent is the fistfight? Spatial bias in the interpretation of human behavior. *Social Cognition, 26*, 833–852.

Maass, Anne, Caterina Suitner, Xenia Favaretto & Marina Cignacchi (2009). Groups in space: Stereotypes and the spatial agency bias. *Journal of Experimental Social Psychology, 45*, 496–504.

Maher, Lynn M., Anjan Chatterjee & Leslie J. Rothi (1995). Agrammatic sentence production: The use of a temporal-spatial strategy. *Brain and Language, 48*, 105–124.

McManus, I. Christopher & Nick Humphrey (1973). Turning the left cheek. *Nature, 243*, 271–272.

Meier, Brian P. & Michael D. Robinson (2004). Why the sunny side is up: Associations between affect and vertical position. *Psychological Science, 15*, 243–247.

Morikawa, Kazunori & Michael McBeath (1992). Lateral motion bias associated with reading direction. *Vision Research, 32*, 1137–1141.

Nachson, Israel, Einat Argaman & Assaf Luria (1999). Effects of directional habits and handedness on aesthetic preference for left and right profiles. *Journal of Cross Cultural Psychology, 30*, 106–114.

Oppenheimer, Daniel M. (2008). The secret life of fluency. *Trends in Cognitive Sciences, 12*, 237–241.

Padakannaya, Prakash, Maharabam L. Devi, Siddiqua Zaveria, Shyamala K. Chengappa & Jyotsna Vaid (2002). Directional scanning effect and strength of reading habit in picture naming and recall. *Brain and Cognition, 48*, 484–490.

Reuter-Lorenz, P. A., M. Kinsbourne & M. Moscovitch (1990). Hemispheric control of spatial attention. *Brain and Cognition, 12*, 240–266.

Rohrer, Tim (2006). The body in space: Dimensions of embodiment. In Tom Ziemke, Jordan Zlatev & Roslyn M. Frank (Eds.), *Body, language and mind* (Vol. 1). Berlin: Mouton de Gruyte.

Schubert, Thomas W. (2005). Your Highness: Vertical positions as perceptual symbols of power. *Journal of Personality and Social Psychology, 89*, 1–21.

Schubert, Thomas W., S. Waldzus & Beate Seibt (this volume). *More than a metaphor: How the understanding of power is grounded in experience.*

Spalek, Thomas M. & Sherief Hammad (2005). The left-to-right bias in inhibition of return is due to the direction of reading. *Psychological Science, 16*, 15–18.

Spence, Janet T., Robert Helmreich & Joy Stapp (1974). The Personal Attributes Questionnaire: A measure of sex role stereotypes and masculinity-femininity. *JSAS Catalog of Selected Document in Psychology, 4*, 43–44.

Spence, Janet T. & Robert L. Helmreich (1978). *Masculinity and femininity: Their psychological dimensions, correlates, and antecedents.* Austin: University of Texas Press.

Suitner, Caterina (2009). *Where to place social targets? Stereotyping and spatial agency bias.* Doctoral Thesis, University of Padova.

Suitner, Caterina & Anne Maass (2007). Positioning bias in portraits and self-portraits: Do female artists make different choices? *Empirical Studies of the Arts, 25*(1), 71–95.

Suitner, Caterina & I. Christopher McManus (this volume). *Aesthetic asymmetries, spatial agency, and art history: A social psychological perspective.*

Taylor, Isaac (1988). Psychology of literacy: East and West. In Derrick de Kerckhove & Charles J. Lumsden (Eds.), *The Alphabet and the Brain* (pp. 202–234). Verlag: Springer.

ten Cate, Carel (2002). Posing as professor: Laterality in posing orientation for portraits of scientists. *Journal of Nonverbal Behavior, 26*, 175–192.

Tettamanti, Marco, Buccino, Giovanni, Saccuman, Maria C., Gallese, Vittorio, Danna, Massimo, Scifo, Paola, et al. (2005). Listening to action-related sentences activates frontoparietal motor circuits. *Journal of Cognitive Neuroscience, 17*, 273–281.

Tversky, Barbara (this volume). *Spatial thought, social thought.*

Tversky, Barbara, Sol Kugelmass & Atalia Winter (1991). Cross-cultural and developmental trends in graphic productions. *Cognitive Psychology, 23*, 515–557.

Vaid, Jyotsna (1989). Asymmetries in the perception of facial affect: Is there a influence of reading habits? *Neuropsychologia, 27*, 1277–1287.

Vaid, Jyotsna (this volume). *Asymmetries in representational drawing: Alternatives to a laterality account.*

Vaid, Jyotsna, Maharaj Singh, Tripti Sakhuja & Gyan C. Gupta (2002). Stroke direction asymmetry in figure drawing: Influence of handedness and reading/writing habits. *Brain and Cognition, 48*, 597–602.

Vallortigara, Giorgio & Leslie J. Rogers (2005). Survival with an asymmetrical brain: Advantages and disadvantages of cerebral lateralization. *Behavioral and Brain Sciences, 28*, 575–633.

Watt, William C. (1988). Canons of alphabetic change. In Derrick de Kerckhove & Charles J. Lumsden (Eds.), *The Alphabet and the brain* (pp. 122–152). Verlag: Springer.

Zebian, Samar (2005). Linkages between Number concepts, spatial thinking, and directionality of writing: The SNARC effect and the REVERSE SNARC effect in English and Arabic monoliterates, biliterates, and illiterate Arabic speakers. *Journal of Cognition and Culture, 5*, 166–190.

Who is the second (graphed) sex and why? The meaning of order in graphs of gender differences

Peter Hegarty and Anthony F. Lemieux

Abstract

In this chapter, we propose that the study of graphs from a social psychological perspective is both warranted and necessary. We review the literatures on both cognitive studies of graphing, as well as the relativist theory of scientific visualization. Extending on these frameworks, we provide a detailed review of our research on graphs that shows (a) a widespread preference to graph men before women, (b) that this preference is influenced by social thought, (c) that this social thought is not easily deciphered when people assess graphs for evidence of bias, and (d) that preferences for graph order change when people draw on different social beliefs about the groups that are represented. We conclude by recommending that these initial empirical studies of what graphs mean should be the impetus for developing a social psychology of graphs.

1. Introduction

What can a social psychology of *graphs* tell us about the ways that space represents social thought? Recent studies have shown effects of reading habits on perceptions of distance (Chokron & DeAgostini, 1996, 2000; Singh, Vaid, & Sakhuja, 2000), agency (Maass & Russo, 2003), beauty (Maass, Pagani, & Berta, 2007), musical pitch (Lidji, Kolinsky, Lochy, & Morais, 2007), number (Dehaene, 1992; Zebian, 2005), and gender (Suitner & Maass, 2007). However, graphs are distinctly *Western* forms of visual representation that only became popular outside of Western scientific subcultures in the 19th century (Beninger & Robyn, 1978; Best, 2005). After graphs became popular, Western statisticians studied how ordinary people made sense of them (e.g., Croxton & Stryker, 1927; Goldenweiser, 1916; Ripley, 1899). Such statisticians advised early on that graphs be designed and scanned from left-to-right (American Joint Committee on Standards for Graphic Presentation, 1915). This advice from speakers of English, who read from left-to-right, is not surprising. However, its very existence troubles easy conclusions that left-right asymmetries in graphical thinking observed today are direct consequences of individuals' reading habits, rather than indirect effects, mediated by the historical advice offered by statistical experts in Western cultures.

How then do graphs particularize Western ways of drawing sociality onto space? Below we report several studies that show that the left-right axis of simple vertical bar graphs implicitly represents semantic information about the social groups depicted. Like the pictures described by Suitner and Maass (this volume), the graphs we describe were spontaneously drawn with men to the left and women to the right. This behavioural preference is theoretically important; graphs represent a *hard* test of the hypothesis that social thought impacts the meaning of the left-right axis of two-dimensional space. We psychologists have been sometimes too quick to make attributions about why laypeople draw and interpret pictures the way they do (Wood, Nezworski, Lilienfeld, & Garb, 2003). We are, perhaps, less inclined to consider how implicit beliefs affect our own scientific conventions for visualizing data, and yet less inclined again to consider how such effects distinguish our *norms* for scientific practice from what we scientists actually do.

In this chapter we first review two traditions that examine the meaning people make of graphs: cognitive psychological studies of graph schemas and Latour's (1990) influential relativist theory of scientific visualization. We next present four phases of our research which show (a) that the behavioural preference to graph men first is widespread, (b) that this preference draws on social thought, (c) that such social thought is not readily deciphered when people inspect graphs for bias, and (d) that behavioural preferences for particular graph orders change when people draw on different social beliefs about the groups that they represent. Throughout we will emphasize how the perspective we are developing differs from both the cognitive psychological view and from Latour's (1990) relativist view, and we will conclude with thoughts for future directions for a social psychology of graphing.

2. Cognitive studies of graphing

In recent decades, cognitive psychologists have taken over the statisticians' task of studying how people make sense of graphs, and have produced an impressive body of work showing how different graphs succeed or fail at communicating particular kinds of information (see Shah & Hoeffner, 2002; Tversky, 2005 for reviews). For example, studies have shown that undergraduates assume that line graphs represent continuous variables while bar graphs represent discrete variables (Zachs & Tversky, 1999). Similarly, pie charts communicate proportions better than bar charts do (Simkin & Hastie, 1987). Graphs are easier to read when relevant data are grouped (Shah, M. Hegarty, & Meyer, 1999), and regression lines are easier to read when the variable of interest, which is typically the dependent variable, is on the Y-axis (Gattis & Holyoak, 1996). The difference between effective and ineffective graphing has real-world implications. For example, pictographs allow patients to extract both accurate numerical information and overall 'gist' (Zikmund-Fisher et al., 2008) and reduce reliance on anecdotal evidence (Fagerlin, Wang, & Ubel, 2005).

Interpreting a graph requires the reader to draw on information that is not directly displayed in that graph. Graphs act as two–dimensional *metaphors* for variables that are more difficult to visualize, such as time (Tversky, Kugelmass, & Winter, 1991) or risk (Lipkus, 2007), and Pinker's (1990) influential model of *graph schemas* describes the implicit knowledge that is typically drawn upon to allow their comprehension. Pinker (1990) described graph schemas as exploiting the perceptual properties of two-dimensional space, Gestalt principles, and conventional knowledge about graph formats. As such, his model allowed, in principle, that the conventional knowledge needed to understand graphs might vary between scientific subcultures. Indeed, as Roth (2003) has shown, scientists often cannot understand the graphs produced in neighbouring disciplines because they lack the conventional knowledge to do so.

Cognitive studies have tended to focus on aspects of graph schemas that are *shared* within members of a culture, rather than those that are subject to disciplinary variation. For example, graph schemas include default 'comparison points' toward which people consistently mutate their memory when they recall a graph's content (Tversky & Schiano, 1989), much like the canonical forms encoded in memory more generally (Allport & Postman, 1945; Bartlett, 1932). Graphs share some, but not all, of their comparison points with other forms of visual-spatial representation. For example, asymmetric curves are systematically misremembered as symmetrical whether they represent rivers on maps or normal distributions on graphs. However, the tendency to mutate lines towards a 45 degree angle occurs when people remember lines close to the identity line $x = y$, but not when those lines appear in maps (Tversky & Schiano, 1989).

Cognitive psychologists have reached mixed conclusions about the extent to which the knowledge that is drawn upon to make sense of graphs depends on cultural conventions, or draws directly on human visual information processing systems. Tversky and Schiano (1989) concluded that internal graph schemas and the graphing conventions that are visible in popular and scientific communications were mutually reinforcing. This interpretation is consistent with Roth's (2003) finding of large differences between Western scientists' understandings of each others' graphs. However, Zachs and Tversky (1999) argued more boldly that the tendency to graph continuous categories with line graphs and categorical ones with bar graphs was universal. In other words, contemporary Western graphing conventions might not be culturally particular forms of interpretation, but *cognitively natural* ones. If this were true, a social psychology of graphs would appear to be of little interest.[1]

3. The relativist theory of graphs' social influence

Ironically, research in the sociology of scientific knowledge begins from the premise that it is precisely the capacity of graphs to appear as direct, unmediated representations of nature that makes graphs most worthy of sociological study. This argument has been proposed most forcefully by Latour (1990), for whom scientific representations (or 'inscriptions') such as maps, tables, and graphs, are crucial tools for enlisting allies within professional battles for the determination of what 'nature' and 'reality' truly are (see also Latour, 1987; Woolgar, 1988). Within this antagonistic model of scientific communication, visual representations such as graphs allow scientists to make 'look, see!' arguments, while freeing themselves from the necessity of literally pointing to the natural phenomena they describe (which is, of course, often literally impossible). Convincing scientific representations allow scientists to build additional arguments, and call for actions, that are in fact predicated on the account of reality that they wish to foreground. In a sense, they allow a scientist to let the visual representation 'do the talking' (and arguing) for her.

---

1 Indeed, Zachs and Tversky's (1999) argument for cognitive naturalism is weaker than it might at first appear. Their experiments used gender to operationalize categorical differences, and age to operationalize age differences. Consequently, the argument that it is natural and species universal to represent categories with bars rather than lines depends on the argument that it is natural and species universal to represent human gender as a dichotomous variable. Historical (Laqueur, 1990), anthropological (Morris, 1995), sociological (Garfinkel, 1967) and biological (Fausto-Sterling, 2000) research and the perspectives of gender minorities in the researchers' own culture (Parlee, 1996) trouble the assumption that this hegemonic belief is either natural or species universal. Of course, a similar argument could be made about age, which may be perceived as continuous or as organized into life stages (childhood, adolescence, etc.).

This relativist view assumes that modern science falls short of its own norms of independence from textual authority. Similarly, historical studies show that while early modern scientists imagined themselves to be liberated from a dependence on text by the direct witnesses of 'matters of fact' in experiments, they rapidly became dependent on a genre of written communication about experiments whose rhetorical value hinged upon its being perceived as non-rhetorical (Shapin, 1998). Latour (1987) argues that sociologists should not study science by evaluating it as 'good' or 'bad' with respective to such prescriptive norms, but by tracking the ways that natural phenomena are 'inscribed' into written and visual-spatial representations, and by observing scientists' trust and interest in those representations. Ethnographic studies of laboratory practices show that science is about "the transformation of rats and chemicals into paper" (Latour & Woolgar, 1979; p. 3), meaning that the natural phenomena that are studied in laboratories are rarely enduring, while trust in their ontological status depends on written records of their happening. Latour (1990, p. 33) has even argued that empirical observation without representation does not constitute science at al; scientists only see something *as scientists*: "once they stop looking at nature and look exclusively and obsessively at prints and flat inscriptions."

Latour (1990) characterizes graphs as both 'mobile' and 'immutable;' they can be transported and modified while retaining the effect of convincing others that they speak directly for a pre-existing solid material reality. When the thing-to-be-represented scientifically is the human mind, these arguments take on particular force; Western empirical philosophy did not allow for a science of non-material mind for several centuries (Mackenzie & Mackenzie, 1974). Latour (1990) understands psychologists to also be reliant on networks of trust in networks of assumptions about representation to structure our interpretations about people's minds. For instance, in Piaget's experiments, water is poured from tall thin beakers into short broad ones, and the child's ability to conserve volume is assessed (Piaget & Garcia, 1989). Latour (1990) follows Cole and Scribner (1974) in arguing that such experiments do not show the emergence of higher cognition, but rather the child's participation in a modern scientific culture in which standardized measurements define abstract properties – such as volume – more than obvious visual differences do. As Latour (1990) tellingly notes, Piaget himself was dependent on modern inscriptions to run the experiments and "without industrially calibrated beakers Piaget himself would be totally unable to decide what is conserved" (page 40–41).

Several content analyses and experiments add weight to Latour's (1990) claims that graphs make scientific claims appear more 'hard' and enrol "allies" in scientific battles for the determination of 'truth.' The amount of space devoted to graph content is higher in natural science publications than social science publications (Cleveland, 1984). Within psychology, those journals that devote the most space to graphs are deemed to report 'harder' rather than 'softer' science by the psychologists who read them (Smith, Best, Stubbs, Archibald, Bastiani, & Roberson-Nay, 2002). This finding is not an artefact of greater quantification in some areas of psychology; journals that contain more tables are deemed by expert psychologists to report *softer* science (Smith et al., 2002). Brain maps appear yet more powerful than graphs in increasing the apparent realism of cognitive neuropsychological studies (McCabe & Castel, 2008).

A radical relativist interpretation of such findings might lead to the conclusion that psychology is an epistemologically vacuous activity. The experiments we describe next are vulnerable to the same relativist criticisms. We never observed a 'graph schema' or looked at a 'mind' directly, but have relied on, and reinforced, a network of social-cognitive assumptions to make inferences about individual mental processes from the graphs that our participants produced. Sociologists of science will not be surprised to learn that we filed the graphs that participants drew quite quickly after we coded them, and began looking "exclusively and obsessively" – as Latour (1990) might predict – at the graphs that SPSS produced from our data. Our experiments would interest relativists little if they were simply one more confirming example of how psychological scientists reifying the mind. However, we think that the graphs that our participants produced also challenge assumptions of Latour's (1990) relativist account about the role graphs play in the social organization of science.

Recall that Latour's (1990) account of graphing assumes that science is fundamentally a battle for the determination of truth. Latour, like many cognitive psychologists (e.g., Tversky, 2005), also describes graphs as *metaphors*, and foregrounds *literalness* as the implicit meaning of graphic communication. These two assumptions are linked, as it is their apparent literalness that makes graphs particularly effective at convincing others that one's account of reality is *the correct account*. At one point Latour describes those dynamics as follows:

> This trend toward simpler and simpler inscriptions that mobilize larger and larger numbers of events in one spot, cannot be understood if separated from the agonistic model that we use as our point of reference. It is as necessary as the race for digging trenches on the front in 1914. He who visualizes badly loses the encounter; his fact does not hold (Latour, 1990, p. 33–34).

This quotation illustrates an irony of Latour's position that we wish to contest. Here, as elsewhere, Latour's metaphors and pronouns presume that science is a masculine activity, a presumption that has been often reiterated in Western scientific sub-cultures (Harding, 1986, 1991; Keller, 1985; Merchant, 1980). Indeed, Latour's pronouns are more androcentric than those used by contemporary psychological scientists (Gannon, Luchetta, Rhodes, Pardie, & Segrist, 1991). We argue that Latour's (1990) theory is an insufficient critical interrogation of graphs precisely because it overlooks the degree to which social thought about *gender* is drawn into lay and professional practices of scientific visualization. This irony is compounded by the fact that *graphs,* those emblems of objectivity, provide the evidence for our argument about the shortcomings of Latour's relativism.

4. Men are positioned first in graphs of gender differences

We first observed a behavioural preference to position men first in graphs and tables in a larger content analysis examining representations of gender differences in empirical psychology articles (Hegarty & Buechel, 2006). Kahneman and Miller's (1986) norm theory had inspired earlier experiments which had shown that group differences tended to be explained by focusing on the particular attributes of atypical groups, implicitly taking more typical groups as the normative standards of comparison (see Hegarty, 2006; Hegarty & Chryssochoou, 2005; Hegarty & Pratto, 2001; Miller, Taylor, & Buck, 1991; and Pratto, Hegarty, & Korchmaros, 2007 for a review). We hoped our content analysis would test these predictions in a real world context, by examining if professional psychologists similarly focused on attributes of women and girls more than those of men and boys when describing and explaining gender differences. The feminist literature on the subtle ways that standard forms of scientific writing might implicitly privilege males' psychology further motivated our study (e.g., Ader & Johnson, 1994; Gannon et al., 1992; Lee & Crawford, 2007, Martyna, 1980; see Hegarty & Pratto, 2010, for a review).

We confirmed our hypothesis; psychologists' published verbal descriptions and explanations did focus on attributes of women and girls. We then turned our attention to the graphs and tables in these articles. Here we found that 74% of these positioned data representing males first and data representing females second.[2] This behavioural preference was not moderated by author gender, the gender distribution of study participants, or year of publication. The reverse preference was observed in only one instance; articles in *Developmental Psychology* tabulated and graphed gender differ-

---

2   By 'first' and 'second' we mean both 'above' and 'below' with respect to vertically ordered data, and 'left' and 'right' with respect to horizontally ordered data.

ences among parents with mothers first 81% of the time. Verbal descriptions and explanations of gender differences among these parents also focused equally on fathers and mothers.

Then as now, we were completely unaware of any specific guidance to psychologists to explain data *asymmetrically* (Bloor, 1991) by focusing explanatory attention on particular groups, or to graph data asymmetrically with particular groups in particular orders. Our initial conclusion was that psychological scientists, like laypeople, thought about gender differences in androcentric ways by constructing men as the norm, and that such androcentric thinking explained both their asymmetric explanations and descriptions, and their asymmetric graphs and tables with equal ease (Kahneman & Miller, 1986, see Hegarty & Buechel, 2006). To explore this hypothesis further, we next examined if novice psychologists (i.e., our students) would similarly graph gender differences asymmetrically. In one experiment, 54 students drew graphs of interaction effects within four categories; fruits, animals, genders, and nationalities (Hegarty, Buechel, & Ungar, 2006). In each case, participants graphed differences between prototypical category members (oranges, horses, men, British people) and less typical category members (kumquats, kangaroos, women, French people). The instructions required that both category members be named in order, and this order was counterbalanced. The results confirmed the hypothesis. Most prototypical entities were graphed on the left rather than the right (68% vs. 32%), and men were graphed to the left of women more often than chance would predict (64% of the time) However, the results also varied across non-human categories. Differences between fruits were graphed 83% of the time with oranges to the left of kumquats as predicted. In contrast, graphs of differences between animals positioned horses and kangaroos on the left with equal frequency (55% vs. 45% respectively).

Our second experiment was a classroom demonstration. Students were asked to hypothesize a gender difference in human behaviour and to conduct an observational study to see if their hypothesis was correct. Mid-way through the semester, the instructor asked the class to write down their hypothesis and to draw a graph of their predicted results. Most students drew graphs of gender differences that positioned men first and women second (68% vs. 32%). Consistent with norm theory, most wrote hypothesis that made women, rather than men, the figure of the sentence (71% vs. 29%). However, in contrast with norm theory expectations these two effects were not correlated with each other.

The third experiment took place in another university classroom and concerned the degree to which graph schemas include gender order as a 'comparison point' (Tversky & Schiano, 1989). Students explained the results of vertical bar graphs of gender differences in cognitive abilities in their own words. The results presented were always stereotype consistent; women had higher verbal competency and men had higher math competency. However, the order of these genders and competencies varied between participants. Three days later, the instructor surprised the students by asking them to draw the graphs from memory. More than three times as many students switched the order of the genders in graphs that initially had women on the left, than in graphs that initially had men on the left. The tendency to graph males on the left acted as a classic schematic 'comparison point' and affected memory for graphs.

Most recently, we returned to a real world context to examine order of information in medical publications. Rudin, Jones, Lemieux & Hegarty (2009) reviewed 501 articles published between 1998 and 2008 in the *Journal of the American Medical Association*. Many more tables than graphs of gender differences were included in these articles (Ns = 292, 52 respectively), and 70% of tables and 60% of graphs positioned men first and women second. This result demonstrates that the phenomenon of placing men before women in scientific publications extends beyond psychology and describes both graphs and tables.

Jointly, these studies establish a widespread international, cross-disciplinary preference to graph and tabulate gender differences with men's data represented first. We observed this preference when shuttling between the 'real world' of the scientific literature, classrooms in both the United Kingdom and the United States, and laboratory settings. However, unlike cognitive studies of other widespread preferences, the preference to position men first does not seem to be 'cognitively natural' (Zachs & Tversky, 1999) or a direct product of the affordances of either the human visual system or a result of Gestalt principles of organization (Pinker, 1990; Tversky & Schiano, 1989). Nor is this preference predicted by relativist arguments that graphs play a role in motivated attempts to recruit allies to a scientist's own worldview (Latour, 1990). Had that been the case, and graph order was a simple projection of self-interest, one might expect that people consistently graph their own gender first. However, we observed no gender differences in any of these studies. If graph order does not simply implicate social motivations associated with self-interest (Latour, 1990), what might it mean to graph men first?

5. The meaning of graph order: From prototypicality to power

We initially hypothesized that graph order preferences were caused by implicit beliefs that men were more prototypical than women. People of both genders more readily call to mind male exemplars than female exemplars for many social categories (Broverman, Broverman, Clarkson, Rosenkrantz, & Vogel, 1970; Eagly & Kite, 1987; Foster & Keating, 1992; Haddock, Zanna, & Esses, 1993; Hyde, 1984; Lambdin, Greer, Jibotian, Rice, & Hamilton, 2003; Moyer, 1997), such that the particularities of men and masculinity are often the normative standard against which people in general are described or evaluated (Ader & Johnson, 1994; Bem, 1993; Miller et al., 1991; Pratto et al., 2007). However, further experiments lead us to revise this interpretation of the graph order preference. In two experiments, we tested whether women would be positioned first when they were prototypical. Participants graphed gender differences in female-normed and male-normed professions (i.e., teachers and professors; McWilliams, Strang, Lemieux, & Hegarty, 2007), and among couples described as parents or as romantic partners (Hegarty, 2009). Men were graphed first whether participants graphed differences among teachers (66%), professors, (67%), parents (66%) or romantic couples (62%). These results contrast with norm theory findings that when women, or other lower power groups, are prototypical within a social cateogry, that the tendency to focus explanation of group differences on the lower power group is mitigated (Hegarty & Buechel, 2006; Miller et al., 1991; Pratto et al., 2007).

At this point, we took heart from findings that scientists often have to receive disconfirming evidence repeatedly before they are willing to abandon their theories for alternatives (Fuselsang, Stein, Green, & Durban, 2004). We considered three other gender-related beliefs that might cause graph order preferences. First, gender stereotypes might structure expectancies that women's and men's interests, physical characteristics, personality traits, and sexual orientations, will form a single index of stereotypical masculinity-femininity (Deaux & Lewis, 1984). Stereotyping research suggested to us that people might simply graph masculine groups ahead of feminine ones. Second, women and men differ in power in most societies (Sidanius & Pratto, 1999), and power can be represented by the left-right axis (Suitner & Maass, this volume). Finally, power can operate by conflating the particular attributes of higher status people with those attributes deemed generalizable to all (Dahrendorf, 1959). Perhaps people graph groups first that they consider to be more important kinds of people.

Our next experiment examined whether the left-right axis in vertical bar graphs represents prototypicality, gender stereotypes, power, or importance (see Hegarty et al., 2010, Study 3). Participants graphed group differences between groups that they chose themselves, and which differed on one of eight attributes; typicality and unusualness, masculinity and femininity, importance and marginality, powerfulness and weakness. Unlike earlier experiments, most graphs positioned groups who possessed a greater amount of the attribute on the left rather than the right (64% vs. 36%). Equivalent proportions of participants graphed groups characterized by more typicality or unusualness, masculinity or femininity, and importance or marginality first (59–67%). However, powerful groups were almost exclusively graphed on the left (93%) while weak groups were graphed on the left in only a minority of cases (42%).

The tendency among participants to graph groups that possessed the attribute to the left of those that did not does not explain the preference to graph men before women. We conclude that this preference likely occurred in this experiment because the instruction to call to mind groups to represent differences on an attribute likely lead people to call to mind groups that possessed the relevant attribute before those that lacked it (c.f., Klayman & Ha, 1987). However, as powerful groups were consistently graphed ahead of weaker ones, while masculine, typical and important groups were *not* graphed first any more than their complimentary attributes, we concluded that beliefs about power are the most likely cause of the preference to graph men before women. Two other findings from this experiment rendered this interpretation more plausible. First, the participants in the masculinity-femininity condition were not permitted to graph gender differences. Among the remainder, a disproportionate number of participants in the *power* and *weakness* conditions spontaneously graphed gender differences. Second, a significant majority of the participants who spontaneously graphed gender differences in this experiment graphed men first.

If it is indeed the case that power is the prime factor that influences graph order, then power should also be a limit condition of the behavioural preference to graph men first. In other words, participants should prefer to graph powerful women first, ahead of less powerful men. We tested this hypothesis by asking participants in Britain to graph differences between members of the British Royal Family. Participants chose both the individuals to represent and the attribute that made them different from each other. Participants who graphed the reigning Queen positioned her first ahead of her kinsmen (Hegarty et al., 2010, Study 4). As predicted, a powerful woman was graphed ahead of less powerful men.

As in pictures (Suitner & Maass, this volume), the left-right axis can represent power in graphs. As men *do* have greater power than women (Sidanius & Pratto, 1999) conventions to graph men to the left of women are not 'biased' in the sense of being erroneous. However, we think that such behavioral preferences are worthy of study; by graphing powerful groups such as men first, scientists and laypeople might by drawing social thought into space to a greater degree than they intend or desire, or than models of graph schemas (Pinker, 1990), or graph's social influence (Latour, 1990) yet recognize. The next phase of our research examined whether laypeople recognize how social thought is drawn down into graph order.

6. Attributing bias to graph order

While conducting the studies described above, participants often seemed surprised when debriefed about the studies' goals. Some asked if the study showed that they were sexist, while others insisted that we were making something of nothing by looking for sexism in graph order at all. Similarly, when we presented these findings to psychology colleagues, some told us that their own published papers showed a preference to graph men first which they had never consciously considered. Others argued that there was no reason to break with convention by graphing women first because graph order carried no semantic meaning. None reported that our account described them poorly and that they had unthinkingly consistently graphed women ahead of men. In short, reactions of both participants and colleagues have sometimes been to conclude that order is a form of bias, and sometimes to conclude that no social thought is drawn down into graph order at all.

To get beyond both of these views, it is worth recalling that theorists who might agree about little else, agree that graphs are *metaphors* (Latour, 1990; Tverksy, 1990). Cognitive research shows that metaphorical and realist meanings are often processed in parallel (Glucksberg, 2003), and confused during recall (Blanchette & Dunbar, 2002; Perrott, Gentner, & Bodenhausen, 2005). As such, the routine habit of graphing men first might play a role in creating and reinforcing mental associations between men and power, within a medium that is understood by its users as literal and non-interpretive (Smith et al., 2002). Imagine that the 'graphs are metaphors' metaphor is right and graphs function like verbal metaphors. If this is the case, then conventions for ordering information in gender difference graphs might carry meaning that might be obscure to authors and readers of scientific papers, and authors of such papers might feel aggrieved if they felt accused of bias on the basis of graph order.

In the next study we examined what graph order implies about a graph's author (Hegarty et al., 2010, Study 5). Participants were presented with graphs of stereotype-consistent gender differences in cognitive abilities, similar to those used in the earlier memory experiment. We prompted participants to query the assumption that graphed data is hard data with written instructions:

> There are some people who think that you can 'lie with statistics', or draw graphs to give readers a particular impression of things. Thus, it may not be the case that the data itself is biased at all, just that the *way* it is presented may be biased.

Participants rated the degree of bias in the graph on a 4-point scale, answered an open ended question about the kind of bias they had detected, and answered forced choice questions as to which gender the author of the graph likely believed to be more important, to be more powerful, and to be more prototypical. They also guessed the author's gender.

One third of participants perceived the graph as 'hard' data (Smith et al., 2002), in that they did not attribute any bias to the graph at all and left the open-ended item blank. About half of the participants described some aspect of the graph, other than the order of the information, as a source of bias. Only one sixth of participants described order as a source of 'bias' in the open ended measure. However, participants who did describe order as a source of bias overwhelmingly judged that the author had positioned first their own gender group, the group that the author deemed more important, and the more powerful gender group. Other participants did not make these attributions about the author.

These findings tell us three things. First, graph order does not typically lead people to think that graphs are biased (Latour, 1990; Smith et al., 2002). Second, the participants that did attribute bias to order consistently understood that bias to favour the group on the left. These two findings suggest that any implicit meanings that are transmitted by the graphs and tables in Western medicine and psychology that position men first are likely undetected by the readers of the literatures that those graphs populate. Third, the attributions that these few participants made were stronger than the conclusions we drew from our own experiments. Most obviously, participants that attributed bias, attributed *in-group* bias, consistent with Latour's (1990) view that graphs are part of a battle between scientists to reify their own definitions of reality. However, neither these participants' attributions – nor Latour's (1990) theory – predicts why women would show out-group bias by graphing men first in the many journal articles and psychology experiments discussed above.

This last study also informs both our participants' and colleagues' initial reactions to our earlier experiments. Scientific authors may communicate more than they desire when they habitually order social groups in graphs, particularly to more skeptical readers. Cognitive psychologists have advised how different graph formats vary in their capacity to communicate different kinds of information (e.g., Shah & Hoeffner, 2002), but out studies suggest that different graph orders may also communicate different kinds of information about authors' beliefs and identities. As bar graph formats require one gender to go before the other, our advice to scientific authors who would prefer to avoid charges of bias is not simple. Graphs with men positioned first may sometimes be interpreted as the work of sexist men. Yet, the format of bar graphs requires one group to be positioned before the other. As such, the best advice we can offer to authors is to risk the attribution that they are sexist women. In a cultural context where scientific objectivity is conflated with the masculinity (Keller, 1985), this appears to us to be the less dangerous attribution to risk. The last phase of our research addressed the relationship between people's knowledge of their own genders and the order of the genders in their graphs directly.

7. Getting yourself in order: Situating personal knowledge in graphs

In the research presented so far, we observed few gender differences. Participant gender explained almost no variance at all in both the content analyses and experiments. While such results are readily interpreted as gender similarities, they could also be interpreted as gender differences; men graphed their own gender first, but women graphed their own gender second. The interpretation of these findings as differences or similarities depends on whether gender is considered to be a category that is relevant to the participants' self-concepts or not.

Cognitive theories of graphing say little about self-relevance, but ethnographers have observed how scientists talk about space in graphs as if they metaphorically inhabited it with their own bodies (Ochs, Gonzalez, & Jaccoby, 1996). For our first study on self-other graphs we asked women and men to graph differences between themselves and a friend of the other gender. Women and men positioned themselves first most of the time and to an equal degree (61% vs. 64% respectively). Given that graph order appears to follow from beliefs about power, and Western people consider themselves better able to control their fate than others are (Heine & Lehman, 1995), this finding was not surprising.

We considered next whether graphing self-relevant information might affect the way that relevant gender differences were graphed. Experiments show that imagining oneself positioned within a map distorts estimates of the distance between different points on that map (Holyoak & Mah, 1982). In this last experiment, we asked female psychology students and male engineering students to draw graphs of differences between themselves and other-gender friends and to graph gender differences on the same dimension. The order of these two tasks was manipulated.

Where gender differences were drawn first, a majority of the graphs drawn by both women and men positioned male groups and individuals first (70% vs. 96.1%, respectively). Where self-other differences were drawn first, most men's graphs similarly positioned male groups and individuals first (73.4%). However, in this condition, less than half of the women's graphs did so (48.1%). Women who drew self-other graphs first subsequently depicted gender difference graphs in a manner that showed an effect of the former (self-other) graphs on the latter (gender difference) graphs. These women drew self-friend graphs with themselves and their male friends first with about equal frequency. Among the women who drew the self-friend graph with a *male friend* first, 77% continued by graphing men first in the gender difference graph. Among the women who positioned *themselves* first in the self-friend graph, 79% continued by positioning women first in their gender graph. Indeed, across the experiment as a whole, 86% of participants "transferred" order across the two tasks in this fashion, while only 14% of participants switched order between tasks. This transfer of order suggests that the gender difference graphs and self-friend graphing tasks were perceived as related. Participants put *their selves* in order, much as professional physicists do when they utter statements like 'when I come down, I am in the domain state' (Ochs et al., 1996). When women put themselves in order prior to graphing gender differences, they were significantly less likely to graph women ahead of men. Correspondingly, when women graphed gender differences first, they largely positioned men ahead of women, and went on to position male friends ahead of themselves.

Such effects of self-knowledge on graph format are not predicted by purely cognitive models of graph comprehension (Pinker, 1990). However, relativist views that analogize science to a masculinist war or competition for the definition of reality (Latour, 1990) do not account for these findings either. Rather, these results call for a theory that describes scientific representation as something that is not habitually affected by identity, but which can become one, and that acknowledges that female and male scientists have different degrees of discordance between their personal worldviews and preferred scientific conventions. While Harding's (1986, 1991) descriptions of the relationship between feminism and science had little to say about graphs per se, her argument that Western science has long conflated men's ways of constructing reality with the objective value-free way of so doing is clearly relevant here. Harding (1991) argued that when women conform to these conventions that they are lead to 'other' themselves. Our finding that women who graph self-friend differences *after* graphing gender differences position themselves *second*, is consistent with this view. Harding further argued that if women – and indeed many men – resist androcentric conventions that new more diverse representations of reality can be developed that constitute 'stronger' forms of objectivity that do not conflate the worldviews of privileged groups with the normative way of viewing the world. Our findings that women escape the convention to graph men first in graphs of gender differences if they graph self-friend differences first adds weight to Harding's (1986) arguments.

8. Conclusions and future directions

In this final section, we consider some possible objections to our conclusions about the social nature of graphing gender differences and propose future directions for research. The first of these issues concerns the *consistency* of this graphing convention. Content analyses showed that men are positioned first across medicine and psychology. However, in our last experiment, male engineers showed a preference to graph themselves ahead of female friends overall, but female psychologists did not. This was also the only experiment in which men graphed men to the left more than women did. The confound between participant gender and academic subject may have affected the results of this last study.[3] Previous research at the campus from which the male engineering students were drawn found that engineering students scored higher than psychology students on a range of prejudice measures, including social dominance orientation, right wing authoritarianism and modern sexism, even after gender differences were controlled (Tee & Hegarty, 2006). As a result, the engineers may have held stronger beliefs about male power which influenced their graph order preferences, and future research might investigate whether individual and group differences in stereotypical beliefs about gendered power affect graph order preferences.

A second set of issues arises from the relationship between graph order preferences and word order preferences in *binomial phrases* (Malkiel, 1959). In English, the phrase 'men and women' is behaviourally preferred over 'women and men' (Cooper & Ross, 1975) and has been prescribed for explicitly sexist reasons by English grammarians in past centuries (Bodine, 1975). Some colleagues have suggested graph order might be influenced by conventional word order. We do not dispute this possibility, but do not think that it renders graph order preferences any more cognitively natural. Word order preferences cannot be directly attributed to nature because of grammarians explicitly sexist prescriptions to name men first in earlier centuries (Bodine, 1975). Second, in an experiment described earlier (Hegarty et al., 2006), a verbal cue to position women first still lead participants to graph men to the left of women most of the time. Third, studies of preferences for the order of women and men's names in same- and opposite-sex couples show that the social thought that is drawn into name order is not the same as the social thought that is drawn into graph order. People, particularly men, name men before women because stereotypes lead stere-

---

3 Other differences, less relevant to our hypotheses, also suggested disciplinary differences in graphing practices. For example, the engineering students often included error bars on the graphs that they drew while the psychologists never did.

otypically *masculine* people to be named before stereotypically *feminine* people in both same-sex and opposite-sex couples (Hegarty, Watson, Fletcher, & McQueen, 2011, see also Wright, Hay, & Bent, 2005). As graph order appears to draw on beliefs about power rather than stereotypical masculinity-femininity, it does not seem plausible that graph order preferences are a cognitively natural corollary of cognitively natural word order preferences.

    A third issue concerns our colleagues' work, described elsewhere in this volume, on the degree to which reading habits condition the way that people read semantic information onto the left-right axis. We do not consider graphs to be ideal media for testing subtle effects of enculturated reading habits on the semantics of space. This is because graphs are distinctly Western forms of representation whose reading has long been proscribed as proceeding from left-to-right. Rather, graphs are interesting because ordering data in graphs appears to many people as a semantically neutral activity, even though authors must inevitably chose to put some groups ahead of others, and habitually do so in ways that are informed by implicit social beliefs without the mediation of conscious thought. Because graphs appear to their users to represent 'hard' data, beyond interpretation (Smith et al., 2002), they represent a 'hard' test of the theory that the experience of space is mediated by culture. This is not to say that the graphing practices of people who read languages that are written from right-to-left are scientifically uninteresting. Rather, future research on the effects of the direction in which language is written on graph order will evidence the extent of the effects of the globalization of initially Western scientific conventions (see also Moghaddam & Lee, 2006). Findings that Arabic speakers graph from left-to-right would show the influence of Western mathematical conventions and findings that Arabic speakers graph from right-to-left would show their limits. In this regard, we are intrigued by colleagues' reports that the Hebrew version of some software graphing programs include default vertical axes on the *right* of the graph, and that Israeli scholars report the effort of changing this default to conform with international conventions as something of an annoyance (Lieberman, personal communication).

    These findings also demonstrate how social power is drawn into scientific representations. At least since Marx and Engels (1978), Western academics have been required to reflect upon the degree to which they are engaged in ideological justifications of power when they write about what power 'really' is with expert voices (see Eagleton, 1991: Hegarty, 2007). Foucault (1973) has made the strongest argument that ways of ordering knowledge in the Western human sciences constitute forms of imminent, covert social power. Foucault described how Western human scientists often behave in habitual ways when they make representations of which the human scientists are not aware themselves. His description of these consistencies did not focus on gender per say, but his notion that there are things that scientists do, but do not know they do as the 'positive unconscious' of the human sciences appears to aptly describe the graph order preferences we described here.

We do not consider our conclusion that beliefs about power affect graph order to be the last word on the relationship between semantic beliefs and graph formats: quite the opposite. We hope it opens up new lines of inquiry by leading social psychologists to investigate the social nature of graphs still further. We are aware that power has many forms and that social relationships are often constituted by different forms of power simultaneously (Pratto, Pearson, Lee, & Saguy, 2008). The shifts in women's graph order preferences in the last experiment are not the only suggestive finding in this regard. Recall also that developmental psychologists graphed mothers first (Hegarty & Buechel, 2006), but laypeople graphed fathers first (Hegarty, 2009). The influence of parents on their children may be more salient to developmental psychologists, while beliefs about traditional patriarchal power shape the graph order of laypeople. While we have emphasized similarities between the ways that laypeople and professional scientists graph gender differences here, these groups may also understand social groups in different ways and graph differently as a consequence. Clearly, there is much more work to be done to examine the way that power is drawn into seemingly objective representations of social life, such as graphs of group differences.

Similarly, throughout this chapter we have reiterated the metaphor common to both the cognitive (Pinker, 1990) and sociological (Latour, 1990) approach to graphs that 'graphs are metaphors.' Because we have understood graph space to be metaphorical, we have used the terms 'first' and 'second' to define order within graphs. Our research neither rules out nor demonstrates an effect of reading habits on graphs, akin to the effects of reading habits on picture construction described elsewhere (Suitner & Maass, this volume). Reading habits likely contribute to graph order preferences, but drawing graph axes in particular locations re-defines graphical space by locating a zero point within it from which space extends. In the first study where participants could chose their own graph formats, all participants in all experiments drew vertical bar graphs. The experiments currently being conducted will inform this question by prompting participants to draw graphs using multiple different formats.

These open-ended questions do compel us to conclude that graphs are much more social kinds of objects than cognitive psychologists allow and that the time is ripe for a social psychology of graphing practices. We do not doubt that species-general characteristics are necessary to account for the emergence of graphing in the modern West. But they are not sufficient to account for the conventions of graphing power onto order that scientifically literate members of those cultures do so readily. There are consistencies to life that are structured by power as well as by nature, and some of them affect the way that we graph people (see Marx & Engels, 1978; Sidanius & Pratto, 1999). However, we cannot agree with the dominant and *androcentric* (Bem, 1993) theory of how graphs are social. Latour (1990) agonistic model of science suggests that graphs are an expression of self-interest, and as such cannot account for the gender similarities and differences described above. Moreover, the graphs that men drew in our studies fit better with Latour's (1990) antagonistic model of science than the graphs that women drew. We recommend that the empirical project of examining what graphs can mean – a project which statisticians began and cognitive psychologists continue – now needs to become a *social* psychology of graphs. We hope the graphs we have described here have intrigued readers to consider why a social psychology of graphing might navigate the social thought in these highly abstract spaces in ways that neither cognitive science nor the sociology of science can yet chart.

References

Ader, Deborah N. & Suzanne B. Johnson (1994). Sample description, reporting and analysis of sex in psychological research: A look at APA and APA division journals in 1990. *American Psychologist, 49,* 216–218.
Allport, Gordon W. & Leo J. Postman (1945). The basic psychology of rumor. *Transactions of the New York Academy of Sciences, 8,* 61–81.
American Statistical Association Joint Committee on Standards of Graphic Presentation (1915). Preliminary report published for the purpose of inviting suggestions for the benefit of the committee. *Publications of the American Statistical Association, 14,* 790–797.
Bartlett, Frederic C. (1932). *Remembering.* Oxford: Oxford University Press.
Bem, Sandra L. (1993). *The lenses of gender: Transforming the debate on sexual inequality.* New Haven, CT: Yale University Press.
Beninger, James R. & Dorothy L. Robyn (1978). Quantitative graphics in statistics: A brief history. *American Statistician, 32,* 1–11.
Best, Lisa A. (2005). An examination of drawings in philosophical transactions (1665 to present). *The International Journal of the Book, 3,* 45–54.
Blanchette, Isabelle & Kevin Dunbar (2002). Representational change and analogy: How analogical inferences alter target representations. *Journal of Experimental Psychology: Learning, Memory, and Cognition, 28,* 672–685.
Bloor, David (1991). *Knowledge and social imagery, 2nd edition.* Chicago: University of Chicago Press.

Bodine, Ann (1975). Androcentrism in prescriptive grammar: Singular 'they,' sex-indefinite 'he,' and 'he or she.' *Language in Society, 4,* 129–146.
Broverman, Inge K., Donald M. Broverman, Frank E. Clarkson, Paul S. Rosenkrantz & Susan Raymond Vogel (1970). Sex-role stereotypes and clinical judgments of mental health. *Journal of Clinical and Consulting Psychology, 34,* 1–7.
Chokron, Sylvie & Maria De Agostini (1996). Reading habits and line bisection: A developmental approach. *Cognitive Brain Research, 3,* 51–58.
Chokron, Sylvie & Maria De Agostini (2000). Reading habits influence aesthetic preference. *Cognitive Brain Research, 10,* 45–49.
Cleveland, William S. (1984). Graphs in scientific publications. *American Statistician, 38,* 261–269.
Cole, Michael & Sylvia Scribner (1974). *Culture and thought: A psychological introduction.* New York: John Wiley & Sons.
Cooper, William E. & John R. Ross (1975). World order. In R.E. Grossman, L.J. San & T.J. Vance (Eds.), *Papers from the parasession on functionalism* (pp. 63–111). Chicago: Chicago Linguistics Society.
Croxton, Frederick E. & Roy E. Stryker (1927). Bar charts versus circle diagrams. *Journal of the American Statistical Association, 22,* 473–482.
Dahrendorf, Ralf (1959). *Class and class conflict in industrial society.* Stanford, CA: Stanford University Press.
Deaux, Kay & Laurie L. Lewis (1984). Structure of gender stereotypes: Interrelationship among components and gender labels. *Journal of Personality and Social Psychology, 46,* 991–1004.
Dehaene, Stanislaus (1992). Varieties of numerical abilities. *Cognition, 44,* 1–42.
Dunbar, Kevin & Isabelle Blanchette (2003). The in vivo/in vitro approach to cognition: The case of analogy. *Trends in Cognitive Sciences, 5,* 334–339.
Eagleton, Terry (1991). *Ideology: An introduction.* London: Verso.
Eagly, Alice H. & Mary E. Kite (1987). Are stereotypes of nationalities applied to both women and men? *Journal of Personality and Social Psychology, 53,* 451–462.
Fagerlin, Angela, Catharine Wang & Peter A. Ubel (2005). Reducing the influence of anecdotal reasoning on people's health care decisions: Is a picture worth a thousand statistics? *Medical Decision Making, 25,* 398–405.
Fausto-Sterling, Anne (2000). *Sexing the body: Gender politics and the construction of sexuality.* New York: Basic Books.
Foucault, Michel (1973). *The order of things: An archaeology of the human sciences.* New York: Vintage.
Fugelsang, Jonathan A., Courtney B. Stein, Adam E. Green, Kevin N. Dunbar (2004). Theory and data interactions of the scientific mind: Evidence from the molecular and the cognitive laboratory. *Canadian Journal of Experimental Psychology, 58,* 132–141.
Gannon, Linda, Tracy Luchetta, Kelly Rhodes, Lynn Pardie & Dan Segrist (1992). Sex bias in psychological research: Progress or complacency? *American Psychologist, 47,* 389–396.
Garfinkel, Harold (1967). *Studies in ethnomethodology.* New York: Prentice Hall.

Gattis, Merideth & Keith J. Holyoak, (1996). Mapping conceptual to spatial relations in visual reasoning. *Journal of Experimental Psychology: Learning, Memory, and Cognition, 22,* 231–239.

Glucksberg, Sam (2003). The psycholinguistics of metaphor. *Trends in Cognitive Sciences, 7,* 92–96.

Goldenweiser, E.A. (1916). Classification and limitations of statistical graphics. *Publications of the American Statistical Association, 15,* 205–209.

Haddock, Geoffrey, Mark. P. Zanna & Victoria Esses (1993). Assessing the structure of prejudicial attitudes: The case of attitudes toward homosexuals. *Journal of Personality and Social Psychology, 65,* 1105–1118.

Hall, James (2008). *The sinister side: A lost key to Western art.* New York: Oxford University Press.

Haraway, Donna J. (1991). *Simians, cyborgs, and women.* New York: Routledge.

Harding, Sandra (1986). *The science question in feminism.* Ithaca, NY: Cornell University press.

Harding, Sandra (1991). *Whose science? Whose knowledge? Thinking from women's lives.* Ithica, NY: Cornell University Press.

Hegarty, Peter (2006). Undoing androcentric explanations of gender differences: Explaining 'the effect to be predicted' *Sex Roles: A Journal of Research, 55,* 861–867.

Hegarty, Peter (2007). Getting dirty: Psychology's history of power. *History of Psychology, 10,* 75–91.

Hegarty, Peter (2009). Unpublished data. University of Surrey.

Hegarty, Peter & Carmen Buechel (2006). Androcentric reporting of gender differences in APA journals: 1965–2004. *Review of General Psychology, 10,* 377–389.

Hegarty, Peter, Carmen Buechel & Simon Ungar (2006). Androcentric preferences for visuospatial representations of gender differences. In Dave Barker-Plummer, Richard Cox & Nuick Swoboda (Eds.), *Diagrammatic Representation and Inference: 4th International Conference, Diagrams 2006* (pp. 263–266). Berlin: Springer-Verlag.

Hegarty, Peter & Xenia Chryssocchoou (2005). Why are our policies so much better than theirs? Category norms and the generalization of policies between EU countries. *Social Cognition, 23,* 491–529.

Hegarty, Peter, Anthony F. Lemieux & Grant McQueen (2010). Graphing the order of the sexes: Constructing, recalling, interpreting, and putting the self in gender difference graphs. *Journal of Personality and Social Psychology, 98,* 375–391.

Hegarty, Peter & Felicia Pratto (2001). The effects of category norms and stereotypes on explanations of intergroup differences. *Journal of Personality and Social Psychology, 80,* 723–735.

Hegarty, Peter & Felicia Pratto (2010). Interpreting gender-related results. In Don McCreary & Joan Chisler (Eds.), *Handbook of Gender Research in Psychology (pp. 191–211).* Berlin: Springer-Verlag.

Hegarty, Peter, Nila Watson, Laura Fletcher & Grant McQueen (2011). When gentlemen are first and ladies are last: effects of gender stereotypes on the order of romantic partner's names. *British Journal of Social Psychology, 50,* 21–35.

Heine, Stephen J. & Darrin R. Lehman (1995). Cultural variation in unrealistic optimism: Does the West feel more invulnerable than the East? *Journal of Personality and Social Psychology, 68,* 595–607.

Holyoak, Keith J. & Wesley A. Mah (1982). Cognitive reference points in judgments of symbolic magnitude. *Cognitive Psychology, 14,* 328–352.

Hyde, Janet. S. (1984). Children's understanding of sexist language. *Developmental Psychology, 20,* 697–706.

Kahneman, Daniel & Dale T. Miller (1986). Norm theory: Comparing reality to its alternatives. *Psychological Review, 93,* 136–153.

Keller, Evelyn. F. (1985). *Reflections on gender and science.* New Haven, CT: Yale University Press.

Klayman, Joshua & Young-Won Ha (1987). Confirmation, disconfirmation, and information in hypothesis testing. *Psychological Review, 94,* 211–228.

Lambdin, Jennifer, Kristen M. Greer, Kari S. Jibotian, Kelly Rice & Mykol C. Hamilton (2003). The animal = male hypothesis: Children's and adults' beliefs about the sex of non sex-specific stuffed animals. *Sex Roles, 48,* 471–482.

Laqueur, Thomas W. (1990). *Making sex: Body and gender from the Greeks to Freud.* Cambridge, MA: Harvard University Press.

Latour, Bruno (1990). Drawing things together. In Michael Lynch & Steve Woolgar (Eds.), *Representation in scientific practice* (pp. 19–68). Cambridge, MA: MIT Press.

Latour, Bruno & Steve Woolgar (1979). *Laboratory life: The construction of scientific facts.* London: Sage.

Lee, I-Ching & Mary Crawford (2007). Lesbian and bisexual women in the eyes of scientific psychology. *Feminism & Psychology, 17,* 109–127.

Lidji, Pascale, Regine Kolinsky, Aliette Lochy & Jose Morais (2007). Spatial associations for musical stimuli: A piano in the head. *Journal of Experimental Psychology: Human Perception and Performance, 33,* 1189–1207.

Lipkus, Isaac M. (2007). Numeric, verbal, and visual formats of conveying health risks: Suggested best practices and future recommendations. *Medical Decision Making, 27,* 696–713.

Maass, Anne, Damiano Pagani & Emanuela Berta, (2007). How beautiful is the goal and how violent is the fistfight? Spatial bias in the interpretation of human behavior. *Social Cognition, 25,* 833–852.

Maass, Anne & Aurore Russo (2003). Directional bias in the mental representation of spatial events: Nature or culture? *Psychological Science, 14,* 296–301.

Mackenzie, Brian D. & S. Lynne Mackenzie (1974). The case for a revised systematic approach to the history of psychology. *Journal of the History of the Behavioral Sciences, 10,* 324–347.

Malkiel, Yakov (1959). Studies in irreversible binomials. *Lingua, 8,*113–60.

Martyna, Wendy (1980). Beyond the he/man approach. *Signs: Journal of Women in Culture and Society, 5,* 482–493.

Marx, Karl & Friedrich Engels (1978). The German ideology, Part I. In Robert C. Tucker (Ed.), *The Marx-Engels reader* (pp. 146–200). New York: Norton.

McCabe, David P. & Alan D. Castel (2008). Seeing is believing: The effects of brain images on judgments of scientific reasoning. *Cognition, 107,* 343–352.

McWilliams, Diana, Megan Strang, Anthony F. Lemieux & Peter Hegarty (2007). *Category norms and androcentrism in the construction and understanding of graphs*. Poster presented at the Annual Meeting of the Association for Psychological Science.

Merchant, Carolyn (1980). *The death of nature: Women, Ecology, and the Scientific Revolution: A Feminist Reappraisal of the Scientific Revolution*. New York: Harper Collins.

Miller, Dale T., Brian Taylor & Michelle Buck (1991). Gender gaps: Who needs to be explained? *Journal of Personality and Social Psychology, 61*, 5–12.

Moghaddam, Fathali M. & Naomi Lee (2006). Double reification: The process of universalizing psychology in the three worlds. In Adrian C. Brock (Ed.), *Internationalizing the history of psychology* (pp. 163–182). New York: New York University Press.

Morris, Rosalind C. (1995). All made up: Performance theory and the new anthropology of gender. *Annual Review of Anthropology, 24*, 567–592.

Moyer, Robert (1997). Covering gender on memory's front page: Men's prominence and women's prospects. *Sex Roles, 37*, 595–618.

Ochs, Elinor, Patrick Gonzales & Sally Jacoby (1996). "When I come down I'm in the domain state": talk, gensture, and graphic representation in the interpretive activity of physicists. In Elinor Ochs, Emanuel Schegloff & Sandra Thompson (Eds.), *Interaction and grammar* (pp. 328–369). Cambridge, UK: Cambridge University Press.

Parlee, Mary B. (1996). Situated knowledges of personal embodiment: Transgender activists' and psychological theorists' perspectives on 'sex' and 'gender.' *Theory and Psychology, 6*, 625–645.

Perrott, David A., Dedre Gentner & Galen V. Bodenhausen (2005). Resistance is futile: The unwitting insertion of analogical inferences in memory. *Psychonomic Bulletin & Review, 12*, 696–702.

Piaget, Jean & Rolando Garcia (1989). *Psychogenesis and the history of science*. New York: Columbia University Press.

Pinker, Steven (1990). A theory of graph comprehension. In R. Freedle (Ed.), *Artificial intelligence and the future of testing*. Hillsdale, NJ: Lawrence Erlbaum Associates.

Pratto, Felicia, Peter J. Hegarty & Jo Korchmaros (2007). How communication practices and category norms lead people to stereotype particular people and groups. In Yoshihisa Kashima, Klaus Fiedler & Peter Freitag (Eds.), *Language-based approaches to the formation, maintenance and transformation of stereotypes*. Mahwah, NJ: LEA.

Pratto, Felicia, Adam R. Pearson, I-Ching Lee & Tamar Saguy (2008). Power dynamics in an experimental game. *Social Justice Research, 21*, 377–407.

Ripley, W.Z. (1899). Notes on map making and graphic representation. *Publications of the American Statistical Association, 6*, 313–326.

Roth, Wolff-Michael (2003). *Toward an anthropology of graphing: Semiotic and activity-theoretic perspectives*. Berlin: Springer.

Rudin, Stephanie I., Michael O. Jones, Anthony F. Lemieux & Peter Hegarty (2009). *Androcentrism in medical journals: The communication of bias through visuospatial displays.* Poster presented at the Annual Purchase College Natural and Social Sciences Student Research Symposium.

Shah, Priti, Mary Hegarty & Richard E. Mayer (1999). Graphs as aids to knowledge construction: Signaling techniques for guiding the process of graph comprehension. *Journal of Educational Psychology, 91,* 690–702.

Shah, Priti & James Hoeffner (2002). Review of graph comprehension research: Implications for instruction. *Educational Psychology Review, 14,* 47–69.

Shapin, Steven (1995). *A social history of truth: Civility and science in seventeenth century England.* Chicago: University of Chicago Press.

Shapin, Steven (1998). *The scientific revolution.* Chicago: University of Chicago Press.

Sidanius, James & Felicia Pratto (1999). *Social Dominance.* New York: Cambridge University Press

Simkin, David & Reid Hastie (1987). An information-processing analysis of graph perception. *Journal of the American Statistical Association, 82,* 454–465.

Smith, Laurence D., Lisa A. Best, Alan D. Stubbs, Andrea B. Archibald & Roxann Roberson-Nay (2002). Constructing knowledge: The role of graphs and tables in hard and soft psychology. *American Psychologist, 57,* 749–761.

Singh, Maharaj, Jyotsna Vaid & Tripti Sakhuja (2000). Reading/writing vs. handedness influences on line length estimation. *Brain and Cognition, 43,* 398–402.

Suitner, Carolina & Anne Maass (2007). Positioning bias in portraits and self-portraits: Do female artists make different choices? *Empirical Studies of the Arts, 25,* 71–95.

Suitner, Carolina & Anne Maass (this volume). Writing direction, agency and gender stereotyping: An embodied connection.

Tee, Nicola & Peter Hegarty (2006). Predicting opposition to the civil rights of trans persons in the United Kingdom. *Journal of Community and Applied Social Psychology, 16,* 70–80.

Tversky, Barbara (2005). Functional significance of visuospatial representations. In Priti Shah & Akira Miyake (Eds.), *The Cambridge handbook of visuospatial thinking* (pp. 1–34). New York: Cambridge University Press.

Tversky, Barbara., Sol Kugelmass & Atalia Winter (1991). Cross-cultural and developmental trends in graphic productions. *Cognitive Psychology, 23,* 515–557.

Tversky, Barbara & Diane J. Schiano (1989). Perceptual and conceptual factors in distortions in memory for graphs and maps. *Journal of Experimental Psychology: General, 118,* 387–398.

Wood, James M., M. Teresa Nezworski, Scott O. Lilienfeld & Howard N. Garb (2003). *What's wrong with the Rorschach? Science confronts the controversial inkblot test.* New York: Jossey-Bass.

Woolgar, Steve (1988). *Science: The very idea.* London: Routledge.

Wright, Saundra K., Jennifer Hay & Tessa Bent (2005). Ladies first? Phonology, frequency, and the naming conspiracy. *Linguistics, 43,* 531–561.

Zachs, Jeff & Barbara Tversky (1999). Bars and lines: A study of graphic communication. *Memory & Cognition, 27,* 1073–1079.

Zebian, Samar (2005). Linkages between number concepts, spatial thinking, directionality of writing, SNARC effect, and the REVERSE SNARC effect in English, Arabic monoliterates, biliterates, and illiterate Arabic speakers. *Journal of Cognition and Culture, 5,* 165–190.

Zikmund-Fisher, Brian J., Peter A. Ubel, Dylan M. Smith, Holly A. Derry, Jennifer B. McClure, Azadeh Stark, Rosemarie K. Pitsch & Angela Fagerlin (2008). Communicating side effect risks in a tamoxifen prophylaxis decision aid: The debiasing influence of pictographs. *Patient Education and Counseling, 73,* 209–214.

Index

abstract (*see* concept)
action
    ~ execution, 6, 136–137, 141
    ~ planning, 6, 136–138, 141
acquisition (*see* learning)
adjectives, 20, 22
aesthetic preference, 7, 231, 235–238, 257–258, 264–266, 269
affordance/s, 80, 135–136, 139, 147, 159, 333
agency/agentic, 4–5, 7–8, 29, 192–194, 199, 277, 279–287, 280, 282–283, 285–287, 289–293, 295–296, 303, 305–311, 313, 315–318, 325
aggression/aggressive, 155–156, 158–159
amodal (*see* representations)
aphasia/aphasic, 198, 190, 283, 305
asymmetry/asymmetries/asymmetric, 1, 4–5, 7–8, 19, 28, 30, 43, 54, 56, 72–73, 169, 171–172, 187, 189–190, 193, 195, 203, 211–214, 217, 220, 223, 225, 231–237, 239, 241, 243, 245, 247–249, 257–262, 263, 268, 270–271, 277, 282, 284–285, 295, 305, 311, 313–315, 318, 326–327, 332
attention, 5, 8–9, 47–48, 51, 60–61, 69, 71–73, 75, 79–80, 82–84, 86, 88–90, 92, 163, 168–169, 172, 195, 198, 211, 214, 218, 224, 233, 239, 241, 259, 261–262, 264, 269, 271, 279, 282, 303, 305, 311–314, 331–332
authority, 153–155, 165, 177, 329

bias
    left side ~, 4, 211, 214, 216–218, 220, 222–224, 235
    right side ~, 268
    spatial agency ~, 8, 277, 280, 282–284, 286, 290, 293, 295, 303, 310–311, 317
brightness, 58–60

cerebral (*see* hemispheric)
chiral, 232, 240–241
closeness, 57, 122, 144
cognitive dissonance, 142
conceptual metaphor/s, 4, 6–7, 39–42, 43–48, 50–53, 55–58, 60–61, 65–66, 70–72, 74–78, 81–82, 84, 86–87, 89–91, 93, 95–96, 146, 153, 165, 169–170, 172, 174
    acquisition of ~, 39, 41, 89
concept/s
    abstract ~, 3, 6, 18, 24–25, 32, 39–47, 51, 72–74, 78, 87–88, 93–96, 169, 172, 295
    acquisition of ~, 47
    concrete ~, 24, 40, 43, 45–46, 72–73
    social ~, 5, 8, 11
construal, 6, 109–110, 115–119, 121–123, 147
culture/cultural, 1, 7–9, 11, 28–30, 39, 41, 45, 50, 56, 58, 60–61, 65, 69–72, 74, 88, 90, 92–93, 153–154, 164–165, 172–173, 175–177, 193–196, 225, 231, 241, 257–259, 265, 269–271, 277, 280, 292–295, 304–305, 311, 315, 327–329, 337, 341

disgust, 132–133, 145
distance, 1–2, 5–6, 9–10, 21–25, 27–28, 32, 58, 65, 70, 79, 109–123, 129–133, 136, 138–145, 147, 193, 268, 284, 317, 325, 338
    interpersonal ~, 111
    social ~, 6, 79, 109–116, 118–119, 129–130, 193, 284
    spatial ~, 2, 6, 9, 109–119, 121, 123
    temporal ~, 6, 10, 109–112, 114–115, 118–119

dominance
- social ~, 155–159, 163–165, 168, 171, 173, 317, 340
- hemispheric (*see* hemispheric)

egocentric, 26, 118–119, 121–123, 200, 257–258, 266–268, 271
elevation, 7, 153–155, 159–165, 172–175, 269
embodiment/embodied, 3–6, 9–10, 28, 32, 40–42, 45, 77–78, 94, 96, 121, 123, 129–131, 133–137, 139, 141, 143, 145–147, 153, 165, 167–168, 172, 174, 200–201, 277, 280, 292, 295, 303, 311
emotion/s, 30, 41, 57, 59, 82, 132, 141, 154, 157, 168, 214, 289
evolution, 1–2, 78, 173, 314

face/s, 4, 7, 29, 56, 66, 82, 85–88, 96, 154, 157–159, 160–161, 193, 195, 211–225, 224–225, 234–236, 238–239, 242, 246–247, 250, 279, 281–283, 286–287, 288–290, 294, 312, 314
- chimeric ~, 4, 214–215, 218–220, 224, 234–235, 312
fear, 141–142, 157, 159, 173
fluency, 58, 133, 218, 292–293, 311, 313

gender, 8, 20, 193–195, 211, 216, 219, 224–225, 280, 284, 286–288, 290–292, 303, 305–311, 313, 315–317, 325, 328, 331–340, 342
gesture/s, gestural, 1, 18–19, 18, 28–30, 43, 48, 49, 78, 156
glucose, 140–141
graphs, 8, 28, 48, 62, 304, 325–342
gravity, 19, 28, 30, 76, 159, 318

handedness, 7, 28, 195, 235, 238–241, 243–248, 285, 295
hemispheric/cerebral dominance/specialization, 231, 240, 257–258, 264–265, 270–271, 295, 311, 314–315
hypotheticality, 10, 109–111, 113–115

imagery, 10, 245, 247
innate, innateness, 158, 173, 176

language,
- acquisition of ~, 78, 96
- Arab/Arabic ~, 21, 24, 28, 48–49, 51, 66–67, 80, 88, 91, 195, 218, 235, 237–238, 248–250, 260, 271, 294–295, 304, 312–313, 315–316, 341
- English ~, 18, 22, 24, 28–29, 48–52, 55, 75, 175–176, 194, 197, 233–235, 237–238, 244, 248, 250, 258–260, 262, 267–271, 292, 294–295, 312, 315, 325, 340
- French ~, 237, 260, 262–266, 294, 332
- German ~, 49, 51, 175, 177, 214, 292
- Hebrew ~, 24, 48–49, 51, 195, 218, 233, 235, 237–238, 248–249, 259–260, 262, 268, 270–271, 294–295, 304, 312, 315, 341
- Hindi ~, 50, 218, 234–235, 242–243, 248–250, 294, 304
- Italian ~, 51, 175, 177, 191, 195, 284, 292, 294, 306, 312–313, 315–316
- Mandarin ~, 50, 55
- Russian ~, 238
- Urdu ~, 195, 218, 234–235, 242, 248–249, 260, 294–295, 304, 312
laterality/lateral, 190, 197, 231–235, 239–241, 246, 259
learning, 7, 17, 47, 55–57, 61, 71–74, 89, 91–92, 96, 166–167, 170, 173–174, 176, 220, 258, 260, 269, 313
- ~ of conceptual metaphors (*see* conceptual metaphors, acquisition of ~)
- ~ of concepts (*see* concepts, acquisition of ~)
- ~ of language (*see* language, acquisition of ~)
likelihood (*see* hypotheticality)
line bisection, 7, 218, 257–258, 260–263, 268–271

memory
  long–term ~, 9–10, 74, 93–96
  working ~, 6, 10, 39, 41, 73–77,
    81–82, 87–91, 93–95, 167
magnitude, 6, 10, 62–64, 66, 138, 233,
  241
mental model/s, 7, 10, 77, 79–82, 86–94,
  96, 202–203
metaphor/s, 4, 6–7, 8–9, 11, 18, 21, 27,
  39–53, 55–63, 59, 65–66, 70–72,
  74–76, 77–78, 81–82, 84–87, 89–93,
  95–96, 113, 129, 135, 146–147,
  153–155, 169–177, 318, 327, 330,
  336, 342
  spatial ~, 18, 21, 50, 113, 146, 318
modal (*see* representations)
motivation, 72, 89, 131, 141, 157, 159

nonverbal, 1, 7, 153–156, 159–160, 162,
  165, 177, 234, 257–260, 268–269
noun/s, 20, 22
number line, 65, 67, 304–305

painting/s, 8, 193, 232, 235–236, 264,
  277–285, 288–291, 294–296, 306
perceptual symbol/s, 95, 165, 168,
  172–176
personal space, 2, 129–130, 144–145,
  266, 317
polite/ness, 111–112
polysemy, 22, 43
portrait/s, 8, 29–30, 192–195, 235, 242,
  277–284, 286–293, 306–307
posture/s, 1, 41, 57, 76, 147, 154,
  156–158, 164–165, 168, 172, 243, 290
power, 1, 3–4, 6–7, 19, 23, 29–30, 43,
  60–62, 78–80, 112, 153–170, 172–177,
  200, 280, 290, 306, 317–318, 333–336,
  338, 340–342

preposition/s, 22, 75, 176–177, 198–199
prototypicality, 333–334

representations
  amodal ~, 10
  modal ~, 10–11, 172, 174

schema/s
  graph ~, 326–327, 330, 332, 335
  spatial ~, 7, 31, 191, 198, 202–203, 306
  image ~, 41–43, 46, 50, 52, 57,
    71–72, 77–78, 81, 91
script direction (*see* writing direction)
simulation/s, 7, 10, 45–46, 78–80, 95,
  121, 123, 135, 165, 167–170, 172,
  174–176, 177, 201, 303, 311, 316
slant/s, 6, 130–131, 133, 136–144,
  146–147
SNARC, 29, 62, 65–68
social group/s, 21, 277, 286–287, 318,
  326, 337, 342
social support, 143–144
stereotype/s, 280, 286–290, 305–310,
  316, 333–334, 336, 340
strength (bodily), 18–19, 30, 154–159,
  163, 168, 170, 286,
symbol grounding, 39–41, 93, 96, 166
symmetry, 30, 76, 211–214, 220, 225, 267

valence, 45, 57–58, 83, 88, 111, 161
violence (*see* aggression)

Whorfian, 200–201
word recognition, 7, 211, 214, 222–225,
  233–234
writing/script direction/directionality,
  5, 7–8, 49, 51, 65, 232, 234–235, 238,
  241, 248–250, 292–295, 303–305,
  307–309, 311–317